HOUSE *of* LILIES

HOUSE *of* LILIES

THE DYNASTY THAT MADE
MEDIEVAL FRANCE

JUSTINE FIRNHABER-BAKER

BASIC BOOKS
NEW YORK

Basic Books
Hachette Book Group
1290 Avenue of the Americas, New York, NY 10104
www.basicbooks.com

Printed in the United States of America

Originally published in 2024 by Allen Lane in Great Britain
First U.S. Edition: May 2024

Published by Basic Books, an imprint of Hachette Book Group, Inc. The Basic Books name and logo is a registered trademark of the Hachette Book Group.

The Hachette Speakers Bureau provides a wide range of authors for speaking events. To find out more, go to hachettespeakersbureau.com or email HachetteSpeakers@hbgusa.com.

Basic books may be purchased in bulk for business, educational, or promotional use. For more information, please contact your local bookseller or the Hachette Book Group Special Markets Department at special.markets@hbgusa.com.

The publisher is not responsible for websites (or their content) that are not owned by the publisher.

Set in 12/14.75pt Dante MT Std
Typeset by Jouve (UK), Milton Keynes

Library of Congress Control Number: 2023950165

ISBNs: 9781541604759 (hardcover), 9781541604773 (ebook)

LSC-C

Printing 1, 2024

Contents

Contents

List of Illustrations

Photographic acknowledgements are given in italics.

1. An early fourteenth-century manuscript illumination depicting the baptism of Clovis. Paris, Bibliothèque Nationale, Paris (Français 2615, fol. 9v, detail). *BnF.*
2. The Holy Ampoule, replacement made by Jean-Charles Cahier, 1820. Musée du Palais du Tau, Reims. *Author photo.*
3. The Holy Ampoule before its destruction. Etching published by J. Sewell, 1793. *Wellcome Collection.*
4. Throne said to have belonged to King Dagobert. Bronze, late eighth or early ninth century. Bibliothèque Nationale, Paris (Inv.55.651). *BnF.*
5. Suger's eagle. Porphyry vase, probably second-century Roman or Egyptian, mounted in silver-gilt for use as a pitcher, *ca.* 1140. Musée du Louvre, Paris. © *RMN-Grand Palais /Scala.*
6. Suger's chalice. Sardonyx cup, Alexandrian, second/first century BC, mounted in silver-gilt, stones pearl and glass, *ca.* 1140. Widener Collection, National Gallery of Art, Washington, D.C. (Acc. No. 942.9.277). *NGA, Washington.*
7. Silver penny (*denier*) issued by Louis VI. Minted in Dreux, 1108–1137. Bibliothèque Nationale, Paris (L 1219 /ROY-5952). *BnF.*
8. The 'Eleanor Vase'. Crystal vase, probably seventh- or eighth-century Persian, mounted in enamel, niello, gold and silver for Louis VII between *ca.* 1140, with later thirteenth- and fourteenth-century additions. Musée du Louvre, Paris. © *RMN-Grand Palais/Scala.*
9. Remnants of the wall built by Philip II Augustus, rue Charlemagne, Paris. *Photo 12/Alamy.*

17. Scenes from the life of Saint Louis IX. Illuminated page from the *Grandes Chroniques de France*, French school, *ca.* 1377. Bibliothèque Nationale, Paris (Français 2813, fol. 265 r). *BnF.*

18. Queen Joan of Navarre-Champagne. Limestone statue from a portal of the College de Navarre, *ca.* 1305. Skulpturensammlung und Museum für Byzantinische Kunst, Bode-Museum, Berlin (Inv. Nr. M 296). *Wikimedia Creative Commons/Daderot.*

19. King Philip IV and his family. Illumination from Raymond de Béziers (trans.), *Livre de Kalila et Dimna,* 1313. Bibliothèque Nationale, Paris (Latin 8504, fol. 1v, detail). *BnF.*

20. Royal seal of Louis X. Copyright © *Archives Nationales, Paris.*

21 (*centre*) Tomb portrait of Clémence of Hungary. Marble, fourteenth century. Cathedral Basilica of Saint Denis, Paris. *Paul Williams/Alamy.*

21 (*bottom*) Tomb portrait of King John I. Marble, fourteenth century. Cathedral Basilica of Saint Denis, Paris. © *Genevra Kornbluth.*

22 (*above*) The death of Saint Louis. Illustration by Jean Pucelle from the *Book of Hours of Jeanne d'Évreux, ca.* 1324-8. Metropolitan Museum of Art, New York. The Cloisters Collection, 1954 (Acc. No. 54.1.2, fols. 165v-166r). *Met, NY.*

22 (right). Joan of Évreux at the tomb of Saint Louis. Illustration by Jean Pucelle from the *Book of Hours of Jeanne d'Évreux, ca.* 1324 – 8. Metropolitan Museum of Art, New York. The Cloisters Collection, 1954 (Acc. No. 54.1.2, fol. 102v, detail). *Met, NY.*

23. A genealogy of the heirs to the crowns of France and England. Illuminated folio from a book made for Margaret of Anjou, 1444–5. British Library, London (Royal MS 15.e.vi, fol. 3r). Copyright © *British Library Board. All Rights Reserved / Bridgeman Images.*

List of Maps

The Capetian Kings of France

Foreword

House of Lilies is the story of a family, for that is what a dynasty is. In this case, that family, the Capetians, ruled a kingdom that became a recognizable antecedent of France as it exists today, in no small part due to their efforts over the three and a half centuries from the dynasty's inception in 987 to its end in 1328. So, this book is about the intertwined histories of this family and of the lands and people that they ruled – or came to rule – during a time of deep and far-reaching changes that shaped much of French and European history right down to the present day. To most readers who did not grow up in France (and to many of them who did) that history is almost entirely unknown, and yet Capetian France not only witnessed but often also originated some of the most recognizable developments of the Middle Ages, including Gothic architecture, crusading, and 'courtly love'. By the thirteenth century, France was the wealthiest and most prestigious kingdom in Christian Europe, and the Capetians were equally renowned for both their military might and their religious devotion, traits they combined when warring against heretics at home and Muslims abroad.

To a very considerable degree, the Capetians created medieval France. By the dynasty's end in 1328, the realm looked quintessentially 'medieval' in many ways, even if that adjective conjures up nothing more precise than soaring cathedrals, reprehensible religious persecution, and powerful kings, but it certainly did *not* look like that in 987 or for a long time after. Gothic architecture, with its high, slender columns, pointed arches, and great expanses of coloured glass, developed in their lands in the mid-twelfth century, a few decades after the First Crusade (1096–99) and around the same time that the persecution of heresy began to build up steam. (Yet it was a Capetian king, Robert II, who oversaw the first burning of heretics, in 1022.) Much of the intolerance and superstition that is often associated with the Middle Ages didn't even really take hold until the turn of the fourteenth century. Nor, even then, did the Church have a stranglehold over people's imagination or behaviour, particularly as it was itself so often internally riven by political and ideological dissension. But it is probably the serious limitations on the power of the Capetian kings and the uneven hold they had over the varied lands that made up their kingdom, especially in the first century or so of their rule, that is most at odds with modern expectations. So, it is worth taking a little time here at the beginning to explain how the Capetians ruled and how that evolved to more closely resemble the stronger kingship of later times.

When the first Capetian king, Hugh Capet, was elected to the throne toward the end of the tenth century, his kingdom – then more properly called West Francia than France – nominally stretched from Flanders in what is now Belgium all the way across the Pyrenees to Catalonia, an area perhaps slightly larger than France today even considering that it did not include Provence. But the king only had direct control over the royal domain lands, and for a long time these consisted merely of a relatively small slice of land centred on Paris. The rest of the kingdom's lands were in the hands of great barons like dukes, counts and bishops, who ruled domains often larger or richer than those of the Capetians and acted largely independently of them. Perhaps most famously the dukes of Normandy came to see their obligations to the kings of France as very limited, and for many years the Capetians had no means of disabusing them of this view. But the Norman dukes were not alone, and in addition to these great magnates there were also other lords of various types whose power was not as extensive as that of the great barons but whose interests and influence had to be reckoned with. Over the eleventh century these lesser lords actually became more numerous, so that power in the kingdom became even more fractured.

In the dynasty's early days, Capetian kingship did not entail giving autocratic commands to be uniformly obeyed everywhere in the realm. Aside from the territorial fragmentation of their kingdom, they did not have a permanent army or administration that would allow them to enforce that kind of dominance. But more importantly they also did not *expect* to rule by command. They expected – and were expected – to rule through cooperation with the realm's great lords, by seeking their advice, by making military and marital alliances with them, and by offering them gifts and lands. If cooperation broke down, they went to war, and indeed the early Capetians were almost always at war with one or another of their great barons, especially those whose domains bordered their own. By the early twelfth century, they were often even at war with petty lords who only held a few castles near Paris. Several decades into the twelfth century, a Capetian supporter outlined his theory that there ought to be a hierarchy of power, with the king at the top, the great magnates beneath him, and the magnates' subjects beneath them, each bound to obey their superior and their superior's superior – an idea that sounds a little like the 'feudal pyramid' that used to be taught in schools. But this was a minority view and an impractical one at that. Practically speaking, powerful people acted in their own self-interest and they often had ties of loyalty to several different individuals, making their political relationships resemble a spaghetti bowl more than a pyramid.

From around 1200, the Capetians became much better able to *make* people, even powerful people, do what they said. In a few explosive decades between 1190 and 1226, King Philip II and his son Louis VIII annexed many of the great baronies to the royal domain, including Normandy and much of Languedoc. At the same time, the Crown started to develop a permanent bureaucracy staffed by trained administrators, and law was increasingly used as a rationale to convince or coerce people into doing what the Crown wanted. By then, a whole Christian mythos had developed around the Capetians, associating them with the crusade, with particular saints, and with special objects of supernatural power. It was even believed that the kings had a miraculously healing touch. This imbued their rule with an aura of divine approval that was hard for opponents to gainsay. Yet, even then and long after, the realm remained a patchwork of lordships of various strengths and sizes with varying obligations toward the Crown, and, if the later Capetians ruled in a more autocratic style than their forebears, their efforts to move too far beyond the old cooperative model of power-sharing ran into stiff resistance and even outright rebellion. The last Capetians kings, who died in such disastrously quick succession as to seem cursed, discovered this to their dismay.

Those last Capetians, a trio of ill-fated brothers afflicted with adulterous wives and mysterious ailments, point to another common characteristic of the dynasty's rule. That is, the importance of personality and personal relationships. Until the dynasty ended with the untimely and heirless deaths of those brothers, the Capetians had had an extraordinarily lucky run, having passed the Crown from father to son in an unbroken line for twelve generations. But, like all medieval dynasties, their power was embodied in the physical person of the king and passed on through marriage and reproduction. The personal was therefore political. The unhappiness of a marriage, the tensions between a parent and a child, or the rivalry between siblings, all such dynamics could have fateful implications for the future of the kingdom. A disgruntled younger brother or a divorce (in the earlier centuries when it was possible) might scramble alliances or lead to war, while the friendship between two young men might make peace between their nations. A king's temperament and his relationships determined much about his rule, and this was as true in the fourteenth century when the dynasty ended as it was in the tenth when it began.

The importance of the family as the centre of royal power also meant that women played key roles in politics. Some of these roles, it is true, were passive and probably unpleasant, especially for young royal women. They were used as pawns to seal marriage alliances, often in faraway places at very early ages to much older men whom they had never met, and as vessels to bear children, sometimes very close together and sometimes to their death, the fatality rate of medieval childbirth being what it was. But once she had married and produced an heir, and sometimes even before, a royal woman often had an active and influential role in affairs of state. These women appear in almost every chapter of this book, as queens sharing (or even contesting) their husband's power, as regents ruling on behalf of their sons, and as lords governing their own lands. These were literate and highly cultured women, too, whose patronage lies behind some of the most important artistic achievements of Capetian France, including one of the first Gothic churches and the spectacular Sainte-Chapelle in Paris. Unlike most European kingdoms, France never had a ruling queen, but it was profoundly shaped by the women of the Capetian dynasty.

Although royal power was personal, it is hard, and can be deemed unwise, to try to access personalities and personal relationships across the centuries that separate historians from their subjects. After all, we can never sit down with Philip II and ask him how he felt when Richard the Lionheart rejected his sister, or why he couldn't even be in the same room as his second wife. Even those sources that do describe how someone was thinking or feeling, like the chronicle that tells us of Louis IX's bottomless guilt over his failed crusade, are reporting at a remove and for their own reasons. But to disregard historical people's humanity and interior lives altogether would be irresponsible, as well as make for dry reading. We know that they, like us, had thoughts and feelings that shaped their actions, though these might have been quite different from those we would expect today. Getting to know the Capetians as human beings and following their family's fortunes over centuries of enormous upheaval reinforced for me as a historian how important it is not to lose sight of individual lives in the broad sweep of historical change. It has also been enormous fun for me to write, and I hope it will be equally enjoyable for you to read.

A Note on Names

I have tried to pare back the profusion of identically named people, especially in the early period, by using different versions of the same name. At the time, these were often used interchangeably anyway. For example, a woman called Adelheid by speakers of Germanic languages in the tenth or eleventh century might be called Adela in Latin or Old French. I have generally anglicized names where English equivalents exist and it does not seem too jarring to do so.

The French kings were sometimes referred to by number even in the Middle Ages, a system that counts forward from the Carolingian dynasty that preceded the Capetians. The most important Carolingian, Charlemagne or Charles the Great (r. 768–814), counts as Charles I, his son Louis as Louis I, and so on. There had been five Carolingian rulers named Louis before the first Capetian Louis was crowned in 1108, thus making him Louis VI. Almost all the Capetian kings have nicknames, like Louis the Fat, Louis the Lion, or Philip the Fair, most of which were current in their own lifetimes or soon thereafter. In French it is more usual to use the nickname than the number, but I have distinguished each king with the same name by number in the text to avoid confusion.

A Note on Places

Much of the modern political geography of Europe was firmed up over the period of this book, so that, by the fourteenth century, many names and borders were roughly the same as those that exist today. But in the tenth century, when this book begins, those transformations were still to come. This makes talking about 'France' rather than 'West Francia' anachronistic at first, a problem I discuss in the Prologue. Much of what is now known as Germany was called the kingdom of the Romans and made up the most important element of what from the turn of the thirteenth century was called the Holy Roman Empire. For the sake of clarity, I call these lands Germany and the western or German empire. For the eastern empire, seated at Constantinople, I use the term Byzantium, though its inhabitants thought of themselves as Romans.

The names of French regions often have adjectival forms that are not intuitively identifiable for an anglophone reader. I have noted these in the text at first usage, but, for the record, people and things from the county of Blois are Blesois; those from Champagne are Champenois; and those from the Languedoc region are Occitan. A special case is Anjou, whose adjectival form is Angevin. This, however, may be confusing for readers used to thinking of the Angevins as a dynasty of English kings. I follow the usage of most medieval historians of France in referring to that English dynasty as the Plantagenets and avoiding the term Angevin except in relation to the county of Anjou and to the thirteenth-century Capetian prince Charles of Anjou and his descendants. It is also useful to know that Burgundy can refer to a kingdom, which overlapped with what is now Provence, a duchy, roughly coterminous with the modern French region, and a county, which we now usually call Franche-Comté. I specify which Burgundy I mean where there is any ambiguity.

A Note on Money

The circulation of money in the form of precious metal coins was in relatively short supply at the beginning of the Capetian period. Coins became much more abundant from the twelfth century onward. Most great French lords, bishops, and some cities could mint their own coins, meaning that a variety of different currencies with coins of different weight and value were in circulation. Capetian coinage began with the issue of silver pennies (*deniers*). By the thirteenth century, a variety of Capetian-issued coins of higher value were in circulation, but values were expressed in one of two French currencies: the pound Parisian (*livre parisis*) or the pound of Tours (*livre tournois*), with their lower denominations of shillings (*sous*) and pennies (*deniers*). One pound was worth twenty shillings, and one shilling was worth twelve pennies. Tournois money was worth 20 per cent less than its Parisian equivalent, that is, 4 *livres parisis* equalled 5 *livres tournois*. Large sums, such as those paid for ransoms, dowries, and diplomatic deals, were usually denominated in silver marks, which was a measure of bullion weight, not currency. At the time of Philip Augustus's death in 1223, a mark was worth 2 *livres tournois* or 1 *livre*, 12 *sous parisis*.

Prologue

Sweet France

There stood a throne of finest beaten gold
Here seated is the king who rules sweet France
His beard is white, his hair is shot with grey
His body is well formed, his features proud
No one would need to have him pointed out

This is how *The Song of Roland*, one of the greatest poems of the Middle Ages, introduces the king of France.[1] The poem was probably composed around the year 1100, when the nucleus of what is now France had been ruled for over a century by a dynasty that we now call the Capetians. Written in Old French and meant to be performed aloud before a noble audience, *The Song of Roland* bristles with references to the weapons and armour, fighting tactics, and chivalric courtesies common at the turn of the twelfth century and tells a story of warfare between Christians and Muslims that would have resonated with those who lived around the time of the First Crusade (1096–99), when Capetian France first staked its claim as a crusading nation. The poem even includes some characters who seem based on near contemporary figures, like Count Geoffrey of Anjou, whose territorial ambitions and marital mistakes feature in Chapter 3, and 'Old Richard of Normandy', perhaps the Norman Duke Richard I or II, whose alliances with the early Capetian kings appear in Chapters 1 and 2.

But the poem's white-bearded and well-formed man sitting upon a golden throne is not a Capetian king. The story is set some three centuries earlier in a golden age when a king called Charles ruled lands that encompassed most of western Europe, stretching from the shores of Catalonia to the forests of Saxony and including most of northern Italy besides. Much of this he had won by conquest, earning him the moniker Charles the Great, *Karolus magnus* in Latin, a title soon so identified with the man that it became part of his name: Charlemagne. So great in fact was Charlemagne's power and so fearsome his reputation, that on Christmas day 800 the pope crowned him emperor, an office that had ceased to exist in western Europe after the collapse of the western Roman Empire in the late fifth century. Charlemagne's fame reverberated down the medieval centuries, especially in France, where his legacy, as we will see, was a celebrated but complicated one for the Capetian kings who followed him. Even today Charlemagne is thought of as the Father of Europe in some quarters, and his mounted statue stands before the cathedral of Notre-Dame in Paris. It is Charlemagne whom *The Song of Roland* places on that 'throne of finest beaten gold'.

Charlemagne's realm was quite different from the French kingdom ruled by the Capetians when the poem was composed, let alone the France of our own day. The heartland of Charlemagne's empire encompassed some of what is now France and Germany, as well as the Low Countries in between, but in his time it was all just called Francia (see map, p. xxv). Francia had grown out of the kingdoms established by the peoples who had migrated west from the Eurasian steppes in the waning days of the Roman Empire. One of these groups, who called themselves Franks, meaning the free or the fierce, settled in what is today Belgium and northern France, territory they later expanded greatly by conquering lands to the south and west.[2] By the late fifth century, the Franks had acquired a line of kings called Merovingians (after their founder Merovech), and around the year 500 the pagan Merovingians became Christian when King Clovis accepted baptism in the cathedral at Reims, an event endlessly memorialized by his Capetian successors. (Today a stone in the cathedral floor marks the supposed site of the baptism.) Known for their long hair, exotic treasures, and violent family feuds, the Merovingian kings ruled

The Frankish Kingdoms

Francia until their eclipse in the early eighth century, when Charlemagne's family began its rise.

Frankish aristocrats who served the Merovingian kings as 'mayors of the palace', Charlemagne's forefathers increasingly governed Francia in fact, if not in name, until Charlemagne's father deposed the last Merovingian in 751, establishing a new dynasty that we call the Carolingians. Charlemagne, who reigned from 768 to 814, combined his astonishing record of military conquest with a knack for innovative governmental experimentation that has shaped European political life down to the present day.[3] Since he could not personally govern the diverse sprawl of territories that he had annexed to Francia, he adopted the long-standing division of the realm into regions each ruled by a nobleman called a count (from the Latin word *comes*, meaning a trustworthy companion). Charlemagne's counts were supervised by men sent out to keep them accountable, and they could be reassigned or recalled in case of rebellion or ineptitude. But, as time went on and the empire lost coherence under Charlemagne's successors, 'counties' tended to become inherited possessions belonging to great aristocratic families who ruled them quasi-independently.

When the ancestors of the first Capetian kings emerged at the beginning of the tenth century the outlines of the organization that Charlemagne had imposed upon Francia and the rest of his empire were still discernible, but invasion and civil war had profoundly reshaped the Frankish kingdom. The Viking attacks that began in the 790s had increased in intensity from the 840s, and by the end of the century Norse ships were an almost continuous presence on the River Seine. Meanwhile, Hungarians threatened the eastern frontier and raided as far west as Iberia, while Arab forces harried settlements from their base on the Provençal coast of the Mediterranean. The realm itself had fractured. In 843 Charlemagne's grandsons accepted a tripartite division of the empire in order to end their civil war. The youngest grandson, Charles II the Bald, had taken West Francia, a kingdom that covered most of what is now France. The middle grandson had taken East Francia, comprising most of modern Germany and Austria, while the eldest brother accepted the lands in between. This middle kingdom was soon re-absorbed and the empire briefly reunited under Charlemagne's great-grand-son Charles III the Fat, but his abdication in 887–8 led to the definitive division of Francia into East and West.

Carolingian rule continued in East Francia until the line failed in the early tenth century and was replaced by a new dynasty called the Ottonians (because most of them were named Otto), while in West Francia Carolingian kings traded the West Frankish Crown back and forth with a family known as the Robertians (after their founder Robert the Strong) until 987 when a Robertian named Hugh was elected king. Later chroniclers gave Hugh the nickname 'Capet', a sobriquet that had actually belonged to his father, Hugh the Great, either because he was known for wearing a short cape or because of his association with the church of Tours, whose patron saint had famously given his cloak (*cappa*) to a beggar.[4] The Carolingians never regained the throne, and West Francia gradually became known simply as Francia (in Latin) and then as France (in French), though for a long time usage was variable and 'France' was often used to refer only to the royal heartlands around Paris (the Île-de-France).[5] Hugh Capet's descendants were to rule this realm in an unbroken line of succession from father to son for the next three centuries and via closely related successor dynasties for another four and a half centuries after that.

Because Hugh's election is now seen as a watershed moment, from which we trace such a long line of direct father-to-son succession, the dynasty's name derives from his (supposed) nickname, rather than being viewed as a continuation of its Robertian predecessors. It is true, though, that the distinction is an artificial one, and in fact the Capetian name is an invention of the French Revolution, not the Middle Ages. It dates to 1793, when a surname for the royal family was invented to make them seem more like ordinary people and Louis XVI was sent to the guillotine as 'citizen Louis Capet'. For a while, the French word *capétien* became a term of abuse for anything that smacked of pre-Revolutionary decadence, though now it simply designates the medieval dynasty that is the subject of this book.[6]

By the time Louis XVI lost his head, France and the francophone world had become much larger than the West Francia of Hugh Capet's day. While Hugh knew that the Earth was round, he and his Capetian successors would have been amazed by the way that French domains had stretched not just beyond West Francia but across seas they had never heard of to lands they had never imagined. Or perhaps they would only have nodded and smiled, for the Capetians were men and women of expansive vision and unbridled ambition. They thought of themselves and their nation as chosen by God to fulfil a great destiny. If they were undoubtedly mistaken in their assumptions and often merciless in their methods, their results were extraordinary. From an insecure foothold around Paris, they built a nation that stretched from the Atlantic to the Mediterranean and from the Rhône river to the Pyrenees mountains, and created the myths and symbols of a most holy monarchy: the Oriflamme banner (said to be Charlemagne's own) that flew above their armies, a miraculously healing royal touch that cured scrofula-ridden subjects, and the fleur-de-lys emblem of a three-petalled lily that adorned not only their castles and their carriages but even the clothing worn by the recipients of their alms.

By 1300, Capetian France was not only the most powerful kingdom in Christendom but also the most prestigious. Building on a tradition of pious works and the persecution of non-believers, Capetian kings were known as the 'Most Christian' and France was proclaimed a new Jerusalem. They and their counsellors developed political ideas and instituted practices of government that endured until the Revolution. Even today, the Capetians' imprint remains visible in myriad ways, from France's reputation as a land of love and chivalry to its close but complicated relationship with neighbouring England, to the ongoing struggle to decide how religious belief and political practice ought (not) to intersect. It was the Capetians who made the Languedoc French, even if it remains also proudly Occitan, and they who wrenched Normandy and Poitou from English hands. It was they who transformed muddy Paris into a splendid metropole and they who are responsible for some of the city's most cherished tourist attractions, including the Sainte-Chapelle and the Louvre. In many senses, 'sweet' France was the Capetians' creation and those who love it are simply heirs to their legacy.

HOUSE of
LILIES

PART ONE

Charlemagne's Long Shadow

(987–1108)

Simplified Capetian family tree, 987–1108

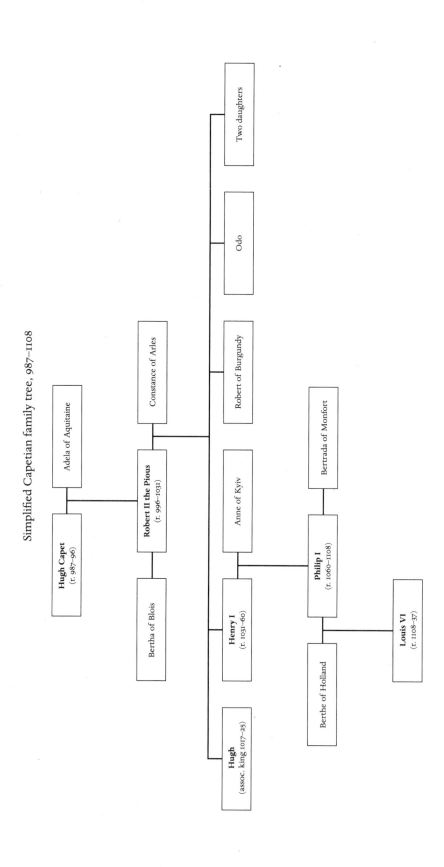

I.

The Rise of the Robertians
Hugh Capet

When the fourteenth-century Italian poet Dante recounted his alleg-orical journey through Purgatory, he told of encountering a man crying out to Saint Mary and weeping 'as a woman giving birth will do'. The tormented soul praised the virgin saint for her poverty and then went on to extol Saint Nicholas for his generosity, lamenting the avarice that had condemned him to his post-mortem place of punishment. Intrigued, Dante asked the poor man who he had been while he still drew breath. 'I was called Hugh Capet back there,' he said. 'From me are born the Philips and Louis by whom France in recent times is ruled. I was the son of a Parisian butcher; when the old kings had died out . . . I found grasped in my hands the reins of the kingdom's government.'[1] The Hugh Capet of Dante's poem then decries his descendants' recent military adventures in Italy and predicts even worse to come from the house of the lilies.

A polemical reflection on the Italian politics of his own day rather than an accurate record of tenth-century Frankish history, Dante's account garbles the Capetian dynasty's origins, perhaps purpose-fully. When Hugh 'of the short cloak' acceded to the throne of West Francia in 987, it was not because the previous line of Carolingian kings had died out and the Crown had somehow fallen into his lap. Rather, Hugh had been unanimously elected to the position by his peers in preference to a Carolingian claimant after careful machin-ations by people more interested in the survival of the imperial dynasty in what is now Germany than in the founding of a new royal dynasty in what is now France. Few of Hugh's contemporar-ies would have considered his coronation a watershed moment, for, far from being the son of a Parisian butcher, Hugh was not even the

3

first of his line to be crowned king of West Francia. That title belonged to his great-grandfather Odo, who became king in 888 after the Carolingian Charles the Fat abdicated due to ill health, not to mention his ignominious failure to deal with Viking attacks. Since then, Odo's descendants, known now as the Robertians after Odo's father Robert the Strong, had traded the throne back and forth with the West Frankish branch of the Carolingians (see figure, p. 5).[2] Closely related by ties of blood and marriage, the Robertians and Carolingians had cooperated as much as they competed, and many in 987 must have thought this arrangement set to continue.

It is true that Odo's brother Robert had deposed the Carolingian Charles the Simple in 922, and when this Charles then killed Robert in battle the following year, Robert's son-in-law Raoul succeeded him. Yet, when Raoul died in 936, Robert's son (the brother of Raoul's wife) Hugh the Great engineered the succession of Charles the Simple's son Louis IV and served as his right-hand man. In return, Louis supported Hugh's adoption of the magnificent title 'Duke of the Franks'. Although Louis eventually shook off Hugh's tutelage and Hugh later went to war against him and even imprisoned him, the two men had reasons for friendship as well as enmity. Each had married a sister of the powerful German King Otto I of Saxony, who had been crowned Western Emperor in 962. The elder princess bore Louis a son named Lothar, and her younger sister bore to Hugh the Great a son called Hugh Capet.[3]

These boys were both in their mid-teens and still considered minors when they lost their fathers in the mid-950s. Their mothers ruled in their stead for a few years, an arrangement not unusual for women of high birth in a period when politics was a family affair. When problems arose, Otto sent their brother, who was the Archbishop of Cologne, to calm things down, but, with the exception of a quarrel over possession of the duchy of Burgundy in central France, the cousins and their mothers got along well enough at first. It was Hugh the Great who helped to guarantee Lothar's succession in 954, and when Hugh Capet's minority ended with his mother's death in 960, Lothar granted him his father's title Duke of the

West Frankish Carolingians, Robertians, Capetians

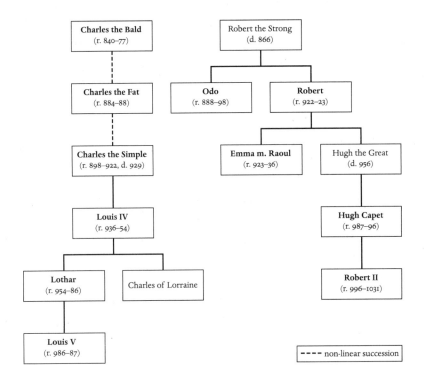

Franks in exchange for his oath of fidelity. Hugh distinguished himself in the military arts, a Robertian tradition, and Lothar made him his general in the war he declared against the Empire in 978.[4]

The *casus belli* was Lothar's claim to the old Carolingian territory of Lotharingia or Lorraine, lands that caused as much conflict in the ninth and tenth centuries as they were to do in the nineteenth and twentieth.[5] Lotharingia corresponded to the 'middle kingdom' sandwiched between East and West Francia when Charlemagne's three grandsons divided up his lands in 843, but it was now under German rulership. Lothar, whose very name advertised his family's territorial ambitions, had claims to Lotharingia not only on his father's side but also because his mother had property there from her first marriage to its previous duke. Otto I, far too strong a ruler to gainsay, had kept West Francia and his nephews under close supervision during his lifetime, but his death in 973 tempted Lothar to try to reclaim these lands from the emperor's inexperienced successor Otto II.

The Lotharingian affair set off a chain reaction that was to culminate in the extinction of Lothar's line in favour of Hugh's, but at first the adventure seemed likely to draw the cousins closer together rather than tear them apart. With Hugh at his side, Lothar led an army said to be 20,000 strong against the young emperor Otto II, forcing him and his pregnant wife to flee the imperial palace at Aachen built by Charlemagne. Leaving no doubts as to their intentions, Hugh and Lothar had their soldiers scale the palace roof and move the bronze imperial eagle atop it to face east, toward the Ottonian dynasty's homeland in Saxony, rather than west toward Lothar's kingdom, where Otto I had placed it years before as a sign of his expansive ambitions.[6] When Otto II answered this attack with an invasion of West Francia the next year, penetrating as far as the hills above Paris, Lothar chased him back to Germany and cut his rearguard to pieces as they fought to ford the River Aisne.

It was this victory that caused the cousins' alliance to unravel. Lothar had no doubt noticed that he alone had triumphed at the Aisne with no any contribution from Hugh's celebrated soldiering, and with so little of substance achieved by this war, the Carolingian must have begun to wonder whether Otto II might not make a better friend than enemy. When Hugh caught wind of secret negotiations between Lothar and Otto, he arranged a secret meeting of his own with Otto in Rome, the news of which inevitably made it back to Lothar and his powerful wife, Emma. They sent men seeking to capture Hugh in the Alpine passes, and he had to make the return journey to Francia in disguise.[7]

Any possibility for a reconciliation collapsed at the end of 983 with Otto II's premature death, blamed by the imaginative chronicler Richer on an exceptionally bad case of haemorrhoids.[8] The late emperor left behind what looked like prey for the aspiring princes:

a three-year-old son, also named Otto, and a young widow named Theophano. Lothar, Hugh, and an Ottonian prince evocatively known as Henry the Quarreller fought over who should take charge of the boy and his empire, but the Empress Theophano was not a woman to be taken lightly. Unlike her late husband, son of an ambitious prince who had risen to an imperial diadem through a combination of luck and skill, she was a princess of Byzantium, the eastern half of the Roman Empire that would continue uninterrupted for a millennium after the fall of its Western counterpart. Nor was it birth alone that distinguished Theophano, for she was also a political strategist of the highest order.[9] Only a few months into her widowhood, she had gained full authority over her little son, to Hugh and Lothar's dismay. But Lothar, still seeking control over his ancestral lands, pressed his claim by capturing the city of Verdun, the Ottonian's westernmost possession in Lotharingia.

Lothar probably just meant to test Theophano's mettle, but this act of provocation made him enemies that proved fatal to his lineage. The Verdun incident exacerbated Hugh Capet's growing disaffection toward Lothar because the city lay in Hugh's sister's lands and her son was captured in the attack. It also alienated the archbishop of the ancient and holy city of Reims, a man named Adalbero, who, like most medieval bishops, was as much a creature of politics as he was a man of God. Archbishop Adalbero had been serving as Lothar's chancellor but, unfortunately for Lothar, Adalbero's brother was the Count of Verdun, ruling it on the Ottonians' behalf. Adalbero himself owed his own prestigious and lucrative career to the Ottos, as did his friend and protégé Gerbert of Aurillac, a monk, polymathic scholar, and future pope, who was at that time teaching in the nearby city of Laon. Keen to demonstrate their loyalty to Theophano and her son, Adalbero and Gerbert began to consider Hugh Capet an interesting alternative to the perfidious Lothar. Hugh was, after all, a better soldier than Lothar and wealthier too, as well as less threatening to Ottonian interests. As Gerbert wrote in 985, Lothar might be king in name, but Hugh was king 'in acts and in fact'.[10]

The clerics' nascent plans for Lothar's downfall were pre-empted by his unexpected death in March 986, aged just forty-four. His passing opened the way for a rapprochement between his line and its Ottonian and Robertian relatives, but his heir, a nineteen-year-old boy named Louis, had neither the time nor the temperament to effect it. The last Carolingian to rule West Francia, Louis V reigned for little more than a year, leaving no legacy beyond criticisms of his character. The monk Gerbert scathingly described him as 'a person most disturbing to his friends but not very disturbing to his destructive enemies', while the chronicler Richer complained of the young king's lax morals and the strange clothes he adopted during his unhappy and short-lived marriage to a southern countess.[11] Even Louis's own mother, Queen Emma, disliked him, calling him an 'enemy' in her letters and seeking protection against him from the Ottonians – and from Hugh Capet.[12] Admittedly, these witnesses are not the most impartial, for the adolescent king spent his short reign waging war against their friends and allies, going so far as to attack Adalbero's see at Reims and to imprison Queen Emma for her Ottonian sympathies. Luckily for them all, on 21 May 987, Louis slipped while hunting in the ancient forest near the city of Compiègne, about 50 miles northeast of Paris, sustaining internal injuries from which he died the next day.

Louis's death handed Archbishop Adalbero an unexpected opportunity to mould the realm's future. The young king had come to Compiègne not only for the excellent hunting to be had in the forests that surrounded it, an amenity that had attracted royalty for centuries, but also because he had summoned Adalbero there to answer for his alleged treasons. These were rumoured to include not only collusion with Theophano against Lothar but also favouring an adulterous affair between Adalbero's nephew and namesake the Bishop of Laon and Louis's mother, Emma. These charges died with Louis, allowing Adalbero and Hugh to summon the realm's great men to a meeting at the nearby city of Senlis a week later, near the end of May 987, to choose a new king, for Louis had left no children behind to inherit his throne.[13] Only his uncle, Duke Charles of Lorraine, remained to carry on the West Frankish line of Carolingian kings.

Charles of Lorraine felt that he was the obvious choice and said as much, but there was as yet no undisputed hereditary right to the West Frankish throne nor any inviolable principle of patrilineality or primogeniture among great families. The past century had shown the importance of blood, but it had also demonstrated that kingship might not follow a direct line of descent. Although kings were drawn from a very small pool of princely families – despite Dante's claim, Parisian butchers were not in the running – leadership qualities and diplomatic advantages carried considerable weight with the dukes and counts, bishops and abbots who gathered in the royal audience hall in Senlis to cast their votes.

With Hugh presiding over the assembly as Duke of the Franks, Adalbero reminded the princes at Senlis that high birth was a necessary but insufficient condition for coronation. In a stirring speech that owed some of its flourish to borrowings from classical Roman authors, he asserted the principle that 'a kingdom cannot be acquired by hereditary right'.[14] A man's wisdom, loyalty, and greatness of spirit should count as much as his lineage. He rubbished Charles of Lorraine as a wicked and faithless man, who had not only disregarded the loyalty he owed to Emperor Otto but also married a woman far beneath him. Her relatives, he claimed, were unworthy even to help Charles onto his horse. By contrast, Adalbero praised Hugh Capet as a man 'famed for his deeds, his nobility, and his wealth', capable of protecting both the kingdom's interests and those private concerns of the great men gathered before him.

Whatever deliberations there were cannot have lasted long. The chronicler Richer reports that Hugh's election was unanimous. On 1 June 987, Adalbero crowned Hugh at Noyon, the site of Charlemagne's coronation as king of the Franks in 768, and from there they made their way to Reims where, on 3 July, Hugh was anointed with the heavenly chrism reserved for the kings of West Francia in the cathedral where Clovis, the first Christian king of the Franks, had been baptised almost half a millennium before.[15]

Through these ceremonies freighted with symbolism and history, Adalbero inaugurated the line of kings that would rule France for the next eleven generations, a feat unmatched by any other royal dynasty of the European Middle Ages (and the reason that the line takes its name from him rather than his Robertian forefathers), but one that seems all the more surprising in light of the archbishop's flat denial of hereditary right at Senlis. In truth, Adalbero was overstating his case. The Robertians themselves had favoured the succession of their first-born sons since King Odo's time, and Hugh himself moved quickly to ensure his own son Robert's position as his heir to the throne.[16] First, he had him crowned as junior king just after Christmas 987, a common practice known as associative kingship that was to endure in France for another two centuries.[17] Then, Hugh began the hunt for a queen appropriate to his son's newly exalted status.

A good match was vital. Ideally, it would add lands and alliances to the dynastic portfolio, enhance the family's prestige, and introduce a skilled political operator to its team. A *mésalliance* like that made by Charles of Lorraine, on the other hand, could doom dynastic ambitions. The Robertians had been careful to marry well, sometimes above their station, as with Hugh the Great's marriage to Emperor Otto I's sister. Hugh Capet's own marriage, to the Duke of Aquitaine's daughter Adela, had brought him a partner in power. He spoke of Adela as 'the companion and sharer of our realm' (*sociam et participem nostri regni*) and entrusted her with diplomatic missions to the imperial court.[18] For his son Robert, Hugh harboured stratospheric ambitions. He ordered Gerbert, now his chancellor, to compose a hopeful letter to Constantinople requesting the hand of an imperial princess.[19] This effort came to nothing, though Hugh soon managed to secure Robert a royal bride, the widowed countess of Flanders, Rozala-Suzanne, daughter of the king of Italy.[20] Robert, however, left her soon after. He thought her too old for his young blood – the same ground on which Louis V's marriage to another widowed countess had foundered – but the attempt perhaps reflects a fatherly effort to give this untested teenager not only a well-born wife but also an experienced consort, a woman who could help him as Adela did Hugh, or even take up the reins of power herself if necessary, as Hugh's own mother had done.

These precautions on Robert's behalf highlight the insecurity of Hugh's position. Duke Charles of Lorraine, still smarting from his rejection at Senlis, was not without supporters, especially in the rich and strategic northeast corner of the kingdom around Reims and Laon, far from Hugh's own powerbase southwest of Paris near Tours and Orléans. Hugh's ascendance provoked them to war. In 988, Charles occupied Laon aided by the townspeople and by old King Lothar's bastard son Arnulf, who was ineligible for the succession on account of both his illegitimate birth and his clerical profession. (The clergy were not supposed to hold lay offices.) Hapless Queen Emma, only recently restored to liberty by her unmourned son's death, now found herself imprisoned by Charles, and her alleged lover the Bishop of Laon, captured at the same time, had to escape under cover of night by rappelling down the city's towering walls.

Hugh's army besieged the city, but Laon's position on a plateau high above their camp on the plain below prevented them from bringing their iron-plated battering ram anywhere near its gates. When the townsmen sallied out to rout his wine-addled troops after a long and fruitless summer campaign, Hugh abandoned the siege and tried subtler means. Seeking to seduce Lothar's bastard Arnulf away from his uncle's side, Hugh arranged for him to become Archbishop of Reims when Adalbero died in 989. (This move inflicted much shock and surprise upon Gerbert, who had expected the honour and even written his acceptance speech.) But Arnulf showed no gratitude and promptly handed Reims over to Charles and his pillaging soldiers, who burned the town and raped the townswomen. Not until 991, when the Bishop of Laon returned to the city under peaceful pretexts, only to arrest Charles and Arnulf and call in Hugh and his soldiers, did the Carolingian threat abate. Imprisoned at Orléans, Charles of Lorraine then simply disappeared from history. The Frankish bishops deposed his accomplice Arnulf, and his see was finally awarded to the long-suffering Gerbert.

But peace could not last long in a kingdom as fragmented as West Francia. The chronicler Richer's intimidatingly long list of Hugh's subjects included not only the Gauls, who lived in what is now northern and central France, but also the Bretons, the Normans, the Aquitainians, the Goths (meaning Catalans), the Spanish, and the Gascons, a hail of names meant to impress the reader with Hugh's power, but which tells us nothing about the real extent of his authority.[21] In fact, with the partial exception of the Gauls, Hugh had only the most nominal sway over these peoples, whose laws, customs, and languages were different from his own, and whose lands sprawled over a territory that extended across the Pyrenean mountains, far into the Iberian peninsula (see map, p. 14). Charlemagne had assembled and ruled this vast and varied realm through his characteristic mixture of military and administrative genius, but his reign was a momentary exception to the normal pattern of medieval power, which was dispersed among great regional princes rather than concentrated in the hands of a king. In these centuries, a king did not rule by fiat. Despite the holy ceremonies of crowning and anointing that marked him out from other princes, a king's status was essentially that of first among equals. He ruled – to the extent that he ruled – through making alliances where he found friends and war where he found enemies.

The king's limited authority and the great princes' liberty of action can seem surprisingly chaotic to us because we are used to strong, centralized states and imagine the much more autocratic kings of much later centuries, but there was nothing inherently 'wrong' with the way power in Hugh's day was divided among many holders and brokered through violence or compromise. People at the time thought it normal, even if they sometimes complained about its more dysfunctional elements. (We do the same about our own political arrangements today.) There were advantages to having power concentrated locally and exercised flexibly, without the encumbrances of later developments like ideology and bureaucracy, especially if you were powerful or under the protection of someone powerful. Although war was frequent, consensus and consultation were the principal ideals underpinning the political order.[22]

But it is certainly also true that the two centuries since Charlemagne's reign had seen some exceptionally difficult developments that reinforced the fragmentation of power and reduced the kingdom's coherence. Partly as a consequence of wars among Charlemagne's heirs, the counties into which he had divided his empire had evolved into territories held by families who considered them their personal property. Counts sometimes opposed – or often just ignored – supposedly superior authorities like kings and dukes, whom they regarded essentially as equals. And because the West Frankish peoples had been left to fend for themselves against invasions by Vikings, Hungarians, and Arabs for much of the ninth and tenth centuries, the population had gradually lost any meaningful sense of belonging to a larger political community.

So, the kingdom of West Francia at the time Hugh came to rule it was not a strong state with neat borders and a hierarchical political system with Hugh at the top. It was simply a loose confederation of semi-autonomous territories dominated by men and women jockeying for power. Only too recently, Hugh himself had been just one of these men, frantically shoring up the Robertian inheritances by sword and fire, brokering alliances where he could and abandoning them when they no longer served. That Archbishop Adalbero had anointed his head and set a crown atop it had transformed him from a duke to a king. It had not transformed the geopolitics of his kingdom nor the cut-throat competition among its princes. As his rivals saw it, Hugh's victory over Charles of Lorraine had simply shifted the balance of power too much in his favour. Countermeasures would have to be taken.

Chief among Hugh's adversaries was Count Odo of Blois. Odo's lands in western France lay between Hugh's and those of Hugh's chief ally, Count Fulk Nerra (the Black) of Anjou, a figure of legend

Royal domain

N

FLANDERS

Noyon
Laon

Beauvais
Rouen
Compiègne
Reims
Verdun

NORMANDY
Senlis
Paris
CHAMPAGNE

BRITTANY
Seine

ANJOU
BLOIS
DUCHY OF BURGUNDY

Tours
Loire

Poitiers

AQUITAINE

Clermont

KINGDOM
OF
BURGUNDY

Bordeaux
Dordogne

Garonne
Rhône

GASCONY
TOULOUSE

Toulouse

NAVARRE

CATALONIA

AL-ANDALUS

0   100 km
0   50   100 miles

'France' at the time of Hugh Capet

even in his own time for his furious temper, merciless soldiering, and extravagant piety.[23] Fulk's family had long sought to limit the House of Blois's expansion on the eastern borders of Anjou. Hugh, too, saw the wisdom of opposing Blois, for the family had taken advantage of Hugh's minority to increase its holdings south and east of Paris, squeezing the Robertian lands that lay almost encircled in its midst. Odo had sporadically supported Charles of Lorraine, and his first move after Charles's defeat was to occupy the strategic castle of Melun on the River Seine south of Paris, wheedling its guardian into handing it over. Hugh recaptured the castle with the aid of Duke Richard of Normandy, who sent his sailors, descendants of the Vikings who had settled in the territory and whom Richer simply calls pirates, down the Seine to assail the island fortress. The treasonous guardian was executed and his wife was left hanging upside down beside him, a shameful death made more so by the way her dress dropped down over her face, revealing everything to the soldiers and sailors looking on.[24]

Fulk Nerra now played his part, harrying Odo's lands over the next year until he was forced to reconcile with the king. But Odo, almost as devious as Fulk himself, was merely biding his time. In 993 he went for broke. With the turncoat Bishop of Laon's help, Odo sought to rid West Francia of the Robertians altogether and to make himself Duke of the Franks. He reminded Emperor Otto III that the West Frankish realm was historically part of the Empire and might rightly be considered the Ottonian's patrimony. Now bereft of his mother, Theophano, thirteen-year-old Otto looked for guidance from his grandmother, the dowager-empress Adelheid. One of the tenth century's most powerful women, Adelheid had ruled alongside Otto I in his heyday and remembered a time when resurrecting Charlemagne's empire seemed a realistic hope. She was also the aunt of Odo's wife, Bertha, and sympathetic to the House of Blois's interests. Richer's chronicle claims that, with the connivance of Odo and the Bishop of Laon, Otto invited Hugh and Robert to Germany to attend a council of bishops, planning to kill them at the border and annex West Francia for himself.[25]

This tale is false: Richer erred in associating this plot with the bishops' council, which took place two years later.[26] But, while not factually correct, the story accurately reflects the entanglement of Church policies and royal politics in Hugh's kingdom. The Frankish bishops' deposition of Arnulf from the see of Reims in favour of Gerbert had set off an ecclesiastical firestorm. The pope had not approved it, or, at any rate, the bribes brought to him by Arnulf's supporters were more impressive than those that Hugh and Gerbert's messengers had to offer. The Frankish bishops stridently asserted their autonomy from papal interference in these local matters, but Otto and his grandmother seemed to support the pope's interpretation. This not only offended the Frankish bishops, but also antagonized Hugh, who rightly saw it as an effort to assert Ottonian authority in his kingdom and an attack on his fragile reign's most solid supporters.

These bishops, all born into great families like Hugh's own, were powerful men, every bit as powerful as the counts and dukes for whom they prayed and composed letters. Although barred by their profession from marriage and the lucrative alliances it might create, they nevertheless possessed great expanses of land and the people who laboured on them. What is more, they controlled the sacred rituals and objects – crown, chrism, ring, sword, and sceptre – that made a king. Hugh repaid them with his support against outside enemies like the pope and the emperor, as well as internal rivals, like the great monastery of Saint-Denis whose monks riled up their subjects against the bishops when they came to interfere in monastic business. Breaking into the hall where the bishops and the monks argued over who should pocket Saint-Denis's tithes (the 10 per cent tax collected on the harvest), the monks' people chased the bishops into the street where they axed the Archbishop of Sens in the back and rolled him in the mud – somehow he survived. Another bishop was so frightened that he ran back to Paris, leaving his dinner steaming on the table.[27]

This fracas could hardly have helped the monks' case with a pious king like Hugh, but his son Robert's influence nevertheless saved

Saint-Denis's revenues. In the great medieval rivalry between the 'regular' clergy – monks whose lives were governed by a monastic rule – and the 'secular' clergy – priests and bishops who lived out in the world rather than enclosed in a monastery – Robert came down on the side of the monks.[28] He was much impressed by the Abbey of Cluny in Burgundy, where the monks practised the latest advances in spiritual discipline and where no bishop save the pope himself could meddle in its affairs. In contrast to the Cluniacs, the monks of Saint-Denis were generally considered a bit dissolute: King Hugh had once been scandalized to discover a naked couple fornicating outside their chapel as he made his way to early morning prayers.[29] Robert calculated that helping Saint-Denis would open the door to imposing Cluny's way of doing things there too.

Conveniently, Robert's aid would also help to cement his dynasty's claim to power, for Saint-Denis was not just any old monastery. Axes, mud, and naked lovers notwithstanding, Saint-Denis had been at the heart of Frankish kingship for centuries before Hugh found himself on the throne. Situated just north of Paris on ground long considered sacred, Saint-Denis was a royal necropolis, France's Valley of the Kings. Founded to commemorate the miracle of the Roman martyr Denis, who had walked there carrying his own recently severed head, the church had been home to Frankish royal burials since the sixth century.[30] So, when Hugh died in his mid-fifties late in 996, it was to Saint-Denis that his mourners naturally brought his body. His corpse joined those of the Merovingian and Carolingian kings and queens of old, as well as those of his own father and his great-uncle Odo, first of the Robertian kings.

Hugh's rule had not gone unchallenged, but his burial at Saint-Denis showed that in death, perhaps even more so than in life, his kingship was accepted as legitimate and his line as royal. Robert succeeded him without controversy. He had already been crowned associate king in 987 and had ruled alongside his father for nearly a decade. Charles of Lorraine's children stayed silent, and Odo of Blois had died earlier in the year, leaving only children still too young to make trouble and a widow whose intentions regarding

Robert lay in a very different direction. Yet, if much about Hugh's death and Robert's succession indicates that their contemporaries considered them rightful rulers, doubts had begun to fester long before Dante told his spurious story of their base origins. Fears of illegitimacy and guilt about Hugh's supposed usurpation were to wrack the souls of his descendants and give ammunition to their enemies right up to the end of the dynasty.

This sorry state of affairs came about mostly because Hugh's chancellor, the scholarly schemer Gerbert, had lost a library book. Richer's *Histories*, the only eyewitness record made of these fateful years, had been written as a present for him, and he put the only copy in his baggage when he moved to Germany after capitulating to papal demands to resign the see of Reims. This setback worked out spectacularly well for Gerbert: while he had once complained that Empress Theophano had not rewarded him 'with even a little villa' for all his efforts on her behalf, now the Ottonians consoled him with the much more prestigious archbishopric of Ravenna, and from there he climbed to the pinnacle of Latin Christendom, being crowned Pope Sylvester II in 999.[31] But when he moved from Germany to Italy, he left Richer's book behind. There it lay forgotten for almost a millennium until it was rediscovered and published in 1839.

The disappearance of Richer's *Histories*, the only contemporary account of the Senlis assembly that elevated Hugh, meant that later writers, especially those hostile to the Capetians, were free to imagine more sinister scenarios. Although a monk from Fleury, a monastery with strong Robertian ties, gave an account similar to Richer's story in 1005, a chronicle composed a decade later at Sens, the most anti-Capetian place in France, imagined that Hugh and Bishop Adalbero of Laon had treacherously kidnapped and deposed Charles of Lorraine, wrongly identified as Louis V's brother and a reigning king, so that Hugh could usurp the throne. Unfortunately for Hugh's successors, it was the Sens version that was repeatedly copied out and incorporated into later chronicles, becoming the standard account of the dynasty's origins.[32] Even in the official royal histories that proliferated in later centuries, Hugh's coronation was misleadingly presented as a shameful act of usurpation against the rightful Carolingian heir, a taint his successors could never fully escape, even when their glory grew almost equal to that of Charlemagne himself.

2

Peace and Love at the Millennium
Robert II

Like all great men of the Middle Ages, King Robert spent much of his life on the road, never staying in any one place long enough to exhaust the resources to be found there, moving from palace to palace and town to town to remind his friends, enemies, and subjects of his power. Among his favourite haunts was Compiègne, a city nestled between the fast-flowing waters of the River Oise and whatever dark mysteries lurked in the primeval forest that crowded up behind it. The Carolingian Charles the Bald had built this palace after he became king of West Francia in 840, and Robert's biographer, a monk from Fleury named Helgaud, noted that its great tower still bore his name.[1] A Merovingian stronghold even before the Carolingians got there, this was an old place, redolent of the faded glories of vanished empires, but the new king embraced this history as his own. He had his eldest son crowned, and later buried, there. But if easy with the old, Robert was nevertheless eager to embrace the new. Finally freed of his father at the age of twenty-six and at liberty to overthrow outmoded practices and question long-held certainties, he embodied the spirit of his millennial generation. As the thousandth anniversary of Christ's life and death approached, many people feared, others longed for, and some prophesied the dawn of a new era. Bold strokes were called for. The Apocalypse might be at hand.

Audacity Robert possessed, but his circumstances and conscience drove him in contradictory directions. Known to posterity as 'the pious' and imbued with an almost saintly power, he gave sight to the blind and cured the sick just by signing the cross over their bodies. It is to him that the Capetian claim to be able to heal scrofula can be traced.[2] He kissed lepers, showered the poor and hungry with alms, and wore a torturous cicile (a garter made of irritating material) cinched tightly around his thigh to remind him of Christ's suffering. So deeply devoted to the crucifixion was he that he adorned his parchment decrees with large crosses, departing decisively from the archaic imperial style that his father's chancery had followed.[3] Educated in the liberal arts by Gerbert at his mother's direction, he knew Scripture and canon law so well that he presided over Church councils and passed judgement alongside the bishops. The first European heretics ever to be burned alive were executed by his order and in his presence. Robert was also twice divorced, constantly at war, and once tried to burn down a monastery because it was in his way. His heart was tender and his disposition kindly, but the times were less hospitable to lovers than to fighters.

The new king immediately ran into trouble by marrying his sweetheart, Countess Bertha, the widow of his father's great enemy Odo of Blois, almost before King Hugh's body had cooled. The affair had begun in the months before Hugh's death, and Bertha, a woman several years Robert's senior, probably seduced the young prince. Hugh had disapproved, as had Pope Gregory V. Hugh's misgivings may have been born from paternal solicitude about an inappropriate match or from concerns about Bertha's Blesois connections, so inimical to Capetian interests. These issues might be dismissed as circumstantial and fleeting, but papal disapprobation was of greater moment, resulting not only from the Church's long-standing rules about marriage but also its growing desire to see those rules enforced. Hugh and Bertha had the same great-grandfather, making the match incestuous within the Church's definition of consanguinity. Worse, they were also 'spiritual kin', for Robert had held one of Bertha's children at the baptismal font.[4]

'Fatally drawn to one another', their passion perhaps made more piquant by the opposition it aroused, the couple forged ahead, earning them – and the French bishops who had married them – sentences of excommunication and anathema.[5] The election of Robert's old schoolmaster Gerbert as pope in 999 afforded them some breathing room, but public opinion was not on their side. Even the abbot of Fleury, whom Robert expected to be sympathetic and whom he sent to Rome to remonstrate with the pope, had a habit of lecturing him (and in public, no less) about this 'infamous copulation'.[6]

As well as causing difficulties with the Church, Robert's alliance with Bertha also alienated Fulk Nerra of Anjou, one of the kingdom's most important barons and one of Hugh's most powerful allies. Their alliance had been built in no small part on their mutual distrust of Blois, which lay between Anjou and the Capetian domain lands. But now that Robert had not only taken up with Blois's widowed countess but also taken on guardianship of her son, the young Count Odo II of Blois, Fulk felt himself out in the cold, infuriated by the way that Robert seemed to favour Blesois interests over Anjou's own. Robert could ill afford Fulk's enmity, for he was already shorter on allies than he might like. His previous marital peccadillo – the repudiation of his first wife Rozala-Suzanne – had antagonized the Count of Flanders, who was the lady's son by her first marriage. Together, mother and son dominated a strategic stretch of northern coastline and were now inclined to use that advantage against Robert's interests.[7] It was a mercy that imperial pressure on West Francia had eased with the death of the heirless Otto III in 1002, but that same year brought new dangers – and opportunities – when Robert's uncle the Duke of Burgundy died.

It looked as though that key principality, long part of Robert's ancestral interests, might slip from his control because the local magnates had passed over the Robertian candidate to replace the late duke, choosing the Count of Mâcon instead. This, Robert could not countenance. War was the only answer. Aided by Duke Richard II of Normandy's army, he invaded Burgundy in 1003 and went so far as to besiege a monastery near Auxerre in order to gain the high ground, forcing the monks to flee and God to intervene with a miraculous fog that foiled Robert's plan.[8] Proving an even more capable general than his famous father, he eventually annexed Burgundy for the Crown, but it was a long, hard slog that required years of effort, as well as willing allies and a mind undivided by domestic distractions.

If Bertha and the Blois alliance were proving increasingly burdensome to Robert as their liaison neared its tenth anniversary, it was probably a lack of babies that led him at last to abandon the relationship. Bertha was not barren. She had had five children by her first husband, and Robert himself was fertile. Children by his third marriage would later demonstrate his potency, but given the habits of the time, he may already have had a bastard or two to prove it to himself and others. The fact that he and Bertha had not been blessed with an heir in all their years together – and according to one later moralist had been cursed with a goose-headed monster baby instead – must have suggested to this man of the first millennium that their relationship displeased God every bit as much as it did his vicar.[9] The death of pliable Pope Sylvester in 1003 sealed Bertha's fate. In 1004, Robert set her aside and immediately married a woman named Constance of Arles. This new marriage solved the baby problem and quieted clerical carping, but it plunged Robert into a morass of personal and political predicaments from which he never extricated himself.

Because Robert's new wife was cousin to Count Fulk Nerra of Anjou, the marriage brought the Angevin family back on side, but in so doing it complicated the Blois alliance. Odo II, now grown to manhood, seethed at his former stepfather's betrayal, though Bertha seems long to have hoped for a reprieve. After all, theirs had been a love match. Bertha had cultivated a circle of friends and followers in the royal household during her tenure as Robert's queen, and these now faced off against the allies and retainers who accompanied Constance from Burgundy. The gaudy way that the new queen's courtiers clothed themselves – and even their horses – aroused the disgust of the northern Franks.[10] But it was their violent perfidy that turned the king himself against his new wife and her allies. In 1008, Constance and her cousin Fulk Nerra conspired to send assassins to kill Count Hugh of Beauvais, Bertha's relative and one of Robert's closest friends, while he was out hunting with the king.

This murder, a mortal sin which Fulk only expiated after a long pilgrimage to the Holy Land, led to Robert deciding to divorce for the third time. When Fulk left for Jerusalem, Robert left for Rome to petition the pope for an annulment, and Bertha followed close behind. But if she travelled in the hope that Pope Sergius IV would rehabilitate her marriage, she was disappointed. Whether because Sergius remained adamant or because the deeply religious king got cold feet, Rome was a bust. Robert stayed married to Constance to the end of his days, making him (and her) very unhappy and enabling her to become one of the most significant players in Frankish politics.[11]

Historians medieval and modern have vilified Constance as 'avaricious and domineering', 'humourless', 'hateful and perfidious', and even 'bestial and insane'.[12] But whatever faults of temperament she may have had, she cannot have found it easy to be queen to a court and wife to a king both still entangled with Bertha. It is true that she proved fertile where Bertha had failed, giving Robert six children, four of them boys, but if this fecundity suggests some affection between the royal couple, they usually lived apart, Robert often in his new palace at Paris and Constance at hers in Étampes. Conscious of her own royal dignity, she excoriated anyone who seemed to disregard it and carried a staff with which to beat those who disobeyed her. When her long-time spiritual counsellor was convicted for heretical beliefs, thus endangering her own religious reputation, she used this staff to strike him such a hard blow that he lost an eye.[13] Fierce as a lion, Constance horded treasure like a dragon. When she discovered the theft of a candelabra, she swore on her father's soul that she would have the negligent guards tortured and their eyes torn out. Her open-handed husband drove her to distraction by giving away gold and jewels and luxurious clothing to the Church and its poor, and Robert had to swear one beggar to secrecy over a silver gift for fear that Constance might find out.[14]

The figures of Robert the munificent and Constance the mean may be overdrawn caricatures, intended by the queen's enemies to undermine her authority, but even if that is true, they do tell us something about how important the poor were becoming to those in power around the year 1000. Poverty, of course, was not a new phenomenon, and in fact there was probably less poverty in Robert's in than there had been a century or two earlier. Since Charlemagne's day, the climate had grown a bit warmer and the crops had produced a bit more bountifully, so people had generally become better off. Although there had been a famine in 1005 so severe that 'mothers ate their babies and sons consumed their mothers', such crises were occurring less frequently than they once had done or were later to do.[15] What seems to have been new about the poor in Robert's kingdom was their vulnerability to violence and the way that the Church and the king tried to protect them from it.

This violence was due to the proliferation of castles, arguably the most important development of the eleventh century. Earlier fortresses had certainly existed, including fortified palaces as well as city ramparts and communal strongholds, and these had, of course, increased in number and importance during the Viking invasions.[16] But the individual fortresses that now dotted the landscape were unquestionably much more numerous than in earlier centuries. And as regional power fragmented further, below the level of dukes and counts, many of these new castles were in the hands of lesser lords of murky, but military, background.[17] Those who were wealthy and enterprising enough increasingly built their castles of stone, but many of these eleventh-century castles were 'motte and bailey' structures, simply a great earthen mound surrounded by a palisade and topped with a wooden tower. Nevertheless, it is practically impossible to dislodge a garrison occupying the high ground. So, even though they were often modest in appearance, these castles enabled their builders to dominate the nearby countryside and those living in it. At their best, they served as a venue where people could go to have their conflicts resolved by the local potentate and, perhaps, as a refuge from danger (though they could not have sheltered many people). But at their worst – and there were many complaints about how often this happened – castles provided a base from which lords great and small could ride out with gangs of sordid supporters to scare the locals into paying them tribute and giving them free labour.

This kind of oppression shocked and angered the clerics tasked with the care of souls, not least because it skimmed off some of the wealth that otherwise might have been directed their way in tithes and donations, and they called on God to protect his flock from this rising tide of violence flowing from the hilltop forts. Bishops summoned the poor of their dioceses to mass prayer meetings held in fields, the only place large enough to accommodate their multitudes. Men and women, young and old, ploughmen and pigboys, dairymaids and dyers, and merchants and matrons too (for 'poor' really just meant 'less powerful than princes'), came together in the open air as if prefiguring a nineteenth-century religious revival. They camped out together for days and nights at a time, talking perhaps of the violence of the lords and the approaching Apocalypse, when the great would be humbled and the meek would inherit the earth. Monks paraded the holy relics of long-dead saints before them, miracles occurred, and the clerics sat down together and wrote rules for the protection of the unarmed. To any whose heart remained hardened, they promised damnation, decreeing excommunication against the oppressors of widows and orphans, the destroyers of carts and ploughs, and the murderers of pilgrims, priests, and merchants. They called this the Peace of God and hoped it would prove more durable than that of men.[18]

The meetings that are grouped together as the Peace of God had begun in Hugh's reign. The first such gathering was probably held in 989 at Charroux in central France, the practice then spreading fitfully first southward to Aquitaine and Catalonia before reaching northern and eastern lands over the next few decades. The simultaneous appearance of the Capetian dynasty, on the one hand, and the rise of these crowds of pleading peasants forced to rely on reliquary processions and threats of excommunication for their own safety, on the other, has reflected badly on the early Capetian kings. It seems as if the Church was forced to step in to mitigate the young dynasty's impotence. Their Carolingian predecessors, after all, had undertaken to protect the powerless as a royal responsibility. Charles the Bald, whose great tower shadowed Robert's palace at Compiègne, had simply decreed the safety of all clerics, peasants, widows, and orphans in the land, something, it is true, that neither Hugh Capet nor his son Robert would have been able to do even if they had wanted to.[19] The early Capetians ruled by making agreements with other powerful people, not by issuing decrees.

Yet, viewing the Peace of God as proof of Capetian weakness is probably wrongheaded, for Robert was not a bystander to the Peace but rather one of its proponents. His favourite monks at Cluny were great Peace advocates, and the movement's aims and rhetoric spoke to his deep religious convictions and experience. Robert knew what power relics held, having commissioned gold and silver vessels encrusted with jewels to hold the precious pieces of holy bodies. Once he even transported the entire corpse of a saint on his shoulders to a more gloriously decorated sepulchre.[20] Of course, personal experience had also given him a keen appreciation of the anxieties suffered by the excommunicated. Robert also realized that the Peace might be usefully employed in advancing his own interests, even against clerics themselves, a thought that also occurred to counts and dukes across the realm who participated in Peace councils. For the great churchmen, especially bishops, were not immune from the strategic demands that pushed the powerful toward violence.

Like their lay counterparts, bishops were often at war for their own purposes. Bishop Warin of Beauvais, who swore an important peace oath before Robert in 1023, sounds no less violent than any petty princeling in his promise to the king that he will not plunder cattle, pigs, sheep, goats, mules or the burdens they carried, nor rob peasants and merchants of their money, nor kidnap them for ransom, nor burn down houses, nor destroy mills, nor loot the grain found in them, nor assail noble women, nor those who walked with them when their husbands were absent, nor attack widows or their priests.[21] In swearing to uphold God's Peace, bishops also engaged themselves to go to war against any who contravened it.

To enforce peace, they could not only excommunicate the violent, but also summon armies to war, and, naturally, who and what might be considered to have violated the peace was in the eye of the beholder. 'Peace' associations could easily become vehicles for violence.[22]

Still, if prayers for peace did not necessary contradict the demands of politics, we should not be too cynical about the motivations of either the great or the humble. This was a time of religious revival and spiritual awakening, a medieval Age of Aquarius that inspired people to transform their lives and to undertake utopian projects. As fast as the castles went up, churches were built even faster. The monk Rudolph Glaber reminisced, 'It was as if the whole world were shaking itself free, shrugging off the burden of the past and cladding itself everywhere in a white mantle of churches.'[23] For a long time, reformers had been pressing to purify the Church of its corruption and society of its sins. For some, anxiety that the year 1000 heralded the world's end and Christ's second coming fanned the fires of devotion and gave urgency to the calls for reform and repentance. Few could ignore the portents now appearing in terrifying number: a rain of blood or of fire here, the sighting of a dragon or a monster there, not to mention astronomical wonders seen the known world over, including the supernova of 1006, an event so spectacular that it convinced the mad and misogynistic Caliph al-Hākim in Cairo that he was divinity incarnate.[24]

It was well known from the Book of Revelation that Satan would be loosed on the Earth after a thousand years, so the millenarian-minded thought it no wonder, and only the fulfilment of things long foretold, that heresies arose hydra-headed to entrap the faithful.[25] Even those unbothered by apocalyptic anxiety saw religious difference as a dire emergency, inimical to the puritanical values of reform. Although unorthodox beliefs had not troubled Christian Europe for many centuries, now it seemed to some that believers in bizarre and deplorable things were meeting secretly to practise ungodly rituals in every cellar and barn in Christendom. Jewish communities, too, became suspect. Those of France were charged with sending secret messages in Hebrew to convince al-Hākim to destroy the church of the Holy Sepulchre in Jerusalem, a wholly unfounded accusation that led to the first pogroms suffered in the West for centuries. Suddenly and fitfully, but irreversibly, Christian Europe was taking on the paranoid and persecutory character that was to bloody its history for centuries to come.[26]

Pious Robert, of course, was no friend to those deemed enemies of the faith. He forced the Jews of his lands to choose between conversion and death, inaugurating an infamous series of antisemitic measures decreed by his dynasty. Yet, his household was itself not immune to the contagion of religious deviancy. In 1022 a knight called Aréfast uncovered heresy deep in the heart of the Capetian court when the queen's confessor Stephen offered to initiate him into a cabal of men and women who denied basic tenets of medieval Christianity like Christ's virgin birth and resurrection, as well as the efficacy of the sacraments and the remission of sins. Stephen and his circle abstained from meat and marriage, but supposedly they also held orgies, sacrificed infants, and worshipped the devil, who appeared before them 'first as an Ethiopian and then like an angel of light'.[27] Aréfast confided these shocking discoveries to Bishop Fulbert of Chartres, who convened a trial at Orléans. At the trial, Stephen and his accomplices refused to recant their beliefs and were sentenced to be burnt alive, the first time that such punishment was prescribed for divergence from the Catholic faith.[28]

Robert presided over the trial accompanied by Constance, whose rage at the outcome robbed her former confidant Stephen of an eye when she struck him in the face with her staff. It could not have calmed the queen that the shadow of Odo II of Blois and his mother, Bertha, hung heavy over the trial, for although the affair was a religious matter, it was also the result of political plotting. Aréfast was an agent of Blesois interests and the brother-in-law of Odo's ally the Duke of Normandy. The Norman duke had, in fact, sent him to infiltrate the sect. The council that met at Orléans to decide Stephen's fate also deposed Bishop Thierry of Orléans, who had been Robert's man and Constance's chaplain, replacing him with Odo's choice, a man who happened to be one of Bertha's grandsons. Odo hoped that toppling Stephen and Thierry might take Queen Constance and her whole faction down with them, and Bertha may have wished the same, though for reasons as intimately personal as strategically political.[29] Surely, now that the pressures of youth were past and the dynasty's continuation assured, the old flame could be rekindled, even at the cost of a literal burning of human flesh? In the event, Constance lost, but Bertha did not win. Robert remained with the wife the Church had chosen and even had another baby with her soon after.

If Robert and Constance loved this new child, named Adela after her esteemed grandmother, the needs of state cut their time with their daughters very short. Robert had given away his first-born girl when she could have been no more than a year old to cement a Burgundian alliance in 1005.[30] Adela, too, was married to the Duke of Normandy almost from the moment of her birth in 1027. When his death only a few months later undid this effort to undermine the Blesois–Norman alliance, she was again shipped off, supposedly still in her cradle, to solve another inveterate problem by marrying the Count of Flanders.[31] Powerful pieces on the chessboard of medieval politics though they might be, little princesses had no say in when they moved or where they landed.

Grown-up princes had more room to manoeuvre. Constance had given Robert four sons, Hugh, Henry, Robert, and Odo. We know very little about the last beyond the strange story that after betraying his family he took to a life of brigandage. Having sacrilegiously stored his spoils in a church, he further insulted its heavenly protector Saint Benedict by using an Easter candle to light his stolen feast and was struck down by the saint with a disgusting illness that soon proved fatal.[32] The career of the eldest brother, Hugh, was more illustrious, but equally tragic. Crowned associate king at Compiègne in 1017 at the age of ten, he was the apple of his parents' eye, but as he grew older he also grew impatient for a full share in the power promised to him. When the German emperor Henry II died, Hugh was considered for the crown of Lombardy, but his father turned it down on his behalf, apparently without consulting him, choosing instead to support the Duke of Aquitaine's son in exchange for a handsome bribe. Nor was Robert as generous with his first-born son as he was with every beggar and blind man who turned up at the palace gates. By the time Hugh reached manhood, his quarrels with his parents had become a matter of urgent concern among the king's councillors.[33] They implored Robert to repair the rift before it threatened the kingdom, and when Hugh died unexpectedly in 1025, Robert and Constance deeply regretted their estrangement from their son. Those who observed their grief first-hand said that they were both 'afflicted almost unto their own death by sadness of heart and mourning'.[34]

Whatever unity the royal couple found in sorrow, however, the question of the succession tore them apart again almost immediately. Although primogeniture was not yet routine practice, Robert had assumed that the crown would now go to Henry, his second-born son. Constance thought otherwise. She had serious reservations about this boy, reservations shared by many, who considered Henry a 'weak and lazy lawless hypocrite'.[35] The queen believed their third son, Robert, to be more suited to royal responsibilities. She probably also thought that his comparative youth made him more likely to afford her power, especially if her fifty-something husband were soon to pass away, as was sadly all too likely at his age. The family quarrel ran on for two years before Odo II of Blois came down on the king's side and Henry was crowned at Reims in 1031. Despite the splendour, the queen's palpable fury at being stymied made the atmosphere most uncomfortable. Bishop Fulbert of Chartres refused to attend because he was 'frightened away by the savagery of his mother', and he was probably not alone in wishing to avoid the occasion.[36]

Having suffered the loss of his son and now an old man by the standards of the time, King Robert must dearly have wished to spend his last years in peace, but he was not to do so. Henry, already eighteen at the time of his coronation, proved if anything more impatient for power than his older brother had been. Egged on by

Constance, Henry and his brother Robert rebelled against their father, who had promised Robert his Burgundian conquest but then delayed handing it over to him. The brothers attacked in a pincer movement, with Henry taking Dreux northwest of Paris and Robert capturing key towns in Burgundy in the southeast. Furious, their father marched his army into Burgundy, where he was only calmed by the Abbot of Cluny's reminder of how his own hot-headed youth had troubled his parents.[37] A greater share in the family funds reconciled the princes to their father, whose death in 1031 freed Henry, at least, from any further reason to rebel.

Like his father Hugh before him and his wife Constance soon after, Robert was laid to rest at Saint-Denis. Widows and orphans, the poor and the lame lined the roads and beat their chests in lamentation for the loss of their pious benefactor. He had not impressed everyone as much. As a satirical poem taunted him, 'Though first among Franks, you are but a serf in the order of kings'.[38] Possessing no formal means of government and few advantages over his rivals, he had ruled only by creating consensus among the great princes when he could and by going to war with them when he couldn't. His innate authority as an anointed king was not negligible, but neither was it sufficient to ensure unquestioning obedience. It was rather his personal charisma as an individual of great – if imperfect – religious devotion that accorded him a place nonpareil in a kingdom throbbing with Christian zeal and eschatological expectations. Robert combined the king's personal piety and the almost miraculous power of his office with the violent persecution of religious minorities. The frailties of his son and grandson put an end to this innovative experiment, but Robert's later descendants were to rediscover its alchemy to explosive effect.

3

A Stormy Season

Henry I

King Henry's reign began with bad omens and worse weather. A lunar eclipse had darkened the sky when his father died, and for three days comets streaked across it, 'portending death and destruction'.[1] Torrential storms beat down upon France as the heavens mourned the old king's passing with a fury equal to that of the wailing throngs lining the route of Robert's funerary cortege. Rain fell so continuously for three years that crops could not be sown and a terrible famine beset the land. Starving men and women walked from town to town seeking alms and shelter but often collapsed too weak to continue on the road, their bodies abandoned to rot unburied in the unceasing rain. Naked corpses were thrown into charnel houses by the hundreds. People ate roots and dirt and carrion, and then in desperation they began to eat one another. In Burgundy, a wild man decorated his hut with the severed heads of those he devoured, and a shameless profiteer in Tournai openly sold human flesh roasted 'like the meat of some beast' in the market square.[2]

As the year 1033 – reckoned to be the millennial-anniversary of Christ's death and resurrection – approached, some who suffered through these apocalyptic storms wondered if they heralded not only the end of the world but also the promise of the new age to come. And perhaps for a few years after 1033, as the rain ceased, the weather turned mild and the crops became bountiful, the kingdom of Heaven did seem almost to exist on Earth. The hope spurred another wave of Peace assemblies, and those who gathered raised their hands to Heaven, crying 'Peace! Peace! Peace!'[3] Yet peace proved elusive, and King Henry spent almost the entirety of his twenty-nine-year reign at war. Although he was lucky on the eastern frontier, where the vagaries of imperial succession meant that Germany ceased to threaten Capetian interests, within France ambitious barons fought the king with the same unbridled ferocity that they inflicted on one another. The lands under Henry's direct control, the royal domain, were restricted to a lozenge of land running from Orléans in the south to Compiègne in the north with Paris at the centre (see map, p. 36). Outside the domain, the king's authority was largely symbolic and even within it he faced challenges. Henry fought doggedly – and sometimes successfully – to maintain his lands and support his allies, but he was beset by a succession of enemies more effective than himself, ranging from that old foe Odo II of Blois to the young Duke William of Normandy, first called 'the Bastard' but later known as 'the Conqueror'.

Henry himself does not stand out from the background of his reign, whose momentous events were rarely of his making, and he is overshadowed by the commanding characters with whom he had to share a stage. His contemporaries seem to have thought him utterly unremarkable and left no descriptions of his personality, save for the remark that his mother and her allies considered him weak and undisciplined. That comment is hardly flattering, and hard to square with Henry's steady if undistinguished tenure as ruler, but it may have more to do with his sexuality than his abilities or integrity. The Latin word *mollis* used to describe him can mean weak, but it also means effeminate or gay. (It is the origin of the English insult 'Molly' and the name 'molly-houses' given to homosexual brothels from the sixteenth century.)[4] Henry was certainly slow to wed, and perhaps purposefully he chose wives too young or far away to present any immediate danger of having to consummate the marriage.[5] But Henry was not entirely immune to feminine charms. He eventually fathered three or four children, a number beyond that needed to ensure the succession, and there is no identifiable male favourite among his entourage likely to have been his sexual companion. Maybe Henry was discreet, a quality in keeping with the general inaccessibility of his character, or perhaps scarred by the emotional and political turmoil produced by his father's sexual entanglements, he just had little interest in intimacy of any kind.

Henry's relationship with his mother, Queen Constance, can hardly have made him desirous of female company. Long openly hostile toward Henry and still hoping to put her favourite son Robert on the throne, she declared open war against Henry almost immediately after her husband's death and made a pact with Prince Robert against his brother. Henry's supposed allies deserted him in droves. Even the minor lords of small castles in the Capetian family heartlands followed Constance in rebellion. As for the great princes, the Count of Anjou and the Duke of Aquitaine were too busy with their own battles to involve themselves. Odo of Blois might have sided with Henry given his natural aversion to Constance and the part he had played in putting Henry on the throne, but Constance bribed him with half of the city of Sens and he then became pre-occupied far to the southeast, where he was attempting to wrest the kingdom of Burgundy from the emperor's grip. It was only the Duke of Normandy who proved of any use to the young king, offering him men and horses when he and a dozen followers straggled over the border, but according to a later chronicler, this 'gift' cost Henry the Vexin, a strategically important territory half-way to Paris and a bone of contention between Normandy and France for the next century and a half (see map, p. 36).[6]

As the weather improved in 1033, so did Henry's fortunes in war. Midway through the year he concluded a treaty with the emperor Conrad II, bolstering the latter's position against Odo of Blois, in exchange for the hand of the emperor's five-year-old daughter and an enormous lion. The lion probably outlived this child bride, who died the next year, but the political alliance at least proved fruitful. Conrad ravaged Odo's lands in eastern France while Henry, a better general than his doubters had given him credit for, pressed Constance hard. Besieged in her favourite palace at Poissy, a place she loved for the fish (*poissons*) that gave the place its name, she escaped by sailing down the River Seine to Pontoise, whence she was immediately forced to flee, this time overland, to the castle at Le Puiset

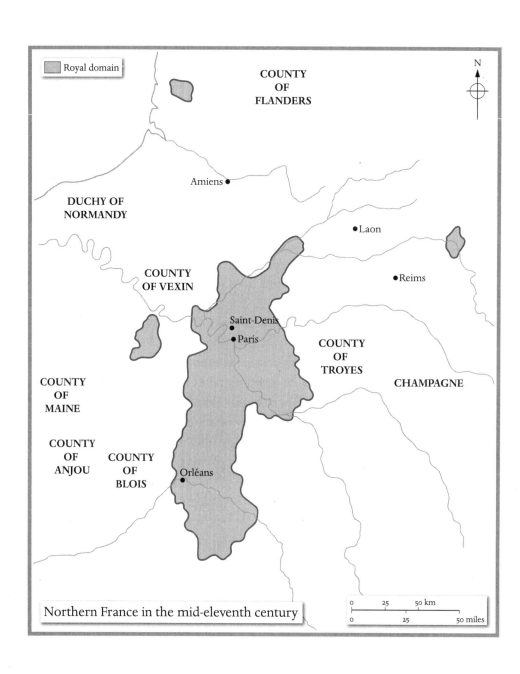

Northern France in the mid-eleventh century

near Orléans, with Henry hard on her heels. Fed up, Henry besieged the fortress, furiously launching his soldiers and his wooden war machines (*machinis*) at the walls and vowing to give no quarter to the hungry, thirsty, and increasingly argumentative men inside the castle. He would at last have slaughtered everyone, had not his mother thrown herself before him and begged for their lives with tears in her eyes.[7] Robert, too, submitted to Henry after a humiliating defeat south of Paris, though as the price of peace he exacted his recognition as the Duke of Burgundy.

Constance's death in 1034 may have come as a great relief to Henry, but if the young king now had peace at home, he had little respite away from it. The regional princes were used to considerable latitude in their dealings and inclined to answer any argument with war. While Henry could depend on the loyalty of the Count of Flanders and the Duke of Normandy – though he did not meddle in their affairs without invitation – he had almost no sway in the far-off Duchy of Aquitaine, and his younger brother Robert now had free rein in the Duchy of Burgundy. The house of Blois, too, remained a problem. Although Odo of Blois died at war in 1037, his sons inherited not only the old family lands of Blois west of Paris but also the rich county of Champagne in eastern France, which Odo had acquired in 1021.[8] The king's own ancestral lands lay in the middle, nearly encircled by the Blesois boys' holdings. But it was Anjou that would take up most of Henry's time and attention over the next two decades.

Situated in western France between the great principalities of Aquitaine and Normandy, Anjou had been ruled by the infamous Fulk Nerra since the time of Hugh Capet. Because his interests had been inherently opposed to those of Blois for decades, Fulk had supported Henry in the 1030s, when Constance convinced Odo to forget old enmities and Henry made his alliance with Emperor Conrad. But having dominated the political scene since the Capetian dynasty's inception, Fulk departed France and then this mortal life, dying on his fourth pilgrimage to Jerusalem in 1040. He left behind an ambitious and acquisitive son named Geoffrey, nicknamed Martel (the Hammer), whose military and diplomatic acumen made him a dangerous rival not only to his neighbours in Aquitaine, Normandy, and Blois, but also to King Henry himself.[9]

Impatient for his father's death and his own succession as Count of Anjou, Geoffrey had taken a short-cut to power in 1032 by marrying the widow of Duke William V of Aquitaine, Agnes of Burgundy. As the daughter of a claimant to the duchy of Burgundy and the granddaughter of an Italian king, Agnes opened up enticing vistas of power to her new husband, but first she aimed to secure positions for the son and daughter she had borne to her first husband. Happily, these aims complemented Geoffrey's own. He needed little convincing to annex Aquitaine on her son's behalf, quashing the claims of the late duke's eldest son, and Geoffrey also found an excellent use for his new stepdaughter, creating an imperial alliance by promising her to the newly elected Emperor Henry III. Once his father (finally!) died, Geoffrey was able to realize a long-held Angevin dream by seizing the city of Tours from the Count of Blois, capturing him along with a thousand of his soldiers. A moralizing monk attributed this victory to the intervention of Saint Martin, who forgave Geoffrey for all that he had stolen from churches in the past, but equal credit should certainly be given to the loyalty long demanded from Anjou's castellans by the late Fulk Nerra.[10]

Geoffrey can have had little love for his formidable father, who once punished his adolescent rebellion by making him walk for miles wearing a horse saddle. When Geoffrey at last fell prostrate before him, Fulk kicked the boy viciously, shouting 'Finally, you are beaten, beaten, beaten!'[11] Still, if Geoffrey chafed at the memory of such chastisement, he must have felt at least grudgingly grateful to inherit the military discipline that the unyielding old man had imposed upon Anjou. Fulk had not only built dozens of castles – and done so in state-of-the-art stone rather than wood – crucially he had also kept control of these fortresses, entrusting them to experienced men of proven loyalty who used them to support the count's interests and who returned them to his possession when requested.

This was the ideal situation: a lord rewarded a man's service by bestowing a castle on him and the man repaid him with his fidelity. According to a famous letter written by Bishop Fulbert of Chartres to Duke William V of Aquitaine, 'fidelity' meant ensuring the lord's safety, keeping his secrets, facilitating his plans, and not betraying him in word or deed.[12] This might seem like a low bar to clear, but it was only through force of personality that Fulk and then Geoffrey enjoyed the fruits of fidelity from their men. Elsewhere, castles and their holders tended to generate violence and political instability as they competed against one another – and the great lords meant to rule over them – to accumulate wealth and power. They slipped beyond obedience to any higher authority, seizing what they and their men wished from monks and peasants, and contributing to the fears of bloodshed and brutality that animated the Peace councils.[13]

Those who now commanded these castles often considered them personal property, even if they supposedly held them on someone else's behalf, and they wanted to keep this property in the family by passing it on to their children. No one entertained any illusions that castles ultimately belonged to the king – the 'feudal pyramid' one might find sketched in an old textbook or on an ill-informed website was a long way from anyone's imagination in the eleventh century – but dukes and counts might still think of the castles in their domains as essentially their own possessions. They considered them commissions to be bestowed for a limited period in service to their own objectives and withdrawn at will. They also felt that no castles should be built in their territory without their permission. Castles erected on the sly were supposed to be knocked down. In practice they proliferated. So, too, did the number of lords to whom a man might pledge himself, making it difficult to determine just where his loyalty lay when there was conflict between them. As one historian summed up, 'in the eleventh century existed only interest, not fidelity'.[14]

In the castellans' defence, it must be said that the great lords in turn did not always fulfil their pledges of loyalty and protection toward their followers. Castellans might champion the fine idea that their relationship with their lords was a reciprocal one of mutual benefit, but the great princes resisted this interpretation. Bishop Fulbert of Chartres had told Duke William V of Aquitaine that, even if a man had done his duty to his lord scrupulously, that lord was still not *necessarily* bound to reward him with lands or castles. The duke himself put it more plainly to one of his men, Hugh of Lusignan. 'You are mine,' he said, 'to do with what I will.'[15] This Hugh had spent much of his life doing his utmost on William's behalf: he had captured castles and horsemen who had rebelled against William. He had broken off a lucrative betrothal because William forbade it. He had left his wife besieged in a castle and his lands under attack when William ordered him to accompany him elsewhere. Despite all this, William had steadfastly refused to reward Hugh with any of the lands and castles that he dangled tantalizingly before him. Only when an exasperated Hugh renounced his faithful service and seized a fortress that William needed did he at last obtain some of the holdings that Hugh considered his own by hereditary right.

This long-suffering lord came from a noble family and bore the quasi-Roman title of chiliarch. He was a great soldier with a thousand men under his command, not some impoverished peasant. Actual peasants found lordship much more difficult to combat. It is true that they had some avenues of advancement open to them, even in this turbulent age of counts and castles. The polymathic monk Gerbert, who had served the Ottonians and Hugh Capet and eventually became pope, had begun his life as a peasant boy in the rugged mountains of central France before the local abbot spotted his talents and sent him to Catalonia for an elite education. Even on a less spectacular scale, the growing importance of trade and the increasing availability of cash in the form of silver pennies afforded new options, especially in the burgeoning towns, to men and women who might otherwise have worked the land. But those able to grasp these opportunities were still exceptions to the rule. The vast majority of people remained on rural estates, where they spent their lives labouring for their lords, many or most of them as serfs.

Serfs were not slaves – and indeed some of them chose the status as a way to advance professionally in a lord's service – but neither were they free. They could not be bought and sold outright, and it is certainly true that, 'compared with the lives of unfortunate slaves in extreme dependency, those of serfs were enriched by a whole fabric of social relations'.[16] But serfs could be given as gifts, donated to monasteries, or transferred to other lords along with the land where they worked and resided. They lived subject to the will of their lords, and their lords received all their property when they died, a source of particular frustration given how the economy had begun to expand on the back of climatic improvement, the reduced threat of invasion, and the growth in trade and the monetary supply. The 'lord's first night', the supposed seigneurial right to rape a new bride, is a myth, but lords did control their serfs' marriages.[17] Because serfs' offspring also belonged to their lord, a serf could not marry outside of the lord's lands without paying a fine, and those who married the serfs of another lord might find their children divvied up between their masters, right down to the last 'little girl in her cradle'.[18]

The plight of serfs caused considerable embarrassment to the rulers of a supposedly just and moral Christian society. 'There is no end to the cries or the tears of serfs,' sighed old Bishop Adalbero (he who in his youth had rappelled down the walls of Laon). But although it was considered a pious act to free a serf, most nobles, including Adalbero himself, justified serfdom as being part of the natural order of things. A popular explanation was that society was divided into three groups: those who fought, meaning nobles; those who prayed, meaning clerics; and those who worked, meaning everybody else. 'Everybody else', of course, did not always find this arrangement satisfactory. We see evidence of their discontent – and the fury with which it was met – everywhere, even in this period, long before the great peasant revolts that came after the Black Death in the fourteenth century. Saints' lives and church chronicles are full of stories about impudent serfs miraculously struck down for their insolence, while in Normandy the punishment that the duke visited upon a peasant rebellion was as awful as anything God could have devised. When their leaders came to speak with him, he ordered their hands and feet cut off and had their bleeding bodies carted back to their followers.[19]

The brutally decisive actions of the Norman dukes had protected Capetian interests since their 'pirates' had sailed up the Seine to Hugh Capet's rescue in the previous century. In Henry's reign, Normandy had proved a useful counterweight first against Henry's mother and brother Robert and then against Geoffrey Martel of Anjou. Henry and the Duke of Normandy had made common cause against Geoffrey. Geoffrey's expansionist efforts threatened the borders of Normandy, and his stepdaughter's marriage to the new emperor had brought him an imperial alliance that dashed Henry's dreams of reviving French claims in Lotharingia. Geoffrey's ascent had been assisted by disarray in Normandy following the death of the reigning duke in 1035, leaving as heir to the duchy a seven-year-old bastard named William. (Legitimacy was not yet strictly a requirement for inheritance in eleventh-century Normandy.) By all accounts, this William was an exceptionally strong and sturdy specimen, but even the hardiest little boy could not have ruled Normandy, a land crowded with castles where the politically inept fell prey to poison.[20]

By 1040, William's guardians had been assassinated and his own life was in danger. Violent family rivalries destabilized the duchy from within and enemies gnawed at its borders from without. Henry himself took the opportunity to seize a border castle. This slap to William's ducal dignity smarted, but the danger from his own barons was of greater moment. Henry and his troops fought for William at the watershed Battle of Val-ès-Dunes in 1047, massacring the rebel barons who had tried to unseat the young duke and setting the seal on William's power.[21] William and Henry then turned to face Geoffrey Martel together in a war that lasted for the next two years. Since Geoffrey remained the only real threat to either man at the end of the 1040s, it must have seemed like an incredible stroke of luck to both Henry and William when he committed a stunning act of self-sabotage by repudiating his wife in

1050. Geoffrey had grown impatient for an heir of his own body, but the divorce cost him both his power base in Aquitaine, which he had ruled on behalf of his now ex-wife's son, and his imperial alliance, which depended on her daughter's marriage to the emperor.[22]

In these reduced circumstances, Geoffrey really ought to have restrained himself from seizing the county of Maine the next year. Although the Angevin counts considered Maine a vassal state, its proximity to Normandy provoked William, now a grown man of powerful build and fearsome reputation. But as the balance of power shifted toward Normandy, Geoffrey found a friend in Henry, who had begun to look nervously at his former protégé, perhaps hearing rumours that William stood to inherit the English throne from childless King Edward and certainly aware that William had sealed a splendid marriage alliance with Flanders, wedding the count's daughter Matilda, a woman of royal and imperial blood far superior to his. Determined to keep the situation in check, Henry abandoned his support for William and struck a deal with Geoffrey, launching an invasion of Normandy in 1053. It was already too late. William was now too firmly in control of the duchy, too commanding a figure, and too effective a general. The Norman barons, once rebellious, now rallied to the duchy's defence. Decisive battles in 1054 and 1057 saw Henry defeated and chased from Normandy.[23] He was still besieging castles and trying to regain lost territory when he died in August 1060.

William's rise points to the fluid and fragile nature of Capetian kingship in the dynasty's first century, when there was so little that set them apart from the realm's other great princes. Indeed, William and his descendants were to prove an almost existential threat to the Capetians, a danger deepened by Henry's infamous and ineffectual successor Philip. But for a long time it was not clear that Henry was to have any successor at all. His second wife, an imperial princess who can have been no more than ten at the time of their betrothal, had died in 1044 along with the baby she had recently borne him. Now in his middle years, Henry badly needed an heir and should really have made a quick match with a likely local lady.

Instead, he took one of the most puzzling marital decisions in medieval history, dispatching ambassadors to the remote and only recently Christianized kingdom of Rus' to ask the Prince of Kyiv for the hand of his daughter Anne. This was a proposal that the prince was only too happy to accept. Born heir to the principality of Novgorod, he had conquered Rus' in 1015 and then embarked on a project of prestigious alliances by marrying his children into the ruling houses of foreign powers. In this way he cemented his dynasty's place in Christian Europe and forged useful ties from Brandenburg to Byzantium. The French marriage can be readily understood as part and parcel of this policy, but what possible advantages Henry could have perceived in marrying an unseen woman from an unknown land are harder to imagine.[24]

Did Henry harbour grand dreams of encircling the Western Empire, perhaps at the urging of the Flemish count or even on the advice of the Polish King Casimir? (The latter had studied in Paris in his youth and was himself married to Anne's aunt.) Was he intrigued by the prospect of a bride from what was then the Far East, one who might add 'a much-needed touch of the exotic to the homespun Capetian dynasty'?[25] Did he savour the idea that news of the marriage would reach Constantinople and make France known in the East just as Rus' wished to be known in the West? (Perhaps it was especially satisfying that Anne was the granddaughter of the Byzantine princess whom Hugh Capet had failed to obtain for Robert some sixty years earlier.) Or did Henry just like it that Anne was so very far away – a round-trip journey for the ambassadors of over five thousand miles – that she was likely to be delayed in arriving, perhaps so much so that death or another insurmountable obstacle might prevent the marriage from ever taking place? Whatever Henry hoped or feared, his Slavic princess reached France at last in 1051. In lieu of lands, she brought to the Crown a dowry of precious presents, including a great red jewel from India or Azerbaijan destined to decorate a reliquary at Saint-Denis.[26] The wedding took place in May, and about a year later Anne gave birth to a son named Philip.

Philip's name has puzzled historians almost as much as his parents' marriage. Although it eventually became a staple for French royalty and indeed a perennial favourite with French people down to the present day, the name is Greek in origin and was virtually unused in western Europe at this time. Anne, an educated woman able to write her name in Cyrillic letters, must have been perfectly aware that she was giving the future King of France an uncommon name evocative of her own Eastern upbringing, and Henry, of course, must have approved or even suggested it. Perhaps they were thinking about the Apostle Philip, crediting with converting eastern peoples just as Anne's own people had recently converted. Perhaps they were invoking Philip of Arabia, considered at this time to have been the first Christian Emperor of Rome. Maybe both were concerned about the growing animosity between the Eastern and Western Churches – soon to split irrevocably from one another in the schism of 1054 – and hoped to position Philip as a bridge across the divide. Or maybe Henry just felt sympathetic toward his new wife, twenty years his junior, probably homesick, and only just learning to speak French, and sought to comfort her with the gift of a familiar name for her first-born son.[27]

That Anne had some part in the naming or at least appreciated the gesture is shown by the fact that the name Philip was to spread first among the allies and associates of her second husband, the courageous if calculating Count Raoul of Valois. Raoul had created a sprawling lordship for himself by marrying first one heiress, invading Champagne to rescue her from a castle where her vassals had imprisoned her in opposition to the marriage, and then another after this first wife's death.[28] At the moment of Anne's widowhood in 1060, Raoul was still inconveniently married to this second lady, forcing him to invent a charge of adultery against her in order to free himself to add Anne (and her dowry lands) to his collection. If the widowed queen was sanguine in the face of these shenanigans, other people considered the marriage 'contrary to laws both human and divine', and Raoul was excommunicated.[29] Although Henry had named Anne co-regent along with the Count of Flanders, the scandal forced her to leave court and her still young son, effectively stripping her of regency powers. Historians have perhaps been overly judgemental in accusing Anne of abandoning ten-year-old Philip I in order to wed her lover, especially as it is impossible to know how much choice she had in the matter.[30] The fact nevertheless remains that a letter addressed to the pope – the only evidence we have for Philip's own feelings – states unequivocally that his mother's nuptials had 'hurt the king very, very much'.[31]

Philip did get his mother back eventually, though at the cost of accepting her new husband's regular presence, a price familiar enough to many modern stepchildren. But although Anne and Raoul again appear as signatories to royal acts from 1065, Anne never regained the regency. Her child was raised and his kingdom ruled by Count Baldwin of Flanders, a man whose wife was Philip's aunt and whose daughter was wedded to William of Normandy. An English chronicler wrote approving of Baldwin's regency that 'being thus placed as mediator between his ward and son-in-law, he was able by a policy of common sense to restrain the ambitions of both nobles and common people'.[32] But neither Baldwin nor anyone else could have restrained William of Normandy's ambitions for long. By the time Baldwin died and Philip gained his majority in 1067, William had crossed the Channel and conquered a kingdom, irrevocably altering the fates of England and France alike. William's exploits shook the foundations of post-millennial Latin Europe, but as Turkish Muslims threatened Byzantium and an infant inherited the Western Empire, even greater storms gathered on the horizon. Unfortunately for France, Philip proved uniquely unsuited to weather them.

4.

Philandering Philip
Philip I

Hope had flown high the day that King Henry had his seven-year-old son Philip crowned as his associate king in 1059. Standing before an audience of princes, prelates, and people 'great and small' who crowded into the cathedral at Reims, the little boy had solemnly read out a pledge to defend the Church and to rule his people righteously, just as a king ought to do. (Old enough to write as well as read, he was made to sign this promise, too.) These expectations outlined, Philip's father had then formally designated him as his successor and the Archbishop of Reims had anointed Philip's forehead with the special chrism sent from Heaven for the use of French kings alone. The throng had shouted its approval, crying out thrice in unison, 'We approve! We want it! Let it be done!' Bishops, abbots, dukes, and counts had come from as far afield as Aquitaine and the Auvergne to witness this rare royal ritual. Only William of Normandy was missing, but if this gave anyone an uneasy feeling, they quickly dismissed it and joined in the celebrations. The archbishop threw a lavish party afterward – not, as he explained later, on the king's account, but just to show off the Church's wealth and generosity.[1]

This archbishop was actually rather fond of young Philip and served as one of his guardians after Henry's death, but, as an adult, Philip's relations with the Church can only be described as disastrous. Excommunicated three times for adultery and unwilling to face the realities of growing papal power, Philip bore the brunt of clerics' reforming zeal. Their animus caused him many problems during his reign, and because they wrote most of the sources their contemptuous characterizations have carried the day. 'Lazy, fat, and

unfit for war' was the stinging judgement of one monastic chronicler, while another called him 'a particularly corruptible man' when it
came to religious matters and Church property.[2] For all that, their
opinions were not unfounded, especially for the second half of Philip's nearly fifty-year reign. The king was not necessarily an indolent
man, but he was certainly a corpulent one, a sign in contemporary
eyes of his undisciplined appetites not only at table but in moral matters as well.[3] More to the point, he was far better at starting wars
than he was at winning them, and he endangered his kingdom as
well as his soul by running off with the Count of Anjou's wife. While
there have been some brave attempts to rehabilitate Philip's legacy,
his reign is generally regarded as the point when the Capetian monarchy hit rock bottom. 'Few kings,' remarked his best biographer,
'have been judged more harshly by historians.'[4]

It does not help Philip's reputation that his long reign encompassed events so spectacular and so unprecedented as to pass into
legend. Philip lived through not only the Norman Conquest of England, but also the First Crusade (1096–9) and the epic struggle
between the papacy and the Empire that set the stage for it. Across
the Channel, William of Normandy forged a kingdom, freeing him
from French overlordship. Across the Alps, Pope Gregory VII hurled
anathemas and armies at the Emperor Henry IV, seeking to bend
imperial authority to the will of the Church in the service of reform.
And across the Mediterranean, ardent Christians and bloodthirsty
adventurers fought the Seljuk Turks who threatened the borders of
Byzantium and the western pilgrims seeking Jerusalem. Philip,
however, had almost nothing to do with any of this. Old King Henry's strengths had been overshadowed by those of the more
interesting and accomplished figures of his time, but it was Philip's
weaknesses on the battlefield and in the bedroom that marked him
out from his contemporaries.

Philip could not, of course, help beginning his reign on the back
foot since William had conquered England a year before he himself
reached majority. William's absence at the king's coronation had signalled his growing disregard for the Capetians' claims to overlordship

in Normandy even before he gained a kingdom and a crown. His coronation in Westminster Abbey on Christmas Day 1066 made him Philip's equal, or so he felt. His fellow Normans agreed, especially when they contemplated the extensive English lands and rich prizes that William proceeded to dole out to his followers. A religious man though a ruthless one, he also gave generously to the Church, and he championed a reforming rigour pleasing to the pope, whose interventions in Europe's princely politics were becoming ever more intrusive and effective. William did do homage, the ritual act of kneeling in submission before one's lord, for the duchy of Normandy in 1060, but it would take more than half a century of war and diplomacy before a Norman duke again bent the knee to a Capetian king.[5]

Philip's only option to counter Norman ascendance was to exploit the incessant quarrels between William and his sons: Robert Curthose, William Rufus, and Henry. The policy's results were mixed at best because Philip tended to favour the undoubtedly audacious and honourable if 'probably plump' and certainly ill-fortuned Robert Curthose over his father and two brothers.[6] Curthose, so called because his fat little legs required short (*court*) trousers (*hose*), did enjoy some early successes against the father who gave him this mocking nickname. In 1077, worry about Robert moved King William to give Philip half of the Vexin in northwestern France after being defeated in Brittany. Robert had grown sick of his father teasing him about his weight and tired of waiting to get his hands on Normandy. When William sided with his younger sons for literally pissing on Robert and his friends from a balcony, Robert exploded in rebellion.[7] Only too happy to help, Philip gave him a castle in the Vexin and a small army of vicious mercenaries. Underestimated by his father (and by most historians ever since), Robert met William in battle and unhorsed him on the field, though honour restrained him from finishing the old man off. Yet despite this demonstration of filial piety and although he was the eldest son, Robert's efforts to claim the English throne upon William's death in 1087 came to nothing. William Rufus made good his father's wish that he inherit England, while Robert had to content himself with Normandy.

Deprived of England and thus also of the English plunder that had greased the wheels of governing Normandy in his father's day, Robert had to seek Philip's help to hold on to both the duchy and the rebellious border county of Maine, where the Norman dukes supposedly held sway.[8] Philip, notorious according to chroniclers for his cupidity, accepted a bribe to abandon Robert when William Rufus invaded Normandy in 1090, leading the brothers to make a peace very disadvantageous to Philip's interests. Philip then joined Robert to interfere in a little war between two Vexin lords that threatened to destabilize the region, but he left him as the fighting spilled over into Maine in 1092, a fateful moment that marked the end of Philip's active efforts to control events in western France.[9] Robert's defeat and capture at the Battle of Tinchebray in 1106 handed control of Normandy back to the English Crown and reconstituted the Anglo-Norman realm as it had been in the Conqueror's day. Philip's failure to get to grips with Anglo-Norman power bequeathed to his successors a perilous and painful legacy. Bristling with castles and crawling with soldiers, the Anglo-Norman border lay little more than a day's ride from Paris, like a knife at the throat of Capetian France.[10]

The Anglo-Normans might not have been such a problem. The Capetians were, after all, used to dealing with strong regional princes. They had survived this far partly by relying on the ritual prestige that came from ceremonies like Philip's coronation but mainly through creating alliances that exploited the rivalries between other great houses. Philip was trying to do something similar by playing William and his sons off against one another. But, for reasons initially political and then intimately personal, Philip could not look to Anjou as a counterweight against Normandy as his father had done. The old count Geoffrey Martel had died childless in 1060, his disastrous divorce in search of an heir having borne no fruit. This circumstance set off an eight-year struggle for the succession that left once-mighty Anjou a shadow of its former self. Philip gained a rich territory southeast of Paris called the Gâtinais in exchange for supporting the successful claimant, one Fulk 'le Réchin', an untranslatable nickname that might mean 'the rich', but then the king squandered the advantages of his Angevin alliance by an act of unforgivable betrayal.

This new Count Fulk was a curious character. Although excoriated by a prudish chronicler for popularizing shoes with long, curly toes, he used his wealth not only to make fashion statements but also to support the Church in its pursuit of reform.[11] This policy made him friends in Rome, under whose protection he placed his county, but he did not live up to the reputation of his grandfather and namesake Fulk Nerra for hard-nosed efficiency or dazzling grandeur (save for the shoes). Aside from writing an inelegant but entertaining account of his family's history, Fulk le Réchin's achievements include papal excommunication for keeping his brother chained up in a dungeon and general disapprobation for casually marrying and divorcing at least three women, one of whom he lost to King Philip's seductions in 1092.[12] This scandal was to cost Philip the goodwill of Anjou, the Church, and modern historians alike.

It was perhaps this lady's allure that led Philip to abandon the war on the Maine frontier in 1092. Despite his support for the Norman duke, Robert Curthose, Philip had kept open a back channel to Fulk le Réchin who dreamt of making Maine an Angevin vassal state as it had been in the golden age of his grandfather. Fulk had previously agreed to help Curthose in Maine in exchange for his permission to marry the young maiden Bertrada of Montfort, but he had since had second thoughts, and now he invited Philip to the city of Tours to discuss matters. Perhaps, as had been speculated, Fulk may even have intimated that, if Philip would give him free rein in Maine, he would give the king free rein with beautiful Bertrada.[13] That seems unlikely given the venomous insults that Fulk spat toward Philip later, but the king may well have gone to Tours with Bertrada on his mind.

Philip had reached a time in his life when change can seem irresistibly attractive: forty years old, father of two, and with three decades of kingship behind him, he had been married to his first wife, Berthe of Holland, for almost twenty years. We can well imagine that he might have been restless and bored, and his wife, says one chronicler, had gained a lot of weight.[14] Philip could persuade himself that leaving her for this younger woman wasn't even a reckless career move. After all, the lands of Bertrada's family lay just southwest of the Vexin, ideally positioned for harrying the Norman frontier. So, although it was only May and the summer campaign season had hardly begun, Philip sent some excuse to Curthose, hoisted his own, increasingly heavy body onto his horse, and rode south to the old city to have dinner with Fulk and his lovely lady.

We can imagine Bertrada, standing at the door to welcome her husband's guests and watching the king and his entourage arrive with the cool calculation of a castellan's daughter who owed her position entirely to her forefathers' foresight and ambition, not their princely bona fides. Said to have nothing good about her except for her face and known for her skill 'in all the astonishing female arts that women use to walk all over their husbands', Bertrada had Fulk wrapped around her little finger for now.[15] But she was well aware that he had unceremoniously discarded his two previous wives. Perhaps she thought it best to take her vengeance in advance. Philip's rapidly spreading middle may have turned her off a little, but she liked his talk and she was keen on his crown. Philip flirted and Bertrada smiled, and a flurry of surreptitious signals passed between the king and the countess as evening fell and the court retired to bed. Some sources say that Philip came to Bertrada that very night, others that it was Bertrada who sought out Philip, others still that it wasn't until the next day that she slipped out, journeying under secret royal escort to rendezvous with the king down the road to Orléans. All agree that, once joined, the pair would never be parted, no matter the reproaches from their former spouses, their spiritual counsellors, or even their subjects.

It was the work of a night and a day for Philip to elope with Bertrada, but the consequences would linger for decades. He had destroyed all of his alliances in a stroke. What successes he had managed to eke out in the first half of his reign fell away in the second.

He had abandoned Curthose for Fulk, but whatever Fulk had offered Philip – if he had offered him anything – living life as a public cuckold outrageously victimized by an abuser of his hospitality was not what the Angevin count had in mind. 'Disgraceful King Philip's adultery,' fumed Fulk, 'has defiled France.'[16] Compounding the collapse of Angevin support in the west was Philip's loss of Flemish support in the northeast, for his humiliated first wife, Berthe of Holland, was stepdaughter to the Count of Flanders and half-sister to his heir. Philip had married her in 1072 as the price of peace after backing the wrong horse and losing a key battle in a war over the Flemish succession. His repudiation of Berthe not only wrecked that reconciliation but also offered the Anglo-Normans another opportunity to profit at Philip's expense. Seething with hatred for Philip, the Flemish count sailed for England where William Rufus, now king despite Curthose's claims, gleefully hosted him at Dover, and there they discussed all the ways they might make Philip pay for past injuries. The count died soon thereafter, but his son (the ex-queen's half-brother) despised Philip even more than his father had. The Bishop of Arras wrote that he dared not travel outside his frontier city for fear that war would break out at any minute.[17]

Philip hoped it would all blow over. He convoked the bishops of France to Paris so that he could be divorced from Berthe and marry Bertrada. Most of them even came and did as they were told. After all, both Philip and Bertrada's previous marriages were technically invalid according to the Church's laws against consanguinity. Philip's first wife was his sixth cousin, and Bertrada was Fulk's fifth, not that Fulk had bothered with such ecclesiastical niceties as annulment when he walked away from his previous marriages. Philip and Bertrada were even more closely related to one another than to their previous spouses, but that would only pose a problem if Philip changed his mind later on.[18] The sad story of Philip's grandfather Robert the Pious's tragic entanglement with Bertha of Blois notwithstanding, powerful men changed wives when they wanted, and their bishops made exceptions to the rules accordingly. They owed their sees to royal favour, for eleventh-century rulers decided whom to appoint when an episcopal vacancy arose. Once a prince had indicated his preferred candidate, the local clergy then held an election *pro forma* and the winner was consecrated either by the area's archbishop or by other local bishops, or even by the pope himself if he happened to be available.

For a long time, all of this had been a mere formality, but secular involvement in investiture, as the process was called, flagrantly violated the canon laws of the Church, as well as the sensibilities of those Christians, lay and clerical alike, committed to purifying the Church of the world's corruption. Rulers objected, and understandably so, that bishops simply wielded too much power to allow the Church a free hand in choosing their occupants. With castles, armies, leagues of land and legions of labourers all their own, bishops controlled all the accoutrements of princely power, in addition to the sacred attributes of their office. The conflict over investiture, not to mention a bundle of other reforming measures virtually designed to raise the old guard's hackles, caused one of the greatest crises of the Middle Ages, a showdown between Pope Gregory VII and Emperor Henry IV. Henry eventually found himself at Gregory's mercy in 1077, excommunicated and forced to stand barefoot in the snow before the Tuscan castle of Canossa for refusing to keep his nose out of Church business and his hands off Church property. (It hadn't helped the emperor's cause that he had called Gregory 'not pope, but false monk' in a public letter he sent around to all the important people in Germany.) If Philip felt a little anxious at the treatment of the emperor, a far more powerful man than he, imperial politics now impinged very little on France, and his own involvement in clerical investiture continued largely unchallenged.[19]

The bishop most in debt to Philip's patronage was Bishop Ivo of Chartres, but it was he who wrecked Philip's would-be marital bliss. Unlike most bishops, scions of great lineages who could call upon their families whenever they hit a spot of trouble, Ivo had come from nothing and owed his elevation to the episcopate entirely to Philip, who, as he readily acknowledged, had basically thrust the episcopal crozier into his hands.[20] His common origins sometimes left him out of sympathy with a status quo that winked at great men's indiscretions or endorsed reasons of state over the claims of conscience, at least in this early period of his career. A principled man of acute – not to say acerbic – intelligence, Ivo nevertheless possessed a pragmatic streak and favoured a more flexible approach to reform than the implacable faction that dominated Pope Urban's circle. Ivo accepted, for example, that kings had a legitimate interest in investiture, but on the subject of Philip's second marriage he was as obdurately opposed as any hardliner in Christendom.

Philip knew he needed Ivo's support, but the bishop was not for turning. Ivo wrote to him, quoting Scripture to say that he would rather 'be thrown into the sea with a millstone around his neck' (Matthew 18:6) than be seen to support Philip's adultery.[21] Piously, he reminded the king that he was only acting in the best interests of his soul. Philip left the bishop to the mercies of a rapacious castellan who imprisoned him, but such privations only strengthened the resolve of a righteous man like Ivo. In the years to come, these unpleasantries with his former patron helped Ivo to shape Church doctrine on marriage in ways that still hamper middle-aged Catholics' attempts at second marriages today.[22] Philip found himself repeatedly excommunicated and France placed under interdict, meaning the Mass could not be celebrated nor the sacraments administered. At a time when religious feeling grew ever more fervent among ordinary men and women, these sanctions lost him the support of his subjects. Church bells fell silent when he and Bertrada approached a town, only to ring out all the louder when the shameful couple finally departed, as if jeering them on their way.[23]

Pope Urban had been shocked by Philip's actions, but he tried to steer a middle path between the king's intransigence and that of the ecclesiastical hardliners. He had no appetite for a French mess dumped on top of everything else on his plate. The papal-imperial crisis over reform had only deepened in the years since Emperor Henry had humbled himself at Canossa. At this point in the conflict, Urban's see and even his personal safety were threatened by a rival pope's imperial supporters, who were forcibly occupying Rome. Further east was another headache, one with even greater importance for the future of Europe. Constantinople, a city packed with precious relics and home to the great basilica Hagia Sophia that dwarfed any church in western Europe, was in danger. Over the last twenty years, the Seljuk Turks had beaten back the borders of Byzantium, and by the time Philip fell for Bertrada, Anatolia had fallen to the Turks. Urban felt a Christian duty to protect Constantinople itself, but he was equally worried that these Muslims would not only overrun the city but also cut off the pilgrim route to Jerusalem. The Byzantine emperor, Alexios Comnenos, had taken to asking Latin Christians for help when they stopped off at his palace on their way to Jerusalem, and early in 1095 he sent messengers to Urban in Italy, imploring his aid.[24]

With the weight of the known world on his shoulders, Urban understandably hesitated to add a French imbroglio to his burdens, but after two years spent trying gently to shepherd Philip in the right direction, he had to admit that Ivo was right. A Frenchman himself, Urban sought the counsel of his countrymen and the comforts of home, undertaking a long sojourn in southern and central France in the summer of 1095, though he remained pointedly outside the lands north of the River Loire that were part of the excommunicated Capetian king's direct domain. As summer ended, Urban wrote to the European clergy, calling them to a council at Clermont in central France to settle the difficult problems that beset the Church and its people.

A dozen or so archbishops, eighty-odd bishops, and ninety or more abbots (each with his own entourage) came from all over the Capetian realm and as far away as Spain, Italy, and the Empire to descend upon Clermont in November.[25] There they decreed excommunication against the French king and his so-called queen, as well as against the German emperor and his anti-pope, and they ordained new peace measures: a truce from sunset on Wednesday until sunrise on Monday when no violence was permitted, for reform and peace continued to be linked and the millennial spirit was not yet extinguished. (That very year, marvelled Fulk le Réchin, stars had fallen from the sky like hail.)[26] As at the Peace councils earlier in the century, crowds of lay people flocked to the fields outside the city where the clerics met in the hope of seeing something extraordinary. They were not disappointed. On 27 November, Urban stood before them and preached the most important sermon of the Middle Ages, one whose exact words no one now will ever know, but whose effect cannot be overstated.

He spoke, it seems, of Jerusalem. Sited at the centre of the world on medieval maps, Jerusalem was where God himself was believed to have lived and died in human flesh. It was the earthly symbol of the Heavenly Kingdom and the place where the Apocalypse was widely expected to begin. Some in Urban's audience had been to Jerusalem themselves, or at least knew someone who had. Since the Christian conversion of Hungary had opened a land-based route to the Holy Land at the beginning of the century, a steady stream of pilgrims had made their way eastward, bringing back stories of the city and tokens imbued with the sacred power of the relics they had touched there. These pilgrims, and the ever-expanding circle of friends, relatives, and acquaintances who had listened with rapt attention to their tales, had a sense of Jerusalem not only as unimaginably exotic but also as comfortably familiar. Were someone to evoke its present peril, they would take it personally.

But what Urban proposed to do about the situation, writes one historian, 'was insane'.[27] Since we have various versions of what he said – medieval sermons were extemporized and only written down later if ever – it is hard to know what exactly he did propose. Still, to judge from the reports we have and what happened afterward, his plan was indeed essentially unprecedented and enormously risky.[28] He clearly exhorted people to undertake the journey east, probably casting the endeavour as a sort of 'armed pilgrimage' against the Seljuk Turks threatening Byzantium and Christian access to Jerusalem. Most of the versions that we have of this sermon describe the cruelties he alleged the Seljuks were committing against Christians in gruesome detail: 'When they wish to torture people to a base death,' one report of the sermon claims, 'they perforate their navels, and dragging forth the extremity of the intestines, bind it to a stake; then with flogging they lead the victim around until, the viscera having gushed forth, the victim falls prostrate upon the ground.'[29] Urban called upon the French, as the descendants of Charlemagne and a people chosen by God like the Israelites of history, to take up arms against the Muslim Turks, followers of Antichrist, and to prepare the Holy Land for the Apocalypse.[30]

The crowd may not actually have shouted 'God wills it!' (*Deus vult!*) in response to the vision Urban laid out, as one chronicler reported, but there is no doubt that they responded rapturously, not only whilst under the sermon's spell at Clermont but in the weeks and months that followed. News of the expedition was spread through electrifying sermons at altars and in market squares, public letters read out to enthusiastic crowds, and excited rumours passed from person to person.[31] The pilgrims (for so they thought of themselves) sewed crosses on their clothing as a proud sign of their intentions, mortgaged their possessions, turned their faces toward the sunrise, and set off down the road to death or glory.

Christians of both sexes, of all social ranks, and from every corner of Europe joined the crowds heading east in the spring and summer of 1096. 'Even the Welshman gave up his forest hunting, the Scot his familiar fleas, the Dane his continual drinking, and the Norwegian his raw fish,' but it was especially those of France who swelled the pilgrim flood.[32] (So French was the crusade that crusaders became known simply as 'Franks'.) Peasants abandoned their ploughs at the urging of a charismatic preacher named Peter the Hermit, who showed them a letter from Heaven and promised to lead them all the way there – and he did, too.[33] Alongside the elated masses journeyed many of the great and the good among French princes. Robert Curthose hocked his duchy to his brother to raise funds for the journey. Count Stephen of Blois, married to Curthose's sister, kissed her goodbye and promised to write, while Count Raymond of Toulouse took his wife with him. Even King Philip's younger brother Hugh cobbled together a small force and shipped out, arriving at Constantinople before many of the others had yet departed in the spring of 1096, when it seemed the whole world was on the move.

Meanwhile in Byzantium, Emperor Alexios had simply been hoping that Urban would scrape together a mercenary force to bolster his own troops in strategic engagements. Instead, Alexios watched with irritation and growing alarm as a series of unruly mobs numbering in the tens, or even the hundreds, of thousands pitched their camps before the towering walls of Constantinople. Reasoning that they were on their way to fight non-Christians, many of the arriving westerners had participated in atrocious pogroms against the Jewish communities they met on the way, their thirst for violence only whetted by the rivers of blood they spilled in the Jewish quarters of Rhineland Germany, where mothers slew their infants rather than surrender them to the Christians.[34] The westerners' 'uncontrollable passion, their erratic nature and . . . their greed for money' disgusted the emperor's daughter and biographer, who wrote – albeit some decades later – of their 'horrible cruelty to the whole population' and the atrocities they visited even upon the babies, whom she claims one contingent impaled on spits and roasted over bonfires outside Nicaea (modern İznik).[35] The crusaders suffered in their turn. For nearly three years they fought, sometimes capturing cities, sometimes losing them. Famine and disease beset them, as well as the unfamiliar battle tactics of the Muslim forces, who cut their armies, filled with the overly enthusiastic but woefully unprepared, to shreds in the rocky passes and arid plains of the Near East.[36]

But in the end, they got what they came for. On 15 July 1099 the Franks pushed a wooden siege engine against the walls of Jerusalem under a hail of fire and arrows, and, crossing from it to the battlements via a hastily constructed bridge, they fell upon the city and unleashed pandemonium. Some inhabitants fled to the top of Solomon's Temple, where ten thousand were said to have been beheaded, while in the streets a massacre of the city's Jews and Muslims commenced. The blood ran ankle-deep as men and women, old and young alike, were slain with indiscriminate fury. Nor did the invaders refrain from pillaging anything they could lay their hands on. A Christian chronicler, present at the slaughter, said they split open the bodies of the dead to pick out any gold coins the victims might have swallowed for safekeeping. The innumerable corpses were piled up and burnt, for 'in the ashes they found the gold more easily'.[37] The Count of Lower Lorraine, Godfrey of Bouillon, found himself proclaimed King of Jerusalem. In centuries to come, Europeans were to rank him alongside Alexander the Great, Julius Caesar, and King Arthur as one of the worthiest men in history or legend. Back in Constantinople, even Emperor Alexios was impressed, and in France, the news was received with rapture.

King Philip, however, had little personally to celebrate. Excommunication had barred him from taking the cross even had he wished to do so, and he laboured under its sentence all through those years of staggering violence and resounding glory, unwilling to give up Bertrada as the price of pardon.[38] He did try. Again and again, he sought absolution, promising to separate from her forever – or at least to see her only under chaperone – but again and again he returned to her. Even after he humbled himself barefoot and penitent in Paris before a crowd of bishops and abbots and was finally received back into the arms of the Church, he could not restrain himself from seeking her out. As time wore on, his old enemies gave him less grief about it. Ivo of Chartres, softened by success and no longer the angry outsider, smoothed over some of his problems, while Fulk le Réchin even hosted Philip and Bertrada together in Anjou. But it was too late to redeem his reign. Feeling unworthy to be laid among his celebrated ancestors in Saint-Denis, Philip chose burial beneath the stones of Fleury at Saint-Benoît-sur-Loire, where he would lie for centuries without so much as a marker.[39] Philip knew he had been a foolish man, and he hated himself for it. He just couldn't bring himself to love God's kingdom, or his own, more than he loved Bertrada.

PART TWO

By Fire and Sword, Prayer and Propaganda

(1108–1180)

Simplified Capetian family tree, 1108–80

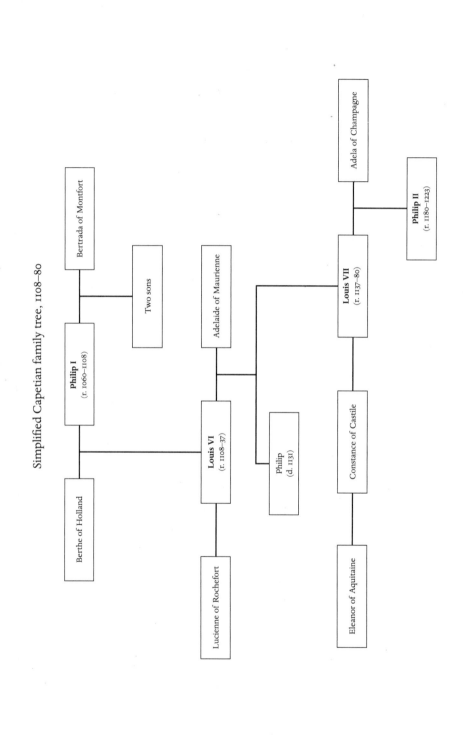

5

The Knight-King
Louis VI

By the time he died in 1137, King Louis VI had run to fat like his father, Philip I. Too heavy for the horses, he had his men carry him on their shoulders through the narrow passes of his kingdom when he went on campaign.[1] But Louis, known to posterity as 'the Fat', resembled Philip only in obesity. If Capetian fortunes reached their nadir under Philip, the reign of Louis VI marks the moment when they changed decisively and durably for the better. Louis combined the two most important ingredients of power at the turn of the twelfth century: he was friendly with powerful men in the Church, and his armies were successful against his enemies on the battle-field, both skills that Philip had conspicuously failed to master. Philip the incorrigible adulterer had squandered the sacred prestige of his dynasty, reportedly losing the miraculous healing abilities that his grandfather Robert had first manifested, and his military ineptitude had dissipated royal lands, now confined to an area around Paris known as the Île-de-France and ringed round with the castles of royal rivals. The great families had drifted further from the royal orbit, preoccupied with their own affairs and border quarrels, while the growing group of lesser nobles saw more opportunities for adventure and advancement fighting Muslims on the frontiers of Latin Europe. As the eleventh century gave way to the twelfth, the action appeared decidedly elsewhere to those living in Capetian lands. But that was beginning to change even before Louis's consecration as king in 1108, performed at Orléans with a haste that shocked contemporaries only a few days after Philip's death, for 'action' could have been Louis's middle name.

Born in 1081 to Philip's first – some would say only – wife, Louis had taken over the kingdom's military affairs in his teens and was already being called 'defender of the realm' and 'general of the army' before his father died.[2] Decades later, his friend and biographer Abbot Suger of Saint-Denis recalled how as a young man Prince Louis could be glimpsed dashing across the realm with his band of knights, now riding south to put out fires (or set them) in Berry or the Auvergne, now rushing back north to the Norman border to tussle with William Rufus or his successor Henry I.[3] With his father plagued by excommunication, rotten teeth, and scabies, the vigorous young prince appeared already more powerful than Philip himself, so much so that Bertrada machinated unsuccessfully to have him imprisoned for life while he was visiting the English court after Rufus's death in 1100. This plot foiled, Bertrada connived with sorcerers and poisoners to put an end to her stepson when he returned to Paris. Only the intervention of a 'hairy doctor from Barbary' steeped in Muslim medical knowledge saved Louis's life.[4] Philip had had his own quarrels with his eldest son, and his own sons with Bertrada to provide for, but he found the episode sufficiently shocking that he finally officially named Louis heir to the kingdom and associate-king in late 1102.[5]

Louis combined his status as king (or king-in-waiting) with that of a knight, having been 'adorned and honoured with knightly arms' a few years earlier (possibly behind his father's back) after acquitting himself well in a war with Rufus over the Vexin.[6] Kings and knights are now both so emblematic of the Middle Ages that it is hard to imagine that at this time the knight–king combination was a relatively novel one. In 1098, when seventeen-year-old Louis received his arms, knighthood had only been a respectable status synonymous with nobility in northern France for a few decades. Before that, a knight was just a soldier of no particular background, valued, but also vilified, for the violent work he did. But as raising armies in the eleventh century came to require great princes to reward their soldiers (these knights) with land, and the knights and their commanders began to view this land as family property, the knights' bloodlines took on a new importance. No longer disreputable, low-born men whose company stained the reputation of their associates, by the late eleventh century knights were welcomed at court and admired for their exploits. Knighthood began to seem integral to noble identity, not inimical to it.

By Louis's day, knights and kings alike had come to share a world view and a way of life we might call chivalry.[7] Evocative now of refined if antiquated behaviour, the word's derivation betrays the knightly class's bellicose origins. Chivalry (*chevalerie* in French) derives from the French word for horse (*cheval*), because knights fought on horseback as the shock troops of the cavalry charge, a key tactic in some of the period's most important battles. The chivalric ethos espoused by these horsemen required that they act honourably (at least toward one another) and that they possess both bravery and prowess, which they demonstrated not only on the battlefield but also in a new kind of military game called tournament. At this early date in its history, tournament was simply a less deadly re-enaction of the cavalry charge, not the elaborate show it later became. Some clergymen took a dim view of tournament's point-less violence – the first papal prohibitions date to the 1130s – but a growing association between chivalry and crusade infused twelfth-century knighthood with a sense of Christian purpose. The homicidal ends of the knightly profession, so obviously sinful, could be not just excused but positively glorified as the protection of the Church and the persecution of its enemies.[8] It is no accident that the *Song of Roland*, with its tales of martial exploits, unfailing courage, and loyalty unto death, not to mention its confident assertion that 'Pagans are wrong, and Christians are right!', emerged at just this moment.

The halo of crusading glory that hovered over chivalric knighthood cannot eclipse the fact that knights' new social status owed much to the inability of eleventh-century kings, especially Louis's father, to prevent the proliferation of castles and the devolution of power to lesser lords lower down the social scale. Philip had been 'too lax to punish tyrants', wrote an Anglo-Norman chronicler, particularly in the later decades of his reign when obesity and obsession overcame him.[9] But Louis, although he endorsed and enjoyed the

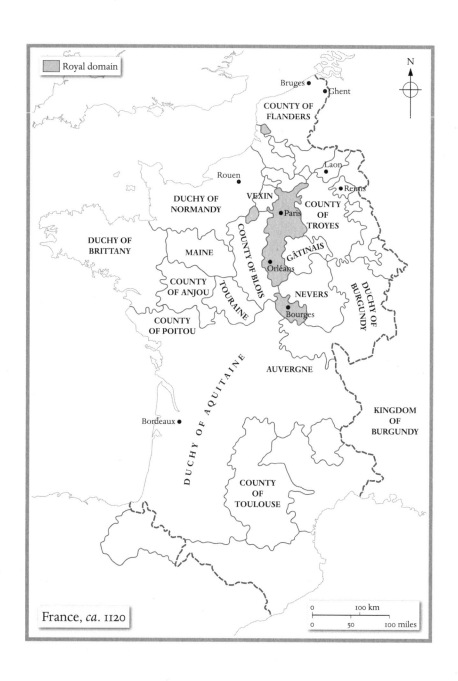

Royal domain

Bruges
Ghent
COUNTY OF
FLANDERS

Rouen
Laon
Reims

DUCHY OF
NORMANDY
VEXIN
COUNTY
OF
TROYES
Paris

DUCHY OF
BRITTANY
MAINE
COUNTY OF BLOIS
GÂTINAIS
Orléans

COUNTY
OF ANJOU
TOURAINE
NEVERS
DUCHY OF
BURGUNDY

COUNTY
OF POITOU
Bourges

DUCHY OF AQUITAINE
AUVERGNE

Bordeaux
KINGDOM
OF
BURGUNDY

COUNTY
OF
TOULOUSE

N

France, ca. 1120

0   100 km
0   50   100 miles

trappings of knighthood, had no truck with upstarts eager to extend their authority at the cost of his own. He was happy to play their games to his enemies' detriment, especially with those along the Norman frontier who chafed at the English king's authority. In his own lands, it was a different matter, and he saw both a sacred duty and a political opportunity in protecting Church property from the 'insupportable and execrable evil' that castellans were wont to visit upon their clerical neighbours.[10]

By taming the castellans' violent ambitions – mostly by acting even more ambitiously and violently himself – Louis gave later Capetian kings the leisure to expand their territory beyond the Île-de-France, to raise the taxes to pay for it, and to create the ideological juggernaut that justified and extended their power. Had he not hammered away at the castellans with fire and sword, his descendants would have spent all their time as he had had to do in his youth, fighting the little wars and petty conflicts that broke out on an almost monthly basis and finding even their own security threatened by men so forward as to think that pillaging the royal palace – a thing that actually happened in 1111 – was fair play.[11] Not that riding about, besieging and burning castles (and sometimes churches, too!) wasn't fun. Louis had a talent for the brutal flourish. Once he cut off the right hands of some enemy soldiers and sent the men back to their commanders, 'carrying their fists in their fists'.[12]

Louis had learned that he could not countenance the castellans from watching the failure of his father's conciliatory approach. Perhaps concluding that their rise was irresistible, Philip had embraced these unruly families whose surnames, like Montfort (strong hill) and Rochefort (strong rock), betrayed their modest if martial origins. That Philip had exchanged the daughter of a count for that of a castellan might be put down to the mysteries of love, but that he married both of his elder sons into castellan families suggests a policy decision born of his dynasty's diminished prestige, as well as the castellans' new position of importance among the kingdom's elite. On Bertrada's advice, Philip betrothed Louis to a little girl from the Rochefort family and put her father in charge of his army.[13]

The castellans' rising star burned all the brighter after the First Crusade, for men of these families had distinguished themselves fighting in that holy war, and the Capetians could not help feeling a little outshone by the returning heroes of Christendom.[14] Louis had been too young to participate and Philip, excommunicated at the time, had been too sinful. While Philip's younger brother Hugh had gone on the crusade, he had returned ignominiously early after the going got tough at the siege of Antioch, before the miraculous capture of Jerusalem rewarded those who stayed the course. So, when Bohemond of Taranto, the blue-eyed and sandy-haired warrior who had raised his banner over Antioch and made himself both its prince and the most eligible bachelor in Christendom, announced his intention to tour France, Philip made the bishops dissolve his daughter's barren and long-unhappy marriage to the Count of Champagne. If the princess, 'beautiful of face and charming of character', had not planned to take another spouse so unseemly soon, Bohemond overwhelmed her defences with 'presents and promises'.[15] She was a prize too precious to let pass.

Bohemond badly needed the Capetian princess's prestige. Although he was now of princely status in his own right, his family were little more than opportunistic adventurers from Normandy who had carved out a position for themselves as warlords in southern Italy and the eastern Mediterranean through violent conquest. His own signature victory at Antioch had been won first by exploiting a Turkish traitor to help him, infiltrating his men into the city over a rickety ladder under cover of night and then by extorting title to the city from his fellow crusaders, who needed Antioch secured to continue on their way to Jerusalem.[16] By 1104, the Byzantine emperor had grown so exasperated with Bohemond that the 'hero' had to fake his own death and travel in a coffin perfumed by a rotting chicken carcass to pass through imperial waters on his way back west to France.[17] Bohemond could wash away the stench of dead poultry, but if an air of dishonour clung to him more doggedly, it didn't dissuade the Capetians from welcoming him into the family with a big wedding in Chartres Cathedral and a fine feast laid on by the Countess of Blois. (Bohemond used the occasion to canvass the guests, looking for recruits for his plans to conquer Constantinople.)[18] In fact, the Capetians doubled-down, shipping Constance's half-sister Cecile off to Tripoli to marry Bohemond's nephew Tancred, a man only a little less famous and nearly as ruthless as Bohemond himself.

At the time of his sisters' marriages in 1106, Louis already possessed a spouse with crusading connections – his Rochefort father-in-law had gone east on the First Crusade and returned there on an ill-fated follow-up expedition in 1101 – but he had never been enthused by the match and had left it unconsummated. When the pope visited France in 1107 in search of support in his seemingly interminable struggle against the German emperor, the young prince took the opportunity of his father's age and inactivity to have the marriage annulled and handed the Rochefort girl over to a castellan husband more at her level. Louis then stayed single for nearly a decade before choosing a bride named Adelaide in 1115. Known as Adelaide of Maurienne for the place of her birth, an old Provençal settlement tucked into the folds of the French Alps, she possessed a pedigree more in keeping with Capetian precedent, being both daughter to the Count of Savoy and niece to the pope. A relatively mature twenty-three at the time of her marriage and perhaps not the prettiest of princesses, she nevertheless had more sway over king and kingdom than had been seen in a Capetian queen since the days of Constance of Arles.

Luckily for Louis, the pair got on much better than Constance and Robert had done. Louis could rely on Adelaide, much as Hugh Capet had relied on his queen, who bore essentially the same name. Like Hugh's Adela, Louis's Adelaide was his companion and his co-ruler, so much so that royal acts bear her name and the year of her reign as well as Louis's own. By comparison with Louis's mother, whose name appears on only three royal acts, Adelaide's appears on forty-five.[19] Married in March 1115, during the Lenten season and therefore prohibited from immediately consummating the marriage, the newlyweds passed some anxious months before Adelaide finally fell pregnant around Christmas and was safely delivered of a bouncing boy in August 1116. In keeping with tradition, the royal infant bore his grandfather's name (Philip), while his brother, born four years later – perhaps after miscarriages or unrecorded still-births intervened – was named for his father. Princes Philip and Louis were followed by six other children, all but one of them male.

Louis's repudiation of his first wife in 1107 marked the moment of his shift away from his father's accommodating policies toward the castellans. That same year he had removed castellan men from the palace offices they occupied under Philip. In their place, he installed men of even more modest origins, giving the honours to the Garlande family, who were noble, but only just. The Garlandes had first appeared at court as if from nowhere in the 1080s as hangers-on who could only dream of rising to the rank of a castel-lan. By the turn of the century, the family had ingratiated itself with Louis, who supported their most dynamic member, Stephen, in his ambitions to become Bishop of Beauvais over the vociferous objec-tions not only of the cathedral's own clerics but also those of Bishop Ivo of Chartres, who considered the man 'an illiterate, skirt-chasing chancer'.[20] The see went to someone else, but when Louis came into his kingdom, Stephen Garlande became France's chancellor and his brothers were handed other palace offices. The Garlande men owed everything to Louis, Stephen especially. His service raised him to the very pinnacle of power. Known in France as Louis's second-in-command, his *vice roy*, Stephen's reputation spread as far as Jerusalem, whose clerics sent a relic of the Holy Cross to Paris just for him.[21]

Louis showered his chancellor with appointments to lucrative benefices, but he always remembered that Stephen was his creature. When, after two decades in office, Stephen forgot which side of his bread was buttered and who had buttered it, Louis, led by Queen Adelaide, put him back in his place with alacrity, stripping him of his titles, razing his houses in Paris, and ripping up his vineyards. That was one advantage of relying on 'men raised from the dust': you could return them to dust whenever it pleased you. Men with posher pedigrees might make faces to see the palace defiled by the presence of hard-working plebs, but Louis realized that there was more to kingship than princely prestige and winning battles (though that was nice, too). He could look to England, where the Domesday survey had shown the Conqueror where all the wealth of his new kingdom lay, right down to the number of eels that could be fished from the marshes and the pen where one Hugh the Donkey 'may keep what he can catch' along the Welsh border.[22] That was the kind of administrative acumen a modern king needed.

The castellans did not help their case with Louis as they colluded with England every chance they got.[23] The new English king, Henry I, was a hard and humourless man. He blinded not only actual traitors but even those who dared to compose silly songs at his expense.[24] Still, if he was not merciful, he was just, and if he was not affable, he was effective, especially in war. When he re-attached Normandy to the English Crown after defeating and imprisoning his older brother Robert Curthose at the Battle of Tinchebray in 1106 – Curthose's crusading credentials counted for nothing with Henry – the castellans were encouraged by King Philip's failing health, Louis's relative youth, and the possibility of struggle over the succession with Bertrada's sons to take advantage of the opportunity to ally with Henry. The southern castellans, not least among them the Rochefort family of Louis's ex-wife, flocked to Henry's side when war threatened again in 1109.

Under contention was the castle of Gisors, whose position on the Norman frontier was to make it the regular object of military ventures for the next century. Gisors had been built by William Rufus during his brief reign and then came into the hands of a castellan called Pagan until Henry took it off him shortly after Tinchebray. As Louis's counsellor and biographer Suger explained, Gisors lay on the north bank of the River Epte, which traced a natural boundary between the Capetians' heartlands and the troublesome Norman duchy. Gisors, a towering fortress representing the finest in modern castle construction, offered easy entry into France for the Normans while repelling French armed advances into Normandy. Henry had to have it. Louis could not countenance the threat. The French king gave his Norman duke an ultimatum: destroy Gisors or give it back to Pagan, a man more amenable to the Capetian's control. Henry naturally found neither option palatable, so Louis named a time and place for negotiations, collected an army, and burned and ravaged Norman lands on his way there, 'giving such gifts', Suger observed ironically, 'in order to facilitate the negotiations'.[25]

When the appointed day arrived, the French and Norman forces faced off on either side of the Epte with only a rickety bridge between them. Louis sent a spokesman across the river to remonstrate with Henry. Since Henry would not agree to abide by the law, as Louis saw it, the French offered to settle the matter through a duel. When the Normans hemmed and hawed, high-spirited Louis offered personally to meet Henry in single combat wherever he wished. Some of the onlookers joked that the flimsy bridge – sure to collapse and dump both opponents in the river – might be a suitable location for the match-up. Louis, prone to veering from bravery into recklessness, thought this an excellent idea. Ever the killjoy, Henry nixed the idea, remarking dryly that he would not hazard losing Gisors for the sake of answering a provocative jest. Nothing decided, the armies retired for the night, but the Normans awoke the next day to find the French had crossed the river, forcing them to flee for refuge to the very castle under contention. Impregnable Gisors protected them, and the kings called a truce.

Peace held until war broke out once more in 1111, when Louis's own barons rebelled under the leadership of Count Stephen of Blois, who was married to Henry's sister and whose lands lay just west of Paris. The war that followed ended in 1113 when Henry crushed the rebellious Norman barons, but the respite lasted only until Robert Curthose's son, William Clito, staked his claim to Normandy.[26] He had been little more than an infant when his father lost the Norman duchy and his liberty at Tinchebray in 1106. Fostered in the court of the Count of Flanders, the exiled boy impatiently awaited the day when he could avenge his father's loss and claim Normandy as his own rightful inheritance. He made his first move as soon as he reached the customary age of knighthood in 1118, inciting the restive lords of Normandy to rebel against overbearing Henry. King Louis, of course, was eager to lend a hand. Both kings adopted a scorched-earth policy. Henry torched the rebellious town of Évreux, including its cathedral and a nunnery, while Louis's forces besieged and burned many of Henry's defences along the Epte. For most of a year, the land was wracked by fire and sword and ordinary people saw their crops carried off by enemy soldiers.

Both sides sought battle, but they seemed always to miss each other until one August morning when Henry's scouts spotted Louis's bannermen setting a monastery's barn on fire. Henry had only 500 knights with him, and Louis even fewer, but the opportunity was too good to pass up. Flat ground, good for the horses, was found nearby on a plain that local people called 'Brémule', and the two armies assembled to face each other, mail-clad, their banners raised, their horses snorting, their war cries echoing on the wind. Louis's armies often relied heavily on common-born foot soldiers drafted from the towns and villages of northern France, an unsung element in his reign's signature military successes, but this time it was the chivalrous cavalry who took the lead.

Eighty of Louis's most valiant knights charged first 'in a bold but careless attack'.[27] The English line shuddered, then absorbed the shock, and the French knights found their horses cut from under them. Though they tried to fall back, they were surrounded and seized. Dismayed and now severely outnumbered, the remaining French forces fled pursued by Henry's men, who captured half of them. An Anglo-Norman chronicler, our best source for the battle, piously opined that 'they spared each other on both sides, out of fear of God and fellowship in arms; they were more concerned to capture than to kill the fugitives. As Christian soldiers they did not thirst for the blood of their brothers', and indeed, only three men lost their lives at Brémule.[28] But, truth to tell, it was not only chivalric Christian brotherhood that prevented a massacre but also the prospect of rich ransoms. A captured man might pay for his freedom, perhaps even quite a lot. Dead ones were only worth what could be stripped from their corpses.

As for King Louis, the chronicle says that he fled the field alongside his men but soon found himself separated from the rest, wandering in a dark wood without his horse or his standard and unsure of the way back to his garrison at Les Andelys. He was still wearing his chainmail tunic called a hauberk, but he had nothing on him that advertised his royal rank. Dazed with defeat and trembling like a leaf according to the chronicler, Louis nonetheless kept enough wits about him to use this accidental anonymity to his advantage. He let a chatty peasant who chanced upon him think that he was just an ordinary knight who had lost his way. This good Samaritan helpfully pointed out the right path and even walked him most of the way there. It was only when they neared Les Andelys and the worried garrison went wild to see its missing king that the man realized Louis's true identity. Henry had paid 20 silver marks to the knight who had captured Louis's banner at Brémule. How much more would he have paid for the man himself? Ruefully, the peasant returned to the forest, regretting the loss of a once-in-a-lifetime opportunity to gain a literal king's ransom.

Louis, too, nursed regrets, for he had bet the house and lost. In the wake of Brémule, he had to concede that the great fortress of Gisors belonged to Henry, and although Henry's heir, William Adelin, took over Normandy and did homage for it to Louis, it wasn't much comfort. Receiving that homage meant recognizing Henry's son's claim to Normandy over those of Robert Curthose's son William Clito, a staunch French ally, and Louis knew that sooner or later young William Adelin would be King of England as well as Duke of Normandy, with all the almost unlimited resources to make the Capetian king's life miserable that his father and grandfather had had before him. Worse still, Henry had recently married William Adelin off to the Count of Anjou's daughter, robbing the Capetian of his usual counterweight against Normandy and raising the spectre of an enlarged Norman sphere of influence, for the girl had brought the county of Maine as her dowry. Louis foresaw only sorrows ahead.

And sorrows there were, eventually for Louis, but first for Henry, who, little more than a year after his victory at Brémule, lost his son in a horrible accident that changed the course of English history. On 25 November 1120, Prince William Adelin and his friends set sail with much gaiety and more wine from Normandy on a fine vessel christened the *White Ship*. Waving off the priests who came to bless the boat with holy water and place the passengers under divine protection, the merry party wagered the crew that they could overtake King Henry's ship, which had set off some time earlier, and a race ensued across the English Channel. The seventeen-year-old prince and his companions urged the drunken rowers onward to greater and greater speed. Not far from shore – but far enough to be fatal – the speeding ship foundered upon a rock that tore through its port side, and the seawater poured in. The moon was new and the night a cold one. Only three men surfaced. None of them was the prince, nor had they seen him. Only one of them, a butcher named Berold, lasted until morning and lived to tell the tale. William Adelin's body was swept out to sea, along with those of the nearly 200 others who had accompanied him. For days and weeks afterward, people walked the shore and strong swimmers were paid to search what they could of the sea, but few bodies were ever found.[29] Henry's hope had become food for the fish.

A personal tragedy for Henry, of course, the disaster also created dynastic difficulties whose ramifications for France and the Anglo-Norman realm can hardly be overstated. Henry had plenty of bastards, two of whom he also lost aboard the *White Ship*, but William Adelin had been his only legitimate son and his obvious universal heir. Now, everything was thrown into uncertainty. Henry, in his fifties and long a widower, immediately remarried, but the union proved barren. Ultimately, he nominated his daughter Matilda as his successor to the kingdom of England, the duchy of Normandy, and all their appurtenances. Henry had already done more than well by Matilda, marrying her to the 'ruthless and hard-faced' German Emperor Henry V, whom she, rather ruthless and hard-faced herself, nevertheless loved deeply.[30] A proud woman, Matilda bore the title Empress her whole life, even after her imperial husband's death in 1125 and her second marriage to Count Geoffrey of Anjou, nicknamed 'Plantagenet' for the jaunty sprig of broom (*genêt*) he wore in his cap. Indomitable Empress Matilda was to spend most of the decade following the death of her father in 1135 trying to defend her right to the English throne against the rather more dubious, if ultimately successful, claims of Stephen of Blois, who was the Conqueror's grandson through his mother's marriage to the Count of Blois. The long and brutal war in England fought between Matilda and Stephen, a period known simply as 'The Anarchy', gave the Capetians some breathing room, though Matilda's son, named Henry after his grandfather, was to shatter their tranquillity. But in 1120 no one could have foreseen these future turns of Fortune's Wheel. Of immediate moment was the fate of Normandy now that William Adelin was no more, while William Clito still sought vengeance for his father, Robert Curthose, whom Henry had captured and deprived of Normandy at the Battle of Tinchebray in 1106 and who had remained imprisoned ever since.

While it was not in Louis's power to release Curthose from prison – indeed, he would die there – Louis did have some ideas as to how Curthose's son William Clito's aims might be satisfied and Henry's unhappiness augmented. In 1123, Louis moved to install Clito as Duke of Normandy, granting him his father's lands and title. Although it had not been to Louis's liking that homage for the duchy after Brémule had been performed by Henry's heir rather than Henry himself, the act had nevertheless been an acknowledgement of Capetian overlordship in Normandy and Louis was arguably within his rights to fill the vacancy that Adelin's death created. Henry, of course, felt that the 'vacancy' was automatically filled by himself, and his animosity toward Clito was such that he could not tolerate the idea of his succession, even though Clito's paternal right was patent and the man himself was much loved by their contemporaries, an easy popularity that made Henry's hatred for his nephew burn all the brighter. The English king threw himself into war with his customary industry, personally instructing the carpenters to build siege towers against the castles of rebellious Normans who sided with his enemies and burning their lands for leagues around.[31]

With Louis thus occupied in the west, Henry connived to open another front in the east, where his son-in-law the emperor mounted preparations for an invasion of France, the first time that the Capetians had had to worry about imperial aggression since the early decades of the eleventh century. In 1122 the emperor had at last laid to rest the long-running conflict with the papacy over investiture that had begun more than fifty years earlier, agreeing to the Concordat of Worms that reserved the spiritual side of investiture for the papacy, leaving the powerful political matters of bishops' landholdings to imperial discretion. Finally freed of this trans-Alpine headache, the emperor could now look for opportunities to expand his lands. At first, he thought to invade Saxony, but changed his mind. 'Evidently in order to aid his father-in-law Henry', as a German chronicler caustically remarked, the emperor instead directed his army toward the French city of Reims near the kingdom's eastern border. The invasion planned for August 1124, however, never materialized. A popular uprising recalled the emperor to Germany before he reached France, and frankly he was relieved at the excuse. His scouts had sent worrying reports about the size of the army that Louis had summoned from all over France, far outnumbering his own reluctant troops.[32]

Louis, impatient for an imperial reckoning that would never arrive, had already left to meet up with this intimidating French army massing on the frontier. Travelling via the road north from Paris, Louis stopped in at Saint-Denis, where his old friend Suger now reigned as abbot. Despite his clerical profession, the good monk had accompanied Louis on many a military venture in their well-spent youth and had no qualms about war's morality, so long as the violence served divine justice, and he knew a way to ensure that God knew that Louis was on his side. Suger invited the king to approach the main altar in the abbey church, where a war banner was laid out amongst the abbey's most precious relics. All medieval armies carried banners as a means to communicate troop positions on the battlefield, and Louis already had plenty of them, despite the one he had lost to Henry at Brémule. But the banner laid on the altar that day was special. It was the standard of the Vexin, significant here not because the territory was a bone of contention between the French and the Anglo-Normans but because it was, in a way, the banner of the sainted martyr Denis himself. The abbey believed, and the Capetians agreed, that ultimately the Vexin belonged to their patron saint. It was Saint Denis, with the abbey acting as his earthly intermediary, who had granted its possession to Louis.[33]

So, when Suger bade Louis to pick up this banner from the altar and carry it into battle against the emperor, a man who only recently had been excommunicated, it was as if Louis was waging war on the saint's behalf. By putting the martyr's flag in the king's hand, Suger recast France's border conflict as a Holy War, and he knew very well what he had done. Writing about these events many years later, he spoke of the French army's eagerness to slaughter the German invaders 'as if they were Saracens', leaving their unburied bodies to the ravens and wolves.[34]

The banner of the Vexin was to fly over French armies for the next three hundred years, while the French battle cry '*Montjoie! Saint-Denis!*' invoked the honour and the aid of the heavenly patron under whose flag they fought. In time everyone came to think of this banner as the same as the legendary flag of Charlemagne known as the Oriflamme.[35] A pure crimson banner said to have been dipped in Saint Denis's own blood and flown from a golden staff, the Oriflamme featured in the *Song of Roland*, where one of Charlemagne's best knights carried it into a desperate battle against the Saracens of Spain.[36] Since *that* banner had been kept at Saint-Denis, supposedly since Hugh Capet brought it back from Charlemagne's palace at Aachen, it was natural that the two banners gradually became thought of as one and the same. This fusion of Holy War with both the old Carolingian legacy that the Capetians were always eager to adopt, and the new chivalric ethos that suffused elites' outlook was to make the Oriflamme a powerful symbol of medieval French identity, imbuing their martial exploits with a sense of divine mission. When Louis took up the saint's banner from the abbey's altar in August 1124, raising the martyr's standard to claim the victory that followed, he took the first step down a path bound for glory and strewn with corpses.

6.

Gothic Fabrications
Louis VI and Louis VII

Prince Philip and his friends raced their horses through Paris on a mid-October afternoon. It was 1131, and fifteen-year-old Philip had been named heir to the throne and consecrated associate king three years earlier.[1] A couple of years shy of knighthood, he had just begun to make a reputation for himself in the mould of his famous father, Louis VI, still hammering away against God's enemies and his own even in his fiftieth year. That very day, in fact, Louis was assembling an army. It wasn't going to be one of those adventurous expeditions down to the southern reaches of the kingdom where the Capetian king was beginning to make his presence felt in regions that had not seen royal authority in over a century. Just a quick raid into the Vexin to remind certain people of the obedience they owed him. Even so, Philip and his friends were keen to go, and they rode hard, as much to prove their mettle to themselves as for the pure joy of being young and rich with the whole world in front of them.

The Paris that they rode through wasn't yet France's capital, nor could any place have been considered such. The Capetians still hewed to the itinerant ways of their ancestors, moving from palace to palace as politics and provisions dictated, but Philip's family was spending increasing amounts of time in the city. Located at the centre of their ancestral heartlands yet close enough to Normandy to keep an eye on that worrisome neighbour, Paris was well served by transportation routes radiating outward to the rest of the kingdom. Merchants, pilgrims, soldiers, beggars, and brigands traversed the wide royal road – originally a Roman construction – that ran through it, heading south to the cathedral city of Orléans and north to Saint-Denis, then onward to the burgeoning towns of Flanders.

But it was the River Seine, flowing northwest from Burgundy through the city before reaching Rouen and emptying into the Channel, that made Paris prosperous.[2] Since goods and people were much more easily transported by water than over land in this era of rare and often impassable roads, rivers like the Seine served as the highways of the medieval world.

The main island in the Seine's middle, known as the Île de la Cité, housed the city's heart. Its western half was dominated by the royal palace, whose foundations dated to Roman times and whose medieval vestiges form part of today's Palais de Justice. King Louis had recently expanded the royal residence, taking advantage of the debauched reputation of the ancient convent of Saint-Éloi to evict the scandal-ridden nuns and tear down some of their buildings, allowing him to add a three-storey tower that soared above the city's low-slung skyline.[3] On the island's eastern side lay the cathedral, at that time still a rather dilapidated Carolingian structure dedicated to Saint Stephen, as well as the bishop's palace and the fine residences of the rich canons who ran the cathedral's affairs. Separating these royal and episcopal zones, a 'street of the Jews', named for the vibrant community that lived along it and worshipped at its synagogue, bisected the island. Leading off from it, a tangle of streets lined with houses, workshops, market stalls, churches, barns, and gardens twisted haphazardly across the densely populated island.[4]

Crossing one of the two bridges over the river to the north, houses and workshops had already begun to proliferate on the marshy Right Bank, while over the single bridge to the island's south the labyrinthine streets of the Left Bank echoed with the rude songs and Latin chatter of young men who had come to Paris to learn at one of the great abbey schools, or from one of the peripatetic professors who lectured wherever they could locate a room. The most famous (or infamous) of these teachers was a cocky man in his middle years named Peter Abelard, whose torrid affair with his brilliant young student Heloise had resulted in an unwanted pregnancy for her and castration for him. The scandal, remembered by Abelard in a suffocatingly self-indulgent autobiography whose contents Heloise contested in a famous exchange of letters, forced both into monastic professions.[5] Although they missed each other terribly, the intellectual life of a medieval cleric was far more to their liking than an attempt at marital bliss might have proved, for 'who', Heloise wondered, 'can concentrate on thoughts of Scripture or philosophy and be able to endure babies crying . . .? Who will put up with the constant muddle and squalor which small children bring?'[6] When the baby came, they named him Astrolabe after a scientific instrument that had recently reached Latin Europe from the Islamic world, and they sent him off to be fostered elsewhere. Abelard passed his days in ecclesiastical controversies with Suger and Saint Bernard and founded a convent where Heloise ruled as abbess, and where she often received letters of advice from her former lover, who always had plenty of it to give.

This was the teeming world of money, power, sex, and scholarship through which Prince Philip and his friends rode at speed in the half-light of a Parisian autumn. A place of unparalleled excitement for an adolescent of twelfth-century Latin Europe, it was nevertheless nothing like the sprawling metropolis of Paris today nor even like the truly great cities of medieval Asia. With a population of perhaps 15,000, relatively impressive for medieval Europe north of the Alps, it was still half the size of Rome and dwarfed by Constantinople (400,000), let alone cities like Baghdad (which Philip had probably heard of) or Hangzhou (which he probably hadn't), whose medieval populations approached one million.[7] Nor was the city of Paris yet fully distinct from the countryside that surrounded it. Only the central island had ramparts. To either side of the Seine the city simply shaded into suburbs that became increasingly rural as you went on. Not even a mile from the palace and Philip would already have reached the city's outskirts, where the press of buildings petered out into the fields that stretched northward toward the hills of Montmartre and domestic animals roamed freely along the unpaved streets.[8]

In such surroundings, Philip might not have been surprised to see a pig suddenly appear and race across his path. But his horse was. It stumbled with enough force to unseat even a boy trained since infancy to stay in the saddle, dashing him against a stone and then trampling his stunned form underfoot. The pig disappeared down an alleyway – back to Hell whence it had come, as some people thought – and Philip's fair-weather friends scattered. It was left to horrified onlookers to take the broken royal body into a house nearby, but nothing could be done for him. The heir to France did not live long enough to see the morning.

Louis and Adelaide received the news of their son's death, as senseless as it was sudden, with grief so profound that 'not even Homer', sighed Suger, 'could have put it into words'.[9] Since Philip had been crowned and anointed his father's successor, he merited a royal burial in Saint-Denis, where he joined the other kings' sepulchres to the left of the altar. The realm's devastated subjects cried their sorrow to the stars and fainted in lamentation at his funeral. But the king and queen had no leisure yet to indulge their grief. They first had to ensure the succession, rushing their second son Louis to Reims, where he was crowned and anointed as his father's new heir.[10] A quiet but cheerful boy of ten, little Louis had never expected to have to carry such a legacy.

In the dark winter months that followed the funeral, after the shock subsided and the adrenaline wore off, Queen Adelaide tried to find a project to keep herself occupied. She settled on founding a convent on the slopes of Montmartre. A sleepy place, set miles beyond the modest sprawl of Paris's suburbs, medieval Montmartre was home to a run-down church dedicated to Saint Denis, whose martyrdom was supposed to have taken place there and had given the place its name: Montmartre / Martyr Hill. Louis, acting on 'Adelaide's pleas and advice', replaced it entirely with a foundation dedicated it to Saint Peter, a choice highlighting the queen's closeness to the papal see, whose most recent occupant but one had been her uncle. In time, Saint-Pierre de Montmartre was to house Adelaide's own tomb, as she probably intended from the project's inception.[11] (Its remnants are still on display there today.) A strong woman in every sense, she lived on for another busy two decades after Prince

Philip's passing, but even the liveliest of mothers feels close to death at the loss a child.

For this monument to mortality, the bereaved couple chose an architectural style 'at the leading edge of modernity', an aesthetic known at the time as the 'French style' but which we now call Gothic.[12] Today, visitors used to the soaring heights of later Gothic buildings may find Saint-Pierre de Montmartre a bit small and dark by contrast, but twelfth-century Parisians entering the church for the first time would have had a very different impression. They would have been surprised at the height of its vaults and the arrange-ment of its windows over three levels, which together lent the church an airy, even celestial, grandeur, and they may have been downright shocked to see that the arches supporting that ceiling were not smoothly rounded, as was the style of monumental build-ings up to this time. Instead, these arches came to a point, as if broken.

Louis and Adelaide's avant-garde taste belies the influence of their friend Abbot Suger, who had recently begun planning his own, much more ambitious, programme of renovations for the abbey church just up the road that the martyred Saint Denis himself had once walked, from the place of his decapitation to the place of his burial. Only with exaggeration can Suger be called the father of Gothic, for its origins are diffuse and other examples were more influential on later builders, but his architectural alterations were nonetheless strikingly novel.[13] Suger himself called them 'modern', though our own association between 'modernism' and minimalism was far from his thinking.[14] To the contrary, Suger's church expressed his predilection for sumptuous extravagance.

Even before he found the funds to begin his building renovation, Suger had the church's walls painted in gold and vibrant pigments – most medieval churches were brightly coloured inside, not the bare, spare spaces we see today – and he spent his abbacy amassing pre-cious objects to decorate its surfaces. Saint-Denis's treasury had long housed the royal regalia and other paraphernalia, including not only the banner of the Vexin but also the sword 'Joyeuse' supposedly carried by Charlemagne and even a throne said to have belonged to the Abbey's seventh-century Merovingian founder King Dagobert (Plate 4). To these, Suger added an ever-growing number of sumptuous textiles, ivories, enamels, and objects of precious metal encrusted with jewels. Much of this treasure has been long since lost or looted, but 'Suger's Eagle', a pitcher formed of a porphyry marble body with head, wings, tail, and talons of gold, has survived to be on permanent display in the medieval gallery of the Louvre. Along with the gilt sardonyx chalice held by the National Gallery in Washington DC, the Abbot's Eagle gives us a glimpse of the opulence that once graced what today might seem an austere if still stunning space (Plates 5 and 6).[15]

Suger had honed his tastes during time spent in Rome admiring the pope's elegant decor, and he considered his aesthetic values entirely compatible with his religious ones. He started his project to welcome the crowds of unruly pilgrims who came to adore Saint-Denis's collection of relics, and he believed the art would enlighten their spirits, as well as delight their eyes. The light from his new stained-glass windows were meant to transport the viewer to the heavenly realm, while the towering, intricately fashioned brass doors he installed for the pilgrims' convenience also functioned, in words he had inscribed above them, so that their bright gleam 'should brighten minds, so that they may travel . . . through that which is material', allowing them to ascend to 'the True Light, where Christ is the true door'.[16]

Suger's artistic ideas have been understood to reflect his equally innovative ideas about hierarchical order in political contexts, as well as in religious and artistic ones.[17] Gothic's perpendicular heights, its use of light, and its clear architectural divisions seem almost to inscribe in stone ideas about how power radiated downward from God himself to the king, ideas that can also be glimpsed here and there in Suger's biography of Louis. The clearest example is a speech Suger put into the Duke of Aquitaine's mouth that portrays the king as sitting at the apex of a feudal pyramid of legal jurisdiction. In Suger's telling, the duke once sought to prevent

Louis from attacking the Count of Auvergne by reminding the king that the count held Auvergne from the duke, just as the duke held Aquitaine from Louis. "'Because the Count of Auvergne holds Auvergne from me, as I hold it from you,'" the Duke said, "'if he does something wrong I have the duty of making him appear at your court on your command.'"[18] This was more a statement of wishful thinking on Suger's part than a description of how the king's power extended not only over his vassals but also over his vassals' vassals. (Anyone tempted to believe otherwise should consider that the duke was only near enough to converse with Louis because he had brought an army into the Auvergne to attack the king but was dissuaded by the size of Louis's own forces.) It did nevertheless help to propagate an important idea about how the patchwork political landscape of local and regional powers might be sewn into a single system of royal government, and Suger also believed that there was a hierarchy among kingdoms as well as within them. Nationalist *avant la lettre*, he claimed that 'it is neither right nor natural that the French should be subject to the English, but rather the English to the French.'[19]

It was during these decades when Suger was elaborating his propaganda in prose and stone that the potent symbol of the fleur-de-lys, or three-petalled lily, first became clearly associated with the Capetian dynasty. Louis VI had his coins stamped with the device, a model followed by his son (Plate 7).[20] The symbol was an old one, traceable to the Carolingians and possibly also to the Merovingians, but it had a new and useful relevance in the middle decades of the twelfth century when the dynasty's power began to flourish in earnest.[21] The flower, whose three petals evoked the Trinity, was also a symbol associated with the Virgin Mary, queen of Heaven, whose cult expanded enormously in the twelfth century. Emblematic of both historic and heavenly monarchy, the lily thus encapsulated the Capetians' claims about their right to rule France not only by right of blood but also through divine favour.[22] Harnessing these half-remembered, half-fabricated associations to the nascent ideology of sacred Capetian kingship was probably not Suger's idea – if it was, one would expect to find some mention of it in his copious writings – but it is certainly true that it was 'during his abbacy . . . in the reigns of his friends, Louis VI and Louis VII, that the lilies began to flower'.[23]

If any cleric might have influenced the Capetians to invent the fleur-de-lys tradition, it was probably Suger's friend and rival, Bernard of Clairvaux (later Saint Bernard). The century's greatest preacher, Bernard spoke movingly in his sermons of the lilies of the field and of Saint Mary and the lilies. Always near the centre of power in France and in Rome, Bernard was the head of a newly founded monastic order called the Cistercians, who became famous for leading humble lives dressed in simple habits of undyed wool. Advocating a return to the poverty of the early Church, the Cistercians presented a marked contrast with monks like Suger, who was rather old-fashioned in his piety even if very advanced in his aesthetics, and Suger perhaps felt a little defensive about his various extravagances in comparison with Bernard's asceticism. In a society where lay people were often more devout than the clerics meant to guide them, the Cistercians' humility attracted enthusiastic support, including that of wealthy donors. The young Louis VII himself was a particularly passionate patron. And so, although they were dedicated to poverty, the Cistercians soon became rich.

Well capitalized by their donors and well placed by their literacy to adopt new techniques in estate administration, the Cistercians led the vanguard of a medieval agricultural revolution. A warmer climate and the spread of a more effective kind of plough during the previous century gave rise to a virtuous economic circle of increased population, bringing more land into cultivation and in turn producing more food to support an even larger number of people. The trend was not uninterrupted. A winter so cold that fish froze solid in their ponds was followed by a soggy summer which destroyed the harvests of 1125, precipitating a terrible famine.[24] Nor was the expansion of cultivation without some trade-offs. Already in Suger's day the forests near Paris were so depleted that only divine intervention allowed him to find trees large enough to produce the beams needed for the new ceiling of Saint-Denis.[25] But it had been his careful management of the abbey's farms, as well as the tolls from the annual fair that Louis granted to his abbey, that provided the surplus to pay for Suger's artistic flamboyance, just as in so many places the growing abundance of food, people, commerce, and coins supported expansion and innovation in realms ranging from manuscript painting to political philosophy.

Even those lowest on the social scale saw improvement in their lives. Increasing population and productivity, as well as the desire to live free of lordship, all contributed to a renaissance of urban life traceable from the middle decades of the eleventh century that was to contribute considerably to the Capetians' power in the decades and centuries to come. Many northern French towns, like Tours, Senlis, or Paris itself, grew atop the vestiges of Roman foundations that had been continuously occupied despite many centuries of depopulation and decentralization, while in the south – still largely outside of Capetian control – cities like Toulouse and Narbonne retained more of their Roman character up to the first millennium and beyond. That the early Church of the late Roman Empire had organized itself into dioceses centred on cities had ensured a continuous role for these settlements as episcopal sees, supporting at least a modicum of commerce, scholarship, and political intrigue even in the most difficult of times. Easier economic circumstances and the twelfth century's growing political stability encouraged these long-dormant seeds to germinate. New towns even began to appear, often developing from the sprawl of houses and workshops that sprang up outside of castles.

Towns drove a wondrous commercial expansion that supplied the ever-increasing demand for goods ranging from locally produced pottery to exotic textiles imported from Byzantium and beyond. As silver coins, like Louis's lily-embossed pennies, came into increasing circulation, the merchants and artisans who populated the fairs and markets hosted by towns came into possession of cold, hard cash. So urban communities used their new economic bargaining power to win concessions from their rulers. With incomes often based on payments in kind, lords, bishops, and even the king himself were receptive to townsmen's offers to replace these old-fashioned and inconvenient dues with a monetary payment in exchange for a grant of rights of freedom and self-government called a commune. Communes were formed by citizens who swore a common oath to protect one another's rights and probably developed out of similar oaths sworn by adherents to the Peace of God. In fact, the Latin word for peace (*pax*) was often used as a synonym for 'commune', and communes were sometimes sponsored by the city's bishop, echoing the episcopal organization of the Peace of God. Lay lords, too, sponsored communes. Louis VI took a dim view of communes in his own domain lands, but he was an enthusiastic supporter of their establishment in the cities of his rivals, approving so many of them that he is sometimes called 'the father of communes'.[26]

Communes were established in most of the larger settlements of northern France and Flanders over the twelfth century, though Paris never had a commune. But they were controversial, especially for the traditional elite who found the political activities of commoners scandalous. 'Now "commune",' sniffed one monastic chronicler, 'is a new and evil name for an arrangement by which all persons are subject to a yearly head tax that they owe their lords . . . all other forms of taxation that used to be inflicted on serfs are abolished.'[27] And communes were politically combustible, sometimes literally so, as at Laon in 1112 when the bishop's decision to suppress the commune provoked a bloody uprising against him. Shouting 'Commune! Commune!', the townsmen murdered him in the cathedral square, leaving his naked and mutilated corpse exposed for days and forcing noblemen to disguise themselves as women to escape from the city, which burned to cinders in the wake of the revolt.

In Flanders, where expansion was most advanced, the inflammatory potential of urban politics had even more spectacular effects. Count Charles, son of a Danish king and a Flemish count's daughter, had taken possession of the county when his childless cousin Baldwin VII died of wounds incurred fighting for Louis in the hostilities leading up to the Battle of Brémule. Count Charles, known as 'the

Good' for his generosity to the poor, especially during the great famine of 1125, was betrayed to his death on 2 March 1127 by members of the Erembald family, who, much like the Garlandes of Paris, had risen from obscurity to capture the county's administration. Descendants of an adulterous liaison between a treacherous serf and the wife of his lord in the mid-eleventh century, the Erembalds' servile origins gave Charles an excuse to remove them from office when their war against a local lord imperilled his peasants. In response, the Erembald men spilled his blood and brains across the floor of Bruges Cathedral and then went on to massacre his servants and supporters wherever they could find them. A war ensued, in which the Erembald faction held fast to Bruges's castle while furious townsmen sought to scale its walls and flush them out with fire.[28]

Since slain Charles had left no heirs, it fell to King Louis (or so he saw it) to end the conflict and choose a new count for Flanders among the numerous candidates who presented themselves. Predictably, he chose his long-time ally William Clito, still landless after all these years but with a claim to the county by way of his Flemish grandmother. The townsmen of Flanders, however, were unconvinced. While Louis held an assembly of barons to 'elect' Clito, the burghers of Bruges and Ghent were holding their own assembly, swearing that they would only elect as count 'someone who both wishes to and can serve what is of common usefulness for the fatherland'.[29] They held out on accepting Clito until he had promised to abolish some tolls and reduce their rents. Clito took up the countship, and the treacherous Erembalds were hunted down and inventive punishments devised for them and their supporters: their chief was hanged alongside a dog whose viscera was wrapped around his neck, while others were beaten until their bones broke, then stretched across a wheel and left to die of exposure. Those who had tried to hold out against King Louis and William Clito in the besieged castle at Bruges were tricked into submission by a promise of mercy, then thrown down one by one from its highest tower.[30]

Clito, however, soon caved in to pressure from the Flemish nobility and reintroduced the tolls he had abolished to gain the townsmen's favour, provoking a rebellion by the townsmen of Ghent, who were soon joined by those of Bruges. Arguing that it was up to the people of Flanders to install or remove their count – an assertion widely considered an early instance of the concept of popular sovereignty – they transferred their allegiance to another claimant, Thierry of Alsace, who promised them peace and free trade in exchange for their support.[31] When Louis angrily summoned the men of Bruges to answer for their rejection of William Clito, they replied tartly that 'the king of France has nothing to do with choosing or setting up a count of Flanders'.[32]

The ensuing war between Louis's candidate, William Clito, and the townsmen's candidate, Thierry of Alsace, who was probably also backed by Clito's uncle and inveterate enemy the English King Henry I, ended abruptly when Clito perished in a minor skirmish at the end of July 1128 and Louis accepted Thierry's countship as a *fait accompli*. The conflict faded into history, but it offered ominous lessons for the future. The problems posed for the French Crown by Flemish townsmen's political ideas, independent actions, and English interests were to plague Louis's successors for centuries to come, contributing much to causing the Hundred Years War in the fourteenth century.

It was not only to the Capetians' north in Flanders that the origins of that great conflagration were now taking shape, but also to their south in Aquitaine. In June 1137, while old Louis VI lay dying of dysentery, his heavy body a misery in that unusually hot summer, Duke William X of Aquitaine perished while on pilgrimage. As sole heir to lands that stretched from the city of Poitiers to the Pyrenees, he left his young daughter Eleanor. Although Aquitaine had never been more than peripherally part of the Capetian realm, Louis had long looked to expand southward. Here was an unexpected chance to do just that on a grand scale. The late Duke William had entrusted Eleanor's guardianship to the king, and Louis VI could think of no safer future for her – or her lands – than to take her under the protection of the Capetian Crown as the wife of his heir apparent. He told his seventeen-year-old son Louis to ride south with Suger and an entourage of 500 knights to Bordeaux, where he was to meet and marry thirteen-year-old Eleanor of Aquitaine.

Barely out of girlhood, Eleanor's existence must have seemed a trivial footnote to the richness of her patrimony. Neither then, nor even much later when she was a grown woman, did anyone imagine her capable of making a decision that could imperil the French Crown and even the kingdom's independent existence. It surprised everyone, including Louis, when she married Henry Plantagenet, Count of Anjou and soon to be King of England, almost before the ink on her annulment from Louis VII had dried. The personal wounds thus inflicted on Louis were grave enough, but the political wounds were to fester long after he and Eleanor were dead. As Eleanor moved from one king to another so, too, moved Aquitaine, lands which could never quite be integrated into England nor excluded from France, a conundrum to which war eventually proved the only solution.

Of course, as the party made its way northward under the too-sunny skies of August 1137, they thought not of war and division but of permanent and peaceful union, that of France and Aquitaine and that of Louis and Eleanor. Wedded in late July, the pair received word of Louis VI's death about a week later and were crowned king and queen at Poitiers in a ceremony designed by Suger to empha-size Aquitaine's union with France.[33] During their journey to Paris – the closest thing to a honeymoon a medieval couple was likely to get – Eleanor made her own, private gesture of unity, pre-senting Louis with a precious crystalline vase she had received from her grandfather. Manufactured centuries earlier in Sassanian Persia from Madagascan rock crystal, the vase had likely been given to him by the Muslim ruler of Zaragoza, a rare gesture of cross-confessional friendship and a stunning example of the winding journeys taken by luxury items in the Middle Ages.[34] Years later, Louis gave the vase to Saint-Denis, whence it made its way many centuries later to the Louvre, where it is now displayed near Suger's Eagle and some of his other treasures (Plate 8).

It may have been some years later, after Suger finally finished his renovations to Saint-Denis in 1144, that Louis gave Eleanor's vase to the abbey. The king and queen had, of course, been invited to the consecration, the medieval equivalent of a 'grand reopening'. The now elderly abbot was not on such good terms with Louis *fils* as he had been with Louis *père*, and the king may have intended the vase as a conciliatory gesture. Louis VII would, in the end, choose burial in a Cistercian monastery rather than interment at Saint-Denis, the second – and the last – time that a Capetian spurned the royal mausoleum.

Suger must have turned in his grave at the sheer ingratitude of the gesture. He had dedicated his life to the twin and, in his mind inseparable, advancement of Louis's dynasty and his abbey. By the time Louis and Eleanor walked through his gleaming bronze doors, Suger's church really did glow with celestial light, lit up in rainbow colours from the stained-glass windows that adorned the chapels arranged like jewels in a necklace around its apse. One window featured panels dedicated to the First Crusade and to a legendary gift of Crucifixion relics, which had passed from the Roman Emperor Constantine to the Carolingians and from that dynasty to Saint Denis, a perfect illustration of France's now pre-eminent place in the political and religious history of Christian Europe.[35] A great fabricator, in every sense of the word, Suger knew well how to weave legend into history and history into legend.[36]

7.

Bread, Wine, and Gaiety

Louis VII

Twenty-five-year-old Louis VII celebrated Christmas 1145 at Bourges, an old Roman city set in rolling hills about a hundred miles south of Paris. Bourges had belonged to the Capetian Crown since its last viscount sold it for 60,000 silver shillings to go on crusade at the turn of the century.[1] Neither of Louis's predecessors had paid much attention to the place, but Louis liked it. It lay near the border of his wife's lands in Aquitaine, and the viscount's old palace, now his, sat impressively atop the old Gallo-Roman walls. (Rebuilt in the fourteenth century by an extravagant duke, the site now houses local government offices.) Louis had passed his first Christmas as king here in 1137, marking the occasion by wearing his crown in the cathedral, a ceremony borrowed from imperial Germany that stressed the divine character of his royal majesty. In the years since, events had prevented him from spending another Christmas in Bourges. Indeed, Bourges had been at the centre of some of the most painful moments of his last few years. But Louis had returned to the city in the belief that all that was behind him now. He hoped that by celebrating this, the ninth Christmas of his rule, as he had its first, he might reset the clock on his reign, if not his life.

Medieval Christmases did not include a tree, of course, and it would be nearly another century before Saint Francis of Assisi invented the nativity scene, but the twelve days from Christmas to Epiphany on 6 January were nevertheless a special time of year. For a devout Christian like Louis, the season marked the moment that God became man, humbling himself as a helpless infant for the redemption of sin. So, it seemed to many a propitious season for miraculous, even magical, transformations.[2] There were those who believed that animals could speak on Christmas night or that it was a good time to tell fortunes. Some people dressed up in strange clothes and did strange things, like ringing bells out of time and lighting flickering little fires that lent an eerie air to the dark nights of medieval midwinter.[3] The clergy, too, adopted a topsy-turvy revelry during Christmastime, honouring the way that God exalted the humble.

On the first of January they celebrated the anniversary of Christ's circumcision by leading a donkey into the cathedral and singing a song to it called the 'Prose of the Ass', shouting 'Hey, Hey, Sir Ass, Hey!' when they got to the chorus.[4] At the time Louis was in the city, Bourges Cathedral was still a cramped eleventh-century building in the middle of a messy collection of houses, granges, wells, and workshops, not the massive Gothic structure there today, so the donkey cannot have been too out of place.[5] Perhaps Louis was there when the donkey song was sung, or even joined in its riotous refrain. But if he felt his heart lift a little at the gaiety, it would have brought him only temporary relief. By 1 January, Louis had fallen out of sorts with the season, for he had hoped to use Christmas at Bourges to launch an expedition to the Holy Land that would absolve him of his many sins. Those hopes had been thoroughly dashed.

For years now, his conscience had been pricked by a growing number of moral missteps. Chief among them was the murder of 1,300 innocent men, women, and children, whom he had allowed to be burned alive in a church where they had sought refuge from one of his wars.[6] The deed had caused widespread outrage, and anyway Louis did not have his father's stomach for violence. Those who knew him described a quiet man, thoughtful toward others and deprecating of his own dignity. A second son, he had originally been destined for a career in the Church, but then the pig had killed his older brother Philip, and Louis became king in his stead. This, too, weighed on him. Philip, five years Louis's senior, already crowned, and nearly a man at the time of his death, must have seemed like a god in little Louis's eyes. Whatever mistakes Louis made (and they were many since he was only a teenager when he became king) can only have confirmed his suspicions that he was not fit to fill Philip's shoes. Louis knew that his brother had made a private vow to crusade – maybe one of Philip's friends had told him, or maybe Philip himself had boasted of it to his impressionable little brother – and he felt, said one chronicler, honour-bound to fulfil that vow.[7]

Some thought a new crusade already overdue, for a Turkish army had captured the Crusader County of Edessa on Christmas Eve 1144. Now a full year had passed and nothing had been done about it, though everyone knew the defence of the Holy Land was France's special responsibility. The people of Jerusalem and Antioch had already sent messengers to appeal to the 'invincible prowess' of the French, and just before Christmas the pope issued a bull directly addressed to Louis, recalling that when Pope Urban had preached the First Crusade 'with a voice like a trumpet', it was especially the French who had answered the call.[8] Now that Edessa had fallen – its castles occupied, its archbishop murdered, its relics dispersed – the pope exhorted the French to follow their ancestors' example and return to the East, lest their valour be questioned.

Louis knew he had no choice but to lead a rescue expedition, but he also knew the decision would be unpopular. Though France's nobles might glory in their ancestors' exploits, the ardent enthusiasm animating the First Crusade had long since cooled in the knowledge that the Holy Land did not flow with milk and honey but rather abounded in bleak struggles and dispiriting compromises.[9] It would take a grand gesture, a performance equal to Pope Urban's sermon at Clermont, to transform his vassals' inertia into action.

Louis had meant Christmas at Bourges to be his Clermont moment. He had invited far more guests than usual to his Christmas court, and he had marked it as a particularly special occasion by wearing his crown in the cathedral, just as he had at that first Bourges Christmas eight years ago. Later that day, his crown back in its coffer but the spectacle still fresh in everyone's mind, he hosted a Christmas feast, and it was probably after that, when everyone was cheerful with rich food and good wine, that the king took a deep breath and 'revealed for the first time to the bishops and magnates of the realm the secret in his heart': he intended to leave his kingdom and go East.[10] No one said anything for a moment. Then, as if on cue, a bishop stood up and spoke passionately about the suffering of Edessa's Christians and the intolerable pride of their Muslim oppressors. This at least got a response from the crowd, who made a loud show of their sorrow. But when the bishop urged them to go with their king to 'fight for the King of all', they again grew quiet.[11] Louis's Christmas show had flopped. It must have been with some awkwardness that he and his guests said their farewells as the season drew to its end. A few of them promised that they would talk to the head of the Cistercian monks, Abbot Bernard of Clairvaux, and see what he had to say about it.[12] But, for now, Louis went away disappointed, perhaps embarrassed, and probably frustrated.

These painful sensations had become all too familiar to the young king since the promising debut of his reign, when he and his bride Eleanor rode together in the southern sunshine. He had gained confidence from some early military successes, putting down communal revolts in Orléans and Poitiers, and Eleanor, too, had grown in assurance as she matured from an adolescent girl into a woman acknowledged as among the most beautiful, and certainly the most influential, in France. Ageing Abbot Suger's cautious counsels irritated them, and Louis looked for a minister more sympathetic to his wishes. He found one in a cleric named Cadurc, who hailed from near Bourges, though no sooner had Louis made him his chancellor in 1141 than an opportunity arose to place his new favourite in an even more helpful position by appointing him Archbishop of Bourges. Unfortunately for Louis, the clergy of Bourges had already chosen a different candidate, and much to Louis's anger the pope had consecrated this rival candidate, observing as he did so that Louis was just 'a boy in need of instruction and correction'.[13] Unwilling to learn this lesson, and indeed 'burning with anger' at the pope's presumption, Louis swore solemnly on relics never to allow the man to set foot in Bourges.[14] Furious in turn at this act of almost sacrilegious disobedience, the pope put Louis's lands under interdict, and for three long years he and his subjects were deprived of the sacraments.

The conflict over the see of Bourges became entangled with another drama unfolding at exactly the same moment: Queen Eleanor's fifteen-year-old sister Petronilla and Louis's fifty-year-old cousin Count Ralph of Vermandois had somehow fallen in love, and since Ralph was already married, he had convinced some sympathetic bishops to annul this marriage on specious grounds. Ralph's would-be ex-wife, of course, objected, as did her uncle Count Thibaut 'the Great' of Champagne, probably the most powerful man in France after Louis himself. His family lands nearly encircled the Capetian's domain, and his brother Stephen of Blois was winning the war to be King of England. Thibaut had grown rich from Champagne's annual fairs, a major motor of the medieval economy, and the generous donations he gave to the Church made him a favourite among the clergy.[15] So when he complained to the pope about his niece's treatment, the annulment was rapidly found illegal and the bishops who pronounced it were excommunicated along with Petronilla and Ralph, who refused to separate despite the danger of damnation. The story might seem to encapsulate the new ideals of courtly love that Eleanor was once supposed to have brought with her from Languedoc, where poets sang of delicate sentiments and impossible yearnings, though, if the literary forms were new, difficult desire is certainly a timeless experience.[16] King Philip and Bertrada at the beginning of the twelfth century or King Robert and Bertha at the beginning of the eleventh could well have testified to that.

Like those tragic pairings of the past, the political and military consequences of Petronilla and Ralph's love were decidedly unromantic. Louis and Eleanor's ire at Count Thibaut had been growing for some time even before the Petronilla affair, for Thibaut had twice failed to bring his army to Louis's aid, as a vassal was obliged to do at his lord's request. The first time, when he put down the rebellion at Poitiers in 1138, Louis had managed well enough without him, but he and Eleanor blamed Thibaut's absence for their unsuccessful expedition in 1141 to capture Toulouse, which Eleanor claimed by right of her grandmother. Louis's anger at these failures and Thibaut's assault, as they saw it, on Petronilla's happiness and indeed her salvation, grew white hot when it became known that Thibaut was sheltering the pope's preferred candidate for the see of Bourges. By August 1142, Louis had invaded Champagne, and when his army reached the town of Vitry, whose unarmed inhabitants fled from the violence of his ravaging soldiers, he ordered the massacre that still haunted him years later.[17]

As the war in Champagne dragged on, Queen Eleanor, too, began to have doubts. She had not yet carried a pregnancy to term, a fact which suggested God's displeasure. Although her influence on her husband's reign during these unhappy early years is hard to prove – the sources are scant and coloured by knowledge of her later actions – she does seem to have gained some say in the kingdom's governance soon after her marriage, and many blamed its 'confused and chaotic' character on her.[18] Certainly, Bernard of Clairvaux faulted her for Louis's aggressive policy toward Champagne and his unwillingness to settle with Count Thibaut or to concede to the pope's wishes for the see of Bourges. When Bernard came upon Eleanor praying for a child during the reopening festivities for Abbot Suger's renovated Saint-Denis in June 1144, he seized the opportunity and promised her that God would finally bless her womb, but only if she dropped her obdurate stance and worked zealously for peace.[19] She agreed, and his prediction proved correct. Once Thibaut and Louis were reconciled and the pope's candidate took up the see of Bourges – though at the cost of Louis breaking his sacred oath never to allow it and incurring yet another sin to weigh on his conscience – Eleanor did at long last bear a child, albeit a disappointingly female one.

The queen was far from alone in agreeing to do what Bernard asked of her. The honey-tongued abbot had a talent for convincing people to do things, and it was he who convinced the kingdom to undertake Louis's crusade. The dubious nobles at Louis's Christmas court had promised to seek Bernard's advice, and he in turn sought guidance from the pope, who was more than happy to have Bernard preach the crusade that spring. Bernard carried out the task with his unequalled eloquence, advertising the expedition as a 'great bargain', allowing its participants to acquire the Kingdom of Heaven at a cut-rate price.[20] At Easter, speaking to a great crowd before the new Gothic church of Vézelay in Burgundy, Bernard and Louis combined their forces and accomplished what the king alone at Christmas could not. Standing on a wooden platform with a cross-adorned Louis by his side, the abbot so moved his audience that he ran out of fabric crosses to give them and had to rip up his own garments to make more.

The Second Crusade, as we now call it, came near to stirring up the same enthusiasm as the First – 'neither sex nor status absolved anyone from going', recalled one English writer – but far more care went into the preparations for this expedition than its predecessor.[21] This was the first crusade led by a king, and kings could not just leave their kingdoms without provision for their absence. Louis spent a year readying his realm and himself for the trials ahead. He entrusted France to Suger, who sent a lieutenant along on the journey to record the great things that Louis was sure to accomplish in the Holy Land, and he collected money from his subjects to fund the journey, only the second time a French king had come close to levying something that might be called a tax.[22] (The first had been a collection to underwrite his wedding to Eleanor in 1137.) The king's ritual preparations were just as careful as his administrative ones. He embarked on the journey from Saint-Denis, where Suger orchestrated one of his elaborate ceremonies. First, Louis healed lepers with his royal touch, and then he entered the basilica, where Suger invested him with the same holy banner of the martyred saint that the king's father had carried against the German empire almost a quarter of a century earlier.[23]

Now, the French king joined his forces to those of the German king, who had also fallen under the spell of Bernard's preaching along with his subjects. But though they mustered huge armies, the Second Crusade was not just a failure, but something of a fiasco. Louis, grumbled one chronicler, 'was not able to do anything useful or memorable'.[24]

Even Pope Eugenius admitted that the crusade had caused 'the most severe injury of the Christian name that God's church has suffered in our time'.[25] By the time Louis got as far as Hungary, he was already out of money and had to send letters to Suger, requesting more funds.[26] The Turks slaughtered many of Louis's troops early in the campaign, and although Edessa's recovery had been the ostensible reason for the crusade, Louis showed so little interest in its rescue that it has been wondered whether the whole expedition was just a pretext for a pilgrimage to Jerusalem, something otherwise difficult to fit in around his many royal responsibilities.[27]

The Franks blamed Greek treachery for their failure, but the crusaders' poor strategy was the real cause of the ignominious outcome. Instead of Edessa, the Latin armies focused on attacking Damascus, an 'incredibly stupid decision', in the words of a normally dispassionate crusade historian.[28] Although in Muslim hands, Damascus had been an ally of Christian Jerusalem for nearly a decade, acting as a bulwark against the much more dangerous threat from Aleppo. Blinded by the binary prejudice of Holy War, the Latin crusaders were unable to appreciate the delicate diplomatic compromises required by the Near East's fractured and unstable politics. Nor did the gamble pay off. The attack on Damascus – 'as ridiculous in execution as in conception', according to the same historian – was abandoned almost before it began. Disillusioned, the Germans set sail for Constantinople, and most of the French went home, leaving Louis and a few followers behind in Jerusalem.

However pleased Louis was to have finally reached his destination, he could not have known much happiness there, for the crusade had destroyed his marriage, as well as his army. He had gone East with Eleanor, who didn't mind the road's hardships or the journey's uncertainty. A vigorous woman who would be active well through her seventies, she welcomed the adventure, not least because it offered her a good excuse to visit her uncle Prince Raymond of Antioch. She and her ladies did not ride to Constantinople bare-breasted like Amazons, as Katherine Hepburn's incomparable Eleanor of Aquitaine recounts in the film *A Lion in Winter*, but something did happen on the crusade that upset Louis and estranged the couple.[29] Much ink has been spilled over whether that thing was an affair between Eleanor and her uncle Raymond, as some later chroniclers hint, or whether those writers were just trying to besmirch the reputation of a woman whose actions had proved so contrary to the wishes of both French and English kings in the decades since. It seems particularly damning that Odo of Deuil, whom Suger had tasked with recording the crusade, ceased his narrative the moment the king arrived at Antioch, though it may be that Louis was more upset at Eleanor's efforts to redirect the crusade toward Aleppo, as Raymond wanted, than anything else that happened during the time they spent in 'constant conversation'.[30]

Affair or no, whatever happened at Antioch angered Louis enough that he forced Eleanor to leave the city and incensed her sufficiently that she raised the possibility of divorce. By the time they returned to France at Suger's insistence in 1149, the pair were barely speaking. It was only the kindly intervention of elderly Pope Eugenius III on the way home that prevented an immediate annulment. Allegedly, Eugenius put them into bed together, and, unusually, Eleanor got pregnant.[31]

Had the baby not been another girl, everything would have been different. Louis had loved being Eleanor's husband once, and he still loved being Aquitaine's duke. He hung on for another couple of years, but he had to have an heir. What Eleanor had or hadn't done in Antioch didn't matter. What mattered was that by 1152 she was approaching thirty and apparently incapable of bearing male children. A council of bishops was convened, the couple were found to be too closely related to be legally married – which they were, as had been well known from the start – and the marriage was dissolved. Louis was the author of the annulment, but Eleanor not only consented to it, 'she seems to have known precisely what she would do' after it.[32] She immediately rode south to Poitou, where not two months later she married Henry Plantagenet, Count of Anjou and Duke of Normandy, a man nine years her junior, whose father she was rumoured to have slept with once. Two years after acquiring Aquitaine through Eleanor, Henry became

King of England by right of his mother Matilda (see figure below) and ruler of an empire that stretched from the southern border of Scotland to the northern border of Spain.

Henry and Eleanor's intensely passionate, if often furiously angry, relationship has never lost its power to fascinate. Each was to inflict such damage on the other and yet to have known such pleasure in one another's company (if eight surviving children in fourteen years is any indication) that we can only conclude that their feelings were strong ones. Of course, Louis also had strong feelings. When he caught word of the nuptials, he ordered Henry, his vassal for Normandy and Anjou, to answer for not asking his permission to marry as he was obliged to do. (Henry didn't reply.) Louis tried invading Normandy, though to no avail, and he held on to Aquitaine for as long as he could, styling himself 'King of the French and Duke of Aquitaine' for another two years. Then he remarried, looking even further south for a bride, this time from Castile. By that time, Eleanor had already given Henry a son, the first of the five boys she would bear him.

Even in their ignorance of X and Y chromosomes, people could

Norman and Plantagenet Rulers

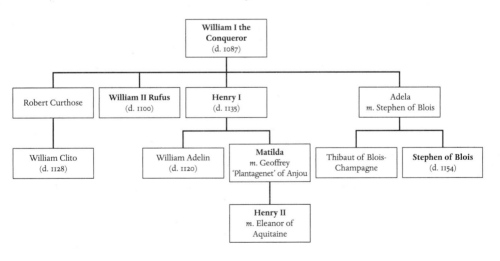

see perfectly well that the procreative fault had lain with Louis, not Eleanor. Nor was this the only way in which Henry Plantagenet outstripped his comparatively colourless Capetian counterpart. The Anglo-Norman realm's long-standing threat to France had been less pressing during the anarchic struggle between Henry's mother, Matilda, and her cousin Stephen of Blois, but with the end of that war it now re-emerged in a more dangerous form. After the failed invasion of 1153, Louis did not undertake military intervention against Henry for another two decades, though he did strengthen his alliances in the kingdom's east, marrying his daughter to the new Count of Champagne, and to the south, where his sister's marriage to the Count of Toulouse undercut Henry and Eleanor's ambitions there. He was well aware that the English king's resources far outstripped his own. It has been estimated that Louis could count on annual revenues of 20,000 *livres parisis*, while Henry enjoyed double that from England alone and much more from his continental possessions besides.[33] Louis himself put it another way: 'the king of England, who wants for nothing, has men, horses, gold and silk, jewels, fruit, game, and everything. We in France have nothing except bread and wine and gaiety.'[34]

In fact, what Louis really had was the moral high ground, and there he bested Henry over and over again. The Plantagenets were rumoured to descend from Satan – indeed, they boasted of it – and they won their domains through bloody civil war and marital policies of questionable morality. Louis, by contrast, had been anointed king 'with the oil given by an angelic hand for the anointing of Clovis', the first Christian King of the Franks six centuries earlier.[35] He possessed the healing touch of his quasi-divine lineage, vassals of the martyred Denis, and he had added crusading credentials to its pious reputation. In 1155 he went on pilgrimage to Saint James of Compostela, and upon his return he took over the Church's peace efforts, convening a council of barons and prelates that guaranteed ten years protection to the realm's churches, peasants, and merchants.[36] When Henry became incensed with his old drinking companion Thomas Becket, finding him a far less tractable

Archbishop of Canterbury than he had imagined, it was to Louis that Becket fled, earning Louis the title *rex christianissimus* (the most Christian king), an appellation the Capetians were to bear proudly for the rest of their days, setting them apart from and above all the other dynasties of Latin Europe.[37] The universal opprobrium that Henry earned when he, accidentally or otherwise, ordered Becket's murder in 1170, and the family quarrels that led his wife and children to rebel against him in 1173, can only have confirmed Louis's sense that he had chosen the better path, however little it had seemed so to others at the time.

When these troubles overtook Henry, Louis had finally had an heir. His Castilian wife had produced yet another girl, but the lady's death in 1160 freed him to marry Adela, daughter of his late rival Thibaut of Champagne. Five years later she gave birth to the long-awaited son. Louis was in his mid-fifties by then, not as old as the biblical Abraham when God at last blessed his wife, Sarah, with a child, but old enough for the comparison to feel apt. The baby, named Philip, was nicknamed *Dieudonné*, God-given. Louis, who once confessed himself 'dismayed by the great number of our daughters', now lavished presents upon the queen's welcome messenger, and bells rang out across Paris as people poured into the streets to thank Heaven for this most precious gift.[38]

Although their new prince was born small and sickly, Louis and his people were right to celebrate. When he grew up, Philip was to outstrip his Plantagenet rivals, claim their lands, and make the French Crown the wealthiest in Latin Europe. Even intrepid Eleanor and her wicked litter of sundry sons would come to fear him in time. Cold, calculating, even cruel, Philip could not have been more unlike his gentle and impulsive father. A century later, a chronicler recalled a famous story that before Philip's birth Louis dreamt of him as a grown man holding a golden chalice filled with human blood. As Louis watched, Philip offered it to the realm's princes, and they all drank deeply. 'What this vision portended,' concluded the chronicler, 'his later deeds made clear.'

PART THREE

A New Rome

(1180–1226)

Simplified Capetian family tree, 1180–1226

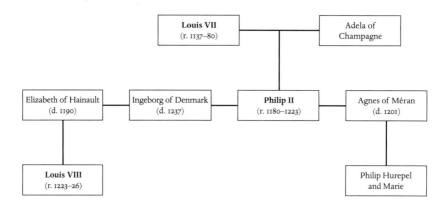

8.

Augustus
Philip II

Fifteen-year-old Philip II had heard a rumour. Maybe he, or his chronicler, had even made up the rumour. It is said that he had heard it from other boys in the palace growing up, though there isn't any evidence for the story before the chronicle says that Philip started telling it, and what was said had certainly never happened.[1] But the story was too fascinating, too frightening, and too useful to Philip for it not to catch hold. The rumour was that every year just before Easter the Jews of Paris lured a Christian boy into the caverns that lay below the city and slit his throat 'almost like a sacrifice'.[2] One of the supposed victims, so it was claimed, was a boy named Richard, who had been about Philip's age at the time of his death. It was said that Richard, who had been not just killed but actually crucified, had become a saint and worked miracles for those who prayed to him.

This story about Richard might have been a little older than the story about the caverns, and Richard, if he even existed, was from Pontoise not Paris anyway.[3] No one had paid this Richard much attention until now, but Philip found the story so compelling that somehow he had this boy's relics collected, housed in silver, and deposited at the church of the Holy Innocents on the city's Right Bank, just off the main road leading north to Saint-Denis. Along this busy and probably dusty thoroughfare outside the church, Philip installed a fountain to encourage passers-by to stop and notice his shrine. Evidently, he wanted people to think about Richard and about his devotion to him. It helped to explain what he had done to their Jewish friends and neighbours.

When Philip began his reign upon his father's death in September

1180, Paris had a substantial and wealthy Jewish population, as did other Capetian cities like Orléans and Bourges. Less than two years later, the Jews were gone, their houses taken over by Christians, their synagogues turned into churches, all at the new king's express command. Philip, said his chronicler, had been planning a strike against the Jews for a long time, and one of the first things that he had done as king was to stage a raid on Jewish houses. One Saturday in February 1181, as the Jews were at synagogue celebrating the Sabbath, Philip's agents arrested them, broke into their houses, and carted away their valuables.[4] A year later, the king ordered the Jews' total expulsion from Paris and other royal lands, cancelled any debts owed to them by Christians, and forced them to sell or abandon their property. By July 1182, every Jew in Paris had left the city or converted to Christianity. As depressingly frequent as such episodes were to become in later centuries, nothing like this had ever happened before in northern Europe. It must have made some people uneasy and in need of explanation.

It was not that Philip had found himself ruling some sort of oasis of medieval tolerance. Antisemitism had established itself firmly in the thought and policy of Christian France in the century and a half since Philip's ancestor Robert the Pious had attempted to force Jews to convert to Christianity.[5] Philip's father, Louis, had condemned relapsed Jewish converts to exile, ordering mutilation or death for those who returned, and he had had a Jew burned for allegedly interfering in a Christian ceremony, telling those who objected, 'I will have these Jews know that they must keep their dogs off the processions of Christians.'[6] Certainly, Louis VII had been no friend to Jews, despite the claims of Philip's chroniclers and some historians to the contrary, but he had censured the burning of thirty-two Jews in Blois in 1171 and he seemed to have no problem with the vibrant Jewish quarter established just a stone's throw from the palace. The kingdom's Christian subjects took a similarly ambivalent line. Jews and Christians did business together. Some Christians worked in Jewish houses as servants. They had neighbourly chats

Royal domain
Plantagenet lands

N

COUNTY OF FLANDERS

Rouen

DUCHY OF NORMANDY

DUCHY OF BRITTANY

COUNTY OF BLOIS

Paris

COUNTY OF CHAMPAGNE

Le Mans

GREATER

Angers

Tours

ANJOU

POITOU

Poitiers

DUCHY OF BURGUNDY

DUCHY OF AQUITAINE

AUVERGNE

PÉRIGORD

AGENAIS

GASCONY

COUNTY OF TOULOUSE

BÉARN

France in 1180

0   100 km
0   50   100 miles

on street corners or in each other's homes. Some ill-fated souls even fell cross-confessionally in love.

Philip disliked ambiguity, and he found these interactions both repugnant and dangerous. His veneration of Richard, an early example of the appalling child murder legend that would be retold to atrocious effect in many places in the coming centuries, reflected a sincere, though paranoid, perception of Christians' vulnerability to imagined Jewish malice. When he heard of another case of a Christian death at Jewish hands some years later, Philip had eighty of the alleged murderer's co-religionists rounded up and executed, probably exterminating every Jewish adult in the community. (He did allow the children, at least, to leave.)[7] Modern observers of whatever religious stripe can agree that the Hebrew chroniclers had good reason to speak of Philip as 'that wicked king',[8] but Philip's own chronicler, a monk at Saint-Denis named Rigord, celebrated these acts as a praiseworthy beginning, one hopefully indicative of the young man's future reign as a protector of the Church and a pillar of orthodoxy.

Rigord, a doctor turned monk whose work provides the backbone of our knowledge about Philip's early reign, bestowed the same 'most Christian king' (*rex Christianissimus*) sobriquet upon him for his treatment of the Jews that his father Louis had earned for sheltering Thomas Becket from Henry II's wrath.[9] Rigord sprinkled the phrase liberally throughout his work and reported miraculous signs linked to Philip, such as that which occurred at his coronation when lamps hanging above the king and queen broke and poured oil over the pair almost as if God himself were anointing them.[10] But if Philip could claim to be just as superlatively Christian as Louis VII had been, 'bread, wine, and gaiety' were not enough to satisfy his appetites, not least because gaiety was not something he valued or perhaps even understood. He kept a quiet court, without any of the minstrels, acrobats, or fools to be found in the halls of other European palaces, and he had those who wasted their time playing games fined if they let fly a blasphemous oath.[11]

What the young king did value and understand was money, and

his persecution of the Jews certainly had as much to do with his love of it as it did with his hatred of them. The first confiscations alone had made him 15,000 marks, a sum equivalent to a year and a half's royal revenue.[12] When he then cancelled all Christian debts owed to Jews, he nevertheless stipulated that 20 per cent of the debt was to be paid to the Crown, making him an 'immense amount of money', and when he finally forced the Jews to leave, he allowed them to sell their goods but kept their real estate and their businesses for himself.[13] All this produced 'an enormous windfall' for his treasury, but Philip soon realized that he had killed a goose laying golden eggs.[14] Having Jews living in one's lands might be religiously objectionable, but it was also very profitable. Unlike medieval Christians, Jews had no religious prohibition against loaning money at interest, which was a necessary commercial expedient and consumer stopgap, and Jews' international networks facilitated long-distance trading and stimulated economic activity, the profits from which could be taxed at much higher rates than those levied on Christians. Such benefits were now accruing to Philip's rivals, to whose lands the expelled Jews had fled in 1182. These realities outweighed Philip's piety and his prejudices. Although meteors rained from the sky to harken the return of Antichrist and, as the chronicler Rigord groused, it was 'against everyone's opinion and his own royal edict', the king eventually invited the Jews to return.[15] The additional revenue did not amount to much, perhaps 1 per cent of his annual income, but it was worth it to him.[16] Ambitious despite his relative penury, Philip needed every coin he could squeeze from every source he could find.

One of his costly projects was the transformation of Paris into a capital city worthy of its name, which was believed to derive from that of a prince of ancient Troy. Odd as the legend may seem to modern ears, educated people in the twelfth century thought that Troy's fleeing refugees had established the European kingdoms after the city's destruction by the Greeks, and this myth became central to French, English, and other medieval national identities.[17] While Paris was still small by medieval Islamic or Chinese standards, the city had grown at breakneck pace over the last century and may have housed a population of 50,000 in Philip's day.[18] The king's predecessors had tried to keep up with its needs, founding a market here, building a new church there, and others had pitched in. Most notably, the Bishop of Paris had begun replacing the old Carolingian cathedral of Saint Stephen with an enormous Gothic church dedicated to the Virgin Mary, known as Our Lady, or *Notre Dame* in French.

The construction of Notre-Dame Cathedral had begun two years before Philip's birth and continued for most of his reign. The new church could be seen from windows of the royal palace, its fresh stone contrasting sharply with the muddy and rubbish-strewn streets below. The muck and the stench – redolent, claimed Rigord, of the city's Roman name 'Lutecia', which derived from the Latin word for mud (*lutum*) – drove Philip to order the citizens to pave the city's four main streets, including that which ran beside the church of the Holy Innocents, where he had installed Saint Richard's relics.[19] Next to the Holy Innocents, he ordered the vacated houses of exiled Jews demolished in order to establish Les Halles, a permanent covered market that would exist until 1969. Philip also enclosed Paris with walls wide and strong enough for a cart to be driven atop its circuit, remnants of which are still dotted around the city. At the walls' northwestern edge, he built a new castle, christened the Louvre. A rectangular fortification with massive round towers at its corners enclosing a central cylindrical donjon, part of Philip's Louvre still stands visible in the museum's basement today, a stark reminder of the building's initial purpose enduring beneath the extravagant additions of the richer and more secure rulers for whom Philip literally paved the way.

The Louvre faced northwest toward the Vexin, whence Philip expected trouble to come. Relations between Philip, a messy-haired adolescent of strong will if few resources, and Henry II, a proven warrior of fifty married to the ex-wife of Philip's father, had begun on a friendly note, at least as Henry saw it. Two of Philip's many sisters had been betrothed to two of Henry's many sons as a

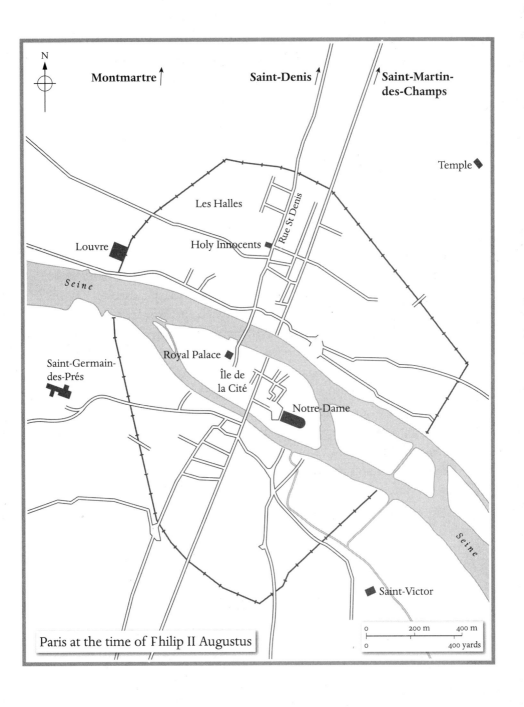

N

Montmartre ↑   Saint-Denis ↑   Saint-Martin-
des-Champs ↑

Temple ◆

Les Halles

Holy Innocents ◆

Rue St Denis

Louvre

Seine

Saint-Germain-
des-Prés

Royal Palace ◆

Île de
la Cité

Notre-Dame

Seine

Saint-Victor ◆

0   200 m   400 m
0   400 yards

Paris at the time of Philip II Augustus

guarantee of peace between the two kingdoms, and Henry sought no immediate advantage when the throne passed to young Philip. He had carried the crown in Philip's coronation ceremony, and in 1183 he gave Philip a princely gift of 'wild beasts collected from all over Normandy and Aquitaine, including young stags, fawns, and wild goats, placed most carefully in a great ship' and sent up the Seine to Paris, where Philip received them 'most kindly'.[20] But, welcome as Philip found such presents, they were as nothing against the needs of his kingdom and the honour of his family.

Both were thrown into peril by the premature death that same year of Henry's eldest son and heir presumptive, another Henry, known as the Young King. Although King Henry's quarrelsome sons had grudgingly accepted his authority since their failed rebellion of 1173, the Young King's death unsettled their arrangement and gave Philip an opening. Philip had immediate cause for complaint in that Henry had neither returned the Norman half of the Vexin that had been the dowry of the Young King's widowed bride, nor had he made his second son, Richard, celebrate his promised marriage to Philip's half-sister Alice. It was even rumoured – and this rumour may have been true – that the wicked old king had seduced her himself.[21]

In the face of such provocations, Philip employed a time-tested Capetian strategy, exploiting the enmities among the squabbling siblings of the English Crown and their intimidating but ageing father. First, Philip befriended Prince Geoffrey, Henry's disgruntled

Sons of Henry II and Eleanor of Aquitaine

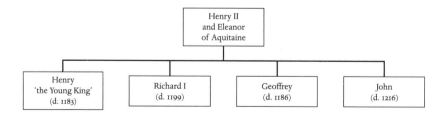

third son, though the plan came to nothing when Geoffrey died in the tournament lists in 1186. (Philip mournfully buried him in Notre-Dame.) His options thus reduced, cold-blooded Philip made common cause with hot-headed Richard, a soldier-poet nicknamed Lionheart. 'At his finest superhuman, at his worst unpleasant and inhumane', Richard would prove most irritating to Philip in the decade to come.[22] Yet although opposites in temperament, the two men were equally superb on the battlefield. When they fought on the same side, even Henry could not stop them.

By the end of 1188, Philip had raised 'an infinitely large army', seized two of Henry's most important castles, swallowed up his dominions in central France, and symbolically chopped down an ancient elm near Gisors where peace negotiations traditionally took place, 'swearing conversations like that would never again happen there'.[23] Sensing the way the wind was blowing, Henry's vassals went over to Philip and Richard over the next few months, and on 3 July 1189 the city of Tours, key to Henry's own ancestral lands in Anjou, fell to their attack. The old king died a broken man only three days later, aware in his last moments that even his favourite son John had betrayed him.[24] Rigord celebrated the outcome as proof of God's favour toward the French king, 'whom the Lord had placed as a bit in Henry's mouth to revenge the blood of Thomas Becket', the quarrelsome Archbishop of Canterbury whose murder Henry had accidentally ordered, but it was for Philip something of a pyrrhic victory.[25] He and Richard had become very close over the years of their contest with Henry. They shared meals, and sometimes they even shared a bed.[26] (What they did there is anybody's guess.) But now that Richard had inherited almost the entirety of his father's realm, Philip already felt the fraying of the bonds that had united them.[27]

There was, however, a more pressing problem to deal with, one that promised a temporary reprieve from the ancient enmity between England and France: in October 1187, Crusader Jerusalem had fallen to the Kurdish Sultan of Egypt, al-Malik al-Nāṣir Ṣalāḥ al-Dīn Yūsuf, known to Christian Europe as Saladin. Richard had immediately taken the cross upon hearing the news despite the ongoing hostilities at home. Thirsty for blood and hungry for glory, he had long been yearning to crusade. Philip did not follow until two months later. Not only more cautious in nature than his English counterpart, he was also more interested in the governance of his kingdom and he lacked the funds that Richard could splash about with such generous abandon. A tax, called the Saladin tithe (*decima Salahadini*), was decreed in England and France in 1188 to support expenses, but while it was collected efficiently in England, Philip's subjects hated it so much that the effort was abandoned.[28] The pope and the preachers were, however, insistent, and with Henry's death and the ostensible end of his Anglo-Norman war, Philip had no reasonable grounds for further delay.

Following in his father's footsteps, Philip departed for the East in June 1190 from Saint-Denis, where he prostrated himself before the holy relics before taking up the banner of the Vexin. 'As has been customary since antiquity for French kings whenever they take up arms against the enemy,' Rigord observed with more piety than accuracy.[29] Its blood-red silk matched the colour of the French crusaders' crosses, distinguishing them from Richard and his men, who wore white ones, and the Flemish, who wore green.[30] The expedition assembled at Vézelay in Burgundy, where Saint Bernard had preached the Second Crusade to such rapturous reception, and then proceeded to the Mediterranean coast. Sailing separately, the two kings met again in the autumn at Messina in Sicily, where they were to winter before continuing onward to Syria. Over those grey and chilly months, the long-suppressed differences between them erupted into the open. Richard was behaving boorishly, mistreating the Sicilian inhabitants and their rulers alike, but it was the thorny subject of Philip's long-unwed sister Alice that provoked the first serious break.

While they were still at war with Henry, Richard had again promised that he would marry Alice, though not until after the crusade. So it was with considerable surprise and anger that Philip learned not only that Richard was not going to marry Alice – due, as

Richard helpfully explained, to her liaison with his late, unlamented father – but that he had also contracted an entirely new marriage.[31] Richard's intended, a princess from the northern Spanish kingdom of Navarre, fetched over the Pyrenees by none other than his indefatigable if aged mother, Eleanor of Aquitaine, would shortly arrive to accompany them to the Holy Land. This really was too much. Philip demanded negotiations, kept his head, and played a bad hand well. The Treaty of Messina, agreed in March 1191, not only wrung out of Richard 10,000 marks as the price of marrying 'whomsoever he likes', but also reaffirmed Philip's rights as overlord of all the Plantagenets' continental possessions, including Normandy and Aquitaine.[32]

Putting Messina behind them, the kings set sail for the East on the spring winds. Philip arrived at the siege of Acre on 20 April 1191, three weeks after leaving Italy. There he waited – and waited – for Richard, who had detoured to Cyprus where he conquered the local Greek potentate, married his Navarrese princess, and sold the island to the Knights Templar before arriving with great fanfare before the walls of Acre in June. Philip must have greeted Richard's bombastic entrance with irritation, but even with their hostility simmering barely below the surface, the pair's old battlefield magic was still there. Acre had been besieged for two years at this point. Once Philip and Richard were on the scene it fell in a matter of weeks. Even when sickness swept through the crusading army, infecting both kings and causing Philip's skin to peel, his fingernails to fall off, and his once luxuriant hair to fall out, they fought on. So ill at one point that they couldn't stand, they shot crossbows at the enemy from their sickbeds, or so the story goes.[33] Exhausted, Acre surrendered on 12 July. A vital port enabling Latin access to the West, its survival in Christian hands helped to delay the ultimate collapse of the crusader states, but anyone could see that there was nothing more that could now be done.

At least, Philip could see that. Taking Acre was hard enough, and crusader prospects elsewhere in Syria looked even less promising. Jerusalem was impossible. Philip had not recovered from his illness – he never fully did, remaining bald and prone to fevers for the rest of his life – and succession issues in Flanders required his urgent attention. Richard was too experienced and too talented a campaigner not to have known at some level that there was nothing more the crusade could accomplish, but his heart could not accept the loss of Jerusalem, and anyway he was enjoying himself too much to leave just yet. While Philip sailed home in July 1191, Richard stayed on for another year and a half, immersing himself in the cosmopolitan cultures of the Levant, defeating but then befriending Saladin, and even suggesting the latter's brother marry his sister.

Philip's comparatively early withdrawal redounded to his shame, one of a growing number of signs that early clerical confidence in his Christian bona fides had been misplaced. Rigord, who once could hardly dip his quill in ink without writing *rex christianissimus*, ceased using the phrase at this point. Even generations later, Philip's precipitous departure was held up as a model of what *not* to do on crusade.[34] Philip didn't much care. His ancestors had relied upon ritual and religion, but he put his faith in money and land. If the crusade had hurt his reputation, it had strengthened him in other, more material ways.

Before leaving France in June 1190, Philip had made arrangements that amounted to a fundamental reorganization and modernization of the kingdom's governance. As set out in an 'Ordinance-Testament' that Rigord copied into his chronicle, the king instituted a new system for the collection of royal revenue that solved his money problems for good. As the Saladin tithe's failure had shown, the French Crown did not possess an effective tax collection system. Up to now, men known as provosts (*prévôts*) had collected the hodgepodge of taxes, tolls, tithes, and other customary duties owed to the Crown. Provosts paid a flat fee to collect these revenues themselves, which saved the trouble and expense of having to collect the money directly but gave the provosts wide leeway to abuse their offices and meant that the Crown did not always have very detailed knowledge of its rights. Over the provosts, Philip now placed a new category of officers called *baillis* (a word not well translated by the English 'bailiff'). *Baillis* monitored the provosts' activities, punished their excesses, and held inquests into royal rights, as well as convening monthly courts to hear judicial cases and collecting the revenue owed from irregular, if rich, sources, such as those due from forests, vacant bishoprics, and 'extraordinary' taxes levied for urgent matters such as war, the marriage of a royal daughter, or the knighting of a royal son.[35] Three times a year, the *baillis* and the provosts brought their takings to Paris and reported to the queen mother and the Archbishop of Reims, whom Philip had named co-regents in his absence. Their staff had the officers' work checked and required any discrepancies to be explained and corrected. After each of these sessions, the co-regents sent a letter to Philip, detailing the trimester's business.

The principle of accountability manifest in the 'Ordinance-Testament' underpinned a revolution in medieval governance that is often called 'administrative kingship'.[36] In France it marked a move away from royal reliance on ritual and prestige (albeit frequently backed up with the sword) to shape the affairs of their kingdom and toward more active and direct involvement in its daily governance through salaried officers. This in turn drove innovations in record keeping, for keeping tabs on these officers required that registers of accounts be maintained from year to year. Philip's efforts on that score suffered an early setback when he lost his baggage, containing most of his documents as well as a substantial amount of treasure, at a skirmish against Richard in 1194. But owing to these setbacks, Philip took a revolutionary administrative course of action, the disaster prompting him to cease the traditional practice of moving the kingdom's records with the king and to establish a permanent chancery and archive in Paris, the kernel of today's French national archives.

Thanks to such innovations, Philip finally began to have the kind of knowledge of and control over his kingdom that the Anglo-Normans had been developing ever since William the Conqueror ordered his Domesday survey a century before. Philip had much ground to catch up, for the legal reforms and administrative advances of Henry I and Henry II had far outstripped his Capetian predecessors' modest efforts in that direction. It was lucky for Philip that Richard was an old-fashioned warrior king uninterested in bureaucratic niceties who spent as little time as possible in England, leaving its administration to drift while Philip forged ahead. French royal administration would never reach the levels of efficiency that its English counterpart did in the Middle Ages, but France was soon to become a much larger, and therefore richer, kingdom than its rival across the Channel. The acquisition of these new lands, combined with the modernization and rationalization of government and finance, at last relieved Philip of his relative poverty. By 1202–3, the first year for which an account survives, his annual income was approximately 115,000 *livres parisis*, a near sixfold increase compared with his father's regular revenues.[37]

Philip's territorial expansion, too, can trace its roots to the Third Crusade, in part because Richard was so delayed in returning from it that Philip had time to envisage a France free from the Plantagenet scourge. Having finally embarked for home in October 1192, Richard was taken captive in December near Vienna by agents of the Duke of Austria, whom he had insulted on crusade, while travelling in disguise to evade ambush by agents of the Count of Toulouse, whose lands he had previously invaded. 'Purchased' by the German Emperor, whose rivals he supported, Richard did not regain his freedom until April 1194, by which time Philip had invaded the Vexin, seized Gisors, and besieged Rouen.[38] Following the Capetians' standard operating procedure toward feuding Plantagenets, Philip made overtures to Richard's younger brother John, who seems not to have had a loyal bone in his body and gladly handed over most of Normandy in exchange for 6,000 marks, the Artois – and Alice.[39] This wedding never came off, not because John had any compunction about taking his father's leavings or even because he was already married, but because he immediately switched sides again when Richard reappeared. Richard quickly regained almost everything he had lost, save Gisors, but he replaced that long-storied stronghold with a new fortification based on archi-tectural principles observed in Syria. Christened *château Gaillard* ('the saucy castle'), Richard intended it not only to guard the fron-tier but also to convey his insouciance toward Philip. Still, this brief period had shown what Philip might accomplish in Richard's absence, and the Capetian must have felt fairly saucy himself when a stray arrow from a crossbow fired from a castle struck Richard in 1199, causing his death through infection a few days later and leaving the Anglo-Norman realm in John's incapable hands.

Richard's return from crusade had been a delayed one, but many of the Capetian's great rivals did not return at all. The Duke of Bur-gundy and the Count of Champagne remained in the Holy Land, the latter becoming titular King of Jerusalem before falling from a window to his death, and others died during the campaign itself. These included the counts of Blois and Troyes and, most import-antly for Philip's purposes, the quasi-independent Count of Flanders. The childless Flemish count's death allowed Philip to float a claim to Flanders, which in the end came to nothing, but the vacancy did enable him to acquire a rich and strategically important territory called the Vermandois. Lying between Paris and Flanders, much as the Vexin lay between Paris and Normandy (see map, p. 124) the Vermandois was to be essential to the next phase of Philip's wres-tling match with the Plantagenets. Philip also took possession of adjoining lands in the Artois and Valois, buttressing his strategic position and his economic one, since these lands were both agricul-turally bountiful and commercially advanced.[40]

Over the next three decades of Philip's long reign, he was to secure such vast new expanses of land as to make these early gains seem paltry in comparison, but they were the first new Capetian acquisitions in decades and impressed the chronicler Rigord so much that he bestowed the imperial title 'Augustus' upon Philip. As Rigord explained, the name derived not only from Philip's birth month but also because Philip had 'augmented' (*augere* in Latin) the realm in the manner of great Roman emperors.[41] The epithet did

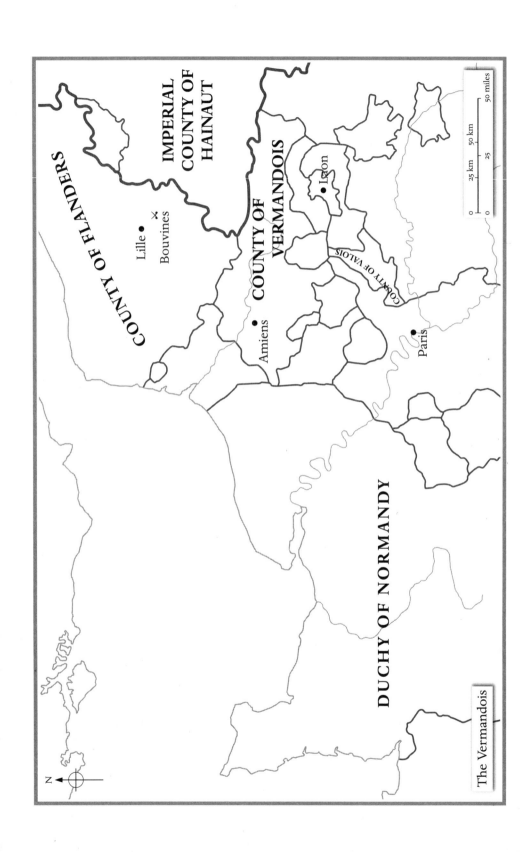

COUNTY OF FLANDERS

IMPERIAL COUNTY OF HAINAUT

Lille •
✕ Bouvines

COUNTY OF VERMANDOIS

Laon •

COUNTY OF VALOIS

Amiens •

Paris •

DUCHY OF NORMANDY

N

0   25 km   50 km
0   25   50 miles

The Vermandois

not catch on among Philip's contemporaries, though modern historians use it almost universally. Philip's own views on the matter seem equivocal. His father and grandfather had sporadically spoken of themselves as 'Emperors of the Franks', a gambit Philip did not employ, but he did cast himself as a successor to Charlemagne, named a bastard son after him, and had Charlemagne's supposed sword 'Joyeuse' carried before him at his coronation.[42] Still, if Philip did not necessarily wish to be considered an emperor himself, he certainly did wish to be considered the German emperor's equal and his kingdom free of imperial control. Although it had been a long time since anyone had tried to enforce France's legal status as an imperial fief that had evolved from the territorial provinces of the Carolingian Empire, the Capetian Crown's twelfth-century successes and the Empire's increasing political disarray definitively closed the question. As the pope put it in 1202, 'this king [Philip] recognizes no superior'.[43]

These legal abstractions took concrete form in the military and diplomatic spheres, where Philip had to contend with the Plantagenets' alliance with the Welf family's claimants to the imperial Crown. Capetian diplomacy favoured the Welfs' great rivals the Hohenstaufen, whose members had held the throne for most of the twelfth century. Richard's captivity in the Hohenstaufen emperor's castles, however, made him receptive to the Hohenstaufen way of thinking, and he owed his freedom largely to his agreement to abandon the Welfs and accept imperial overlordship in England.[44] The growing closeness between Richard and his Hohenstaufen captor left Philip few choices for allies to protect his eastern flank. He could not simply change sides and champion the Welf cause since the Welfs were closely related to the Plantagenets, so he cast further afield, ingeniously alighting on King Cnut of Denmark as a bulwark against both England and Empire. Cnut had both a fearsome navy and an ancient if tenuous claim to the English throne, and while he obdurately refused to put these at the French king's disposal, Philip's English rivals didn't know that.[45] Unwed since the death of his first wife on the eve of the crusade, Philip sealed the alliance by marrying Cnut's sister. In so doing, however, he made a serious mistake, perhaps the most serious mistake of his reign, one that would plunge both king and kingdom into a religious and legal imbroglio that took two decades to resolve. On 14 August 1193, Philip married Ingeborg of Denmark – and repudiated her the very next day.

9.

The Danish Witch

Philip II

'*Mala Francia! Mala Francia!*' ('Wicked France! Wicked France!'), cried the Danish princess.[1] Having spent only three months in the kingdom, Ingeborg of Denmark had as yet little French and had to fall back on Latin to express her pain and anger. Her interpreter had just translated the sentence of the bishops and barons who had assembled in the royal hall at Compiègne in November 1193 to investigate her genealogy. They had said that she could not be married to King Philip for they had found her too closely related to his first wife somehow. They were a little vague about the 'how' – and later they had to admit they'd made it up – but fifteen men had sworn it was the truth, even if ten of them were suspect witnesses.[2] Her marriage was thus invalid, as if it had never taken place at all. The Archbishop of Reims, uncle to the king, had been tasked with breaking the news, and he must have heard Ingeborg's cry with a certain sense of shame and then perhaps with alarm when she added '*Roma! Roma!*', an appeal to the pope himself for justice.

Sister to the King of Denmark with the royal blood of England and Rus' running through her veins, Ingeborg had not expected this when she disembarked on French shores in August. It is safe to say that no one had. Drawn by her famous beauty and breeding, Philip had rushed impatiently to Amiens to meet his eighteen-year-old bride. The wedding was immediate, and a coronation ceremony took place the next day, the Archbishop of Reims himself placing the reginal diadem upon Ingeborg's unblemished brow. Everything was going according to plan. 'But wow!' (*sed mirum!*), exclaimed the chronicler Rigord, 'that very same day, Philip began to hate this wife whom he had so long desired'.[3] During the coronation, he had 'turned pale and begun to tremble, and almost could not make it to the end of the ceremony'.[4] The town was full to bursting with guests – the Bishop of Tournai had a hard time even finding a place to stay – but whatever feasts and entertainments had been planned were cancelled. People must have milled about in confusion, trying to find out what was going on. Philip offered no explanation. He just told Ingeborg's attendants to pack her things, sent her to a run-down Merovingian monastery outside Paris, and began trying to undo the marriage.

Why Philip did this is one of the great mysteries of medieval French history. At the time some people, albeit 'unserious' ones, said it was because she had bad breath or because Philip had found her not a virgin.[5] Rigord and other chroniclers blamed the devil, while modern historians have floated theories ranging from Philip's disappointment with the Danes' diplomacy to his 'personal proclivities and neuroses'.[6] Philip's lawyers offered various but unsatisfactory rationales over the twenty years that he fought to be free of Ingeborg. When their genealogical excuse proved fallacious, they floated the marriage's non-consummation, and when that failed in the face of Ingeborg's unwavering testimony to the contrary, they tried claiming that while penetration *had* occurred, ejaculation had not, for the king had been made temporarily impotent by witchcraft or sorcery.[7] The Church ultimately rejected this explanation, but Philip's claim of penetration without ejaculation via magical means attempted to thread a very narrow legal needle. It was a last-ditch effort to avoid the consequences of an entanglement that his predecessors might have got away with but which his own historical circumstances made inescapable.

That something *had* happened on the wedding night, perhaps something whose implications only became clear to Philip several hours later, seems clear since he was fine until mid-morning the next day, and that this thing shook the king to his core is evident. Philip may have been angered by the Danes' unwillingness to deploy their ships against England – though an English chronicle reports that the king already knew this before agreeing to the marriage – and he may well have wished to keep the 10,000 marks that made up Ingeborg's dowry.[8] He was, after all, a bad-tempered and avaricious man. But while a calculated turn-about might explain Philip's immediate post-nuptial actions, it does not explain his steadfast refusal to be in Ingeborg's presence in the years and years that followed, even when it would have cost him little and gained him much just to have her sit at his side. Philip's seemingly inexplicable behaviour suggests an uncontrollable emotional revulsion, a feeling of shame and disgust that the king, a private and emotionally unexpressive individual, could not face long enough to overcome. He did try, once, to have another attempt at sex with Ingeborg, travelling down to the monastery where he had confined her in the weeks after the wedding, but he left her bedroom 'after a very short while, so much did he hate her . . .'[9]

If the claim of sorcery should perhaps be understood as an explanation approximating Philip's own understanding of what had happened, one that he was too embarrassed to admit until he ran out of options, it is also true that it was the only legal avenue open to his lawyers once genealogy had been ruled out. The Church understood magically induced impotency to be a temporary condition, one not disproved by evidence of virility at other times, such as by the existence of children.[10] But Philip had been married once before, to a woman named Elizabeth of Hainaut, and that union *had* produced children, including a son who was about six at the time of his father's marriage to Ingeborg, as well as stillborn twins whose birth killed Elizabeth. By the time his lawyers resorted to claiming magical impotence, Philip's third – and to papal eyes bigamous – marriage in 1196 had produced two further children, while a later liaison with a mysterious 'damsel from Arras' gave him an illegitimate son.

Although Philip's sexual inability with Ingeborg was an exception to his otherwise proven potency, his cruelty toward her had precedent in his relations with his first wife Elizabeth. She had been only ten when they married in 1180, but by the time she was fourteen he was already trying to divorce her. The grounds for annulment, as a later chronicle suggests, may have been that Elizabeth had not yet produced an heir, a charge that would have been unfair as well as unkind.[11] If Philip had followed the Plantagenet practice of consummating marriage with a young adolescent girl only once immediately following her first menstruation, which average medieval females experienced at twelve, and not establishing regular sexual relations until some years later, he could not yet have had any reasonable expectation of pregnancy.[12] His real purpose had probably been to punish Elizabeth's father over Hainaut's support for the Count of Flanders against the wishes of the queen mother and her faction from Champagne. Bereft of familial protection because Philip had moved against her quickly and quietly, Elizabeth had fought back desperately but shrewdly. Trading her precious robes for humble garments, she walked barefoot through the streets like a penitent sinner, praying at the churches and calling out to God and the people to save her. Roused to pity by this spectacle, lepers and poor people congregated noisily in front of the palace, demanding Elizabeth's rescue.

Ever sensitive to a softening in his subjects' support and perhaps impressed by this evidence of the young queen's ingenuity, Philip capitulated. Although the well-informed chronicler to whom we owe this story remarked that 'he did not visit her bed' in the immediate aftermath, he must soon have resumed sexual relations with her since she bore a daughter a year or two later.[13] This baby died young, but in 1187 the young queen triumphed, giving Philip a son named Louis. Couriers were sent to every corner of the kingdom to announce the news, and there were bonfires in the streets of Paris for a week as people danced all night in celebration.[14] Elizabeth's glory was only brief, for she died in childbirth less than three years later, just shy of her twentieth birthday. Although a striking woman, unusually tall for the period, with beautiful blue eyes and poetic tastes, she could have left little impression on two-year-old Louis. Philip, however, never forgot her. In his mercurial fashion, he had apparently grown fond of her as they reached maturity together. He had her buried with splendour near the main altar in Notre-Dame, her coffin surrounded by those of their infant children. On her silk-wrapped breast was laid a silver seal engraved with her image, crowned and holding a sceptre in her left hand and a Capetian lily in her right, a sign in death of the honours that she had fought so hard to secure in life.[15]

Ingeborg was no less determined than Elizabeth to have her due as a queen, a wife, and, as she hoped, a mother, but it was Pope Innocent III who proved nearly as obdurate an obstacle to the dissolution of Philip's second marriage. Innocent had been elected in 1198, five years after Ingeborg launched her initial appeal, at a point when her cause seemed all but lost. Innocent's immediate predecessor, a well-meaning but ponderous nonagenarian, had taken three years just to respond to Danish appeals against the annulment. Not until 1196 was the French clergy ordered to review the evidence for the dissolution, and this belated action had negligible effect. Too intimidated by their king to do anything else, the French clerics had reaffirmed the annulment, 'like dogs too scared for their skins to bark', as the increasingly disillusioned Rigord sniped.[16] Philip married a German duke's daughter named Agnes of Méran the very next month, and by the time Innocent came to the papal throne Agnes was already expecting their first child.

The *fait accompli* did not dissuade Innocent from what he saw as his divine mission to defend Christian marriage. In the decades since the divorce of Philip's father from Eleanor of Aquitaine, not only the Church's law but also its theology had become less forgiving of marital experimentation. Marriage had become the key metaphor to describe the relationship between the Church, imagined as a bride, and Christ, her metaphorical bridegroom. Human marriages were made in the image of that divine union between Christ and the Church and must therefore be as indissoluble as that eternal one.[17] No longer would great men be able to set aside a wife at will in the way that so many of Philip's predecessors had done. Innocent was even willing to mitigate the Church's long-standing definition of incest to make marriages more stable by reducing the prohibited degrees of relationship from seven to four. While this still meant that anyone sharing, for example, the same great-grandmother was prohibited from marrying, it did sharply reduce the number of ex post facto 'discoveries' of prohibited relations that had provided a convenient excuse for so many royal annulments.[18] That reform would not be codified until the Fourth Lateran Council of 1214, a watershed moment in medieval history and the culmination of Innocent's reign, but from the very beginning of his pontificate, this new lawyer-pope intended to make an example out of Philip. According to the pope's medieval biographer, after his election he sent one of his cardinals to France with three tasks: firstly, to send aid to the Holy Land, secondly, to make peace between France and England, and thirdly, to make Philip return to Ingeborg.[19]

Caught between two such uncompromising characters as Innocent and Philip, the cardinal made the best of a bad job. At the end of 1199, he convoked a council at Dijon, a city that lay outside of Philip's lands, which reversed the findings of the earlier assemblies invalidating the Danish marriage on genealogical grounds. The Dijon council ruled that Ingeborg and Philip were not too closely related, and because they had exchanged vows, they were married. Philip's new marriage was therefore adulterous and illegal. He was ordered to quit his new wife and to return to Ingeborg immediately. If he did not comply by 13 January 1200 – about the length of time it took this decision to be announced in Paris – the entire realm would be placed under sentence of interdict, meaning that the churches would be closed to the laity.[20] Priests would still perform the two most urgent sacraments, the baptism of infants and the confession of the dying, but marriages would not be celebrated nor the Eucharist administered. Holy water would be unavailable. Sinners would receive their penances at the church door. If a priest read the Bible aloud, he should be careful that no parishioner could hear him.

Philip felt hard done by. He complained to Innocent that he had been more harshly treated than his father, Louis VII, the Emperor Frederick I, and even King John of England, all of whom had been allowed easy disposal of a wife deemed surplus to requirements. Innocent replied patronizingly that those cases had been different, and anyway, he was only acting for the benefit of Philip's immortal soul.[21] But Philip was loath to give up his new partner, Agnes of Méran, for the union was a happy one and she was fertile.[22] Although her first child was female, he had reasonable expectations that she might yet give him a son, a hedge against the premature death of his frail first-born, Louis. Nor was Philip without clerical support in France. While some French clerics, including the Bishop of Paris, complied with the interdict, others went about their duties as if nothing had happened.[23]

The interdict was annoying to Philip, but its half-hearted enforcement was the worst of all worlds from a papal point of view. As the months dragged on, Innocent dispatched another cardinal to France to convince Philip to put aside Agnes and to see his Danish wife. Surprisingly, Philip agreed. Perhaps he had begun to feel the pressure or perhaps he was merely toying with the Holy See, as has been speculated.[24] He did, however, make another attempt to overcome his compulsive aversion to Ingeborg. Releasing her from the austere fortress where he had sent her in retribution for the interdict, he met her quietly at a hunting lodge west of Paris, the first time he had seen her in seven years. But that was as far as he could go. He had promised the cardinal that he would treat Ingeborg as his wife and queen. Instead, he now asked for a new council to rule on the Danish marriage, promising to set aside Agnes, who was pregnant once more, until it had deliberated. It is unclear whether the cardinal fully communicated the temporary nature of the agreement to Innocent, but Philip never allowed the council to reach a decision anyway. To everyone's further astonishment, he walked out of the council and took Ingeborg with him, only to deposit her in the castle of Étampes and ride off again.

What Innocent would have done in response to Philip's effrontery must remain a matter of conjecture, for he had not had time to craft a strategy before word arrived that Philip's 'concubine' Agnes had died shortly after giving birth to a son. She had not been Philip's first choice for a third wife. Indeed, she was his third choice. He had been turned down by Princess Joan of England, who thought his treatment of Ingeborg boded ill for her own happiness, and his second choice decided to marry a former suitor while making her way to Paris.[25] Philip had, however, loved Agnes as well as he was capable of loving anyone, and she had fulfilled her most essential duty to him by bearing a boy. His kingdom now had an heir and a spare. That is, if Philip could prevail upon Innocent to remove the taint of bastardry from the boy. This, Innocent proved surprisingly willing to do. Partly, he hoped that a rapprochement would ensure Philip's support for his preferred candidate in an upcoming imperial election, but he was also aware of his papal responsibility to ensure the political stability of Christendom. Innocent had worried from the first that Philip's aversion to Ingeborg imperilled the fate of the kingdom should little Louis die and the heirless realm 'fall to foreigners'.[26] Agnes's death removed a major impediment to the resolution Innocent was seeking, and he was happy to trade the legitimation of her children in prospect of an end to the Danish dispute. Ingeborg, too, must have expected that her ordeal was finally over.

Naturally, Philip dashed their hopes. To Innocent's chagrin and Ingeborg's agony, Philip refused to release the queen from her confinement at Étampes, let alone to treat her as his companion and consort. Nor was her captivity a gilded one. The castle at Étampes, situated southwest of Paris, existed to guard the vital route to Orléans. It was a military fortress, not a palace. A donjon tower built by Philip's father, and still extant today, dominated the complex. During the years that Ingeborg spent there, Philip had encircled it with a wall, a measure that perhaps reflects his insecurities toward his wife as much as it does his defensive requirements. Ingeborg complained bitterly of the austere existence that Philip imposed upon her there. In a letter she sent to Innocent in 1203, she lamented that she had no companions except for those whom Philip sent to berate her. She believed herself to be under surveillance at all times and was not permitted to receive visitors or letters from Denmark. A deeply religious woman, she was deprived of all but the most basic spiritual care. Even her physical needs were neglected. She claimed to be nourished only with 'the bread of tribulation and the drink of anguish' and to have scant clothing or, at least, nothing fit for a queen. She said she was not allowed to bathe and had no one to bleed her, a medieval medical practice thought essential to maintaining good health. No Christian woman, she concluded, should be treated like this. Nonetheless, she professed herself ready to act as a loving wife to the husband who had behaved so cruelly toward her. He remained, she said, close to her heart, 'like a bundle of myrrh between my breasts'.[27]

Ingeborg's insistence that she was still ready to love and cherish Philip even after a decade of mistreatment may seem pathetic, evidence of her victimization not just by Philip but also by a culture that valued women only as wives and mothers. That is true in some ways, but her words were also carefully crafted and meant to appeal to her powerful papal advocate. Her conviction that her relationship with Philip ought to be an emotional and sexual partnership as well as a legal and political one exactly fitted the new model of Christian marriage that Innocent advocated and partly originated. Ingeborg did not hit upon this approach by accident. Her correspondence with Innocent and his predecessor demonstrates remarkable fluency in marriage law and uses turns of phrase that Innocent himself later adopted.[28] Since she was a literate woman noted for her reading, it is possible that Ingeborg composed the letters herself. But even if she did not personally dictate this letter, its rhetoric shows that someone in her inner circle knew how to appeal to Innocent's conviction that human marriages should be genuinely loving ones, as well as indissoluble unions in the way of the Church's marriage to Christ. Although celibate himself, Innocent was a dedicated pastor with a keen interest in the lives of the laity, and he understood the importance of sex to a marriage's happiness, even if he found the act itself rather appalling.

Innocent's pastoral concerns may help to explain why Philip and his lawyers introduced their claim that witchcraft had made the king impotent with Ingeborg. Innocent was not alone among clergymen in valuing healthy sexual relations among married laity. While in the early Middle Ages the Church had encouraged abstinence even between married couples, more recently it had moved away from that position, even as it enforced clerical celibacy with increasing rigour. Husbands and wives were said to owe one another a 'conjugal debt', meaning sex, which neither could deny the other without mutual consent.[29] As one of Innocent's letters warned Philip, 'it was not right for spouses to defraud one another [of the conjugal debt], lest they fall into Satan's snare' by committing the sin of lechery.[30] (It was around this time that Philip had his affair with his 'damsel of Arras', as perhaps Innocent caught wind.) The pope's insistence on marital sex meant that what Philip had to prove was not that he *would not* have sex with Ingeborg. That was just refusal to pay the conjugal debt, a blameworthy act but not grounds for annulment. What he had to prove was that he *could not* do so. He had to show that, as far as Ingeborg was concerned, he was sexually bankrupt; there was no prospect of her receiving what he owed.

Philip's lawyers first floated bewitchment or sorcery in 1202, as hope faded for an easy resolution following Agnes of Méran's death and the legitimation of her children.[31] Philip may have wanted to marry again or perhaps just wanted to be free of the pestering papal letters that alternatively castigated him for his treatment of Ingeborg and patronized him with pastoral advice. That the blame for Philip's inability was laid on sorcery does not necessarily mean that Ingeborg was meant to have cast the spell, but Philip was disinclined to clarify that point. Given his unremitting revulsion toward her, he may well have considered her at fault. What Ingeborg herself thought about the sorcery story is unknown. It is not mentioned in the tale of woe she sent to Innocent from Étampes, and she may not have known about it until Innocent mentioned it in a letter several years later when he gently broached the possibility that she might be ready to capitulate.[32] She was not. The calumnious accusation did not weaken her resolve. Perhaps she considered it ridiculous.

Philip nonetheless continued to pursue the case for another decade. Magical impotence remained a central plank of his strategy, though at one point he became so exasperated that he begged

Innocent to dissolve the marriage on any grounds, whether because they were too closely related, or because he was bewitched, or because Ingeborg wanted to enter a convent (she didn't), or 'by any other means whatsoever by which marriages are usually dissolved either in your time or those of your predecessors'. To this outburst Innocent responded mildly that he would consider it – the wheels of papal justice turned slowly – but in the meantime Philip ought to exert himself to show Ingeborg some 'conjugal affection'.[33]

Innocent's last ruling came in 1212, nearly twenty years after whatever happened on that fateful wedding night in Amiens. The pope chose to believe Ingeborg's interpretation that sex had happened, not Philip's that it hadn't. Philip's claim of penetration without ejaculation was deemed not only 'an insane falsehood' but a legal irrelevance.[34] He and Ingeborg had become one flesh, however briefly and unhappily. What God had joined, no man might rend asunder. This much Innocent could do. But it was still up to Philip to accept the judgement. That he finally did so the next year in April 1213 was a political decision, meant to keep Innocent from interfering in an invasion of England that Philip had planned for that summer and to sweeten the Danes at a moment when England was entertaining ambassadors from Norway.[35] It neither reflected nor engendered a change of heart toward the Danish woman. Ingeborg was no Elizabeth to him. Philip never lived with her, let alone shared her bed. She had the honours of a queen, but never those of a wife.

Ingeborg was now thirty-seven. Her blonde hair must have begun to grey, her fair face to wrinkle, and her unused breasts to sag just a little. The eighteen-year-old girl on the threshold of a brilliant future had vanished with hardly a trace. Philip had robbed her not only of wealth and power, but also of her only chance at companionship and motherhood. Whatever sin (if any) she had committed there in the secret hours of their first and only night together, her punishment had surely been an unjust and excessive one. Yet Philip refused ever to forgive her. Although he left Ingeborg 10,000 *livres parisis*, a sum sufficient to keep her in queenly clothing, fine foods, and skilled doctors for many lifetimes, it was only half that which she had brought as dowry from Denmark. As his will airily observed, he had deducted money from her share in order to pay back the sums he had unjustly taken from other places.[36] But Ingeborg, gracious as a queen should be, did not hold a grudge against the family into which she had married or even against the husband who had rejected her. In the margin of a richly decorated prayer book with illuminations expressing the legitimacy of her queenship, she recorded her genuine joy at the news of a great French victory won by Philip in 1214 (Plate 11).[37] Philip may never have considered Ingeborg his wife, but she always considered herself France's queen.

10.

Trial by Battle
Philip II

Philip was hot, tired, hungry, and worried. It was midday on Sunday, 27 July 1214 and he and his army had been on the move since dawn, beating a hasty retreat from the Flemish border and hoping to reach the safety of Lille's castle walls before the enemy caught up with them. It wasn't looking good. Harried by skirmishers, the rearguard had sent messengers begging him to slow down. He believed himself outnumbered and his enemy impatient for battle. Philip and his company had just crossed a bridge over the River Marcq, near a place called Bouvines in northeastern France. He sat down in the shade of an ash-tree, a welcome refuge from the sun that shone so fiercely that day, ate his lunch, and wondered what to do.[1] Although he was not a particularly religious man, Philip thought he might as well pray on it. The modest church of Bouvines usually welcomed peasant parishioners, not royal majesties, but it was out of the sun and Philip was out of options. He was shocked but not surprised to find himself facing battle on a Sunday. The Church reserved the day for peace, but the needs of war took precedence for princes, and Philip himself probably wouldn't have hesitated to sully the sabbath if he had had the advantage. Still, at prayer in the cool shadows of the chapel's shelter, he hoped the Lord would take umbrage at the enemy's effrontery and give the French an edge in the confrontation to come.

After all, the army chasing Philip was led by an excommunicate, Otto IV of Brunswick, who claimed the imperial throne against Frederick II Hohenstaufen, the rightful heir, at least in the opinion of Philip and Pope Innocent. Otto, son of a Plantagenet princess and a Saxon duke, was King John of England's nephew and his close conspirator. John, himself only recently freed from ex-communication, was down in Poitou, making mischief in the southwest so as to divide the French forces, but England had other friends in the northeast, especially the Count of Flanders and the Count of Boulogne, who ruled the coastal areas that Philip needed to launch his planned English invasion. Like Judas, betrayer of Christ, they had betrayed their natural lord Philip, pledging their fealty to England and receiving handsome bribes in return. They had designs on Philip's kingdom. Their war had been going so well that they had already divided the spoils to come. The Count of Flanders would have Paris for himself. The Count of Boulogne was to add the Vermandois to his already extensive lands. As for Otto the would-be emperor, he hoped that Philip's imminent defeat would remove a bastion of Hohenstaufen support, allowing the whole edifice to crumble.

The armies that met at Bouvines that day were large for the time, both numbering around 8,000 men, about 1,200 of whom were knights.[2] The German and Flemish armies were buttressed by the mercenaries from Brabant, famous for their courage and cruelty, while Philip had the Duke of Burgundy's forces and those led by some lords from Champagne, as well as dozens of minor lords and simple knights from the Picard region of northern France, each with his company of followers on foot and horseback. Alongside them marched the communal levies drawn from the towns and villages. They had pledged to fight for the king in exchange for tax exemptions and rights of self-government, but many of them thought of military service as their privilege as well as their duty. They were mostly on foot, armed with knives and staves, while the nobles were mounted and carrying swords and lances, though one count trusted to a billhook that day. The bellicose Bishop of Beauvais, who as a cleric was forbidden from shedding blood, carried a mace. (He had other nobles take credit for his kills.) Those who could afford it were wearing iron armour, those who couldn't, boiled leather. The armies clanged and creaked and sweated in the midday sun as they arranged themselves for the onslaught to come.

Every man, and even many of the horses in this hot and anxious mass, was marked out by the colours and emblems of his family, city, or nation. In this age before uniforms, these heraldic designs helped distinguish friend from foe on the field and identified who was worth keeping alive for ransom. Philip himself was decked out in fleurs-de-lys, which he held sacred, having sworn to uphold 'the honour of the lilies, a symbol of the duty entrusted to him by God'.[3] Above this 'whirlpool of tangled signs' floated the banners of each contingent, commune, or noble lord, offering a 'delightful spectacle' to the eyes.[4] Their beauty lifted men's hearts, but, in the absence of radio and satellites, they also communicated field positions, and like the emblems decorating the soldiers marching under them, they had a deeper meaning. Otto's banners, like his shield, were painted with black eagles, a symbol of empire that went back to the Romans.[5] Philip's own personal banner was spangled with golden lilies against an azure background, and his army marched under the scarlet banner of the Vexin, now 'commonly called the Oriflamme', as Philip's chaplain and chronicler tells us.[6] Its stark simplicity contrasted with the ornate design of Otto's army's ensign. Decorated with a dragon and flying from a staff topped with a golden imperial eagle, Otto's flag was meant to strike fear into the beholder. Philip's chaplain remembered with a shudder how the dragon's horrible mouth opened in a rictus grin, the wind filled its wings, and its long tail streamed behind it.[7]

French forces had not faced a pitched battle of this kind since Louis VI's humiliation at Brémule almost a century before. That defeat had cast a long shadow, perhaps leading his successors to avoid direct confrontation in the field, but in fact, most medieval commanders preferred not to engage in battle. It was simply too risky. Much better to gradually wear down the enemy with sieges, skirmishes, and raids on the unprotected fields and villages that paid for nobles' wars and lifestyles. Not only were the odds of this strategy of attrition calculable and manageable, it also better served medieval warfare's main objective, which was not to win or lose all but to bring the opposition to the negotiating table in a flexible frame of mind. After all, the ties of family and fidelity were so entangled that one was often fighting one's father-in-law, nephew, or erstwhile vassal, and the political landscape was so changeable that today's mortal enemy could be tomorrow's boon companion.[8] Philip's youthful intimacies and later enmities with Richard Lionheart were proof enough of that.

A battle by contrast was a toss of the dice, winner take all. An army might have every advantage – a better general, more men, the high ground – and still find itself routed. But although wise soldiers shied from battle, all men claimed to seek it. It was not just the glory, fame, and riches that might be won. It was also that victory or defeat in battle could be deemed God's judgement on the matter. That an ill-timed fall or a well-placed strike could decide a kingdom's fate might be put down to chance, but those who believed in miracles, as most medieval Christians did, might see the hand of God at work, especially if the result was unexpected. This was still a time when an intractable lawsuit might be decided by a judicial duel, the parties vowing to fight to the death and trusting their bodies and God's favour to prove the right of the matter. Battle was a judicial duel writ large.[9] Increasingly, the Church turned its back on duel and other judicial ordeals, like the carrying of a hot iron or the test of cold water, seeing them as sacrilegious efforts to 'tempt' God into intervening in human affairs.[10] Pope Innocent was to outlaw clerical participation the very next year.

But for those convinced that right was on their side and who had exhausted all other avenues of redress, duel remained attractive and in frequent use.[11] Philip, recently restored to Innocent's good graces by reconciliation with Ingeborg, and now the victim of his enemy's choice to violate the sabbath, could have felt reasonably sure that God sided with him. Perhaps he even reminded God of these facts in his prayers at the little chapel of Bouvines. As for his opponents, so sure of their right were they that the Flemish soldiers had sewn crosses onto their clothing, as if this encounter were some sort of Holy War.[12]

Emerging from his devotions and arming himself in haste, Philip found the lines already drawing up and the Oriflamme moving toward the enemy with the communal levies hurrying behind it. He spurred his horse to a gallop to catch up with it, placing himself in the centre of the front line opposite Otto, as if it were only they who were fighting that day. To their right and left their great allies faced off. Or so some chroniclers liked to tell the story of the Battle of Bouvines, as if it had been fought man to man, a series of individual encounters between famous knights and powerful lords, of whom only a dozen or so are even named. 'They all fought as champions,' claims one chronicler, who recounted the battle in verse as a list of their deeds: 'Gauthier, the Castellan of Rasse / Throws himself in before the others / Followed by Eustache of Melnghin / On a powerful horse / Then came Baudouin Buridan . . .'[13]

It cannot have been like that, and reading between the lines of even the most chivalrous chronicles shows that it wasn't. The thousands of unnamed soldiers and sergeants who made up the armies' vast majority had a very different experience from the 'fleshy and phlegmatic' Duke of Burgundy, who was succoured by his followers at every turn, or the Count of Saint-Pol, who stopped to catch his breath on the battle's shady sidelines.[14] They had no leisure to rest or even to choose their targets as the ambitious knights seeking greater glory did. Their job was to kill or to die in the service of killing. On foot, they worked up close, seeking a chink in a great man's armour, sliding a knife through the hole in his helmet, slitting a horse's belly so its rider fell to their mercy.

According to an English chronicler, the Count of Boulogne unhorsed Philip as payback for past wrongs, but according to Philip's own chaplain, who was there singing psalms that day, it was a crowd of German foot soldiers who pulled Philip off his horse with their iron hooks.[15] Prone, with most of his own guard engaged in front of him, Philip had only his armour to protect him. He was saved by his standard bearer, who twirled the fleur-de-lys banner over and over to signal the emergency as the royal trumpeter sounded the alarm. A solitary knight jumped from his horse to chase off the rabble, and Philip regained his steed.

Not so lucky was Otto. Unhorsed three times in the afternoon's course, the third time he turned and fled, abandoning his dragon standard on the field. Even worse fared the Count of Flanders. Struck to the ground and wounded all over, he was taken captive, tied up, and left to await Philip's pleasure. Those with him were either killed, captured, or 'shamefully saved by flight'.[16] As for that other traitor, the Count of Boulogne, he fought on even as his allies fled the field in increasing numbers. Only when a common sergeant, fighting on foot, sidled up to his horse and plunged his sword into its guts 'all the way up to the hilt', did he falter at last.[17] The horse staggered and fell, trapping Boulogne's leg under its body. Blows rained down upon him from every side. A mere boy ripped the count's helmet off and wounded him in the head, then went for his stomach. Had not one of the king's councillors happened by just then, Boulogne would have died a horrible death. What happened to him in the end was worse.

With Otto's retreat and the counts' capture, the day belonged to Philip. He had his trumpeters call back the French still out hunting for blood or ransom on the unfamiliar paths by which the enemy took flight. They had left behind treasure enough, and Philip did not want it lost or squandered. Their baggage wagons, some of them two storeys high with interior rooms 'splendid enough for a wedding chamber' and stuffed with gold, silks, and other riches, were plundered and shared out among the army.[18] The prisoners were brought before the king. By law and custom, they deserved beheading, recounted the royal chaplain, for they had committed *lèse-majesté*.[19] But Philip was unwilling to let them off that easily. The counts of Flanders and Boulogne were loaded with chains – Boulogne's so intricately connected and so short that he could not move more than half a step – and sent to Philip's darkest prisons. Boulogne disappeared into a dungeon in Péronne, a city he had coveted for himself in the event of Philip's demise. Flanders, too, got his wish for Paris. He was immured in the Louvre. Both were to languish captive for years, Flanders because he could not fulfil his promises, Boulogne because 'there was no one to intercede for him'.[20] Flanders at last obtained his freedom in 1227, but Boulogne died in prison, probably by his own hand.

Otto's dragon standard had been trampled to shreds, but the golden eagle that topped the staff on which it had flown was recovered, repaired, and sent back to Germany to Philip's Hohenstaufen ally, Frederick II. This prize was accompanied by a message from Philip that this imperial symbol had been 'transferred' to him by 'divine favour'.[21] The idea that the Western Empire, once Caesar's then Charlemagne's, could be transferred – notionally by God through His vicar the pope – was a commonplace of medieval political philosophy. Its touchstone was an eighth-century forgery known as the Donation of Constantine.[22] Philip's chaplain, who related this story, was keen to stress this idea since Frederick was Innocent's preferred candidate and Philip's victory on his behalf demonstrated the French king's Catholic bona fides as a defender of the Church. But just as Rigord, whose work this chaplain continued, gave Philip the imperial title Augustus, this chronicler considered Philip at least Frederick's equal in dignity and France as much a new Rome as Frederick's empire.

Philip's chaplain celebrated the king's progress toward Paris as a Roman victory procession, reporting that, although 'at that time, only the city of Rome was offering applause to its king . . . now trumpets sound in every street . . . knight, bourgeois, villein, all shine under the purple', the colour of ancient Roman and medieval Byzantine emperors. Even peasants are now 'resplendent in imperial adornments'.[23] Philip paraded his prisoners in chains through the city gates and along the streets in the way that a victorious Roman general would have, and while he did not have a triumphal arch erected in the manner of his imperial predecessors (or his much later successor Napoleon), he did found a monastery dedicated to Holy Victory.

The imperial pretender Otto, having fled in ignominy, was to die in obscurity. But it was King John of England who suffered the worst defeat at Bouvines because the whole thing had been designed to serve his interests. An English chronicle refers to the multinational forces assembled there as the King of England's army and tells us that John had wasted 40,000 marks on the project.[24] John had sent his illegitimate half-brother William Longsword to Flanders as his lieutenant – William was captured and ransomed back to England – and Otto along with the counts of Flanders and Boulogne were England's allies. John had planned their war to be one arm of a pincer movement trapping Philip from the north as John moved up from the south. Philip had, in fact, been more worried about John's army than the northern forces. He had sent the pick of the kingdom's knights south under the command of his son Louis. A once frail boy who had become a hardened soldier and a promising general, twenty-seven-year-old Louis increasingly replaced his father in the field. In the weeks just prior to Bouvines, Louis had confronted John besieging a Capetian castle in Anjou and defeated him with an inferior force.

Philip's unlooked-for victory at Bouvines not only set the seal on the defeat of John's summer strategy. It also confirmed the result of the entire disastrous decade and a half of the Plantagenet king's reign. Since John had come to the English throne in 1199 upon the death of his brother Richard, he had made a number of serious mistakes, most of which Philip had been able to capitalize on. John's erratic personality and taste for treachery did not endear him to his contemporaries in England. The road from Bouvines to his capitulation to the English barons' demands for the Magna Carta at Runnymede the next year was 'direct, short, and unavoidable'.[25] John's difficulties in France, however, were as much to do with the realities of geopolitics as with his character flaws or policy failures. As King of France, Philip was simply in a much stronger position there than John was. Being John's sovereign lord for the Plantagenets' continental possessions meant that he had legal leverage of a sort increasingly important in the rule-based society that coalesced at the turn of the thirteenth century.

John had acknowledged his 'full vassalic subordination' to Philip's lordship in a treaty agreed at Le Goulet in May 1200 which paused the first phase of their enmity.[26] There, he had performed homage to Philip for Normandy, Anjou, and Aquitaine, and he also paid 20,000 marks as a 'feudal relief' (*rachatum*), a kind of death tax paid by vassals upon inheriting a fief. This was the first time that a Plantagenet king had agreed to pay a relief for his continental holdings, but it was not at all the first time that one had recognized Capetian superiority.[27] Although in the early twelfth century Plantagenet kings had had their sons perform homage, Henry II himself had done homage for Normandy in 1183. Richard, too, had given Philip homage for all his continental lands during his rebellion against Henry in 1188–9 and had explicitly recognized their unequal positions in the agreement they made before going on crusade together, referring to Philip as 'my friend and lord (*dominus*)' whereas Philip referred to Richard as 'my friend and vassal (*fidelis*)'.[28] Despite their frequent military encounters, the Plantagenets' efforts to get around the Capetians' political and legal advantages as their feudal lords had always been 'pretty feeble', and from 1200 onward John's acceptance of the French king's superiority became more marked.[29] Diplomatic correspondence between the two countries began always to put Philip's name first, a small but serious sign of mutually acknowledged positioning.[30] Soon thereafter John had presented Philip with a golden opportunity not only to exercise his sovereign prerogatives over him but to begin to dismantle the Plantagenet empire.

The occasion was John's marriage to Isabelle, heiress to the county of Angoulême in southwestern France. Isabelle, a beautiful and vivacious if sometimes vicious woman, fascinated John, a man infamous for his unrestrained sexual appetites. Unfortunately for John, she was already promised to the Count of Lusignan, a descendant of that Hugh of Lusignan whose difficulties with the Duke of Aquitaine appear in Chapter 3, and a powerful lord in his own right. With Isabelle and her county thus snatched from them by their overlord, John, the outraged Lusignan family had appealed for justice to John's overlord, Philip. This was a political ploy as much as a legal manoeuvre. At the turn of the thirteenth century, most of those wronged by their lord had to lump it, for there was not yet a systematic hierarchy of judicial appeal in France, nor were the Capetians, then or ever, interested in adjudicating the petty complaints of all the subjects of their realm. They were, however, very interested indeed in listening to a powerful family like the Lusignans whose opponent was also their own. Philip had summoned John to answer the Lusignan appeal in the spring of 1202, and when John failed to appear as required, Philip had condemned him to forfeit his French fiefs.

The sentence of forfeiture marked the beginning of a new and fruitful Capetian strategy of confronting the Plantagenets through the courts, as well as on the battlefield. Whereas war was always subject to the vagaries of fortune and the mystery of God's will, the Capetians always had the upper hand in the courtroom. Because the Plantagenets held their continental lands from them as vassals subject to their lord's justice, the Capetians had both the political and the jurisdictional authority to make them obey. It is true, however, that this legal leverage had its limits, and therefore it was always employed strategically. On paper (or parchment) Capetian rights were watertight, which lent their actions a legitimacy that mattered to both their supporters and opponents, as well as to supposedly neutral parties like the pope or emperor. But if challenged, these rights could only be enforced, and their legitimacy confirmed, by the sword. Philip's judgement that John forfeit his fiefs for contumacy had thus been understood not just as a judicial decision but as a declaration of war, and war had immediately ensued.

Philip had immediately seized several castles on the Norman border and activated his alliance with John's nephew, seventeen-year-old Arthur of Brittany. The son of John's late elder brother Geoffrey, Arthur had a claim to the English throne that rivalled John's own. Philip now affianced Arthur to his own four-year-old daughter, whose birth to Agnes of Méran had been legitimized the previous year. In exchange, Arthur did homage for Brittany, Maine, Anjou, and Aquitaine, promised Philip Normandy and the Touraine outright, and went to war, laying siege to John's nearly eighty-year-old mother Eleanor of Aquitaine (who was, of course, also Arthur's grandmother). John, whose loyalty to his mother was perhaps the only bond he never betrayed, had rushed to rescue her and captured Arthur and many of his supporters. This victory could have been conclusive, but John squandered its fruits by mistreating his prisoners, especially Arthur, who disappeared mysteriously, most likely murdered at John's command. John's barons recoiled before this barbarous action, and Arthur's former vassals came over to Philip in droves. By March 1203, Philip enjoyed the support of some of the most important lords in Normandy, Poitou, and Touraine.[31]

In the summer of 1203, Philip had taken Maine and Anjou. Counties once independent, then Norman, they were now and forever after to be French. Then he had turned his attention to Normandy. In September he laid siege to Château Gaillard, the 'saucy castle' erected by Richard Lionheart, first with boulders hurled by his war machines, then with flame, and finally by famine. John had done nothing to relieve the siege or to counter Philip's victories – one English chronicler said people thought he was bewitched or else too busy in bed with Isabelle of Angoulême – and he sailed away back to England at the end of the year.[32] That winter Gaillard's stalwart garrison survived on water, wild plants, and the occasional stray chicken, devoured feathers and all, but their walls at last fell prey to Philip's mines and machines in March 1204.[33] The rest of Normandy followed soon after. It was as a supposed prophecy of Merlin had predicted, 'The sword (Normandy) was separated from the sceptre (England).'[34] In August, Philip moved south to take Poitiers. He now possessed all of the lands north of the River Loire that Henry II had bequeathed to his sons. Only Aquitaine, whose venerable duchess Eleanor died that same year, remained. Established in 1154, the Plantagenet empire had lasted barely half a century.

Philip still had the Ingeborg affair to contend with, but the decade between 1204 and the Battle of Bouvines was a period of explosive Capetian expansion that would have impressed his predecessors at least as much as the acquisition of Normandy itself. The two great eastern fiefs of Champagne and Flanders had both lost their counts early in the century and were inherited by minors. Philip kept the infant heir to Champagne in tutelage under the dowager-countess until he reached adulthood, and he married the twelve-year-old heiress to Flanders to a Portuguese prince with an arguable claim to the county on his mother's side, from whom he expected loyalty and gratitude. These expectations were disappointed. The sudden expansion of the lands under Philip's direct or indirect rule had upset the balance of power, leaving many sympathetic to the new Count of Flanders when he complained the king had short-changed him in favour of his son and heir, the future Louis VIII. When Philip then sealed his earlier acquisition of the Vermandois upon the heirless death of its last countess in 1213 and consolidated his military conquest of the Auvergne in central France the same year, eyes had naturally turned to the powers most likely able and willing to rein in the rampant Capetian: the *soi-disant* Emperor Otto and his uncle, King John.[35]

Although John had never resigned himself to the losses Philip had inflicted upon him, he had been unable to start remedying the situation for some time. The war of 1202–4 had exhausted the resources of his treasury and the patience of his men, and then he had become embroiled in a struggle with Pope Innocent over the see of Canterbury that led to a six-year interdict on England. But as discontent grew in France against Philip, John had begun preparing for a war of reconquest, concentrating on firming up alliances in the Low Countries, where ties to Otto were strong and ports plentiful. For England, the loss of Normandy meant that the Plantagenets now lacked harbours in northern France, and 'for the first time since 1066 control of the sea became a military requirement'.[36] Naval concerns had motivated the alliance that John had concluded with the Count of Boulogne, whose lands hugged the Flemish coastline and whom John sent to burn Philip's fleet the next year, scuttling the Capetian's plans to invade England. The Count of Flanders, too, had formally abandoned Philip and given his homage to John in England at the beginning of 1214. Philip ravaged Flanders in return. John then began his campaign in the south that spring, and the stage was set for the campaign that culminated in Philip's miraculous victory at Bouvines that summer.

English and German chronicles tend to be understandably circumspect about Bouvines, where French accounts can give the impression that Philip, if not France, lived happily ever after. As one put it, 'After this, no one dare wage war against him, and he lived in great peace and the whole of the land was in great peace for a long time to come so that his officials could exact much and his son's officials even more from all the land he had come to hold.'[37] Ever-increasing tax revenues were indeed probably Philip's idea of a happy ending, and Bouvines does mark the beginning of the most successful part of his reign. In defeating John and acquiring most of his continental lands, Philip had dramatically expanded the royal domain, and the acquisition of Normandy allowed him to comprehend and then to copy its efficient administration, so lucrative for its ruler's treasury.[38]

Philip had at last overcome the Plantagenets' power and could live content to the end of his days. His son Louis contemplated gains even greater than these. He had a claim to England by right of his wife, and he was aware that the pope would welcome his help in Languedoc, where a war was raging more fiercely than any that Philip had fought. These were big dreams. Unrealistic ones, Philip might have said. Philip had always been a careful king even if he was also a courageous one. His first rule was not to over-extend his forces. He cashed in his winnings before laying another bet. He saw no need to wage another war now that he had won this trial by battle. Louis and his brilliant young wife, Blanche, were not like that. They had not been born into adversity as Philip had. They thought the world was theirs to conquer, and they were not entirely mistaken about that.

II.

New Horizons

Louis VIII

The winds of May 1216 blew contrary to Prince Louis's purpose, keeping his ships in France and delaying the invasion on which he staked his hopes. Short of stature, with his mother's fair complexion and plagued since infancy by poor health, there was a physical frailty to him that belied the nickname 'Lion' bestowed upon him for his military acumen and his fierce ambition. Nearly thirty, Louis chafed to think that his father had already been king at half his age, but the old man, who had passed his fiftieth birthday the previous year, showed no signs of slowing. He had not even had Louis crowned associate king, omitting a ceremony that had safeguarded the lineage in every reign since Hugh Capet's and for reasons that no one can now decipher.[1] Perhaps Philip felt the succession was so secure that it was no longer necessary. Perhaps he thought there was still plenty of time left. Perhaps he did not trust this son of his, so different in temperament from himself. Or perhaps he believed it best to leave some ambiguity about the succession since he had a second son, Philip, who resembled his father in more than just name, not least the unruly hair that earned him the sobriquet *Hurepel* (bristling pelt). Be that as it may, Prince Louis considered himself more than ready for recognition and rule. In France, Philip did not even allow him free rein in the lands of Artois he had inherited from his mother, but England offered a tempting prize.[2] The previous autumn, King John's discontented barons had offered Louis the English crown. He just had to get across the Channel to accept it.

Once the winds improved and his fleet at last made its way across the water to land at Thanet on 21 May, everything turned easy, at least for a while. Anticipating the invasion, John had been at Dover castle, but, ever the unsteady general, he immediately turned its custody over to the garrison when he heard that Louis had arrived and moved to Winchester. Louis marched his 1,200 knights unimpeded to London, where the city greeted his arrival with rejoicing and swore its fidelity to the Capetian prince. He took several castles unopposed, then followed John to Winchester, where he hoped to capture the English king. Since John had once again fled his arrival and left the city in flames, its citizens, too, were all too happy to pledge loyalty to Louis. The remaining English barons who had supported John now came over to Louis's side. Even John's illegitimate half-brother William Longsword, who had been his stalwart lieutenant and fought at Bouvines, foreswore himself in favour of Louis. King Alexander of Scotland, too, offered Louis his loyalty, an early instance of what would become a long partnership between the two nations against their common enemy. By September the Scots had marched all the way to Dover, where they joined Louis's forces besieging the stronghold.[3]

Incredible as it may now appear, Louis's invasion was not an illegitimate power grab, or at least, he and his supporters were keen that it not seem so. They trumpeted the claim that Louis had a right to England through his wife Blanche. The daughter of the King of Castile, Blanche had Plantagenet blood through her mother, one of Henry II and Eleanor of Aquitaine's daughters. It was Eleanor, in fact, who had brought Louis's wife Blanche to France. The marriage between Louis and Blanche of Castile had sealed the Treaty of Le Goulet in 1200 that confirmed John's submission to the Capetians for the Plantagenets' continental possessions. The royal chronicler put the argument for Blanche's claim into verse, and Blanche, an enthusiastic and instrumental supporter of the invasion, probably believed her right to England to be real.[4] Although there were several other claimants whom we might expect to have taken precedence, not least her older sister and her younger brother, Blanche was not a woman who easily imagined any limit to her prerogatives.[5]

That the marriage now constituted an excuse for the invasion of

England must have seemed a bitter irony to John, but the English barons' support for Louis's claim through Blanche was due more to John's accumulation of political mistakes than to any heartfelt belief that the English crown should descend through the maternal line to settle on the head of a Capetian prince. John had ridden roughshod over his subjects' rights and expectations, driving them to rebellion. His barons charged him with the murder of his nephew Arthur of Brittany, an accusation that was probably true and that had contributed much to his loss of Normandy in 1204. They also complained that he had given the kingdom of England to the pope and received it back as a fief in 1213, an act that put England under papal protection but which the barons considered an abrogation of their rights to participate in the governance of the realm. John's refusal to observe his barons' privileges or to obey the customary checks on royal power had led them to force his endorsement of their rights in the Magna Carta at Runnymede in 1215. That Pope Innocent III then declared the Magna Carta void only further inflamed baronial anger, and Louis sent messengers down to Rome to lay out the righteousness of his claim.[6] (Innocent was unmoved and ordered Louis excommunicated.)

Since it was the accumulated illegitimacy of John's rule rather than any innate legitimacy of Louis as an alternative that had made the English barons invite a Capetian to be their king, John's unexpected death through dysentery and exhaustion in October 1216 undermined the invasion's raison d'être.[7] John had left behind a legitimate male heir of his body, the nine-year-old Henry III, and a child-king of direct Plantagenet lineage who could be properly guided by well-chosen regents was a much more palatable option to a baronage seeking its liberty than an adult Capetian who had proven himself a dangerous adversary on the battlefield. Louis sent for reinforcements from France to buttress his ebbing army, but these were slow in coming. Not wishing to be seen as breaking the truce agreed after Bouvines and unwilling to tangle with his old adversary Innocent, Louis's father, Philip, had publicly disapproved of the expedition, whatever he may have thought about it in private.[8] Now he refused all aid and would not speak even a word to his son.[9] Louis returned to England with only a few more knights, though he had acquired one of the new, more accurate and forceful catapults called a trebuchet. The machine caused a stir since 'not many had then been seen in France'.[10] It did not, however, give him the decisive advantage he had been hoping for.

Less than a year after Louis launched his invasion, most of his forces were destroyed in May 1217 at the Battle of Lincoln, called 'second only to Hastings as the most decisive battle in English medieval history'.[11] The sad survivors straggled down to Louis at Dover, and in France the news caused castles to echo with the sounds of tears and wailing.[12] It was left to Louis's wife, Blanche, who took a keen interest in all things military, to try to save the situation. Defying her father-in-law's opposition, she raised a fleet for her husband's rescue. Threatening to pawn her children if Philip interfered, she travelled personally to Calais and worked energetically to put together an expedition bound for the Thames estuary.[13] All in vain. Those ships that survived a storm off Calais on 24 August were wrecked by an English fleet sailing from Sandwich. The noblemen captured in the engagement were ransomed, of course, but the rest of those aboard who were not crushed or blinded by the stones and lime hurled by the enemy's mangonels had their throats slit when boarded or were drowned after their ships splintered and sank. The head of Louis's infamous admiral Eustace the Monk was affixed to a lance and paraded around the Kentish countryside.[14]

Enraged, Louis nevertheless had to recognize reality. He returned to France late the next month with little to show for the adventure, though rather more than one might have expected since the English felt obliged to pay him £10,000 sterling for his troubles. His life in Philip's shadow seemed set to continue interminably. Philip was suspicious of him and his friends and kept all the young nobles on a short leash. Louis's main comfort was his wife, a close companion since they were married at the age of twelve, an expert lieutenant as she had proved during the invasion, and a sexual partner with whom he enjoyed great pleasure, if their large litter of children is any indication. In flagrant rejection of the dreariness of Philip's court, the pair were given to hunting, feasting, watching tournaments, and listening to excitable preachers predicting the Apocalypse.[15] During this post-invasion hiatus, for which we have few sources, Louis must have employed himself in these usual occupations, and he was clearly glad to see his wife again, for, a little over a year after his return, Blanche gave birth to their seventh child, a boy. Perhaps in a fit of dark humour, they named him John.

Louis was at last released from his purgatory when Philip died at the age of fifty-seven on 14 July 1223. Comets had streaked across the sky at dusk for eight days to presage his passing.[16] The change he had wrought in his kingdom over the forty-three years of his reign cannot be overstated. 'Hammer of the Normans and Aquitainians', as one contemporary called him, Philip had returned France to a state and a size not seen 'since the days of Charlemagne'.[17] It must have felt disorientating to be without Philip's presence at the head of the kingdom, no matter how much some had wished him gone, but mourning soon gave way to rejoicing with the double coronation of Louis and Blanche a few weeks later.

Such a celebratory occasion had not presented itself for decades. The holy ampoule of oil, said to be 'sent by God from Heaven to Saint Rémi for the anointing of Clovis, first Christian king that ever was in France', was brought out, and the festivities knew no bounds, though there were some squabbles as to who should pay for what.[18] The city of Reims was packed with France's great clergy and high nobility, all tricked out in the most outrageously expensive robes. They wore purple and samite silks, decked with gold fringe. Despite the August heat, these robes were trimmed in sable, ermine, or the soft white fur called vair that covers squirrels' bellies.[19] The party continued upon Louis's return to Paris. Rich and poor, old and young, his subjects thronged the flower-strewn streets where there was music and dancing all day and into the night.[20]

Tight-fisted Philip must have turned in his grave at the expense. Before his death, he had summoned Louis and given him not just the usual advice about upholding justice, protecting the Church, and so on, but also admonished him 'to safeguard his treasure as best he could, for without treasure one cannot secure one's lands'.[21] His will, too, was explicit on this point. The enormous fortune of 190,000 marks that he left Louis was earmarked for 'the protection of the kingdom' or for a crusade.[22] Philip had spent his whole life amassing money. He did not want it dissipated in the pointless entertainments that so amused his son and daughter-in-law.

Philip needn't have worried. Louis VIII had a sense of manifest destiny to rival that of any nineteenth-century American pioneer. He had grown to manhood riding the crest of his father's great wave of conquests, and his English invasion had only whetted his appetite for further expansion, despite its ignominious end. Naively, King Henry III of England had expected the return of Normandy, for Louis had given a pledge to that effect when extricating himself from the English adventure, but the messengers that Henry sent to the Capetian king returned with the infuriating reply that, since John had lost his lands through legal judgement, they were gone for good. Louis threatened another invasion if Henry pressed the point.[23] Henry backed down, but Louis's attention now turned toward Poitou, almost the last Plantagenet possession in France, whose annexation Philip had had to leave incomplete when he seized John's lands in 1204. The truce with England that had been renewed at the pope's urging in 1220 was about to expire, and Louis had concluded an alliance with Poitou's most powerful lords. He spent the spring of 1224 calling up his forces. From Burgundy to Brittany, the realm's soldiery flocked to his summons, and at the end of June he led them across the River Loire and into the southern lands that had been so long denied him.[24]

Louis was bound ultimately for the city of La Rochelle on the Atlantic coast. A rich entrepôt for the shipping of wine, salt, and other goods, its real draw was the strategic utility of its great port to the naval warfare that now dominated the struggle between England and France. Founded by Eleanor of Aquitaine's father almost a century earlier, its deep harbour could host a veritable armada of great ships and the town itself was well situated and protected from easy attack. Occupants of such a rich prize, the citizens had perhaps assumed they would be rescued, but young King Henry was helpless to intervene. Busy with a baronial revolt at home, he was besieging Bedford while Louis invested La Rochelle. The city held out for three weeks, its walls subjected to the might of Louis's war machines. In Paris, Queen Blanche, the ageing but ever loyal Ingeborg of Denmark, and the visiting Queen of Jerusalem led a wailing procession through the city streets to win God's favour for Louis's endeavour.[25] Miraculously, the city capitulated the next day. Each of its nearly 1,750 adult male inhabitants was made to pledge his undying allegiance to Louis and his heirs.[26]

Satisfied with Poitou's submission, the king returned north but ordered his lieutenants to push on further south into Gascony, where they met with stiffer resistance. Bordeaux and Bayonne refused to surrender to the French, and Louis's men had neither the will nor a way to force the issue. Gascon loyalty and a rescue expedition from England the next year kept this, the last remnant of the Plantagenet empire, from falling into French hands until the end of the Hundred Years War in the fifteenth century. As the story goes, it also assured claret permanent pride of place on English tables, in preference to the formerly famous Poitevin wines exported from La Rochelle.[27]

Louis, whom a later chronicler describes as 'never having hardly any rest', was not done.[28] Having annexed Poitou, he now cast his gaze even further south to Languedoc, lands in which his predecessors had almost never ventured to assert their authority. In the twelfth century, the region had known almost incessant warfare among its great families, often calling upon alliances with the kings of Aragon or England, but only incidentally involving the Capetians.[29] A brief period of peace around 1200 had been followed by an even more brutal eruption of violence. Since 1209, war had been raging between northern French troops and the southern inhabitants with a cruelty that had shocked some people and delighted others. Whole cities had been burned to the ground and their entire populations massacred. For this was no ordinary war and its aims were not – or not only – those of expansion and conquest. This was a crusade in the literal as well as the figurative sense of the term, called by none other than Pope Innocent III to annihilate the enemies of the faith. Only this time, these infidels were not unfamiliar Muslims in faraway lands, but European heretics whose lands adjoined those of the armies that assembled to attack them.

The Albigensian Crusade, named for the southern city of Albi whose inhabitants were thought to be especially heretical, had been called to combat two heretical sects known to be particularly prevalent in Languedoc. One, the Waldensians, was committed to living simple lives of poverty in the mould of the original Apostles. The other, known as the Cathars, presented a more radical challenge to Catholic doctrine, believing not in 'one God, creator of Heaven and Earth, of all things seen and unseen', as the Catholic profession of faith proclaimed, but in *two* powers, one good, who had created the spiritual world, and one evil, who had created the material world. There is considerable disagreement among historians about whether Catharism even existed outside the minds of paranoid Catholic clerics – my own view is that the sources clearly show a fairly organized network of people holding these beliefs for several decades before the beginning of the Albigensian Crusade and the persecutions that followed it – but there is broad consensus that it was the challenge that heresy in any form presented to the Church's authority that led Innocent to call a crusade.[30] That is, it was at least as much a question of power that motivated persecution as it was of belief.

From the point of view of an authoritarian like Innocent, a particularly vexing feature of Occitan heresy was that these heretics had the support of the Languedocian nobility, especially that of Count Raymond VI of Toulouse, whose domain encompassed not only that city and its province but a collection of territories that extended across the River Rhône into the Provençal lands of the Holy Roman Empire. The Count of Foix and the viscounts of Béziers–Carcassonne were also strongly suspect. While most of Languedoc was nominally part of the kingdom of France, some of its lords and cities owed their allegiance to Aragon or the Empire, and culturally these were lands very different from those that the Capetians ruled north of the River Loire. Occitan was a language more closely related to Catalan than to French. The region was more urbanized than northern France, and its forms of law, lordship, and inheritance were different. The people gravitated toward Spain and the Mediterranean littoral, not toward Paris.

The prospect of incorporating these lands more securely into the Capetian domain might have tempted a less pragmatic ruler than King Philip, but when Innocent asked for his aid against the heretics in 1208, Philip had had his hands full with King John and coolly rejected the request. It had been left to a collection of northern French knights and barons led by the head of the Cistercian order to subdue the heretical South. They brought to the venture the same indiscriminate violence that had marked some of the worst excesses of the Holy Land crusades. Their first major act was to sack and burn the city of Béziers. If no one actually cried, 'Kill them all, the Lord knows his own!', as an imaginative German monk nowhere near the action claimed, they did indeed indiscriminately massacre most of the city's inhabitants.[31] (Granted, according to the same monk, the citizens had behaved poorly, peeing on a copy of the Gospels that they then catapulted over the walls at the besiegers.)

Similar scenes of hair-raising violence were enacted across the region in the years that followed, turning Languedoc into a war-torn land of terror. The venture was soon entrusted to the leadership of a distinguished veteran, one Simon de Montfort, a descendant of that castellan clan that had produced old King Philip I's Bertrada over a century before. Although only a minor lord in his own right, Simon was a superb general. He reduced nearly the entirety of Languedoc to his mercy, hanging, burning, blinding, or drowning those who got in his way. By the end of 1215 Innocent had disinherited the Count of Toulouse and granted Simon his lands and titles.[32]

Yet the Occitan resistance did not give up. The hundreds of Languedocian lords dispossessed by the northern crusaders and the people brutalized by their crusade revolted against this overreach. They flocked to the banners of the great southern princes, and the city of Toulouse rose up against the pretender Simon, mobilizing its entire population against his siege. 'Noblewomen . . . little girls and men's wives' were sent to work the mangonels hurling destruction upon the crusaders outside its walls, and it was one of their boulders that smashed Simon's head open in June 1218.[33] He had been the heart and soul of the French crusading effort, and neither his wife, Alice, who had talent and grit, nor his son Amaury, who did not, could take his place. With him out of the way, the lords of Languedoc began to take back their patrimony, and by the time Innocent's successor Pope Honorius wrote to Louis asking for his help, the Occitan insurgency had almost completely succeeded.

For many on both sides of the struggle, the war had been as much about conquest as it had about Catharism or Catholicity. Count Raymond VI of Toulouse, his successor Raymond VII, and the other great southern barons had repeatedly sought to reconcile themselves to the Church, only to have their overtures rebuffed and ever more onerous conditions imposed. Raymond VI had even joined the crusade, but that did not stop his disinheritance. Honorius seems to have had some qualms about the opportunistic side of the affair, and he would have preferred to direct resources toward the Holy Land rather than the Languedoc. Consequently, he dithered, first inviting and then disinviting Louis's intervention, until the southern bishops pressured him into ensuring their rights over dispossessed heretics' property.[34]

Louis also had his own hesitations. He was not sure how long a crusade might take or how much money it might cost him. He worried about invasion from English-held Aquitaine in the south and about an impostor, who claimed to be a long-lost Count of Flanders escaped from a Bulgarian dungeon, wreaking havoc in the north.[35] But, zealous Christian that he was, he did want to 'turn the conquering Toulousain armies into ashes, to make the true faith dare to show its head, to abolish profane rites, and to exile all heresies from the realm', as his father's chaplain urged him in a dedicatory poem.[36] He also wanted the land. In January 1226 he at last accepted Honorius's invitation and took the cross.

Louis already had some experience in Languedoc, having ventured south twice during the reign of his father: once briefly in 1215, against his father's wishes, and again in 1219, at his father's request in order to deflect the possibility that Count Thibaut of Champagne might replace Simon de Montfort as leader of the crusade. (Philip was worried that Thibaut, who was poised to inherit the throne of Navarre in northern Spain, might assemble a patchwork empire of southern lands sufficient to menace Capetian France, and Philip had not worked his whole life to get rid of the Plantagenets just to find a new threat on his doorstep.) Neither campaign had amounted to much. Louis's accomplishments were limited to massacring the rebellious inhabitants of Marmande and abandoning a siege of Toulouse shortly after joining it. Philip's chaplain commented sourly that the 1219 expedition had brought back 'less praise than blame'.[37]

The 1226 expedition was to be an entirely different story for three reasons.[38] First, this crusade's objective was clear, legitimate, and acceptable to those who counted: Amaury de Montfort and Honorius had already signed over Simon de Montfort's conquests to Louis. Louis, who had only to make the claim good, therefore had the support of his barons, who declared their approval and promised their aid 'for however long he pursued the affair', and his prelates, who confirmed that Louis could quit whenever he wanted.[39] Second, and arising from the first, Louis's army was not a hodgepodge gathering of poorly trained and shoddily armed enthusiasts held together by individual commitments of varying intensity in the manner of many crusading forces. It was rather 'the royal army in the service of the church'.[40] This was not a permanent force – France's first standing army was still several centuries in the future – but it was composed of troops and commanders who had fought together for years and who were veterans of several successful campaigns. Third, and perhaps a reflection of this army's reputation, few people in Languedoc wanted to fight. Nearly twenty years of brutal warfare had taken their toll on its inhabitants. Aware that Louis led an 'almost invincible' army that made

England and the Empire tremble, they had no appetite for further struggle.[41]

Such was the enthusiasm in northern France, however, that a flock of 'old men, young boys, and women, as well as the indigent and infirm' had to be sent home before the army marched south from Bourges in May.[42] Louis had had the expropriation and disinheritance of heretics and their protectors publicly proclaimed through the South the month before, and even before he departed, panicked letters had begun arriving from Languedoc's lesser lords.[43] They had proffered their submission and pledged their fidelity to Louis and the Catholic Church, handing over their castles as surety for their good behaviour.[44] The Count of Roussillon had written from the safety of Barcelona to offer Louis his 'person, land, and men for the extirpation of the enemies of the faith and the avenging of the Saviour's injuries'.[45] The city of Béziers, still sparsely populated to judge from the paucity of its letter's signatories, pre-emptively surrendered on 29 April.[46] As the army marched southward, messengers brought word of further submissions. It seemed that nowhere and no one was willing to contest Louis's conquest.

The king met resistance only when he came to the great walled city of Avignon on the Rhône in Provence in the second week of June. Even during the siege that took up much of that dry and miserable summer, when disease ravaged the army, 'flies from Egypt' tormented them, and the city's machines rained rocks down upon them, a steady stream of southern lords continued to arrive in the camp, promising their loyalty to Louis 'against all men and women, living or dead'.[47] Avignon held out until September, with the demolition of its fortifications and 6,000 marks exacted as the price for its surrender. The delay used up the campaign season, costing Louis the opportunity to test his siege train against Toulouse, the last important bastion against his conquest, but the whole of Languedoc was already effectively his. In October he drew up provisions laying the foundation of Capetian rule in the South. Then he headed northward, planning to winter in Paris with his pregnant wife,

Blanche, and their boisterous young household. He never made it back, dying on the road home on 8 November 1226, aged thirty-nine. A chronicler's story that Count Thibaut of Champagne poisoned the king to get hold of Blanche is salacious, but the truth is probably more prosaic.[48] Louis's health had never been good, and the dysentery that most likely ended him was as much an ever-present danger to medieval commanders as it was to their troops.[49]

Louis had ruled for only three years, among the shortest of Capetian reigns, but he had completed his father's transformation of France. The insecure and impecunious realm that Philip had inherited in 1180 had become by 1226 the largest, the richest, and the most powerful kingdom in western Europe. And Louis left a more promising legacy than even Philip could have imagined. The third Capetian king to crusade, Louis's death while still on campaign made him almost a martyr in the eyes of the Church and his more devout Christian subjects, restoring the dynasty's 'most Christian' reputation. His wife, Blanche, upon whom the regency now devolved, came from a Castilian lineage almost equally distinguished by its victories over Iberia's Muslims. But it was their heir, a boy of twelve named Louis, who was to bring the Capetians to the height of their Christian glory. His programme of equal parts profound piety and pitiless persecution would confirm the Capetians as the most prestigious lineage in Christendom and their kingdom as a New Jerusalem.

PART FOUR

A New Jerusalem

(1226–1270)

Capetians, 1226–1270 (simplified)

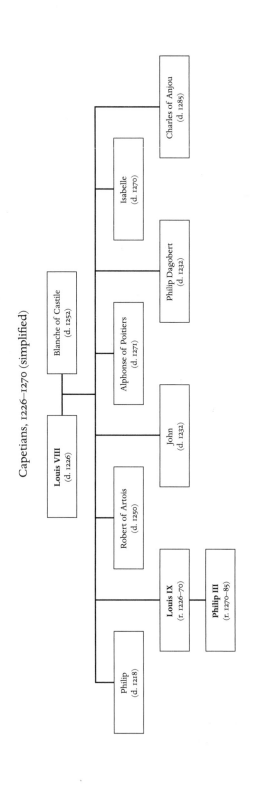

12.

Of Babies and Barons
Blanche of Castile and Louis IX

In a warm room dimly lit against the late winter gloom of 1227, the widowed queen laboured to give birth for the last time. She was surrounded by her close friends and servants of long standing, those who had assisted in her previous births and miscarriages. Midwifery had only just begun to emerge as a profession, and male doctors did not yet enter the birth chamber. If the situation went awry, it would have been one of these trusted companions who used a well-oiled hand to turn a mispositioned infant or to tug, ever so gently, at a retained afterbirth. Even without such agonizing interventions and even for a woman like Queen Blanche, now giving birth for at least the eleventh time, the experience was inevitably excruciating. Women tied amulets around their thighs inscribed with magical verses meant to draw the baby forth and cried prayers for mercy to the Virgin Mary, who alone of women was thought to have been spared the labour pains with which God cursed Eve.[1]

Made more in the mould of Eve than Mary, Blanche of Castile felt every pang. Her thoughts on the experience can be gleaned from a densely illuminated Bible that she commissioned featuring unusually graphic depictions of childbirth. In one, illustrating the birth of Jacob and Esau to Rebecca from the Old Testament, a naked woman lies on a bed, her mouth opened wide in a scream, her hands thrown over her head, gesturing and grasping the headboard in anguish as she gives birth to the twins (Plate 13).[2] The inclusion of such evocative images suggests that Blanche did not want her agony erased. To the contrary, she was proud of her pain, not least because it produced the key to her power. Unlike her older sister Berenguela, who governed the kingdom of Castile in her own right as well as on her son's behalf, Blanche was only able to rule France because she was mother to its king.[3]

The baby born to Blanche that day in 1227, a boy she named Charles, would grow into perhaps 'the most colourful figure in thirteenth-century Europe' and certainly a force to be reckoned with in his own family and beyond.[4] Given Anjou as his own territory, he would one day also rule the kingdoms of Sicily and Jerusalem. But most of Blanche's babies did not even live to see adulthood, let alone to taste real power as this one would. Her first, a daughter, had died in infancy, as did the twin boys that came several years later.[5] (Perhaps it was their birth that the graphic illustration of Rebecca's pain recalled to her.) Just the previous year, in 1226 while her husband Louis was busy with his crusade, she had lost another son before his first birthday, and there may have been other stillbirths or miscarriages. Nor was surviving infancy any guarantee for the future. Several other of her offspring died in later childhood. The most painful of these losses had probably been that of her eldest son, Philip, who was eight when his parents laid him to rest beside his grandmother Elizabeth in the nave of Notre-Dame. Such repeated grief took a toll. For her feelings, we might again look to her artistic patronage: the illuminations of her Bible, which show the agony of mothers watching the death of their children, like those of the Holy Innocents slaughtered in Bethlehem, and Blanche's foundation of the Cistercian monastery of Royaumont, which came to serve as a mausoleum for royal children in the same way that Saint-Denis housed the remains of their fathers.[6]

Despite all this grief, Blanche was primarily occupied with raising children, not mourning them, for she possessed such prodigious fertility that even having lost seven, five remained to her. The eldest of the survivors was named Louis. Born in the miraculous year of Bouvines, he was now approaching adolescence and had been crowned King Louis IX after his father's death the previous year. There was only one surviving daughter. Born in 1225 and second youngest of the family, she was called Isabelle, a French version of her grandmother Elizabeth's name. The others, all boys, were given

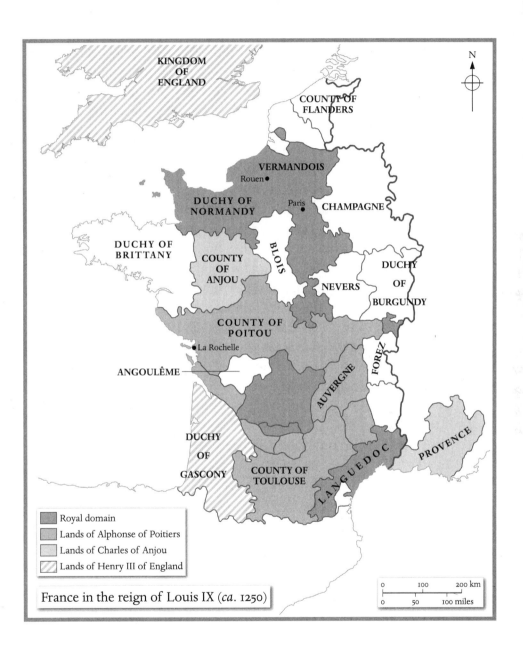

N

KINGDOM
OF
ENGLAND

COUNTY OF
FLANDERS

VERMANDOIS
Rouen •

DUCHY OF
NORMANDY   Paris •   CHAMPAGNE

DUCHY OF
BRITTANY

COUNTY
OF
ANJOU   BLOIS

NEVERS   DUCHY
OF
BURGUNDY

COUNTY OF
POITOU

• La Rochelle

ANGOULÊME

AUVERGNE   FOREZ

DUCHY
OF

GASCONY   COUNTY OF
TOULOUSE   LANGUEDOC   PROVENCE

Royal domain

Lands of Alphonse of Poitiers

Lands of Charles of Anjou

Lands of Henry III of England

0   100   200 km
0   50   100 miles

France in the reign of Louis IX (*ca.* 1250)

the names Robert, an old Capetian favourite, Alphonse, after Blanche's Castilian father, and, of course, this newborn Charles, a provocative decision worth pausing over.

To a thirteenth-century person, the name Charles evoked that of Charlemagne, *Karolus Magnus* in Latin or Charles the Great. With its inescapable associations with the Carolingian dynasty from which Hugh Capet had supposedly usurped the throne, Charles was a name the Capetians had never used for a legitimate son.[7] They had been giving their sons the name Louis, which also had strong Carolingian associations, since the end of the eleventh century when it was given to the future Louis VI. But while Louis was the name of Charlemagne's successor and several of his descendants, including the last Carolingian king of West Francia, Louis V, the name was originally a Merovingian one. The name Louis is a variation of Clovis, the first Christian king of the Franks, whose heavenly chrism, as the chroniclers never tired of repeating, was used to anoint the kings of France.[8] The adoption of a Merovingian name for the Capetian heir was entirely consistent with the growing devotion to the Merovingians, especially at Saint-Denis, where its founder, King Dagobert (d. 639), was a favourite of Abbot Suger. In fact, one of Blanche's children, the first to be buried at Royaumont, was called Philip-Dagobert. The name Charles, however, was a different matter. No western dynasty had used that name until the Carolingians, and none had used it after that line was extinguished.[9]

Charles's name reflected the new Capetian confidence engendered by the victories of Philip II Augustus and extended by his son Louis VIII's recent conquests. The story of Hugh Capet's alleged usurpation of the throne from the Carolingian Charles of Lorraine in 987 had not been forgotten. Far from it. Even the loyal monks of Saint-Denis responsible for writing France's semi-official chronicles always included it in their accounts. But it had been a very long time since that story was any danger to the dynasty. More importantly, Philip Augustus's achievements had so astonished his contemporaries that he was considered a new Charlemagne. Poems were composed to this effect, and contrived Carolingian paraphernalia like the Oriflamme proliferated. Around that time, too, a claim began to circulate that Philip's heir Louis VIII, father to Blanche's baby Charles, was himself a Carolinigian, for his mother, the nearly divorced Elizabeth, had Charlemagne's blood in her veins, as had Philip Augustus's own mother.[10] This story ran counter to an old and often-repeated prophecy that the crown of France would leave Capetian hands after seven generations, presumably to return to the Carolingians. In other words, the game was supposed to be up after Philip Augustus died. Instead, the Capetian and Carolingian lines were considered fused in the person of Louis VIII. The prophecy was thus fulfilled in an unexpected way, as all good prophecies are, and in a way that made everyone happy, as is less often the case.

By now the Capetian dynasty, with its unvarying custom of eldest sons succeeding their fathers, was so well established that no one genuinely questioned the right of Blanche's son Louis to rule even though he was still a minor of twelve. Like his father, Louis had not been crowned associate king during his father's lifetime, nor did anyone see a need to hasten young Louis's coronation after his father's death. Whereas, a century before, Louis VI had had to rush in unseemly haste to Orléans to be anointed by the first available bishop, to ward off any challenge from his half-brothers, and had hurried his second son immediately to Reims after the death of his first heir, Blanche took several weeks to prepare Louis IX's stately progress toward Reims, stopping along the way so that the boy could be knighted.

There were a few notable absences at the ceremony, but the only credible challenger for the crown, Louis's half-uncle Philip Hurepel, participated in a place of honour, carrying the royal sword before the boy king as he processed to the altar. That Philip Hurepel eventually joined the baronial revolt that beset Blanche in the first few years of her regency was not because he questioned her son's right to the throne but rather because he, like the realm's other great princes, thought she should have shared her power better. As a chronicler put it in plain terms, 'They were jealous that Queen Blanche seemed to have control of the king and kingdom.'[11] Though

Philip Hurepel's right to the throne was floated, at least according to a couple of chroniclers, he was slow to join the rebel barons and never became their leader.

The fomenter of that faction was rather Duke Peter of Brittany. A direct descendant of Louis VI, married to a Plantagenet princess, and one of the most powerful men in the kingdom, Peter had naturally expected a role in the regency, 'with its joyous prospect of high prestige, rich rewards, and vast power', just as Philip Hurepel had.[12] Unlike Philip Hurepel, however, Peter of Brittany had strong reasons to be disloyal to the new king and his mother. Although cousin to the Capetians, Peter's interests lay firmly in the orbit of his wife's Plantagenet family. Brittany, a wild land whose inhabitants spoke a Celtic language rather than a Romance once, fiercely guarded its independence against the expansionist Capetians, and its dukes had been traditionally rewarded for their loyalty to the English king with the wealthy barony of Richmond in Yorkshire.[13] In 1226 Peter had betrothed his daughter to Henry III, and the next year he and a few other disaffected barons led an army to face off at Tours against young King Louis and his regent-mother, the latter only recently risen from childbed. Dissension in the rebel camp had forced Peter to agree to a disappointing treaty, but in 1229 he was back, invading the lands of Blanche's ally (and reputed lover) Count Thibaut of Champagne.

Philip Hurepel had been on Blanche's side in 1227, even if he already resented her and exacted a cash payment for his loyalty, but in 1229 he joined the rebels.[14] He had concluded that Blanche was not going to cut him in on the regency, and like his cousin Peter he hoped to win enough in war to improve his position in peace. He was also thoroughly fed up with Thibaut of Champagne, as were most of the realm's nobles. 'Gilded with envy [and] freighted with felony', according to one rebel song, Thibaut had joined the rebels in 1227 only to abscond to Blanche's camp at Tours in the middle of the night, an act entirely in keeping with the rumour that he had treacherously poisoned Philip Hurepel's half-brother, the previous king Louis VIII, the year before in order to sleep with Blanche.[15]

Philip Hurepel increasingly viewed Peter of Brittany's manoeuvring as more likely to bear fruit than hanging around and hoping for the best from Blanche. Peter had a plan to make off with the entirety of Champagne by marrying Thibaut's cousin and invading the county, and he and his friends may have enticed Philip Hurepel to join them with the promise that they would make him king.

If, as a chronicler claimed, Philip Hurepel was not smart enough to see through Peter and his plans, failure soon proved their frailty.[16] An effort to capture Blanche and Louis outside Paris was foiled by local people, who lined the road to conduct them to safety.[17] Peter's marriage did not come off because the pope forbade it, and Blanche put Louis at the head of a large army to chase the invaders out of Champagne. The rebels next tried their luck in Normandy, again with little success. Hoping to shore up his prospects in England, Peter did homage to Henry III for Brittany and invited him to reconquer the lost lands of his father. Henry and his fleet landed in Brittany in May 1230, and he led his army into Poitou, where 'he lost many of his men, expended a great deal of money, and recovered little or nothing of his lands'.[18] Blanche summoned Peter to answer for his treasons, pronounced his fiefs confiscate, and raised an army to expel him from the Norman fortresses he was occupying. The next summer she invaded Brittany, spending nearly 25,000 *livres parisis* to fight Peter to a truce that confined him to Brittany for the next three years.[19]

The conspirators had one last trick up their sleeve, attempting to cut off the head of Blanche's support by offering Thibaut of Champagne the hand of Peter's daughter, whose previous engagement to Henry III had gone nowhere.[20] Thibaut, true to his fickle nature if nothing else, readily agreed to marry her. The plan was risky, for the queen had custody of the girl and would obviously oppose the marriage, but also romantic, capturing not a few of the conspirators' imaginations. Thibaut himself even wrote a song about it.[21] The two were to meet in Champagne at a place appropriately called Val-Secret. Of course, a secret like that could not be kept. The pope refused to grant dispensation for the marriage, which was consanguineous, and a messenger intercepted Thibaut on the road with a royal command not to marry the Breton woman unless he wished to lose everything he owned, which he did not.[22] By the time the truce expired in 1234, Peter of Brittany was in a very difficult position. Thibaut had returned to Blanche's obedience, Philip Hurepel had recently died in a tournament accident, and Henry III was too indebted to support further expenditure of men or money. Peter had no recourse but to make his submission.

Blanche had not just survived but thrived as regent, though as 'a single woman in a strange country' she had not been expected to.[23] The belief that only an adult man could rule a kingdom had incited the rebellions that, at least initially, seemed to confirm that consensus. As a chronicler commented darkly on the early chaos of her regency, 'And thus was the proverb of Solomon fulfilled "Woe to the land whose king is a boy!" France's attackers saw indeed that the kingdom's government was in the hands of a woman and a boy . . . thus they concluded that it was bereft of aid and counsel.'[24] One of the songs composed as propaganda for the revolt invited its listeners to consider 'How much France is debased . . . when it is entrusted to a woman, and such a woman as well you know.'[25] The song goes on to repeat the gossip that Blanche and Thibaut of Champagne were lovers, for her enemies accused her not just of incompetence and overreach, but also of sexual impropriety. She was said to have bedded not only Thibaut but also the papal legate who had accompanied her husband on his fatal crusade. 'Polluted with their seed,' accused a chronicler, 'she violated the boundaries of widowed honour.'[26]

Were the rumours true? Blanche's modern biographers doubt it. Blanche was a beautiful and lively woman used to her late husband's frequent attentions, but if an affair or two thus seems perfectly understandable, her reputation for fervent piety argues against it. Famously, she once told her beloved son Louis that she would rather see him dead than guilty of a mortal sin, especially adultery.[27] That Thibaut wrote poetry about Blanche, as well as about his Breton betrothed and many other things besides, doesn't mean he slept with her, and as for the legate, he was not actually in France all that long.[28] In any case, there was no pregnancy, though Blanche's robust fertility would have made it hard to avoid even as she approached middle age. That was indeed how she defended herself. Innocent or otherwise, she became so fed up with the allegations that she stripped down to her shirt in a session of the royal council and stood on a table 'so that everyone could see that there was no baby in her belly'.[29]

The gossip against Blanche probably tells us less about her private life than it does about how she navigated public power through her relationships with great men, a necessary recourse even for a woman of her tireless talents.[30] Her friendship with Thibaut had been forged in her late childhood when they were living at Philip Augustus's grim court, she as a young bride prone to tears, and he a child of seven or eight, sent to Paris as half-fosterling, half-hostage for his mother's good behaviour as regent of Champagne. Thibaut, whose Navarrese mother probably taught him the Spanish that was Blanche's native tongue, did sometimes ignore his self-interest 'in exchange for a few smiles and kind words' from the woman who had been coming into her first bloom when he, twelve years her junior, formed his earliest memories.[31] The Mediterranean culture she shared with Thibaut also gave her common ground with Raymond VII of Toulouse, helping to smooth the sharp edges of their political rivalries, too.

Although there were never rumours about Raymond, he was often in Blanche's orbit as an adult, visiting Paris to see her and his daughter Joan, who was being raised at the royal court as Thibaut had been. Joan had been affianced to Blanche's son Alphonse, a marriage made to seal a treaty that was to turn most of Languedoc not just into a fief of the Crown but its direct possession. The acquisition of the County of Toulouse, accomplished in its essentials under Blanche, is only overshadowed by the annexation of Normandy among the major principalities – Anjou, Artois, Poitou, the Auvergne, and others – absorbed by the Capetians in this great period of the realm's expansion. It was with good reason that the eminent French medievalist Robert Fawtier disregarded Blanche's sex to count her as one of the kings of France.[32]

Not that Blanche made no mistakes. Her worst error was probably to have driven the students and masters at the University of Paris to revolt in 1229 when she punished their unruliness with excessive force. The Capetians had long been advocates of the scholarly communities that grew out of the cathedral school and the monastic studios scattered on the south bank of the Seine, especially as they became a conduit for ambitious young men of modest means looking to make a career in royal administration. Philip Augustus's chaplain had celebrated how Philip and his father, Louis VII, had so favoured the scholarship of Paris that the study of letters flourished in the city just as it had once done in Athens and Egypt.[33] Philip is often considered the founder of the University of Paris because he granted the scholars a charter in 1200 that recognized them as a privileged community, soon after which Innocent III gave them a bull of incorporation.[34] (The Latin term *universitas*, from which we derive the word university, simply means a corporate body.) Having corporate status gave the scholars special legal privileges, and they derived further protection from the fact that, because Parisian scholars were considered clergy, they could only be tried by an ecclesiastical court and were exempt from secular rulers' jurisdiction. The students' special status did not, however, prevent them from engaging in the kind of rowdy fun that might make a modern frat boy blush. Medieval university students, who were by definition exclusively men, were infamous for their bawdy songs, their spendthrift ways, their drinking and wenching, and especially their violence.[35]

Blanche therefore should not have been surprised – and should certainly have known that she had no recourse – when some students celebrating Mardi Gras 1229 got so drunk that they attacked a taverner, pulling at his ears and tearing at his hair. Driven out by the poor man's neighbours, the students collected some clubs and swords and came back the next day with friends to destroy the tavern. They then proceeded, in the words of a nineteenth-century historian, 'to amuse themselves in the fashion now in favour only with the lowest roughs in the lowest quarters of London and Liverpool'.[36] The disgusted locals appealed to the Crown, and instead of leaving the business to the university's authorities to clean up as was their right, Blanche sent in her mercenaries. Rough men, more 'accustomed to inflicting the worst cruelties' than policing civilian situations, they killed several innocent students, wounded others, and forced the rest to flee for protection to the university's authorities.[37]

Outraged, the university masters went on strike, and when that didn't wring an apology out of Blanche, the students and masters alike packed up their belongings and left Paris for other centres of learning. Some of them went just down the road to the University of Orléans. Some went further afield to the newly established University of Toulouse. Others accepted an invitation from Henry III and joined the burgeoning scholarly communities establishing themselves at Oxford and Cambridge. The masters swore that they would stay away for six years if Blanche did not recant, and the students composed rude songs about her supposed affair with the papal legate because he had asked Blanche to punish them. 'Oh! We are dying!' ran the lyrics of one, 'Prostrate, beaten, drowned, despoiled/The legate's damned dick makes us suffer.'[38] The legate found himself not only ridiculed, but also in trouble with the pope, who had once been a Parisian student himself and who disagreed with Blanche's actions in the strongest terms.

A later chronicle credits sixteen-year-old Louis IX with the scholars' return to Paris. Louis, it says, feared that if France lost the university, 'then the lily, sign of the kings of France, would have been terribly deformed. For since God and our Lord Jesus Christ wish the kingdom of France to shine with faith, wisdom, and chivalry more than other realms, the kings of France usually bear on their arms and banners a lily of three petals,' each petal of which stood for one of these qualities.[39] Losing the university would pluck the petals of faith and wisdom from the French flower, and we can imagine how the last petal, chivalry, would droop dejected from its denuded stem. If the metaphor's logic seems a little tortured, the scholars' 'Great Dispersal' did cost the Crown considerable prestige. Contemporaries considered Paris a 'new Athens' for its learning, and its fame fostered the idea that the ancient world's glories now flourished in Capetian France. The scholars' absence was also expensive in more material ways, since the city's merchants missed out on supplying them with wine and women as well as parchment, ink, and other provisions. After a couple of years, a flurry of angry papal bulls in support of the scholars, and perhaps young Louis's appeal to the lilies, Blanche caved in. Soon the Left Bank's libraries and lecture halls, as well as its boarding houses, brothels, and bars, were once more filled to bursting.

Blanche's battle with the scholars belies her religious piety, which was profound, if in some ways profoundly unpleasant. Forged in the fires of Christian Castile and its wars to conquer the remaining lands of Muslim Iberia, Blanche's beliefs had a distinctly persecutory edge, one she seems to have shared with or given to her husband, an eager crusader. As one historian who studied the matter closely has suggested, Blanche may have been behind the harsh policy that he initiated toward France's Jews, a departure from the relative tolerance that Philip Augustus had adopted after his early experiments with expropriation and expulsion.[40] Soon after Louis VIII came to the throne in 1223, he issued a decree that eliminated the usury (interest) owed on loans made by Jews, diverted the repayment of past loans to the Jews' lords, the king among them, and curtailed Jews' freedom of movement. Certainly, Blanche did not oppose this shift in policy, for as regent she issued orders reaffirming this approach in 1227 and 1228 and then expanded it in one of the most significant Capetian edicts ever issued.[41]

At the castle of Melun in December 1230, she held a large assembly, perhaps a Christmas court, attended by her son the king, Thibaut of Champagne, Philip Hurepel, and a host of other barons. There they again agreed to eliminate usury and to limit Jewish mobility more strictly, requiring any lord who found a Jew from another's land to return that Jew to his own lord. Further, they agreed that 'wherever anyone discovers his [own] Jew, he can capture him as if he [the Jew] were his own serf'.[42] The comparison here between Jews and serfs did not mean that French Jews *were* serfs, whose property and marital decisions belonged to their lords, but it did mean that they were *like* serfs in that their lords could forbid their movement, and even the well-educated sometimes thought that Jews belonged to the Crown in the same way that serfs belonged to their masters.[43] In suggesting this equivalence, Blanche's measure laid the foundations of a pernicious legacy and by giving it the force of law she set the Capetians on a course to use antisemitic persecution to demonstrate and develop their authority as sovereign rulers. Unlike all previous royal decrees, which were really just agreements between the Crown and whichever barons could be coaxed to consent to them, the decree that Blanche issued at Melun in 1230 was more ambitious. It required all the barons, consenting *or otherwise*, to obey the clause restricting Jewish movement and to help the Crown to force others to do so. For that reason, it is widely considered 'the first Capetian piece of legislation worthy of the name'.

Of course, legislating barons' behaviour was one thing, enforcing it quite another. King Louis, still a minor of sixteen when Blanche began legislating on his behalf, was to struggle with that conundrum for much of his reign, inventing new solutions and creating new problems as his father's and grandfather's conquests cohered into a much-expanded kingdom that covered most of what is now France. His mother was more than happy to help, though Louis felt rather ambivalent about her efforts to remain in power, at least at first. He was a recently married man of twenty when Blanche handed over the reins in 1234. She nevertheless remained by his side and at the centre of power for nearly two more decades. When Peter of Brittany capitulated later that year, he submitted himself to both 'my lord Louis, illustrious king of France, and his mother, the illustrious queen lady Blanche'.[44] The parents of Louis's bride had similarly promised joint submission to the king and his mother's judgement when the pair were married.[45] Suspicious of the bride herself, a strong-willed woman from Provence named Marguerite, Blanche kept the newlyweds apart as much as possible. They had to steal secret meetings with one another in the stairwell of Pontoise castle, and Blanche prevented Louis from going to Marguerite when she begged for his comfort in childbirth.[46] (Perhaps Blanche felt she'd survived worse, even with no living husband to call upon.) In time, Louis would come around to his mother's way of thinking. He usually did. His great rebellion against her, as we'll see, was just the fulfilment of everything she'd taught him.

13.

Chosen Ones
Louis IX

King Louis IX could hardly wait. He had received word that a price-less treasure from Constantinople had at last made its way to France, arriving in Champagne on its way to Paris. In haste, he gathered his mother and brothers, assembled an entourage of barons and bishops, and hurried south to meet the monks entrusted with it. Intercepting them on the busy road midway between the great market city of Troyes and the ancient ceremonial city of Sens, Louis immediately ordered the monks to reveal the precious cargo that they had guarded on its voyage across the Aegean and Adriatic seas from Constantinople to Venice, whence they had carried it overland across the Alpine passes to Provence, finally crossing into the French kingdom nearly a year after they began the trip in the autumn of 1238.[1] Now, on 10 August 1239, Louis was at last to lay eyes on the fruit of their labours.

With as much ceremony as could be mustered in the middle of such a well-travelled thoroughfare, the monks handed Louis a wooden box. Inside it Louis found a silver box, and inside the silver box he found one made of gold. Nestled carefully in this golden box lay an even greater treasure, the Crown of Thorns said to have been worn by Jesus himself during the Crucifixion when Roman soldiers satirically hailed him as 'King of the Jews'. Miraculously evergreen (as some people claimed), the Crown never dried out or lost its vitality, a sign of the eternal life granted to true Christians and a useful feature for a relic whose thorns were often distributed to friends and allies.[2] Now finally in the relic's presence, Louis, his mother, and his brothers gazed upon it with tears streaming down their cheeks, 'as if they were seeing God himself crowned with these very thorns'.[3]

Louis's subjects were just as deeply moved to welcome the Crown relic as the king himself, or so said Archbishop Gautier Cornut of Sens, who had accompanied Louis and wrote an account of the Crown's acquisition. He remembered how people had lined the road and run to meet the procession led by the barefoot king and his eldest brother, Robert, as they carried the Crown into the city of Sens. With its buildings decked in tapestries, its bells tolling, and its citizens crowding into the streets, Sens welcomed the Crown with jubilation. Although only those few townspeople who managed to push their way into the cathedral actually saw the Crown when it was briefly brought out of its boxes and 'unveiled for the people', for many it was exciting enough to know it was nearby, even if only overnight.[4] The next day the Crown continued its voyage by boat, sailing down the rivers Yonne and Seine to Paris, where again great crowds came out to meet it in the fields and it was displayed for general admiration from a pulpit near where the Bastille monument stands today. Once more barefoot, the king and his brother Robert carried the relic to Notre-Dame and then to the private royal chapel in the palace itself. Those who hadn't yet glimpsed the Crown had to content themselves with embracing the pulpit outside Paris where it had been displayed.

Today the Crown of Thorns, the very same over which Louis wept, is kept in the treasury of Notre-Dame Cathedral, where it was deposited in 1806 after escaping the Revolution's anti-religious violence. In Lent, it is brought out regularly for the veneration of the faithful and the inspection of the curious alike. Louis IX and his mother envisaged something perhaps equally public but far more spectacular for the relic's new French home, something befitting the Crown's status as the ultimate symbol of Christian royalty. For them, the Crown of Thorns embodied both the heavenly kingship of Christ and the 'most Christian' kingship of Louis and his line, Christ's representatives on earth. Transferred from Constantinople to Paris, the Crown was further proof that the dynasty was worthy of the dignity that had once belonged to Rome, to Charlemagne, and to Byzantium.[5] It was, in short, a 'sublime manifest of the essence of Capetian sovereignty', and it required a home worthy of such symbolism.[6] In its honour, Blanche and Louis decided to replace the royal chapel dedicated to Saint Nicholas with a two-storey, purpose-built Sainte-Chapelle (holy chapel) that would soar above the Paris skyline and glow with the rainbow light of stained glass like a giant reliquary.

Since the thirteenth century, the Sainte-Chapelle has been many times renovated and repainted, robbed of its relics, and deconsecrated, but it still dazzles its visitors. Climbing from the lower chapel, which was reserved for palace functionaries, to the upper chapel, where the Crown of Thorns was kept, you arrive in a space that feels like it was made from light itself. The opulence of the chapel's decoration, the airy height of its vaults, and the great expanses of stained glass that line the walls overwhelm modern visitors perhaps just as much as they did medieval ones. In Louis's time, the chapel's beauty made it instantly famous. The pope, who had never been there, quoted Classical poetry to describe it as a chapel whose 'construction surpasses the material', while those who had actually visited it compared the experience to entering Paradise (Plate 16).[7]

This celestial sensation was not reserved only for the royal family and its peers, like Henry III of England, who loved the chapel so much (and thought it so surprisingly compact) that he said he wanted to bring it home with him in a pushcart.[8] Even common-born people visited the chapel, perhaps in great numbers. Although the Sainte-Chapelle was built for private devotion within the palace precincts on the Île de la Cité in the very heart of Paris, it was also intended for public consumption, a signal reminder that the Capetians possessed the most royal of relics. The Capetians wanted people to see their chapel. Louis prevailed upon the pope to encourage the public to visit the Sainte-Chapelle by offering indulgences worth nearly fourteen years' relief from punishment in Purgatory.[9] But even those never lucky enough to enter the Sainte-Chapelle could see it from all over Paris and beyond. As tall as Notre-Dame itself, the chapel's 'remarkable verticality' distinguished it from the surrounding buildings.[10] In later manuscript painting it is marked out from the rest of the palace by the whiteness of its stone and the delicate pinnacles that decorate its heights (Plate 15).

Those who did venture inside must have been initially overcome not only by the chapel's glittering glass and its blood-red walls, but also by their proximity to its unparalleled collection of Crucifixion relics. By the time of the chapel's completion in 1248, these included not only the Crown of Thorns itself but also a large piece of wood from the Cross, the reed given to Jesus as a satirical sceptre to match his satirical crown, the spear that pierced his side, the sponge that quenched his thirst, and some drops of his blood, as well as some of his mother's milk.[11] As new visitors got their bearings in this over-powering space, they may have begun to notice the messages encoded in the chapel's elaborate decoration. Strewn with coronation scenes and littered with French lilies, its enamels, murals, statuary, and especially its stained glass spoke simultaneously of celestial, biblical, and Capetian kingship. Although a screen positioned halfway down the chapel separated most medieval visitors from the clerics and royalty allowed to approach the altar, it did not block their view of the immense windows that are the chapel's glory. Nearly 50 feet in height, they light the chapel from above and line the walls with Old Testament scenes that were meant to be read as prefigurations of the Capetians' own history, or even as a 'political and moral self-portrait' of Louis himself.[12]

Moving clockwise around the chapel, the stories in the stained glass begin with episodes from the Book of Genesis, which take up the window to the left of the entrance on the north wall, and progress through Exodus and other books of the Old Testament on both sides of the chapel. The windows under which the queen and the queen mother sat are dedicated to the stories of the biblical heroines Judith and Esther, both models for medieval queens, while those that rose above the king's own seat tell the stories of the law-giving leader Moses and the holy warrior Joshua.[13] Behind the altar and above the lily-crowned reliquary holding the Crown of Thorns itself, the chapel's central window depicts the Crucifixion. Directly opposite on the back wall, scenes from the Last Judgement decorated the large rose window (long since replaced) that blossomed above the chapel's central entrance. And to the right of this apocalyptic rose, in the public part of the chapel nearest the entrance, the last great window told the only non-biblical story in the chapel's glass, that of the kings of France and the Crown of Thorns. Positioning Capetian history just before the Apocalypse as the last stop on the journey to Christian salvation, this 'Royal Window' – whose glass was mostly replaced in the nineteenth century – features King Louis himself along with his mother, Blanche, and his brother Robert carrying the Crown on its journey to the heart of the Capetian kingdom.[14]

Louis and Blanche had no compunction about inserting themselves and their family into sacred history. They and their supporters viewed the Crown of Thorns' acquisition as a sure sign of divine favour toward the Capetians and their kingdom. A Latin poem celebrating the Crucifixion relics equated Paris (*Parisius*) with Paradise (*Paradisus*) and portrayed France's capital as spiritually superior to Jerusalem itself.[15] Archbishop Gautier of Sens claimed that God 'specially chose' France for the Crown's home in the same way that He had chosen the promised land of Israel, and the pope noted that God had seen fit to 'crown' Louis by entrusting His own Crown to the Capetian's keeping.[16] God must indeed work in mysterious ways, for the facts were not just more mundane but even somewhat sordid. Louis had acquired the Crown of Thorns for the astronomical sum of 135,000 *livres* by purchasing it from the Venetians, who had received it in pawn from an impoverished Byzantine emperor, whose dynasty, which was Franco-Flemish, not Greek, had been put on the throne after the scandalous sack of Constantinople by Western crusaders in 1204. This chequered history did nothing, however, to detract from the widespread belief that the Crown's presence in Paris demonstrated that Louis and his people were now God's chosen ones.[17] As the pope wrote to Louis shortly after the Crown arrived in Paris, God chose to heap honours upon France 'before all other peoples of the earth' just as once He honoured the Israelite tribe of Judah, a nation that 'prefigured' (*prefigurativa*) Louis's kingdom.[18]

This gratifying conclusion nevertheless raised an obvious if troubling question. If the (Christian) French were a new Chosen People, what then of the old Chosen People, the Jews? The Capetians' answer dovetailed neatly with long-standing Catholic doctrine regarding the Jews, who were said to have lost their divinely chosen status when they refused to recognize Jesus as the Messiah and were as a result replaced by Christians. When it came to the admirable Jews of the biblical past, the Capetians could choose to present their Judaism simply as a prequel to Christianity. Although stories from Jewish history filled the Sainte-Chapelle's stained glass, the figures would have 'looked Christian' to a medieval viewer, for only one of them wears the pointed hat that distinguished Jews in medieval art.[19] Louis thought that a similar kind of erasure might also be practised on modern French Jews. He encouraged them to convert to Christianity, rewarding those who did so with substantial payments and royal favours, and even standing godfather to some of them.[20] The vast majority who did not convert, however, he viewed as an obstinate people wedded to erroneous ways of thinking. No longer chosen, they required correction and containment, if not outright eradication.

Just two months before the Crown of Thorns' arrival in August 1239, Louis had received word of a letter from the pope reporting disturbing passages found in the Talmud, a sprawling compendium of Judaic teachings that serves partly as an interpretative guide to the written Torah, or as Louis might have termed it, the 'Jewish Old Testament'.[21] A recent Christian convert from Judaism had brought these Talmudic 'errors' to Pope Gregory IX's attention, and now Gregory wanted all copies of the Talmud seized, investigated, and burned if necessary. Several other kingdoms had received similar letters, but only in France were the pope's instructions carried out. One Saturday in March 1240, while the Jews were at synagogue, all the Talmudic writings that could be found in Paris were collected and carted away. Among those who undertook the task must have been some of the university scholars who had been taught to read Hebrew by Parisian Jews. For their services, the Jews were now thanked by a trial to determine whether their holiest scriptures, without which it would be essentially impossible to practise their religion, should be destroyed.

Held outside in a courtyard of the palace with university masters as judges, the Trial of the Talmud proceeded through a series of tricky questions posed to the defendants, a process somewhat similar to the way that the Church's inquisitors questioned accused heretics.[22] The convert responsible for showing the pope the Talmud's problematic passages, one Nicholas Donin, acted as the prosecution, while the prominent Parisian scholar Rabbi Yehiel served as the Talmud's lead defence attorney. This Donin had an axe to grind with the local Jewry. Once a promising Talmudic scholar himself, he had been exiled from the community for heresy fifteen years earlier. Now he used his insider knowledge to paint the Talmud in the most objectionable colours. Was it not true, he asked, that the Talmud orders Jews to harm Christians? Did it or did it not contain insults against the Virgin Mary and Christ himself? Wasn't there even a passage that claimed Jesus was in Hell and immersed in boiling excrement?

Rabbi Yehiel parried these thrusts as best he could. A vast and varied miscellany compiled over centuries, the Talmud contains all sorts of things, including these passages that Donin had cherry-picked for their explosive effect on his Christian audience. Yehiel could blunt the impact of the passages advocating harm to Gentiles by saying that they were remnants of a time when Jews lived among untrustworthy pagans, not among the kind and civilized Christians of France, and by pointing out the ways in which modern Jews helped their Christian neighbours, not least by teaching Hebrew to interested scholars like those now sitting in judgement upon them. The bit about Jesus covered in boiling excrement was a little harder to explain away. From a Jewish standpoint, Jesus might be considered

'one of the worst heretics that the people of Israel have ever produced' and deserving of such punishment,[23] but since the university
masters were unlikely to accept that logic, Yehiel offered them an
expert dodge. He claimed that the Jesus mentioned in this passage
referred not to the Christians' Jesus, but to another man by the same
name who had lived two centuries earlier. To any unconvinced by
this convenient explanation, he pointed out that two different people
might have the same name, for 'not every Louis born in France is
king of France!'[24] The joke went down well, at least according to a
Hebrew account, but in the end it didn't matter. The Talmud was
condemned and sentenced to destruction.

In June 1241 wagons loaded with dozens or even hundreds of Talmuds and other Jewish books torn from rabbinic libraries across
northern France were driven to a pyre prepared in the centre of
Paris.[25] There, the books were publicly consigned to the flames as
the city's Jews looked on with deep distress. France had once been a
flourishing centre of Jewish scholarship. The great Talmudic scholar
Rashi had made his home in Champagne at the turn of the twelfth
century, and Paris had been famous for its rabbinical disputations at
the turn of the thirteenth. The community had lost some of its
vibrancy as increasingly antisemitic policies took hold, but many
young men still came to Paris to study under famous rabbis like
Yehiel.[26] The Talmud's condemnation did not entirely end this tradition, but the destruction of so many books was a heavy blow,
keenly felt. 'I will shed tears until they swell like a river,' ran the
dirge written by one of Yehiel's students. 'I marvel that food contin-
ues to delight my tongue / After I witnessed how they gathered
plunder from you / Into the centre of a public square, like booty . . .
and burned the spoils of God on high.'[27] But this was only the beginning of a very dark period for France's Jews, for King Louis approved
of violence not just against Jewish books, but also against Jewish
bodies.

Louis had not attended the Talmud's trial himself, sending his
mother and Archbishop Gautier in his place. He was probably busy
with news of a rebellion in Languedoc at the time, but he may have

welcomed the opportunity to absent himself since he 'so loathed the Jews . . . that he could not look at them'.[28] He was against any airing of Jewish beliefs, even show trials where condemnation was a foregone conclusion. Although the Talmud's trial was a unique event, public disputations between Jews and Christians happened more frequently, serving both to demonstrate the 'errors' of Judaism and to show off the rhetorical talents of scholars from both religions. (Argument had been raised to an art form not only in the Christian universities of thirteenth-century Europe but also in its Jewish yeshivas.) Louis feared that hearing sophisticated Jewish reasoning might sway simple Christians from the faith. He spoke approvingly of a knight who had broken up one such disputation by attacking a rabbi who denied Mary's virginity, since, as one of his friends remembered, Louis advised killing Jews in place of arguing with them. 'When a lay man hears the Christian faith abused,' the king said, 'he ought not defend it except by the sword, which he should thrust into the offender's belly as far as it will go.'[29]

Louis's extremism put him out of step with his mother and other influential people in court circles. Blanche was certainly not fond of Jews, but neither did she treat them with her son's bottomless hatred.[30] Her friend Archbishop Gautier, who had presided with her at the Talmud's trial, had cordial relations with Jews and may have stayed the sentence's execution since it was only carried out after his death.[31] Blanche herself seems to have been better disposed toward the Talmud's defenders than we might expect from her earlier curbs on Jewish moneylending and Jews' freedom of movement. The Hebrew account of the trial shows her taking Yehiel's side at several points and promising to protect him. Blanche's ambivalent attitude mirrored that of the Church itself. Although Innocent III had pre-empted the Nazis by seven centuries in ordering Jews (and Muslims) to wear a distinguishing sign on their clothing, and the Church made Jewish lives very hard in many other ways, official Catholic doctrine held that the Jews should be allowed to exist and to practise their religion, if only as 'a witness to the truth of Christianity that the Old Testament embodied and prefigured'.[32] Pope

Gregory IX's successor even decided that the Jews could keep the Talmud, so long as the 'blasphemous' passages were censored. But Louis was willing to go well beyond what others thought normal or his mother thought wise. His counsellors warned him that the rigorous way he enforced usury prohibitions was bad for business and reduced the kingdom's wealth, but he refused their advice, preferring that Jews leave his land than lend money at interest.[33]

Louis's religiously radical zeal would only deepen as he grew older, but in his youth he was outshone by his sister Isabelle. In 1244, at the age of just nineteen, Isabelle broke off her betrothal to the future Holy Roman Emperor so that she could found a Franciscan nunnery and live as a holy virgin, much to Blanche's surprise, the pope and emperor's annoyance, and Louis's eventual admiration.[34] Although the king first rued the loss of this imperial alliance, he was very close to his headstrong sister and much in sympathy with her extraordinary spiritual impulses. People later imagined them as living side by side in the heavenly kingdom, and both were posthumously credited with miracles.[35] Louis was canonized as a saint, and Isabelle was beatified (the next best thing). Louis must have been quite impressed by his much younger sister's extravagantly pious gestures, if perhaps also a little apprehensive about how those acts annoyed their mother. Blanche had to bribe Isabelle to eat by promising to give forty *sous* to beggars for every mouthful she took, and although Blanche lovingly dressed her daughter in costly silks and precious jewels, Isabelle rejected 'the robes and royal clothes and all suitable decorations . . . to acquire for her soul the adornments of virtue and humility'.[36]

Isabelle and Louis undoubtedly adored Blanche – she was a warm mother, if a domineering one – but they, rather domineering themselves, needed some space to grow up. Like many children who love and admire impressive parents, they rebelled not by violating their mother's deepest convictions but by taking those convictions to extremes. Although Isabelle was Louis's junior by eleven years, it may have been she who showed him how at last to break free from their mother and realize 'the integrity of his own selfhood'.[37] It was only a few months after Isabelle, having recovered from an illness, made her astonishing decision not to marry, despite all its diplomatic disadvantages for a royal family with no other brides to give, that Louis announced a fateful decision of his own, a decision that would require all his kingdom's resources and risk its safety, but one that would finally let him leave his mother behind and follow his heart. Louis had decided to go on crusade.

Like Isabelle, Louis made his stand after a serious illness. As the chronicles tell it, he had been so poorly at the end of 1244 that a maidservant thought he was dead. Louis, too, thought that he was going to die. He vowed to himself that if God should heal him, he would take the cross. Louis, now thirty years old, 'had found the perfect means both for expressing his fervid Christian piety and for charting his emancipation from the dominance of his advisors, especially his mother'.[38] Blanche's joy when she saw her son recovered turned to shock and sorrow when he told her of his vow. She 'mourned as if she had seen him lying dead', and never gave up trying to dissuade him, demanding to know 'how her heart could withstand their separation . . . it would be as hard as stone, if it did not simply break in two'.[39] Blanche might have reacted differently, for she had crusading in her blood. Born in 1188, the year after Saladin captured Jerusalem, she had gloried in her father's resounding victory against Muslim forces at Las Navas de Tolosa in 1212, a battle that turned the tide of Christian conquest in Iberia, and she celebrated her husband's subjugation of heretical Languedoc on the Albigensian Crusade. But widowed by that same crusade and serially bereaved by so many of her children's deaths, she could not now bear to risk losing Louis, too.

The kingdom's nobles were not quite as adamantly opposed to Louis's crusade as the queen mother was, but neither were they uniformly enthusiastic. Although a steady stream of crusaders continued to head to the Holy Land, recent expeditions had met with variable success. The Fourth Crusade, which had diverted to attack Constantinople in 1204 and ultimately brought the Crown of Thorns to Louis, had done little to shore up the crusader states, and a more recent effort partly led by Blanche's old admirer Thibaut of Champagne in 1239 had been only somewhat more successful. Jerusalem, returned to Christian hands by treaty in 1229, had been lost again in 1244. The remaining crusader states found themselves clinging on to the Levantine coastline and squeezed between two seemingly insuperable powers: the Muslim Ayyubids centred on Egypt and supported by the fearsome slave-soldiers called mamluks, on one hand, and a terrifying people known as the Tartars (i.e. the Mongols) who burst on the scene in the 1220s and seemed poised to conquer the entire Eurasian continent, on the other. But neither the mamluks nor the Mongols nor even his mother could keep Louis from heading straight for the storm.

Louis had every reason to expect success, not only because God had given him the Crown of Thorns, signalling France's status as the new Israel, but also because he had now proven himself in battle. In 1240 his men had put down a rebellion by the Viscount of Béziers, and he had personally suppressed a much more serious uprising in 1242, when Count Raymond of Toulouse joined with Henry III of England in a war against Louis and his brother Alphonse, now Count of Poitiers. Louis's victory at the Battle of Taillebourg put an end to Raymond and Henry's hopes of reclaiming territory lost to the Capetians earlier in the century. Louis could feel as confident in his generalship as he felt of God's special favour. He also now knew that the succession was safe. His wife had recently provided the realm with an heir and already had another baby on the way. A crusade was certain to prosper, especially since Louis was willing to put all of his considerable resources into making it the best-planned crusade of all time. To prepare his kingdom morally and financially, he reformed the realm's government, commissioning his favourite friars to stamp out corruption among his officers, and he raised enormous sums of money from the towns and the clergy.[40] The king even built a new port on the Mediterranean at Aigues-Mortes for the sole purpose of assembling his crusading fleet. Louis and his project seemed invincible. What could possibly go wrong?

1. An early fourteenth-century manuscript illumination depicting the baptism of Clovis, first Christian king of the Franks, at the turn of the sixth century. Above him a dove brings down an ampoule filled with holy oil from Heaven.

2. The Holy Ampoule, said to contain the oil brought from Heaven for the anointing of Clovis. This is a replacement for the ampoule that was destroyed during the French Revolution.

3. Etching made in 1793 of the Holy Ampoule before its destruction.

4. The bronze throne said to have belonged to the seventh-century Merovingian king Dagobert was kept in the treasury of Saint-Denis in the Middle Ages.

5. Among the treasures that survive from Saint-Denis in the time of Suger and Louis VI, this pitcher for use in the Mass was made from a Roman porphyry vase that Suger discovered while renovating his church in the new 'Gothic' style.

6. Suger's chalice, made from a sardonyx cup crafted in ancient Alexandria, was used to celebrate Mass at the altar dedicated to Saint Denis, where kings took up the Oriflamme.

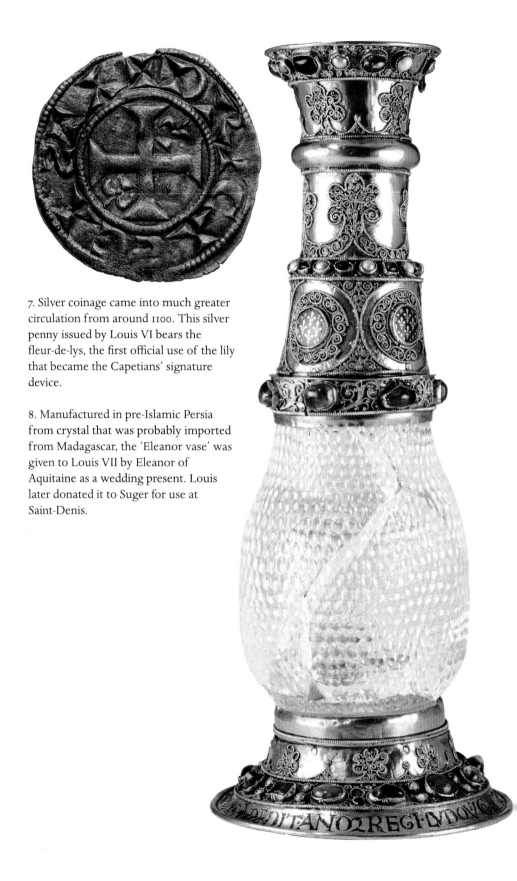

7. Silver coinage came into much greater circulation from around 1100. This silver penny issued by Louis VI bears the fleur-de-lys, the first official use of the lily that became the Capetians' signature device.

8. Manufactured in pre-Islamic Persia from crystal that was probably imported from Madagascar, the 'Eleanor vase' was given to Louis VII by Eleanor of Aquitaine as a wedding present. Louis later donated it to Suger for use at Saint-Denis.

9. Remnants of the wall Philip II Augustus built around Paris, standing in the Marais district by the rue Charlemagne.

10. Some remains of Philip II Augustus's Louvre, visible at the Musée du Louvre today.

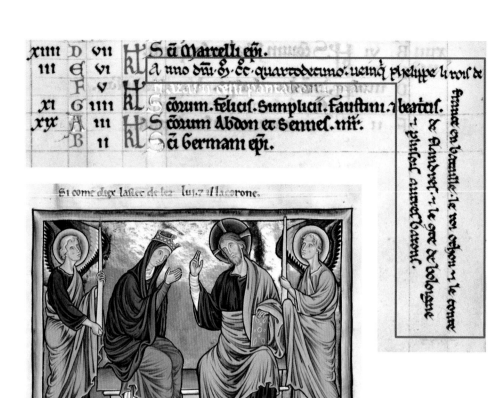

xiiii D vii   KL S cū Marcelli epi.
iii   E vi   KL a nno dūi q̄ cc quartodecimo. uenꝗ ꝑhelippe li rois de
       F v   KL naʒaʒ i cenꝓ pantaleōi m
xi   G iiii   KL S cōnum. felicis. simplici. fauſtini. z beatus.
xix   A iii   KL S cōum Abdon et Sennes. m̄r.
       B ii   KL S cū Germani epi.

france en bataille. le roi oʒhon z le cōte
z ꝑhelipꝓ autreʒ barōs.
z flandres. z le ſire de boologne

Si come dieu lastrce de les lui. z il la corone.

Si come li apoſtle enſeueliſſent noſtre dame.

11. *Main image, left*: an illumination from the Psalter of Queen Ingeborg of Denmark made around 1200 shows the coronation of Mary as Queen of Heaven (*above*) as the Apostles entomb her body (*below*). *Inset, above*: detail of a note inserted in the Psalter's calendar about the Battle of Bouvines, which reads 'In the year of the Lord 1214, Philip the King of France vanquished in battle the King Otto and the Count of Flanders and the Count of Boulogne and many other barons.'

12. In the upper panel of this illumination from one of the four lavishly illustrated *Bibles moralisées* associated with the thirteenth-century royal court, Blanche of Castile gestures animatedly toward Louis IX, while in the panel below a cleric points at an artist working on a manuscript formatted with the roundels characteristic of the *Bibles moralisées*.

13. Detail of childbirth from Blanche of Castile's *Bible moralisée*. The vignette reads: 'Here is Rebecca, from whom [came] the children Jacob and Esau. The one was good and the other bad.'

14. Stained glass from the cathedral of Tours depicting the translation of the Crown of Thorns to France. *Left*: Archbishop Gautier Cornut of Sens displays the crown to a commoner. *Right*: Louis IX carries the crown with his brother Robert of Artois following behind him.

15. View of the palace complex on the Île de la Cité in Paris from the Left Bank in the early fifteenth century, with the great round tower built by Louis VI in the middle and the Sainte-Chapelle on the far right.

16. *Overleaf:* The interior of the Sainte-Chapelle.

17. This illumination from a manuscript made for King Charles V of France around 1377 shows iconic scenes from the life of Saint Louis IX, including his birth to Blanche of Castile (*top left medallion*), his burial of crusaders' bones (*bottom left medallion*) and his flagellation by his confessor (*bottom right medallion*).

18. Queen Joan of Navarre-Champagne, wife of Philip IV the Fair. A highly educated woman with an important book collection, she is depicted holding a miniature version of the college that she founded in her will. Her death was blamed on diabolic dealings by the Bishop of Troyes, who was rumoured to be the son of an incubus.

19. King Philip IV, shown flanked by his sons, his daughter, and one of his brothers, probably Charles of Valois. This illumination is from Queen Joan of Navarre-Champagne's copy of the Indian fables of Kalila and Dimna.

20. Royal seal of Louis X. Louis did not have a seal made for himself as king of France until six months after his father's death, an unusual delay that suggests he did not feel ready for the crown.

21. *Below*: tomb portraits of Clémence of Hungary, Louis X's second wife, and their son King John I, who died a few days after his birth.

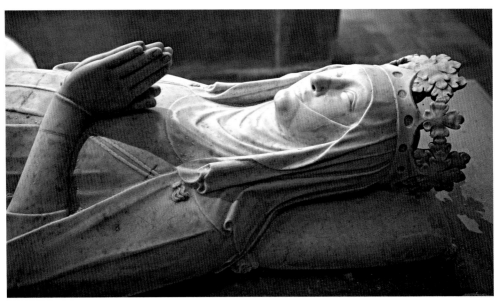

22. *Above*: an illustration from a book of hours owned by King Charles IV's wife Joan of Évreux shows the moment of Saint Louis's death (*left*), while figures mourn and cavort in the margins. Decorated by the artist Jean Pucelle, the book marked a watershed moment in Gothic manuscript painting towards a more sophisticated and realistic style. *Right*: detail of an illustration in the book, showing Joan at the tomb of Saint Louis.

23. A genealogy of the heirs to the crowns of France and England in the form of a fleur-de-lys, this illumination was made for the English King Henry VI's wife Margaret of Anjou in 1444. It shows the descent from Saint Louis of the direct Capetians (*centre*), the Valois (*left*) and the Plantagenets (*right*), which come together in the person of Henry VI (*bottom centre*).

14.

Death on the Nile

Louis IX

The river was full of corpses. The French and the Egyptians both looked on as the bodies, bloated and fish-bitten, floated downstream and piled up against a low bridge that lay between the two camps, filling the river 'from one bank to another, and as far upstream as one could cast a small stone'.[1] As the dead began to rot and stink, the water became undrinkable and the air unbreathable. King Louis paid a hundred men to pull them out. It took them a week to clear the backlog. The genitals of each corpse were examined. Those bodies found to be uncircumcised were buried in a trench with Christian prayers. The rest were assumed to be Muslims. They were tossed back in the river on the other side of the bridge and left to make their way seaward or to be eaten by eels with a taste for man-flesh. These eels, remembered the king's friend and fellow crusader Jean de Joinville, were all the French army had to eat for Lent that year, and he thought it was this cannibalism at one remove that made the army so sick.

It was February 1250 and Louis was trapped on the banks of the Nile, caught halfway between the coast and Cairo. He was facing a numerically and tactically superior Egyptian army that had already killed his eldest brother, Robert, slaughtered the cream of the Knights Templar, and cut the crusaders off from their supplies. Wounded and malnourished, he and his troops were rife with dysentery and scurvy. In his history of Louis and the crusade, Joinville recalled that men cried 'like women in labour' when surgeons sliced away their gangrenous gums and that the king himself was so afflicted with diarrhoea that the bottom half of his drawers had to be cut away for convenience's sake.[2] When Louis at last ordered the retreat, the crusaders' efforts to fight their way out resulted only in death or capture. Less valuable prisoners who refused conversion to Islam were slaughtered *en masse*. (Joinville himself claimed only to have survived by pretending to be the king's cousin.) Loyal to his people, Louis stayed with the army's rearguard as the French fled northward along the Nile but he was captured after a battle on 6 April that saw thousands of French killed or captured and the sacred Oriflamme torn to shreds.[3] Louis, so sick he could barely stand, had been carried to the house of a Parisian lady who lived nearby and left to await death or his captors' pleasure. Clapped in irons and threatened with torture, he agreed to an enormous ransom and the surrender of what little he had conquered in Egypt.

How had it come to this? In August 1248, Louis had left his mother in charge of France and set sail accompanied by his wife, Marguerite, in a fleet of over 100 great ships carrying many of the realm's greatest barons, around 2,500 knights, 5,000 archers, 7,500 infantrymen, and an uncountable number of servants and camp-followers.[4] Since Louis's efforts to interest other nations in the enterprise had come to nothing, almost all of his followers were French. The army wintered in Cyprus, where the crusade's success seemed almost guaranteed by the vast provisions of wine, grain, and money that Louis had stockpiled there. While in Cyprus, a promising new alliance seemed on the horizon when the king received envoys from the Mongols, who (it was said) had converted to Christianity and promised to aid the crusade by attacking the caliph of Baghdad, or so Louis understood.[5] From Cyprus, the crusade was bound for Egypt. Home of the Ayyubid sultanate that now dominated the Levant, Egypt had been considered a strategic gateway to the Holy Land since the Fifth Crusade (1217–21) made it a target. Like that earlier, ill-fated expedition, Louis's forces began their invasion by landing their fleet before the city of Damietta, where a branch of the Nile washes into the Mediterranean.

On 5 June 1249, with the blood-red banner of Saint-Denis flying in front of him, Louis had leapt directly into the sea, wading fully armed in water up to his armpits and onto the beach where the

French were awaited by a contingent of mamluks. All around him, his troops struggled through the shallows with their weapons on their shoulders, some working to force their reluctant horses out of their boats and into the water. (The French had not secured any flat-bottomed landing craft and so had no other way to reach the shore than this ignominious slog.)[6] Despite these inauspicious beginnings, the crusaders took the beach with minimal casualties and then entered Damietta almost without a fight, its defenders having mysteriously abandoned it. The crusaders thought it miraculous. Their victory had been won 'not by force or strength of arms', according to the Master of the Knights Templar, 'but through the operation of divine power and grace'.[7] The Egyptian Muslims were taken aback. 'This was a terrible disaster,' wrote the Arabic chronicler Ibn Wasil, 'the like of which had never happened . . . despair fell upon the whole of Egypt'.[8] Back in France, there were celebrations and processions, and Blanche of Castile wrote to notify Henry III of her son's victory with smug jubilation.[9]

But once in Damietta, Louis made a serious mistake. He had only a short window of opportunity before the Nile's annual flood began and made a march into the interior impossible, but rather than immediately moving toward another target, he stayed in Damietta for over six months. He waited partly for the last of his three brothers to arrive, but also because he had come to Africa intending to put down roots, perhaps even imagining that he might annex Egypt through crusade just as his father had done with Languedoc three decades before.[10] In his ships he carried not only weaponry and victuals but also farming equipment to work the land, for, as Louis later explained to the mocking sultan, 'I made a vow and an oath to come here . . . but I took no vow or oath to leave.'[11] Even much later, after the Nile had drowned his dreams, he still cherished fantasies of an Egyptian future, remarking to a rather mystified Joinville that he would certainly have accepted the sultanate if the Muslims had offered it to him.[12] The half year of inactivity in Damietta did allow Louis to found a (short-lived) bishopric there and to fortify the town as his base on the Nile, but it also annoyed the restless young men who relieved their boredom in fruitless raiding parties, sapping some of the crusade's vitality and allowing the enemy time to regroup and fortify their own positions.[13]

Louis's expansionist vision for Egypt may also explain his poor choice for the expedition's next objective when it finally moved on from Damietta. Many of his advisors recommended attacking Alexandria, Egypt's chief port, 200 kilometres west along the Mediterranean coast. If the Ayyubids were to suffer its loss after that of Damietta, they might have agreed to surrender Jerusalem in exchange for the cities' return. This was a swap that had been offered to leaders of the Fifth Crusade when they held Damietta alone, and one that was offered again either by or to Louis – here, the Muslim and Christian sources differ – as the crusade was failing.[14] But if Louis really did want to conquer Egypt for France, as well as retake Jerusalem, forcing concessions through a coastal strategy would not satisfy his ambitions. Only destroying the seat of Ayyubid power at Cairo would suffice. And so, on 22 November, the army headed, not west along the coast for Alexandria, a route that would have allowed them to be resupplied across the Mediterranean, but instead south along Damietta's branch of the Nile toward Cairo, just as the hapless Fifth Crusade had done before them.[15]

Louis's favourite brother Robert was a particularly enthusiastic advocate of the Cairo plan because, as he said, 'if you wish to kill the serpent, you must first crush its head'.[16] But Robert, on whose reckless pride the crusade ultimately foundered, misjudged the situation. He failed to consider that Damietta had offered so little opposition because of a political vacuum that proved only temporary. The sultan had been gravely ill – in fact, he died the very day the French set out for Cairo – his heir was absent in Anatolia, and his widow, the redoubtable sultana Shajar al-Durr, did not as yet have command of the mamluks. Robert was well acquainted with the misfortunes of the Fifth Crusade, which came to grief when the army became trapped almost exactly where Louis found himself subsisting on man-eating eels twenty-eight years later. Robert (correctly) blamed that disaster on the earlier crusaders' disregard for

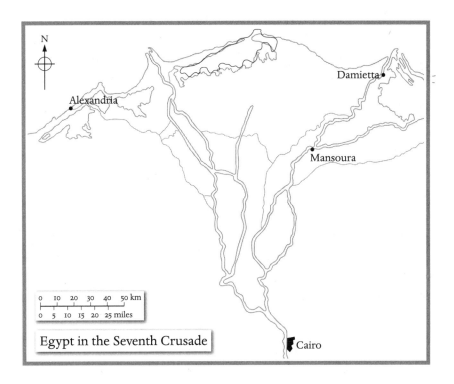

N

0 10 20 30 40 50 km
0   5 10 15 20 25 miles

Egypt in the Seventh Crusade

Alexandria

Damietta

Mansoura

Cairo

the Nile's annual flood, which made the way impassable. As he wrote to his mother, Blanche, he 'believed that the army ought not to leave [Damietta] until the river subsided . . . for the Christian people suffered much harm in that region on the previous occasion'.[17] He thought that setting out in the dry season would ensure better success. As it turned out, a shallow Nile just meant that nimbler Egyptian craft easily overcame Louis's fleet of large ships.[18] But Robert didn't live long enough to learn that.

While the French dallied in Damietta, Egyptian forces had fortified the town of Mansoura about halfway down the crusaders' chosen path along the Nile to Cairo. Although Louis's army reached the area at Christmastime, it could not attack for over a month because Mansoura lay on the other side of a deep canal that met the Damietta branch of the Nile outside the city. Louis ordered the canal to be dammed so that a causeway could be made between the two camps, protecting its construction from the enemy's catapults with moveable wooden towers. But the Egyptians destroyed the dam faster than the French could dig it and incinerated the towers (and those inside) with Greek-fire hurled from their catapults that exploded 'like a thunderbolt falling from the sky', causing Louis to sit up in bed and pray for deliverance, and Joinville to imagine dragons.[19] The French cannibalized some of their ships to find enough wood to replace the towers, only to have them burned down once more and the damming work undone. The stand-off went on for weeks, leaving many crusaders dead from fire, crossbow shot or the occasional raiding party, and the army no closer to Cairo. Not until 8 February did the French at last find a way to cross over the canal.

Tipped off about a ford lying further downstream, the French swam their horses across the canal at daybreak and fell upon the unsuspecting Muslim camp installed before Mansoura. The king's beloved but 'intemperately rash' brother Robert led the vanguard with his company followed by the Knights Templar and a good quarter of the French forces.[20] They chased a Muslim contingent right into the town but were separated among its narrow, winding streets and came under attack both by the sultan's mamluks and Mansoura's inhabitants. They were slaughtered almost to a man. The Templars lost nearly 300 of their best knights, and Robert perished defending himself in a house where he'd taken shelter. His body was never recovered.

Somehow, Robert had managed to send word to Louis of his predicament, but Louis couldn't get there in time. The battle in the Muslim camp outside the city raged too hot. The king was cut off from his company and forced toward the bank of the river, which was 'strewn with lances and shields, and full of horses and men, drowning in the water'.[21] Single-handedly, he saved himself from capture or death, slashing with his great sword of fine German steel at the six Egyptian soldiers who had taken hold of his horse's bridle. The French had left half their troops in the camp on the other side of the canal, but these were now helpless to rescue their companions, and the crossbowmen who might have covered the cavalry had all been in the ill-fated vanguard slaughtered in Mansoura.[22] The French took heavy casualties on the field and lost most of their horses. Joinville remembered a knight riding by with a face wound so severe that it left 'his nose dangling down above his lips'.[23] Yet by nightfall, the crusaders seemed somehow to have won. Although the French had suffered shocking losses, those on the Muslim side were apparently even worse. Cairo was in an uproar. Receiving word of the battle by carrier pigeon, its citizens imagined that the very 'ruin of Islam' was at hand.[24] Back at Mansoura, the Egyptians abandoned their camp, and the French went to sleep in the enemy's pavilions that night.

The battle had been fought on Mardi Gras, the last day of revelry before the penitential weeks of Lent began, and, as Ash Wednesday dawned, Louis discovered his victory to be ephemeral. That morning, he and his army were ambushed in their beds, fighting them off only with great difficulty in their wounded and exhausted state. (Joinville was too injured even to don his mail shirt.) The attack was the prelude to a long and painful period. 'From that day forward,' Louis later wrote to his subjects, 'everything turned out contrary to our desires.'[25] The Egyptian army launched a huge assault just three days later, using the captured arms of Louis's slain brother Robert to encourage the belief that the French king himself was already dead. Again, the French repulsed them, but the battle killed many on both sides, a loss the Egyptian army could absorb far more easily than the French. The crusaders' situation deteriorated rapidly once the Egyptians used their camels and their superior knowledge of the Nile waterways to launch an attack on the ships supplying the French from Damietta.[26] It was then that the gangrene, the scurvy, the dysentery, the hunger, and the hopelessness set in. By the end of March, the French had lost two-thirds of their men and Louis, at last, took the bitter decision to sound the retreat that ended in his and his army's capture.

With the king in captivity, it fell to Queen Marguerite to organize Damietta's evacuation and raise the enormous ransom – equal to nearly one and a half times the Crown's annual revenues – demanded for the French king and army's release.[27] When Louis had left Marguerite at Damietta in November, she was already in an advanced state of pregnancy, and she went into labour only a few days after hearing news of the calamity. (Her servants nicknamed the new baby 'Tristan', meaning sadness, in lamentation for the disaster.) Marguerite's marriage had soured since the early days when she and Louis would bypass Blanche to meet for secret trysts on the stairs of Pontoise castle. Louis had made Marguerite swear an oath of loyalty in 1242, perhaps because he thought her too sympathetic to her sister, who had married Henry III to become Queen of England. He may even have taken her with him on crusade because he didn't trust her – or because Blanche didn't – though it's clear enough from their eleven children that he also enjoyed her bed.[28] The crusade had not measurably improved their relationship, despite the baby, for Louis told his Muslim captors that he was not sure that Marguerite would pay his ransom. 'She is her own woman,' he shrugged.[29] But in the crucible of his captivity and despite her own 'state of both physical and moral exhaustion', Marguerite showed herself as loyal and as able a lieutenant as ever Blanche had been.[30]

By the time that the king and the other captives were brought downriver to be handed over a few weeks later, Marguerite had managed to ready the surrender of Damietta, the collection of the French ransom, and preparations for departure. When the mercenary-minded Genoese and Pisan sailors who had supplied most of the crusade's ships wanted to weigh anchor immediately upon hearing of the king's capture, she convinced them to delay until the army's return so that the French would have transport out of Egypt. Summoning them to her bedside only a day after delivering her baby, she begged them to take pity on her, but when this appeal to feminine vulnerability left the Italians impassive, she bought up the city's entire supply of victuals to keep them fed at a cost to the royal treasury nearly equal that of her husband's ransom.[31] Admittedly, the treasury was not quite sufficiently stocked to pay the crusaders' ransom on top of this expenditure. When Louis and his men arrived to count the ransom on 7 May, they found themselves 30,000 *livres*

short and had to break into the chests where the Templars, a banking order as well as a crusading one, kept their depositors' money.³²
The cash was handed over on 8 May. Marguerite had already set sail
two days earlier without waiting for her husband. Having spent the
last month in a whirlwind of activity and terror so great that she
made her bodyguard swear to kill her if the Muslims overran Damietta, she must have felt intense relief as the African shoreline faded
from view.³³

Sailing aboard one of the Genoese galleys retained by his wife,
what Louis felt was anger. Normally a man of good cheer and great
patience, he could not make sense of what had happened. He
blamed himself – and that guilt would only grow as the years wore
on – but he also blamed other people. In the letter he wrote to his
subjects later that summer, he laid the debacle at the feet of 'our
sins' (*nostra peccata*).³⁴ These sins were not only his, but also those of
the other crusaders and Christian society at large. He had not had
the help he needed. A war between the papacy and the empire had
prevented the emperor and his subjects from taking the cross, and
not all among Louis's army had behaved themselves with the
honour, sobriety, or chastity he expected of them. Some of them
had renounced their faith and gone over to the Muslims.³⁵ Now,
most of the remaining crusaders abandoned Louis to return France,
while he and his two surviving brothers Alphonse of Poitiers and
Charles of Anjou headed for the crusader port of Acre with those
few men who remained loyal to the cause. But even those who
stood by Louis irritated him. No one on board had prepared clothes
or bedding for him, so he was left to sweat in a fur-lined suit of black
satin given to him by the sultan and to lie on a mattress also provided by his captors, humiliating reminders of his defeat. And he
was out of sympathy with his brothers, especially the ebullient
young Charles, who distracted himself on board by gambling at
dice with a friend. Enraged at this show of venal frivolity, Louis
threw the game into the sea.³⁶

Life in the Levant did not entirely cool his fury – he remained so
irascible that Joinville promised to serve him freely for a year if

Louis just agreed not to get angry with him[37] – but it did distract him from despair and even offered hope for redemption. Louis had originally intended to return to France relatively soon after his arrival in Acre, but over the summer he changed his mind. He saw the necessity of remaining in the East to secure the release of the thousands of Christian prisoners still stuck in Egypt. Despite Marguerite's good offices, there had not been enough ships for those too poor to pay their passage, and many of the sick and wounded were too fragile to move.[38] Louis also held out hope that recent political turmoil among the Muslim states of the Near East might turn to Christian advantage. During his captivity, mamluk soldiers had overthrown the new Sultan of Cairo, perhaps partly in order to get their hands on the crusaders' ransom money, but also because his erratic personality and impolitic actions threatened their commanders.[39] In his place, they installed the widowed sultana Shajar al-Durr, who, like the mamluk themselves, was of Turkish slave origins. The coup had had no immediate effect on the French in Egypt (other than terrifying those who witnessed it), but it did create a rift between Cairo and the sultanate of Damascus that the Christians might be able to exploit. Louis wrote to his subjects back in France that these new developments made him optimistic about the tantalizing possibility of 'other advantages for the whole of Christendom' beyond merely holding on to what they already possessed.[40] He was not ready to give up after all. Overruling his counsellors' objections, he sent his brothers back to France to help their mother Blanche run the kingdom, spent freely to replenish his army with soldiers from the Christian lands of the Eastern Mediterranean, and settled in to do what he could for the defence of Christendom.

Louis asked his subjects to send reinforcements, reminding them in ringing tones of France's special status among Christian nations. 'You in particular,' he exhorted, 'being descended by blood from those whom the Lord chose as His special people to win the Holy Land . . . Make your actions recall those of your forebears, who among the nations were particularly devoted in promoting the faith.'[41] Processions were organized and weekly sermons preached throughout France. Some peasants, who said they were 'sent by God to avenge King Louis of France', even mounted a popular crusade.[42] Calling themselves the Shepherds and carrying banners painted with the Virgin Mary and the Lamb of God, they marched into Paris, where Blanche initially welcomed them, but then the movement disintegrated into attacks on clerics and Jews and had to be dispersed.[43] Blanche had been eager for any help at all for her son, for the Shepherds' enthusiasm, short lived and disruptive as it was, was not widely shared. Songs, chronicles, and diplomatic letters alike reported disillusionment, loss of faith, and apostasy among Christians across Europe and even 'in sweet France' following the defeat.[44] If God was on the crusaders' side, then why would He allow them to be so utterly humiliated? 'It is possible,' writes one historian, 'that the *débâcle* of 1250 provoked a genuine crisis in crusading history.'[45] At any rate, relief efforts were not forthcoming.

Left to his own devices and unable to mount another great campaign, Louis spent his time rebuilding the fortifications of several key crusader cities and regulating their contentious internal affairs, for his prestige far surpassed that of any other Christian prince in the region.[46] Rulers of other religious persuasions also sought him out, looking to gain any advantage in the ever-changing landscape of Middle Eastern politics. Little or nothing of lasting diplomatic importance was gained in these exchanges, but Louis did acquire a store of exotic presents that gave him an appreciation for the luxurious wonders available in Asia and Africa. From the leader of the Assassins, who hoped Louis might rein in the Templars and Hospitallers, he received a rose-scented casket filled with exquisite crystalline carvings, including figures in the form of an elephant and 'an animal called a giraffe'.[47] (Sadly, these long ago disappeared.) The mamluk Sultan of Cairo gave Louis a real elephant, which the king later passed on to Henry III of England.[48] The Mongols, too, sent presents, but their diplomacy was especially disheartening to a man still hoping for miracles.

Although the Mongol court had welcomed the emissaries that Louis had sent from Cyprus in 1249 in the optimistic belief that the 'Tartars' had converted to Christianity and were planning to join forces against Islam, it turned out that there had been no conversion and no plan for an alliance. What was on offer was rather an 'opportunity' for the French to submit to Mongol power. The emissaries' diplomatic gifts had been received merely as a down-payment on the tribute that Louis was now expected to send regularly, and when they returned to Louis in 1251, they carried a letter demanding this tribute. Louis ignored the letter, but, as Joinville's account assures us, he 'bitterly regretted that he had ever sent his envoys to the Great King of the Tartars'.[49] He did still harbour sufficient hopes about the Christian conversion of central Asia to send a Franciscan friar to evangelize among the Asian peoples, and he had some success himself in this vein, sponsoring converts from Islam to Christianity in Acre and supporting them with money and favours just as he did with converts from Judaism back in France. He even brought these new Christians back with him when he, at last, returned home.[50]

Louis delayed his return for a long time, much longer than many in France thought prudent. Blanche, already in her sixties when he departed, kept a handle on things as best she could, but the kingdom was restive. 'Among nobles and commoners alike,' reported an English chronicler, 'the French King's name began to seem very shameful and to be reviled as hateful because he was so badly beaten by the infidels in Egypt.'[51] Blanche begged Louis to return. She had already lost Robert to the massacre at Mansoura, and in 1252 her younger son Alphonse, sent back to France to help her, had fallen seriously ill and recovered only very slowly. Later that year her own health began to fail. When Louis departed for his crusade, she had tearfully predicted that she would never see him again.[52] She was right, as usual. But even her death in November 1252 and the disorder that followed it did not induce him to return.

What finally brought Louis back to France was money. His time in the Holy Land had cost the treasury around 400,000 *livres*, a sum only dwarfed by the enormous expenses incurred in initially preparing the crusade's departure.[53] Fourteenth-century accounts by the royal exchequer put the total cost of the venture at over one and half million *livres*.[54] Already in 1251 one of Louis's knights had let slip to Joinville that the king was 7,000 *livres* in debt.[55] In 1253 the Crown ran out of funds and had to borrow 100,000 *livres* from Italian bankers.[56] Louis's crusade had not bankrupted the country – thirteenth-century France was far too rich for that – but it had taken a serious toll on royal finances, as well as on those of his subjects, who had had to underwrite the cost. The Crown's budget had been cut to the bone, and it would take some time for it to recover. When Joinville later approached Louis about a relief force that had once been promised to Constantinople, Louis replied that 'his funds did not allow it, for whatever great reserves of money he might once have had in his treasury, they were now completely exhausted'.[57]

Louis, Marguerite, and the three children born to them during the crusade set sail for home on 25 April 1254. They left behind them lands where Latin Christian influence was almost extinguished. Compared with the new Mamluk sultanate, which would rule Egypt until the sixteenth century, and the Mongol empire, which had conquered China and would soon overrun Baghdad, the remaining crusader cities along the Mediterranean coastline were infinitesimally small and unimportant. They would not survive the century in Christian hands. The age of the great Holy Land crusade had ended with Louis's return to France. From now on, those who wished to fight non-Christians would mostly go to the Baltics and Prussia, where the Teutonic Knights fought the pagan peoples of the north, or to Spain, where the Christian conquest of lands long Muslim continued apace. There would be no further grand expeditions to the East until that mounted against the Ottoman Turks in 1396, a fiasco resulting in the utter destruction of the Christian forces at Nicopolis. Even so, the dream died but slowly. Every French king since Louis VII had been a crusader, and French kings continued without exception to take the cross for another century after Louis IX. Plans for a new Jerusalem crusade, some of them more plausible than others, were floated from time to time, though to no effect.[58] Louis IX himself was desperate to try again and would die while making the attempt. But no Capetian King of France would ever again set foot in the Holy Land.

15.

A Guilty Conscience

Louis IX

Louis returned to France a changed man. 'After the king's return from overseas,' Joinville tells us, 'he lived with such a disregard for worldly vanities that he never wore ermine or squirrel fur, nor scarlet cloth, nor were his stirrups or his spurs gilded.'[1] He slept on rough skins instead of silk, and in place of relaxing pastimes, he now devoted his attentions to the poor and the sick. On Sundays, he walked barefoot from church to church through the muddy streets of whatever town or village he happened to be in, distributing alms while dressed 'like the poorest of the poor'.[2] Under his humble garments of plain and sombre colours, he wore a hairshirt, 'though his confessor told him many times that such penance was hardly suitable to his station'.[3] He insisted that his confessor beat him for his sins with thin metal chains that he wore folded up in a little ivory box at his waist (Plate 17). He fed 120 paupers at his table every night and founded hospitals for the dying, homes for reformed prostitutes, and even a special asylum for the blind of Paris whose inmates later wore a fleur-de-lys badge on their tunics as a sign of Capetian patronage.[4] Not content with mere monetary charity, Louis knelt down before poor men to wash their feet, even cleaning 'between the toes where the grime was hiding', and he kissed lepers, though even Joinville protested that this was too disgusting.[5]

Louis had honed this new and punishing form of piety during the years that he had spent in the Holy Land, where every stone reminded him of God's own life and death in human flesh, and every day that passed further confirmed the destruction of his crusading dreams.[6] During that time, as no miraculous victory materialized to redeem his humiliating defeat in Egypt, he had become increasingly convinced that the crusade's failure was his fault. The king thought that he must have displeased God in some way for his careful plans to have resulted in such comprehensive catastrophe. The only explanation must be that God was punishing him, and he returned to France in July 1254 deeply depressed.

Although his delighted subjects feted his return with a party 'the likes of which Paris had never seen', Louis stewed in his misery.[7] 'I could bear it with equanimity,' he said to a well-meaning bishop, 'if I alone could suffer hatred and adversity and my sins did not affect the whole Church. But alas! All Christianity has covered itself in confusion because of me.'[8] He realized that he would have to do penance for his sins and change his life to win back divine favour. He had already begun some penitential practices while overseas. As a captive in Egypt, Louis had punished himself by lying on the ground with his arms outspread as if crucified. In the Levant, he carried the 'half-rotten, hacked-off limbs' of fallen soldiers to the grave with his own hands and didn't even hold his nose, as Joinville marvelled.[9] These were early markers of the kind of life dedicated to the mortification of the flesh that Louis would lead in France in the decade and a half of life that remained to him after his return.

But even if his confessor whipped him until the blood flowed – and sometimes he did – Louis knew that changing his own life would not be enough. Because he was not just a man but also a king responsible for the realm entrusted to him by God, he had to reform the way he ruled his kingdom as well as how he lived his life. Louis's crusade's failure 'was linked in his mind to his failure to be as careful in his governmental responsibilities as he ought to have been,' writes one of his historians. 'It followed from this that what his sins as a personal ruler tainted, his virtues in personal rulership might redeem.'[10] Louis's conscience told him that his frenetic efforts to organize the crusade had run roughshod over his subjects' rights and bankrupted not a few of them. In total, the crusade had cost the kingdom an amount equal to five times the Crown's annual budget, most of it squeezed out of Church coffers and commoners' pocketbooks.[11] Although the pope had given Louis permission to levy a 5 per cent tax on Church revenues, he had taken twice that, and there were rumours that he had been profligate with that money while being tight-fisted with his own.[12] Just the preparations alone to move men and materiel from Paris to the Mediterranean in the initial stage of the crusade had dispossessed and angered local people in the army's path. Louis had been harangued by a local hermit about good governance as soon as he stepped back onto French soil, advice accentuated by hearing plenty of local protests about his pre-crusade behaviour as he made his way northward through the kingdom to Paris that summer.[13] Over the months that followed, he mulled over in his mind how he might right these wrongs.

By November 1254 he had come up with a plan. Ordering investigations (*enquêtes*) into his own misdeeds and those of his agents, the king sent monks and other trustworthy men out to solicit complaints and make amends.[14] The investigators turned up pages and pages worth of grievances. For the construction of Louis's new port on the Mediterranean alone, people told of houses torn down and trees felled to build guardhouses for the crusade's transport convoys, dovecots destroyed, and dowers unjustly seized.[15] Louis compensated each of his injured subjects individually, and then he took steps to reduce the Crown's ongoing burden on the Church. He was especially careful to stop relying so much on royal rights to enjoy hospitality from bishops and monasteries while he was travelling through his realm.[16] Hospitality might sound like a minor inconvenience, but it was not just a matter of hosting the king himself but also of feeding and housing all of the friends, family, and servants who accompanied him (plus their horses), a prospect that could become very expensive indeed. Local people might suffer, too, because the bishops and abbots collected money from them to support the visit. Sometimes mattresses and linens were even stolen from people's houses to provide sufficient bedding for the king and his entourage. Louis had determined not to abuse his office, and with a sensitivity rare in a leader of any period he worried about how even his mere presence might be unintentionally oppressive.

And yet, his moral rigour could be oppressive in other ways, for

Louis thought that it was not only he who required redemption and reform, but also his subjects, whether they wished it or not. At almost the same moment that he sent out his investigators, he also issued a sweeping law intended to restore France and the French to spiritual health. Later known as the *Grande Ordonnance* of 1254, this law became a touchstone of medieval French government and made Louis's reign a reference point for how later generations thought a realm ought to be ruled.[17] Louis's law took aim at the corruption that tempted the officers who governed his kingdom's provinces, far away from his watchful eye. He forbade his officers from accepting gifts and from marrying into local families who might influence their decisions, and he required officers to remain in their provinces for a while after their terms ended so that any complaints against them could be aired and investigated. He repeated his mother's measures restricting Jewish usury and Jews' freedom of movement, again ordered the Talmud burned, and banned Jews from telling fortunes or making magic amulets. To his Christian subjects, Louis forbade going to taverns and playing dice or other games of chance, and he prohibited prostitution, ordering that the women's own property should be confiscated right 'up to their tunics and overcoats'.[18] Like his grandfather Philip Augustus, he also banned blasphemy, but he punished the crime more seriously than Philip, who only fined those who took the Lord's name in vain. In the Levant, Louis had sentenced a blasphemer to stand atop a ladder wrapped in pig's guts up to his chin.[19] Now back in France, Louis had a Parisian blasphemer branded on the lips, 'as a perpetual reminder of his sin and as an example to others'.[20]

The ferocity of Louis's justice frightened and appalled some people – even his confessor's biography sounds a little ambivalent about the branding – but it also won him praise. His commitment to justice became one of the hallmarks of his reign. Even in a remote monastery in central France far away from Paris he was known as 'Louis the Just'.[21] Joinville remembered with affection how Louis would sit under an old oak tree at Vincennes or in a public garden in Paris, wearing no adornment except a simple cap of white ostrich feathers, and personally settle the disagreements of his subjects.[22] But despite the endearing informality of Joinville's famous story, justice in Louis's France was increasingly professional, not personal. 'Louis was a king of the written word', one whose government was becoming increasingly bureaucratic.[23] The royal court was becoming an institution not entirely dissimilar to the courts of our own day. Known as the Parlement of Paris, it grew out of royal assemblies called *parlements* where great men came together to talk (*parler*) about the realm's business, to hear petitions, and sometimes to have the king judge conflicts between them.[24] In England, similar assemblies developed into Parliament, which mainly existed to give the Crown (often unwelcome) advice and eventually to make laws, but in Louis's France the judicial character of *parlements* became paramount. After he returned from crusade, men with university training increasingly took over its day-to-day functions, and the Parlement of Paris gradually became France's highest judicial court, receiving cases from all over the kingdom, a role it retained until the Revolution.

Louis's approach to justice was undoubtedly advanced for his time. He outlawed using torture 'even against poor people' in Languedoc because it induced false confessions, and he forbade deciding cases through judicial duel in his own lands, instructing his officers to consult witnesses and documents instead of having the parties square off.[25] But Louis made these changes not only because he wanted his courts to use a better standard of proof, but also because he abhorred violence (between Christians anyway). He said that he issued his *Grande Ordonnance* because he wanted his subjects to enjoy 'peace and quiet' (*pacem et quietatem*), and he believed justice was the surest road to that end.[26] Louis devoted considerable attention to settling his barons' conflicts with one another after the crusade, and at the beginning of 1258 he announced that he 'had prohibited all wars in the realm', a step of potentially revolutionary importance in a world where lords great and small habitually resorted to violence against one another.[27] The ban had no impact at the time because it had no realistic path to enforcement, but it was a foundational step toward greater royal control over internal violence on a par with Louis VI's curbs on the castellans in the early twelfth century.

Louis wanted peace abroad as much as he wanted it at home. He himself never fought another war against a Christian opponent. He sought instead to settle relations with his most troublesome neighbours. A few months after issuing his ban on internal warfare, he made a watershed treaty with France's closest Iberian neighbour after a war between the city of Montpellier and its lord, King James I of Aragon, a war which had nearly drawn France in.[28] In a treaty agreed at the town of Corbeil south of Paris in May 1258, James gave up most of his various lands in the Languedoc in exchange for Louis abandoning ancient French claims to Catalonia, where James reigned as Count of Barcelona.[29] (The Capetians had inherited the overlordship of Catalonia from the Carolingians, but the claims had been a dead letter since the dynasty's inception because Hugh Capet had failed to answer the pleas of a beleaguered Count of Barcelona.)[30] Further skirmishes would ensue, not least when Louis's successor invaded Aragon, but although Montpellier itself belonged to James's descendants for a century longer and James retained some other scattered French territories, the Treaty of Corbeil essentially set the border with Spain at the Pyrenees, giving France territorial unity in the south at a time when the Capetians were still consolidating their hold over the lands won in the Albigensian Crusade.[31]

Louis's attempts at solving France's troubles with England had less durable success. In fact, there is a case to be made that his 'solution' ultimately caused the Hundred Years War. But at the time it also seemed likely to produce a permanent peace. Louis had been trying to find a path to peace since he and Henry III had met for the first time in December 1254, when Henry was in France on pilgrimage and Louis was embarking on his efforts to redeem his soul and reform his realm. The two kings had much in common. Married to sisters, they were both profoundly pious men who kissed lepers and dined with paupers. They discovered that they had a natural friendship at odds with the ancient antipathy between their houses. For his part, Henry was in a particularly receptive mood to accept Louis's overtures. Although he had long nursed hopes of reviving the empire of his forebears, styling himself Duke of Normandy and Count of Poitou and twice invading France in a fruitless effort to win it back, Henry had become increasingly embroiled in efforts to secure a Sicilian crown for his second son and in conflict with his barons, who were sick of continental campaigns that drained England of men and money.

Several years of diplomatic wrangling were required before a settlement could be codified, but at last in 1259 the terms of the Peace of Paris were agreed. In exchange for 134,000 *livres tournois* and some territorial concessions bordering his remaining continental lands in Gascony, Henry agreed to give up all claims to all the lands he and his father had lost to the Capetians earlier in the century.[32] What remained to him was to be held in vassalage from the Crown of France. Crucially, this made him subject to French justice in these lands and meant that the Parlement of Paris would hear appeals from Gascon courts, giving the Capetians the legal means to confiscate Gascony should the occasion arise. That eventuality would come to pass before the century was out, but for the moment it looked like the old enmity might finally be extinguished. Henry, his wife Eleanor of Provence, two of their children, and an extravagant entourage of barons, bishops, knights, and servants crossed the Channel and journeyed to Paris to meet Louis at the end of November. The English party lodged at the palace, where Louis set aside his asceticism and entertained them lavishly. On 4 December, in the frigid air of the palace orchard, Henry bent the knee before Louis and did homage for the little that was left of the Plantagenet empire.[33]

Accepting Henry's homage and ending the threat of invasion made excellent political sense, but the Peace of Paris appalled much of France. In the borderlands that Louis ceded to Henry, the treaty was considered such an act of betrayal that even two centuries later the inhabitants remembered that their ancestors lost their love for

Louis from that day onward, and they claimed that his feast day was never celebrated there after he was canonized.[34] Elsewhere, Louis's subjects objected to the taxes that he levied on them to pay off Henry, particularly since the demand followed a couple of years of catastrophically bad harvests. Louis's barons, outraged at the loss of these border territories, wondered if he was acting out of some misplaced guilt over the deeds of his forebears. Louis assured them that he had settled with Henry in order to 'establish love between my children and his, who are cousins and future kings', and that making Henry his vassal was well worth what he traded away to do it.[35]

Louis may have been right about that, but his barons' annoyance was not unfounded. Louis had not only ceded territory without asking them their opinion on this occasion, in general he listened to their advice much less than a medieval king was expected to do. He preferred the innovative and moralizing ideas of church prelates, like his friends Guy Foucois (the future Pope Clement IV) and Bishop Eudes Rigaud of Rouen, both of whom helped shape his reform programme. And, of course, Louis was constitutionally unable to live and let live. That he made peace between barons at war and settled their conflicts, as supporters like Joinville liked to portray it, is another way of saying that he meddled in their business. Many were not keen on such meddling. Louis's reforms looked to them not like advances in just and efficient government, but like the tyrannical theft of their rights and privileges. In the same year that he angered the barons with the Peace of Paris, his actions against Enguerran, Lord of Coucy, for hanging three boys caught poaching rabbits became a *cause célèbre* among France's resentful nobility.

Twenty-two-year-old Enguerran thought executing the poachers was well within his rights, as did the nobles who assembled in Paris to hear his case. In the palace hall where the case was heard, almost all of them came physically over to his side, leaving the king standing almost alone. But Louis, 'hot with justice', as a chronicle describes him, didn't care what they thought of him. He wanted to hang Enguerran the same way Enguerran had hanged the boys.[36]

Only with great difficulty could the nobles persuade him to lessen the penalty. It was still steep. Enguerran, who had been imprisoned in the Louvre, was forced to found two chapels for the boys' souls, stripped of his jurisdiction over the forest where the boys had been poaching, fined 10,000 *livres parisis*, and sent on a three-year pilgrimage overseas. Interference at this level was unheard of; innumerable petty criminals found themselves at the end of a rope on their lord's orders every year and nobody said a word. The case was only brought to Louis's attention because the three boys, Flemish speakers who had come to the area to learn French, were under the protection of a local abbot. But the principle of the thing enraged lords used to liberty in their own affairs, and it worried them that a lord like Enguerran, who ruled a rich and extensive fief, could find himself so rudely treated.[37] 'Sweet France can no longer be called that', lamented the lyrics of a song addressed to France's nobles. 'Now she is known as the land of subjects . . . I would much prefer to remain master of my fief.'[38]

Louis's ostentatious personal piety caused as much upset as his rigorous approach to justice.[39] A particular point of contention was his devotion to two new orders of friars, the Dominicans and the Franciscans. Dedicated to poverty and preaching, they attracted enthusiastic support from lay people eager to return to the simplicity of early Christianity and to fight heresy. By the time Louis died in 1270, the Dominicans had established ninety convents in France and the Franciscans almost 200.[40] Louis himself had founded a number of these houses in France, as well as two in the Levant, and he gave generously to his sister Isabelle's monastery for Franciscan women, where he was a frequent visitor. (It was to Franciscan and Dominican establishments in Paris that he donated the fine paid by Enguerran de Coucy.) Dominicans and Franciscan tutors educated his children, and he always had at least one Dominican and one Franciscan confessor. He himself approached the Franciscans to ask for their prayers 'not in royal pomp, but in a pilgrim's habit', and he placed himself among the brethren when they sat down for their supper.[41]

But not everyone loved the friars as much as Louis did, and many people hated how much influence they had over him. Louis's financial measures, especially the heavy taxes he had levied for the Egyptian crusade, had largely exempted the friars at the expense of the more established orders, like the late queen mother's favourite Cistercians.[42] Once at the cutting edge of Christian devotion, the Cistercians' relatively comfortable existence in well-endowed monasteries looked positively dissolute next to the friars' lives of absolute poverty and street-corner preaching. Louis did not curtail the Crown's generosity to the Cistercian monasteries his mother had founded, but he did not create any new Cistercian houses himself. The friars' interference at the University of Paris – as clerics from other orders saw it – also made them serious enemies, and this, too, created challenges for the king, who was a devoted protector of the university but found himself the target of propaganda preached by an anti-fraternal Master. Even Louis's servants considered his devotion to the friars ridiculous. 'Brother Louis! Brother Louis!' they snickered to themselves when they thought he couldn't hear them.[43] Louis left them to it. It was just one more burden he had to bear. But he could not bypass his wife's objections when she discovered his secret plan to resign his crown to become a friar himself.[44] This was a bridge that even Louis would not be allowed to cross.

Queen Marguerite was able to prevent Louis's plan because the Church required spousal permission if a married person wanted to join a monastery, since it would mean leaving the conjugal debt unpaid. But the royal sex life did fall prey to Louis's penitential practices anyway. If he felt 'an inordinate movement of the flesh' in Marguerite's presence, he would get up and walk briskly around the room until he calmed down, a practice that seems to have worked.[45] Although eight children had been born to them between 1240 and 1254, only three were born in the sixteen years after the crusade, one of whom was probably conceived before they sailed from Acre. Even assuming Marguerite's fertility declined rapidly before she reached forty in 1261, it was a meagre harvest. Marguerite still had some political pull. Her influence can be detected in both the Peace of Paris with England and that of Corbeil with Aragon. But whatever direct personal influence she had once enjoyed over Louis had disappeared. Her pleas for mercy did nothing to prevent him from sentencing a noble adulteress to the stake for murdering her husband.[46] Nor could she change the simple way that he now dressed, though it was unsuitable for a king and certainly out of step with her own, more elegant style.

If Marguerite found Louis hard to live with, their children probably felt equally oppressed by their father's expectations. Louis made them accompany him on his early morning barefoot walks to shower alms on paupers dressed in the same humble style as himself, and he gave them copies of the whip used in his own flagellations.[47] (Whether they used them or not is another question.) He wrote them instructions about how to bear the burdens of royalty with justice and virtue and told them bedtime stories about the good kings and emperors of old, as well as the bad ones who lost their realms to greed and luxury, examples they should avoid so that 'God does not get angry at you'.[48] He hoped his daughter Blanche would become a nun. (She wrote to the pope to make sure she didn't have to.) And he planned for two of his sons to become mendicant friars. (They didn't.)[49] Louis meant well by all of this. Certainly, he loved his children. The death of his eldest son and namesake to a sudden illness at the age of fifteen seems to have caused him genuine grief to judge from a letter he sent to the Bishop of Rouen in its wake.[50] But he was not a warm father any more than he was a tender husband. Joinville, who knew the king perhaps as well as anyone and liked him, too, remarked that 'he had never once spoken to me of his wife and children' during the whole five years they were on crusade together, and he concluded pensively, 'it does not seem right and proper for a man to be so detached from his own family'.[51]

Louis felt no need to consult his family, or anyone else in the kingdom for that matter, when he began to consider undertaking a new crusade in 1266. Already past fifty and so frail that Joinville had to carry him on occasion, Louis must have felt that time was running out. The situation in the Levant was equally critical. One by one, the crusader cities were falling to the mamluks. Caesarea, whose walls Louis had refortified at his own great expense, was lost to them in 1266. Jaffa and Antioch were not far behind. France's barons were unenthused by Louis's new crusade, and even Joinville refused to go, but the king's brothers Alphonse of Poitiers and Charles of Anjou were willing to help. Alphonse had been planning a new crusade almost from the moment he had returned to France after the first one, and Charles, recently crowned King of Sicily after defeating the Hohenstaufen claimants in battle, had ambitions in the Mediterranean's east and problems in its west. A calculating man, Charles may have doubted that Louis's gamble would pay off, but at least he 'could hope to make it brief and profitable to himself'.[52] Charles offered his islands as a staging point in the Mediterranean and his engineers to build siege engines, and Alphonse raised funds from the rich lands of Languedoc by selling his serfs their freedom, confiscating Jewish property, and doubling people's taxes.[53]

Louis took the cross for the second time in March 1267 before his great reliquary in the Sainte-Chapelle. Then he undertook one last effort to clear his conscience and redeem his realm. Once more, he outlawed blasphemy, having the prohibition cried monthly in every town and marketplace and ordering even children of between ten and fourteen years old to be stripped naked and beaten for the offence, and he came down hard on the Jews, forcing them to listen to Christian sermons and to wear a piece of felt 'or other cheap material' in the shape of a wheel on their clothing to distinguish them from Christians.[54] He launched another round of investigations into his officers' behaviour and settled all the conflicts brought to his attention.

By March 1270, he was ready to depart. Like every crusading Capetian since his great-grandfather Louis VII, he started his journey barefoot before the altar at Saint-Denis, where he took up his pilgrim staff and the sacred banner of the Vexin 'according to the ancient custom of French kings'.[55] That night he stayed at Vincennes and bid adieu to Marguerite for the last time. Then he headed south toward Cluny in Burgundy. By June, he was at Aigues-Mortes on the Mediterranean, where eighty ships awaited him. In July he set sail in the flagship *Montjoie* first for Sardinia and then onward to the crusade's ultimate destination, which was . . . Tunis.

The 'effectively absurd' choice to target Tunis, so far away from Jerusalem or even Egypt, was kept secret until the fleet was under way and it caused consternation when it was finally revealed.[56] The decision is often blamed on Charles of Anjou whose Sicilian kingdom lay so close by, but it may equally reflect the sketchy state of French geographical knowledge or Louis's hope of converting the Emir of Tunis to Christianity.[57] Whatever the explanation, the plan turned out badly. 'The nightmare of Egypt happened all over again,' said the great French medievalist Jacques Le Goff, 'but this time it was worse.'[58] The army landed on the African coast at the end of July and passed its time skirmishing with the enemy while Louis awaited Charles's delayed arrival. He was still expected when dysentery set in and the soldiers began to die in their scores. Louis's son John-Tristan, who was born in Damietta during his father's captivity, died on 3 August. A few days later the papal legate died. 'Many others died, too, some of fever, others of a stomach flux, because of the bad air and lack of meat and clean water,' wrote a monk of Saint-Denis.[59] On 25 August 1270, Louis, too, succumbed. Laid out on a bed of ashes in the shape of a cross and clad in a hairshirt, he spent his final hours giving last-ditch instructions for the emir's conversion and praying to France's patron saints. The queen's confessor claimed that even at the end he still whispered longingly for Jerusalem.[60]

With the king's death, the crusade soon collapsed. Late to arrive, Charles of Anjou kept it going until October, but then they gave up. The survivors straggled back across the Mediterranean to Italy. Louis's corpse was boiled in wine and water 'until the bones separated white and clean from the flesh' so that his remains could accompany them in a box bound for burial in Saint-Denis.[61] His heart and entrails, however, stayed with Charles in Italy, where they immediately began performing miracles, safely delivering a healthy baby boy to a woman who had been in labour for seventeen days, and curing the invalided abbot of the Sicilian monastery of Monreale where the king's viscera were brought to rest and where they remain today.[62] Charles, who had finally made port in the very hour of Louis's passing, certainly loved and mourned him. Chronicles say he had to be forcibly pried away from his brother's corpse and could barely master himself to look presentable in public afterward. He believed sincerely in Louis's sanctity and that of the whole Capetian dynasty.[63] But Charles was also a forward-thinking man if ever there was one. He wanted to secure a potentially powerful relic in advance. Charles would not live to see Louis canonized, but it was already well known that there was a case for Louis to be made a saint.

If Louis's reign had split opinion whilst he lived, his time was soon regarded as a golden age. In death the king's virtues loomed even larger than they had in life. His first crusade had humiliated and humbled him. It had also harmed his reputation. Even the pro-Capetian chroniclers at Saint-Denis had to admit that his first crusade had 'brought great shame and great reproach to the kingdom of France'.[64] But Louis's long years spent disciplining himself and his kingdom had redeemed that failure and won him admiration. Enough, at least, that his death might seem like a martyrdom rather than a miscalculation. 'If God died on the Cross,' reasoned Joinville, 'so did Saint Louis; for when he died at Tunis it was the Cross of the Crusade that he bore.'[65] That France had prospered under Louis, its towns growing, its population booming, its fairs and markets filled with interesting and even exotic goods to be purchased with the king's good coinage, didn't hurt either. 'Much was France rich and at peace in his time,' wrote a later chronicler, and that was true, especially compared with the terrible times that came after.[66]

PART FIVE

Reign of Terror

(1270–1314)

Capetians, 1270–1315

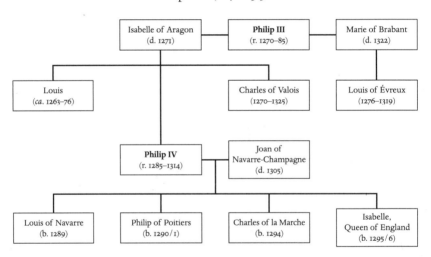

16.

An Unhappy Childhood
Philip III and Philip IV

King Louis IX's reputation long outlived him. The tomb in Saint-Denis where his bones were brought to rest was the site of miracles from the moment he was interred. The blind, the sick, and the lame came to be cured, and some, like the laundress Nicole whose friends carried her paralysed body to the royal grave, actually got better.[1] Stories like Nicole's helped to convince the churchmen who heard Louis's case for sainthood, and, after the long process of questioning witnesses and verifying the sixty-three miracles claimed for him, the pope authorized his canonization in 1297.[2] Reverence was thus transformed into worship. Churches dedicated to him sprang up throughout France. In the Sainte-Chapelle, special masses were devised to honour him as a peacemaker and an ideal king.[3] His life and rule became a touchstone of French identity and a demonstration of the superlative Catholicity of the nation for centuries to come. Even today, Saint Louis's legacy lives on in the names of cities from Missouri to Mauritius. At last, the Capetians had someone who could rival, or even replace, Charlemagne in the firmament of Frankish rulers.[4]

Louis's son Philip III had succeeded him immediately upon his death, but it was Louis's grandson, the future Philip IV, who saw himself as the true heir to Louis's legacy. Born in 1268, Philip could not have remembered much if anything about his grandfather. He had hardly learned to speak and walk by the time Louis sailed away to Tunis, but Philip spent the rest of his life trying to be what he imagined Louis to have been. As king, he would reissue Louis's moralistic measures against blasphemy and duelling, as well as the anti-corruption measures from Louis's *Grande Ordonnance* of 1254, and he would speak of his grandfather often when he made laws, promising his people that whatever new restriction he was enacting followed the example of 'our illustrious ancestor, Louis, the most Christian king of the French'.[5]

Yet, for all that Philip IV literally worshipped Louis, his grandfather's legacy was a double-edged sword. Philip was never able to meet the expectations that Louis's example had set, and his critics used Louis's memory as a stick to beat him with. Philip's great enemy Pope Boniface VIII used the occasion of Louis's canonization to show Philip all the ways in which he did not live up to Louis's example.[6] Louis's own friend Joinville, who began his memoirs during Philip's reign, agreed. He warned Philip that Louis's sainthood brought great honour to the Capetians but 'great dishonour to those of his line who choose to do evil; for people will point a finger at them and say that the saintly king, from who they have sprung, would have shrunk from acting so ill.'[7] Still, so much did Philip wish to associate himself with Louis that he tried to move Louis's remains from Saint-Denis to the Sainte-Chapelle.[8] Forced to settle for part of Louis's head (minus the lower mandible, which stayed at Saint-Denis), he had the royal tombs in Saint-Denis re-arranged so that his own would lie next to Louis's. His own father's sepulchre, made in materials 'distinctly inferior to those of the heroes of the dynasty who had immediately preceded him', had to be shunted off to the side to accommodate him.[9]

Historians have often shared Philip IV's apparent disregard for his father and namesake, Philip III. A recent French biography ranked Philip III among the weakest kings of France and wondered if he might have been brain damaged by a difficult birth with primitive forceps.[10] Philip probably wasn't as bad as all that. He was pious, polite, and apparently handsome, but no one could argue that he was an impressive man or an effective king.[11] 'Infantile' was the judgement of one chronicle; 'unlettered' or even 'illiterate' was that of another.[12] Well-meaning but unintelligent despite efforts to give him an excellent education, Philip III was easily influenced.[13] He had promised the queen mother, Marguerite, to obey her until he turned thirty, an oath that King Louis, perhaps still mindful of his own mother's interventions, made the pope absolve. But after Louis's death, King Philip fell prey first to the designs of Louis's old courtier Pierre de la Broce and then to those of his ambitious uncle Charles of Anjou, King of Sicily.

Young Prince Philip's other familial relationships were no less fraught than those with his father. His mother, Isabelle of Aragon, had accompanied Louis IX on crusade and died, pregnant with her fifth child, while returning from the venture in Italy. Having been so young when he last saw her, Philip probably had no memory of her face or her voice. What he knew of her was probably limited to the beautiful alabaster likeness later carved for her grave at Saint-Denis. And, of course, Philip never met his still-born baby brother. Of his three remaining full siblings, only his younger brother Charles of Valois survived to adulthood. His older brother Louis, heir to the throne, had died in 1276, and his younger brother Robert passed away shortly thereafter. Their father had remarried two years earlier, and there were rumours that his new queen, Marie of Brabant, had poisoned them so as to move her own son, also named Louis, closer to the throne. Even if Philip, then just eight, didn't know that his stepmother stood accused of killing his brothers, he must have felt that death lurked around every corner.

To be sure, the poisoning rumours were probably just rumours. Unchecked by the firm royal hand of a Blanche or a Louis, Philip III's court was rife with malicious gossip, especially at a moment when the arrival of a new queen threatened to overturn existing factional alliances. A chronicler at Saint-Denis suspected that the king's dear friend Pierre de la Broce had started the whispering campaign in order to temper the vivacious young queen's influence, and maybe he was right.[14] A surgeon from the lower ranks of the lesser nobility, la Broce was not a 'poor man' as a hostile chronicler claimed, but he had risen to the office of royal chamberlain entirely through Philip's favour.[15] His sway over Philip was such that the king did nothing without his advice. Philip's evident infatuation with his pretty new wife threatened la Broce's position, but he may

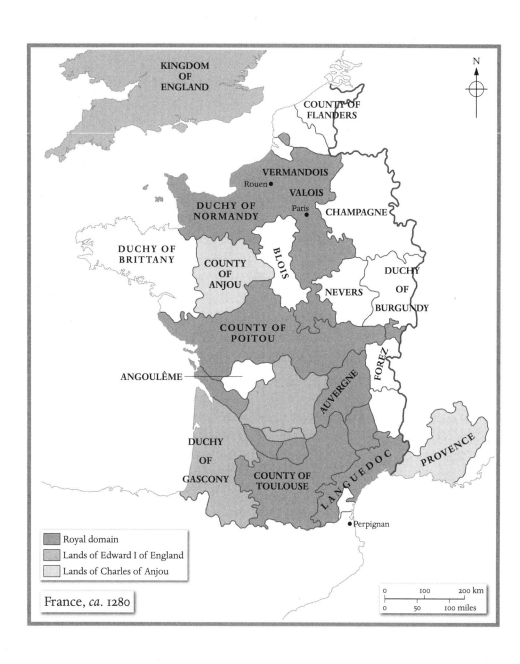

KINGDOM
OF
ENGLAND

COUNTY OF
FLANDERS

VERMANDOIS
Rouen •

VALOIS

DUCHY OF
NORMANDY

Paris •

CHAMPAGNE

DUCHY OF
BRITTANY

COUNTY
OF
ANJOU

BLOIS

NEVERS

DUCHY
OF
BURGUNDY

COUNTY OF
POITOU

ANGOULÊME

AUVERGNE

FOREZ

PROVENCE

DUCHY
OF
GASCONY

COUNTY OF
TOULOUSE

LANGUEDOC

• Perpignan

Royal domain
Lands of Edward I of England
Lands of Charles of Anjou

France, *ca.* 1280

0   100   200 km
0   50   100 miles

N

also have felt some genuine concern about the unflattering contrast Marie made with Philip: not only was she a highly cultured patron of the arts while he was 'unlettered', but her family trumpeted its direct descent from Charlemagne at a time when the old prophecies reminding people of the Capetians' questionable origins had begun to surface once more.[16]

Threatening a queen, especially such a high-born woman backed by the might of a rich and powerful family in nearby Brabant, was, however, a dangerous business. What's more, la Broce's high-handed ways had made him enemies, especially with the great men of the kingdom, who had to shower him with presents to make any headway at court. Marie's supporters began circulating a competing rumour: Pierre de la Broce was the king's lover, and the little princes' deaths had been God's punishment for Philip's 'sin against nature'.[17] Various prophetesses and charlatans arose, claiming to have mystical knowledge of the affair. As the stories swirled, a dying man entrusted a box with la Broce's seal to some monks who brought it secretly to King Philip. No one who saw that box opened was ever allowed to say what they saw inside, but whatever it was, it was damning. Marie was exonerated and la Broce executed like a common thief.[18] At some point, young Prince Philip heard about this episode, and it seems to have impressed him deeply. At that time, sodomy was a crime often prohibited but rarely prosecuted.[19] When Philip grew up, it was a charge that he would lay against his most hated enemies.

All in all, the court cannot have been an easy place to grow up. It is unsurprising that the little boy who lost his mother and his brothers in such an environment matured into a 'humourless, stubborn, aggressive, and vindictive individual' wracked with fears about his own salvation and his dynasty's legitimacy.[20] In middle age he would see conspiracies everywhere, even among his own children. Philip IV was nicknamed the 'Fair', a moniker that has confused generations of English-speaking students, who assume it means that he was even-handed or just. In fact, it is a translation of the French *le bel*, or handsome, a description of his blond complexion. He was thought at the time to be among the best-looking men in the world. But few people then or since have thought of Philip as 'fair' in the moral sense of the word.

Among the few redeeming features of Philip's childhood were his relationship with his surviving brother, Charles of Valois, who though lacking in both talent and luck would be his lifelong companion, and his friendship with the little Countess of Champagne, Joan of Navarre. Five years his junior, she was betrothed to Philip from the age of two and brought to Paris to grow up alongside him.[21] Eleven years old when the marriage took place in 1284, Joan brought to her young new husband not only the rich county of Champagne but also the kingdom of Navarre in northern Spain. The counts of Champagne had ruled Navarre since Count Thibaut IV – the one who had so admired Blanche of Castile – inherited it from his maternal uncle in 1234. The kingdom was small but strategically located. In the wrong hands, it could be a serious threat. Philip III had tried (and failed) to cross the Pyrenees to invade Castile in 1276, and Languedoc was not so long pacified as to be safe from an opportunistic ally in Iberia.[22] And then there was the English possession of Gascony, always a sore spot. Marriage to Joan provided young Philip with political – as well as emotional – security.

The importance of Iberia to Capetian fortunes had led Philip III to marry Isabelle of Aragon as stipulated in the Treaty of Corbeil agreed between their fathers in 1258. Two decades later, it moved him to undertake a dubious crusade against the Aragonese kingdom, accompanied by his seventeen-year-old heir and namesake. This affair was closely tied to the interests of Louis IX's last living brother, Charles of Anjou. As King of Sicily, Charles ruled both that island and a large part of southern mainland Italy, but when his restive Sicilian subjects staged a bloody coup known as the Sicilian Vespers in 1282, King Pedro of Aragon saw an opportunity to make good his wife's claim to the kingdom. Backed up by his powerful navy, Pedro invaded southern Italy the next year. Pope Martin IV, fearing to have the Aragonese king on his doorstep, excommunicated Pedro, declared his lands forfeit, and offered Aragon to France as a crusader's conquest.[23]

Pope Martin saw his way clear to bestowing the authority of a crusade on the Aragonese venture because Charles held Sicily as a papal fief. Pedro's invasion could therefore be seen as an attack on the Church itself and on the pope as its head. Although considered morally suspect by many, such 'political crusades' against Christian rulers had grown increasingly frequent since the Albigensian Crusade had shown how effective – and profitable – they could be. But Philip III's war with Aragon proved to be just as catastrophic as Louis IX's more traditionally focused crusades had been. The Aragonese having blocked the usual passes, the French had to cross the Pyrenees via a 'strange path, so covered in thorns and brambles that it seemed no human had ever been there'.[24] They only got as far as besieging Girona before their supply lines failed and Pedro's naval superiority won the war at sea. The crusaders' most durable acquisition was dysentery, and the king, having been carried back over the Pyrenees in a litter, died in Perpignan on 5 October 1285.[25] Not yet eighteen years old, Philip IV left his father's corpse in his retainers' care and rode north to take up the sacred burden of kingship.

The kingdom that he inherited had problems as deep-seated as those of the new king himself. Like his father, Louis IX, Philip III had spent freely, but the Crown had acquired no new sources of revenue and the underlying economic health of the kingdom had deteriorated. Although France's population had doubled since the days of Louis VI the Fat in the 1100s, that growth had begun to stall around the time that Philip IV was born. Part of the problem was overpopulation. France may not have been so crowded that it had more mouths than its fields could feed, as was the case in some parts of England, but many families teetered on the brink of subsistence. Probably more than a third of Paris's 200,000 inhabitants were considered too poor to pay taxes.[26] Worse was to come. While Philip's predecessors had enjoyed a period of favourable weather conditions known as the Medieval Climatic Anomaly, the climate now entered a new phase of unpredictable conditions, shorter growing seasons, and harsher winters.[27] At Saint-Denis, the royal chroniclers remembered how the Seine burst its banks in 1281, washing away the Petit-Pont, and then flooded even more catastrophically in 1297, such that 'one could find the like neither in the memories of living men nor in written texts'.[28] For most people, a worsening climate meant less food and fuel. For the Crown, it meant fewer taxes.

With these diminished resources, Philip faced increased expenditures, especially for war. A long period of peace with that 'ancient enemy' England was drawing to an end. The ineffectual Henry III had posed little threat to the Capetians. He observed the terms of the 1259 Peace of Paris and did homage for Gascony without incident. In 1272, however, Edward I succeed Henry. Decisive where Henry would have dithered, Edward presented a much more dangerous prospect. Trouble might still have been avoided, for Edward, fully occupied on the Welsh and Scottish marches, did not want conflict with France. It was Philip, driven by his insecurities, his stubbornness, and his grandiose idea of royal majesty, who forced Edward into a war in Gascony.

The conflict stemmed from a disagreement about French jurisdiction over lands and subjects that the English king considered his. In 1292, Gascon sailors from Bayonne and English sailors from the Cinque Ports had seized and sunk French ships off Normandy. The Norman fleet gave as good as they got, chasing off Anglo-Gascon ships while streaming blood-red banners from their masts, 'a sure sign of mortal war between mariners'.[29] Philip told his subjects to desist, but after the Gascons raided La Rochelle he ordered Edward, as his vassal, to arrest the men of Bayonne. When Edward hesitated to do this, Philip flew off the handle. He confiscated the duchy and sent his notorious one-eyed lawyer Pierre Flote down to Gascony to deal with the fallout. And fallout there was. The Gascons resisted the French seizure. Philip's agents acted violently in turn, and Edward's officers treated them as if they were criminals. That one of Philip's men was known only by the nickname 'Cheese' (*Fromage*) suggests that the Anglo-Gascons were probably not far off in their assessment. Sentenced to hang, Cheese and his companions tried to appeal to French justice, but their executioners stuffed their mouths with sticks so they couldn't speak and threatened local notaries with torture and death if they transmitted those appeals to the French king.[30]

Philip considered that his English vassal had now twice denied his superior authority. He charged Edward with *lèse-majesté* (essentially treason) and sent soldiers to garrison the estuary castles near Bordeaux, threatening the vital English wine trade. The Gascons countered by sending ships to Libourne and readied an assault by sea to retake the fortresses. The people of Saint-Émilion rioted against the French. With the situation spiralling quickly, Edward sent his brother Edmund to smooth things over with Queen Joan and the dowager-queen Marie in Paris. By the terms they worked out, Edward agreed to hand over some Gascons, to marry Marie's daughter Marguerite, and to accept a skeleton occupation force in Gascony. Philip invaded anyway. An army marched into the duchy under the king's brother Charles of Valois and the Constable Raoul de Clermont and settled in for a long occupation.

The Gascon war of 1294–7, described as 'one of the most peculiar conflicts of the Middle Ages', cost far more in money than it did in men.[31] There were no major battles, and the navies equipped at great expense on either side of the Channel only sporadically harried the coasts, without ever launching the intended invasions. But Philip spent more than 40,000 *livres tournois* a year on the campaign, and the total English costs have been estimated at £400,000 sterling.[32] The men who sat, bored and restless, in the castles of the Bordelais had not only to be fed and equipped. They had also to be paid. Kings had long since realized that the forty days of military service owed by a vassal to his lord were insufficient for modern warfare, and lords often baulked against sending their subjects to the royal army, especially in the restive Languedoc where Philip sought to recruit forces.[33] Even men from the nobility's upper ranks, like the Constable Raoul de Clermont, now made war as a profession, not a pastime. Much money also went toward cementing alliances with foreign powers liable to distract the enemy's attention. France's 'auld alliance' with Scotland, which would prove so troublesome to England for centuries to come, was forged in 1295. A Parisian chronicle claims that the Scots were so pleased that they put a fleur-de-lys on their coins in celebration.[34]

Building navies, underwriting soldiers' salaries, and bribing foreign princes pushed both Philip and Edward to experiment with new and unpopular ways of raising money. The heavy taxes that Philip imposed were so hated that even sympathetic chroniclers compared them to a 'new serfdom', and the common people nicknamed them 'evil exactions' (*maletotes*).[35] Philip also fiddled with the metal content of the currency (an expedient thought tantamount to fraud), and both kings resorted to taxing the clergy. Clerics had been widely considered exempt from secular taxation, except in order to fund crusades, since the Saladin tithes levied by Philip Augustus and Richard Lionheart in 1190. Papal permission was needed in all other cases, though, so long as the project was one the pope supported, this permission was generally granted. But while both Philip and Edward had come to agreements with their kingdoms' respective prelates, they had left the pope himself out of these discussions.[36] The newly elected Pope Boniface VIII was not one to see his authority ignored or his revenues misdirected. In 1296 he reminded Philip and Edward of their duties in a scathing broadside that excommunicated them both, setting in motion a bitter struggle with France that ultimately cost Boniface his life.

The Gascon war might have continued draining the two kingdoms' treasuries indefinitely had not border problems in both realms forced a truce in 1297. Edward had to turn his attention to Scotland, where William Wallace was leading an uprising for independence that would occupy Edward and his descendants' attention for the foreseeable future. In France the issue was Flanders, a region that posed problems for Philip similar in many ways to those with which Scotland confronted Edward. Just as many Scots were unwilling to submit themselves to English rule, the common people of Flanders did not really feel themselves part of the kingdom of France. In fact, although the County of Flanders was a French fief, its people had compelling reasons to ally with England instead. While only the nobility of Flanders spoke French, ordinary people spoke Flemish, which was a Germanic language rather than a Romance one and very close to the English spoken in London. The common people of Flanders were also unlike their French counterparts, in that, while France was still really a kingdom of villages, Flemish life had long revolved around the region's cities. Commercial powerhouses, these cities – Bruges, Ghent, and Ypres – were built on trade in woollen cloth that was woven in Flemish homes and workshops but sold as far away as Italy and Asia. The raw material for their precious cloth trade was English wool, which was produced in such quantity and quality as to be England's most valuable export.

The Flemish Count Guy of Dampierre, a man in his seventies, had had his differences with Edward I, who had slapped an embargo on English wool exports to Flanders. Being a French vassal meant that Guy could not disobey Philip – let alone connive with his enemies – without risking the confiscation of his fief, if not his life. But Flanders not only had commercial and cultural commonalities with England that inevitably pushed it toward an alliance with Edward, its people also had a tradition of popular politics and outright rebellion sharply at odds with Philip's autocratic tendencies. Stretching back to the citizens' alliances formed during the succession crisis of 1127, when Louis VI had sought to install his own candidate as count, Flemish workers were accustomed to act communally and sometimes violently in political matters.[37] Their guilds doubled as battalions, keeping chests of weapons at the ready. When summoned, workers became soldiers, assembling in the public squares, shouting under the banners that proclaimed their trade, and brandishing the iron-tipped clubs that made them dangerous adversaries. So important was this military aspect that these guild assemblies were known as 'weaponings'.[38] Flemish cities were riven by factional conflict at the best of times, not least because those who worked in the less skilled and poorly paid parts of the wool trade resented and sometimes revolted against the bosses who suppressed their wages and shortened their hours. (Medieval workers often wanted to work longer so as to make more money, whereas their bosses wanted to limit the amount of goods they produced so as to drive up the prices.) But when threatened by an outside enemy, workers and bosses stood shoulder to shoulder.

Aware that the Flemish situation was delicate, Philip had tried to keep Count Guy sweet. Philip understood the importance of Flemish wealth to his coffers, and he knew without having to look at a map that he did not want his attention divided between Gascony in the southwest and Flanders in the northeast. At the beginning of the Gascon affair, he had granted Guy part of the war taxes levied on Flanders, but these were hard to collect and Guy found Philip's interventionism on behalf of his unruly subjects intolerable. In January 1297 he signed a treaty pledging mutual aid with England and renounced his fealty toward Philip. Unfortunately for Guy, the Scottish war prevented Edward from fulfilling his side of the bargain, and Philip used the respite from Gascony to pour troops into Flanders, 'destroying everything around Lille by fire and sword', capturing Count Guy and his sons, and sending them to prisons scattered around France.[39] When a truce pausing the war expired in 1300, Philip sent an army under his brother Charles of Valois to occupy the entire county and then installed his wife's uncle Jacques de Châtillon to rule it as a military governor.

Having so easily subjugated the territory, Philip now committed a serious error. Customarily, medieval kings dealt with rebellions by following punitive measures with a magnanimous show of royal forgiveness, so in May 1301 Philip and Queen Joan set off on a tour of Flanders, intending not only to punish the wicked but also to win back their people's love through the priceless gift of their royal presence. Philip and his ministers, however, knew little and cared less about the mercantile values and proud temperament of the craftsmen and merchants who populated Flemish cities. Mindful of their pocketbooks, Flemish commoners objected not only to the fines that Philip imposed but also to the costs of providing royal guests with presents, feasts, and entertainments. The citizens of Ghent claimed – though probably with some exaggeration – to have spent over 28,000 *livres* on the festivities, while those of Bruges grumbled with particular bitterness about the expensively decorated clothing they had presented to the royal entourage.[40]

Infuriatingly, the costs were not shared out equally among all the citizens. Rather, the patricians who dominated the Flemish town councils decided to protect their own fortunes while the common masses paid for most of the festivities. Discontent at this state of affairs was eloquently articulated by a weaver called Peter the King. Evocatively described by an Italian chronicler as a 'poor man, short and skinny, blind in one eye, over fifty, and ignorant of French and Latin', Peter made speeches in the public squares that nevertheless found a ready audience among the Flemish workers and petty traders of Bruges.[41] The patricians took this seriously. They had long experience of the strikes, sabotage, and outright rebellion that Flemish commoners undertook when angered, and they found a ready friend in the proud and unforgiving aristocrat Jacques de Châtillon. Their violent efforts to suppress Peter the King and his followers, however, only inflamed tensions further, and over the winter of 1301–2, Flemish society became increasingly polarized between the patricians and noble French loyalists who called themselves the 'Lilies' (*Leliaarts*), on the one hand, and the common people who rallied behind the return of old Count Guy, on the other.

Jacques de Châtillon, on whose stiff-necked and short-tempered character Flemish and French sources alike agree, was not one to back down. No doubt encouraged by Philip's zealous lawyer Pierre Flote, who had accompanied him to Flanders, he destroyed part of Bruges's walls and exiled Peter the King's supporters in punishment for the unrest. In his hauteur, he underestimated both the strength of feeling among the commoners and their ability to mobilize an effective opposition. On the evening of 17 May 1302, with hundreds of French troops billeted in private houses all over Bruges, the commoners organized a massacre. Having secretly welcomed the exiled citizens back to the city, they waited until the sun rose, and then they killed every French person they could lay their hands on. Those Frenchmen who tried to pass themselves off as Flemings were found out when they could not pronounce the Flemish password 'shield' without an accent and were then executed on the spot.[42] Jacques de Châtillon and Pierre Flote had to flee the city with only the shirts on their backs and the horses galloping beneath them.

The so-called 'Matins of Bruges', like the Sicilian Vespers before it, presented such a challenge to Capetian authority that the Crown could consider no response other than war – as soon as he heard the news, Philip ordered every armed man available to head for Flanders – but, just as the Aragonese adventure had ended in sorrow and death for the French, Philip's reaction to the Flemish rebellion led to one of the worst calamities of his entire reign.

The Flemish, buoyed by popular support and willing contributions of money, retook most of the county by the end of June, and in July they turned their attention to besieging the fortress of Courtrai (Kortrijk in Flemish), not far from Ypres. There, the concentration of their forces attracted the bellicose French commander Robert II of Artois. Robert, son of Louis IX's bold brother whose reckless charge at Mansoura had sealed the Egyptian crusade's doom, is often blamed for following his foolish father's example by rashly engaging the Flemish in battle on 11 July 1302 and thus inviting one of the worst defeats in French military history. But in truth, it was the only option open to him. Robert had tried alternative assaults in the previous days and could only advance further into Flanders by taking Courtrai.[43] His confidence in his troops was not unreasonable. Dominated by noble knights whose proud lineages stretched back to Bouvines – and who could afford the costly warhorses and heavy armour necessary for cavalry service – Robert's army was probably the very best any European kingdom could have produced. Arranged in battle array beneath their chivalric ensigns, they could not have presented a greater contrast to the Flemish forces now facing them. 'Rustics, few in number, almost unarmed relative to the French, and unused to battle', the Flemish were mainly foot soldiers, guildsmen who had downed tools earlier that summer to fight for their liberties under the humble pennants of their trade.[44]

The smashing victory won at Courtrai by the Flemish infantry largely came down to its advantageous position and the marshy terrain, unfavourable to cavalry, that the French had to cross to get to them. Compounding the difficulty, the Flemings had dug trenches and camouflaged them with brush. Robert had encountered this tactic before, however, so it was not so much Flemish cunning as French over-confidence in their cavalry's invincibility that brought about his downfall. The cavalry's charge, meant to destroy the Flemish lines, foundered on the treacherous ground, allowing the nimble Flemish foot soldiers to pick off the unhorsed riders. The rearguard retreated in disarray while the flower of French chivalry, says a Ghent chronicle, was turned to muck and manure.[45] Among the French fallen were some of the most important and experienced figures in Philip's kingdom, including Robert II of Artois, Jacques de Châtillon, Pierre Flote, and the Constable Raoul de Clermont. In the aftermath, Flemish soldiers stalked the field, finishing off the wounded and looting the dead. The golden spurs they took from the French nobles' corpses were hung as trophies in Courtrai's cathedral, where they remained until recaptured by the French eighty years later. Their significance as a symbol of Flemish commoners' victory over French nobles was such that the confrontation at Courtrai was christened the 'Battle of the Golden Spurs'.

It might be an overstatement to claim that 'Courtrai was the great crisis of Philip's reign', as the American medievalist Joseph Strayer would have it.[46] If the treaty that Philip made with Edward in 1303 was not as advantageous as it might have been in 1297, nor was it anywhere near as punitive as the English might have demanded in the wake of the Flemish debacle. Philip married off his half-sister Marguerite to King Edward and his daughter Isabelle to the crown prince (also an Edward). Isabelle's future son, they agreed, could do homage for Gascony. The union between seven-year-old Isabelle and young Edward would not take place until the girl turned twelve, when girls were believed mature enough to consent to marriage, but since King Edward 'instantly and forever after ardently adored' Marguerite, binding affection between the two kingdoms seemed assured.[47] The treaty put an end to the Franco-Scottish and the Anglo-Flemish alliances, and in 1304 the French army finally beat the Flemish into submission at the Battle of Mons-en-Pévèle. Count Guy died in prison the next year. Philip was thus able to force the Flemings to agree to a peace extremely unfavourable to them at Athis-sur-Orge in 1305. The rebellious cities were to pull down their walls. Three thousand of Bruges's inhabitants were to go on pilgrimage in penance for the Matins of Bruges. Flanders also promised to provide Philip with an army of 500 men-at-arms a year, a punishing annual rent of 20,000 *livres*, and an enormous indemnity of 400,000 *livres*.[48]

These victories turned out to be worse than illusory. In time, they revealed themselves as the seedbed of future calamities. The Flemish never accepted the way that the terms agreed at Athis disregarded their victory at Courtrai, and their disaffection toward France only grew stronger under their new count, Robert of Béthune. For their part, the English continued to find it a vexing contradiction that their sovereign king held a fief in submission to the French Crown. The baby Edward born to Isabelle was to make that situation incomparably worse, leading to the war that ravaged France for over a hundred years. The necessary military expenses required to deal with Flanders, and eventually with England, could not be borne by the increasingly immiserated masses, who were asked to underwrite not only the kind of cavalry France had mustered at Courtrai but also the enormous numbers of infantry whose advantages that battle had shown. In 1305, however, this was all still to come. At the time, Philip must have felt that events had confirmed his greatness. By then, he had brought even the pope to heel.

17.

Angels and Antichrist

Philip IV

On 24 June 1303, one of Philip's clerks surveyed the crowd from his perch atop the royal dais. Packed as tight as could be into the palace's grand gardens below, the townsmen of Paris sweated in the summer heat. Alongside them jostled a throng of mendicant friars and minor clergy and as many villagers as could be rounded up from the nearby countryside. Among them were an Italian merchant, keen to acquire what news he could for his patron in England, and a canon of Saint-Victor, making notes for a chronicle in praise of King Philip.[1] Above this motley assemblage, the king, his sons, and the great prelates of France stood solemnly in their ceremonial robes on the dais where the clerk had just risen to speak. The crowd stirred slightly and quieted. Announcements were about to be made and demands imposed. Philip's ever impassive face gave nothing away, but the assembled masses thought they probably knew what it was about, and they were eager to hear what the king's man was going to say.

Little more than a year before, in April 1302, many of them had stood in Notre-Dame to hear the Crown's *consigliere* Pierre Flote reveal Pope Boniface VIII's unholy designs against France and its king. Flote, who was to die at the Battle of Courtrai three months later, had shocked the crowd by telling them that Boniface was claiming that Philip held his kingdom from the pope, though, as all good Frenchmen knew, France was Philip's by the grace of God alone. Flote wasn't exaggerating (much). Philip had angered Boniface by arresting the rebellious Bishop of Pamiers, who had compared Philip to a giant owl, brought up Hugh Capet's supposed usurpation, and talked excitedly about a Languedocian rebellion, among many other offences.[2] Feeling Philip had no right to treat churchmen in such high-handed fashion, Boniface had issued a bull – patronizingly entitled 'Listen, son' (*Ausculta fili*) – that did indeed imply that Philip was subject to the pope.[3] Boniface was even threatening to have Philip censured before a council of French bishops. Astonished in turn by the pope's effrontery, Philip had circulated a public letter addressing Boniface as 'you utmost fool' (*tua maxima fatuitas*), and his hot-headed cousin Robert II of Artois had tossed the bull into the fire.[4] Little was known about the bull's contents in France until Flote spun them into a polemic for the audience assembled in the cathedral.

The reaction of Notre-Dame's assembly to Flote's account had been as heated as Philip's to the bull. 'Vehemently stirred up' by what they heard, France's nobles had addressed an angry letter to the pope.[5] Their ancestors, they protested, had not shed their blood for the faith to see France's freedoms disregarded and her honour impugned in such a fashion. What was going on 'were not things that pleased God' nor things that anyone expected to happen, 'except with Antichrist' (*fors avecques Antechrist*).[6] Equally appalled, France's towns had sent their own strongly worded letter. The clergy, for their part, had carefully reported the strength of feeling among their compatriots and urged Rome to greater caution. Heedless of the warning, Boniface doubled down on his earlier claims to dominion over France, issuing another bull in November that extended those claims to the entire world. It closed with the ringing declaration that salvation requires 'every human creature to be subject to the pope'.[7]

Philip considered this new bull unhinged but could only fume ineffectually. It fell to his chief minister, Guillaume de Nogaret, to hatch a plan to deal with the problem. 'A man of action, words, and moral imperatives, a razor-sharp thinker, an inspired zealot who wrote and spoke with oracular conviction, a controller and manipulator, endowed with a prodigious memory and immense energy', Nogaret had replaced Pierre Flote at Philip's side after Courtrai, and believing himself inspired by God, he more than matched his one-eyed predecessor's predilection for inventive ruthlessness.[8] In a violent diatribe read before the royal council in March 1303, Nogaret rehearsed Boniface's crimes and recommended that a Church council be called to depose him.[9] Boniface, he said, was a 'manifest heretic' who had obtained the pontificate by nefarious means, whereas Philip had been 'anointed for the execution of justice . . . like an angel of God'.[10]

Nogaret was no fool, but where he wanted to rush in, Philip feared to tread. Deposing a pope was an almost unheard-of expedient. The German emperor Henry IV had tried it at the height of the Investiture Controversy two hundred years earlier and found himself deposed in turn. Philip sent Nogaret to Italy but took no public action until a papal envoy bearing letters of excommunication was caught at the kingdom's border and the king was forced onto the offensive.[11] If the excommunication became public, his vassals would be allowed to defy his lordship and his enemies could declare war with impunity. He suppressed the letters, jailed the envoy, and then summoned France's three Estates – the clergy, the nobility, and the townsmen – to assemblies for discussing the business of the kingdom.[12] That business was Boniface, and the situation was worse, far worse, than any loyal Frenchman could possibly have imagined.

The townsmen gathered in the palace gardens on 24 June, however, had not been so much invited to 'discuss' as to be told what to think. Nogaret's protégé and colleague Guillaume de Plaisians had already laid out the case against this perfidious pope to the kingdom's nobility and great clergy at an assembly ten days earlier. 'Boniface, who now occupies the Holy See,' he had told that crowd, 'will be found a perfect heretic according to the heresies, prodigious facts, and perverse doctrines hereafter mentioned.'[13] Twenty-eight allegations had followed, ranging from the spiritual – 'He does not believe in the immortality or incorruptibility of the rational soul' – to the sexual – 'He is a sodomite and keeps concubines' – to the satanic – 'He has a private demon whose advice he follows in all things.' But that was not all.

There were also accusations that Boniface had impugned the honour of France and Frenchmen. Boniface had 'not been ashamed to assert that he would rather be a dog, ass, or any other brute than a Frenchman'. Boniface had 'called the French, famously a most Christian people, heretics'. And Boniface had 'long harboured an aversion against the king of France, in hatred of the faith, because in France there is and ever was the splendour of the faith, the grand support and example of Christendom'. On 24 June this same (or similar) catalogue of infamy was recited in French before the masses assembled in Philip's garden. A prominent Parisian then rose to ask their endorsement of Philip's position against the pope. After what they had heard, how could they have done anything other than shout 'Yes! Yes! Yes!' (*Oïl! Oïl! Oïl!*)?[14]

As the summer of 1303 wore on, Philip's ministers continued to drum up support for the plan to send Boniface before a council of cardinals. Ministers were dispatched to visit monasteries. A great assembly of the clergy was called in Paris for July. And the three Estates were summoned to meetings in the capital cities of Languedoc. The towns naturally nominated representatives, but the nobles and the clergy were expected to come in person or Philip would know the reason why. One lord sent a proctor in his stead, explaining that he could not make the journey 'on account of the infirmity and the ponderosity of his body', an excuse that the Crown seems to have accepted.[15] But when the Abbot of Aurillac begged off because of a broken leg, the Crown's local *bailli* was sent to examine him for signs of malingering. Only once he had assured himself by 'frequent palpitation' of the broken leg and after consulting two doctors and a surgeon 'for greater certainty' was the poor man left in peace.[16]

Those who hesitated to support the king against the pope were subjected to pressure. The Dominican monks in Montpellier who asked to consult their superior before deciding were taken aside one by one for questioning and given three days to leave the kingdom when they proved obdurate.[17] Two of them later recanted, but many others, especially foreign-born clergy, chose to leave France rather than oppose Rome. The head of the Cistercians himself chose exile and honour (as he saw it) rather than bow to Philip's demands. Still, most people, whether for fear of Philip or otherwise, added their names to the long list of those calling for a council against Boniface. Over 100 towns and nearly 500 monasteries and convents sent individual letters of support. In standard language provided to them by the Crown's clerks, they praised Philip as 'the Church's pugilist' and demanded that a council be called to judge Boniface's 'many enormous and horrible crimes'.[18]

Letters like these were still arriving in September when Nogaret made his move. He had been in Italy since the spring, investigating avenues for action. The idea of a council was one thing, bringing Boniface before it quite another. But on 7 September, Nogaret was forced to act. News had reached him that Boniface was about to proclaim Philip excommunicated, exactly the scenario that Nogaret needed to avoid.[19] Luckily, Nogaret had local help to call upon in this emergency. The Colonna, an old patrician family from Palestrina near Rome, had an ongoing feud with Boniface's family, the Caetani. Since 1297, during Philip's first tussle with Boniface over clerical taxation, the Colonna had been seeking to draw France into the feud. After Boniface antagonized the relationship by removing two Colonna men from the cardinalate, they had sent messengers to Philip to warn him that Boniface was '"the son of perdition", in other words, Antichrist', and they had addressed letters to French archbishops and the University of Paris questioning Boniface's right to the pontificate.[20]

Boniface had asked the Colonna cardinals 'whether he was pope?' (*utrum sit papa?*) in a reprimanding letter.[21] This was meant as a rhetorical question. Of course, he was pope. But the Colonna seized the opportunity to interpret his words literally. They used the remark as proof of a conspiracy theory: Boniface did not believe that he really was pope because he had been elected after forcing his predecessor, Celestine V, to abdicate and then killed him for good measure. Celestine had been a man of humble origins and holy habits. After his death, he was canonized and even considered an angel on earth.[22]

While it was unknown for a pope to abdicate, Celestine had surely just preferred the simple life to papal pomp and politicking. Boniface *had* placed him under house arrest, but since Celestine was in his nineties his demise could hardly be considered premature or surprising. But for those disposed to mistrust the Caetani family in general or Boniface in particular these convenient circumstances only confirmed their strongly held suspicions. Celestine's alleged deposition and murder were numbered among the charges against Boniface read out at the assemblies, charges that Nogaret certainly had a hand in crafting based on the Colonna's claims. The Colonna were thus delighted to learn that Nogaret was making a move against the pope.

Before the sun rose on 7 September, Nogaret found himself riding at the head of some 300 men under the fleur-de-lys and alongside a brutal young scion of the Colonna family named Sciarra. Nogaret was on 'the business of Christ', as he later explained, and his expedition was destined for the hilltop town of Anagni some 70 kilometres southeast of Rome.[23] Anagni was the Caetani family seat, and Boniface used a palace there as his semi-official residence when he needed to escape Rome's summer heat. But Anagni's inhabitants had little love for him. They might even have been in on the plot that morning, for the town's gates were left open overnight.[24] When the army passed through them at dawn, the townspeople did little more than wipe the sleep from their eyes before joining the invaders. Crying 'Death to Pope Boniface!' and 'Long live the King of France!' – or so says a later chronicler – they followed Nogaret's lily-spangled banners to lay siege to the pope's palace.[25]

Boniface's household servants held off the attack with crossbows and stones long enough for the pope to ask terms from Sciarra. But the Colonna replied with the impossible demand that he resign the pontificate and hand himself over. The pope could only exclaim 'Oh my! This is a hard offer!'[26] When the truce expired without a deal later that afternoon, the attackers broke into the palace with fire and sword. Despoiling the palace and pillaging all the treasure they found in its ornately tiled and elegantly frescoed rooms, eventually they came upon Boniface. Abandoned by all but one of his retainers, he had nevertheless got himself up in his papal robes and tiara and was sitting there majestically enthroned with a cross and the keys of Saint Peter in his hands when the invaders burst in upon him.[27] (That, or he was found weeping miserably in despair; accounts differ.) Sciarra may not have slapped him – the source of that story is suspect – but his lackeys certainly handled him roughly.[28] Resigned to death, Boniface simply offered up his throat for the knife.

But now that they had the pope in their power, Nogaret and Sciarra disagreed about what to do with him. Nogaret probably meant to cart him back to France or at least hang on to him until the much-heralded council could convene. Sciarra, however, probably wanted to kill him. A rumour went around the town to that effect anyway. The townspeople refused to countenance such a stain upon Anagni's honour, let alone to run such a risk of excommunication and interdict. Only two days after helping Nogaret and Sciarra capture the pope, they changed sides and drove out the occupiers. According to Nogaret's later testimony, they even killed some of them and wounded others.[29]

Miraculously rescued, Boniface blessed the town's inhabitants with tears in his eyes, ate the bread and drank the wine its women brought him, and then he ran back to Rome as soon as he could find an armed guard to escort him. But if he thought he would feel safer in the city, he was wrong. He had naturally planned to undertake a 'great vendetta'.[30] Instead, he found himself moving from palace to palace, trembling with fear and wracked with sorrow. Rome was in a tumult, expecting new outbreaks of violence any day. Most of the powerful families were not on his side. He couldn't even leave to go elsewhere, for thieves and bandits stalked the roads. Everything was still up in the air at the end of September when the Bishop of Lincoln's man at the curia wrote to his master, 'God knows what will happen, but I don't.'[31]

What happened was that Boniface died suddenly on 11 October. He was seventy-three but had shown no signs of flagging until the 'outrage at Anagni'. Most people, then as now, thought it was the shock that killed him. One account claims he went mad and 'gnawed at his arms like a dog' in his final hours.[32] That story may not be true (though other chronicles tell the same tale), but the Anagni affair was atrocious enough without it. Philip professed himself appalled. Nogaret spent the next eight years excommunicated. Neither of them ever really felt completely at ease about the matter. But thanks to a stroke of luck, they got off lightly. Although Boniface's successor, Benedict XI, summoned Nogaret, Sciarra, and their followers to Rome to answer for their actions at the beginning of July 1304, the pope himself died little more than a week later. His successor, who took the name Clement V, offered Philip and his ministers a more pliable prospect.

A Gascon by birth and most recently Bishop of Bordeaux, Clement hesitated to subject himself to Rome's unhealthy climate and its unpredictable politics. He spent the nine years of his pontificate moving around southern France. The closest he got to Italy was Avignon. In this city on the Rhône, conveniently situated in the empire but just across the border from France, he decided to stay, as did all of his successors for the next seventy years. There was nothing terribly scandalous about this at the time. Slandering the Avignon papacy as a 'Babylonian Captivity' started as Protestant propaganda two centuries later.[33] 'Rome is where the pope is' (*ubi est papa, ibi est Roma*) was already a common adage. That Clement was French, as were all of the Avignon popes who followed him, and that Avignon was more convenient than Rome for the French did not necessarily mean that he was beholden to the French Crown.[34] But it helped. Although Clement tried to hold his own against Philip and his aggressive advisors, it was a losing battle, especially as Philip had lost what little affability he ever possessed.

Just two months before Clement's election, Philip's wife, Joan of Navarre-Champagne, had died after some months of illness. She was only thirty-two. An impressive if elusive woman, she once personally defended Champagne from invasion astride a warhorse and owned an extensive book collection, including a Castilian translation from Arabic of the Indian fables of Kalila and Dimna (Plates 18 and 19).[35] She left money and land in her will to found the Collège de Navarre at the University of Paris and chose a simple burial in a Franciscan church over interment at Saint-Denis. Philip could hardly imagine life without her. Joan had been his companion since the difficult days of his childhood, and she had rarely left his side in their twenty-one years of marriage. Philip had trusted her as much as he could trust anyone. He had named her sole regent in the event of his death because of his confidence in her 'noted faith, proven fidelity, and innate zeal' for the kingdom's welfare.[36]

It must have gnawed at his heart that their last years had been distant ones. He had publicly humiliated her during their tour of Languedoc in 1304 by making her return some silver vases from Carcassonne, a gift that he considered tantamount to a bribe.[37] She, in turn, had been appalled by the marriages he was contemplating for their sons, with women too closely related to them according to the Church's law and of questionable character besides.[38] Joan had to indicate her burial wishes in a secret letter, revealed to Philip only after her death. Philip was enraged by the affront – he had planned for their burial side by side – but so much was he affected by her passing that he is said to have considered abdication, hoping to escape his grief by going on crusade. Eventually, he resolved to remain in France as king, but he never married again, and in his solitude he sank into a morass of angry paranoia.[39] The realm knew much more peace in Joan's day, mourned a poet-chronicler, than it ever did afterward.[40] From this point onward, Philip's government, never a gentle one, truly became a reign of terror.

A rumour arose, as they so often did in Philip's France, that the queen's death had not been an accident. Bishop Guichard of Troyes had hated her, hadn't he? She had raised him from the dust of their native Champagne, then cast him down again. He had already been suspected of poisoning the queen's mother in 1302 after allegations of abetting a financial fraudster's escape to Italy. That case had been dropped when the accusers recanted, but Queen Joan had nevertheless collected 40,000 *livres tournois* from Guichard not long before her untimely end.[41] This time, Guichard had supposedly reserved the poison (made of scorpions, toads, and poisonous spiders) for Philip's son and heir Louis and his beloved brother Charles of Valois, both of whom luckily survived. The queen, however, he was said to have killed through magical means.

With the help of a demon, a witch, and a hermit, Guichard had made a waxen model, baptized it in her name, and pierced it all over with a pin. When that only made her ill, he trampled the figure underfoot and then threw it into the fire, this time to fatal effect, or so said the Crown's accusations against him. (Like those made against Boniface, these allegations were collated and read out before a public assembly in the palace gardens.)[42] After investigation and the interrogation of some 300-odd witnesses, the charges against Guichard grew to include not only murder and sorcery but also forgery, usury, sodomy, keeping a nun as a concubine, and even being the bastard son of an incubus with whom his mother committed adultery.[43]

Philip had Guichard imprisoned in the Louvre, and since clerics were exempt from lay justice, he demanded that Pope Clement try him for his crimes. Clement managed to stall long enough for the main accuser to be hanged after confessing to perjury, leaving the trial in disarray.[44] Guichard took refuge in Avignon, and his see was transferred to Djakovo in what was then Bosnia and is now Croatia.[45] Apparently, this was as unappealing as it sounds since he never took up the position and died still in France six years later. Guichard had a hard time of it but got off relatively unscathed in the end. Perhaps Philip – or Nogaret, whose hand is detectable in all of this – never really believed the charges against him, or perhaps this common-born dabbler in the demonic was just not worth the time. Others were not so lucky.

Those most unfortunate to fall foul of Philip were the Knights Templar. Founded after the First Crusade as a novel combination of knight and monk for the defence of the crusader states, the Templars had been the toast of Christendom for nearly two hundred years. Richly endowed with properties from pious donors devoted to the crusade, they also ran an international banking system on a scale unprecedented in Latin Europe. Their reputation had suffered with the fall of Acre, the last crusader city, in 1291, but they remained rich, powerful, admired, and deeply woven into the texture of elite Christian society. Yet even they could not stand against Philip.

In a coordinated raid on 13 October 1307 the king's agents burst into the Templars' hostels at dawn and arrested every single brother they found in France. Under torture so severe that many of them lost their reason and some even died of it, the imprisoned Templars confessed to a litany of crimes: they were heretics. They denied Christ. They spat on the crucifix. They peed on it. They trampled it underfoot. They worshipped idols, or maybe a cat. They were sodomites. And so on.[46] Proceedings were initiated against the order across Europe, though with far less violent zeal than in France.

Pope Clement doubted the charges and had to be intimidated into pursuing the investigation. Philip convoked more public assemblies in the palace gardens following the arrests and a year later at Tours, where 2,000 men gathered to hear royal propagandists incite public opinion against the Templars just as they had against Boniface VIII. This mob then followed the king to Poitiers, where Nogaret's protégé Plaisians personally harangued Clement about the sins of the Templars and warned him against impeding their punishment.[47] When the Templars' fate was at last decided at the Council of Vienne in 1311–12, Philip showed up outside the town with his sons and brothers accompanied by a menacing force of 'veteran nobles and magnates'.[48] The combined weight of the confessions, public opinion, and Philip's forces decided the matter. Two centuries after its foundation but only half a decade after Philip began its persecution, the Templar order was suppressed and disbanded. Its wealth was given to the Knights Hospitaller, another military order of even older vintage. Dozens of Templars went to the stake in Paris. and a few were burned in Capetian lands elsewhere. The order's surviving members passed the rest of their days in a monastery, if they were lucky, or in prison, if they were not.

The accusations against the Templars were certainly false. It was not a case of 'where there is smoke, there must be fire'. Although 'men may tell truth as well as lies under torture', only where torture was used were confessions extracted and only the mildest accusations of wrongdoing had any corroboration from other witnesses.[49] Whether Philip believed the wild claims his ministers ventilated with such vehemence is, of course, another matter. He was a suspicious and superstitious man, but also one with reasons to wish the Templars ill. Not least, he stood to gain financially by their demise. The Templars had been the Capetians' bankers since the mid-twelfth century, and the royal treasury was kept at the Temple in Paris. (Several streets and a Métro stop still bear its name today.) They also held deposits from many other people – as they had protested when Joinville raided their chests to raise Louis's ransom in Damietta – as well as their own considerable funds intended to underwrite their crusading activities. Philip may have thought he was going to be able to keep the Templar wealth his agents had confiscated at the time of their arrests, and when that assumption proved unfounded and the Hospitallers gained instead, Philip charged the Hospital 200,000 *livres tournois* in expenses.[50]

Always short of money, Philip was willing to do all sorts of things to get his hands on more. He had reduced the bullion content of his coins and pocketed the difference between their face value and their actual worth, introduced harsh new taxes, and taxed the clergy when he shouldn't have, and in 1306 he fell back on an old Capetian favourite, expelling the Jews and seizing their property, an expedient that may have netted him somewhere around 110,000 *livres tournois*.[51] But it probably wasn't money alone that motivated him to move against the Templars. Philip, remarked one historian, 'did not like to be dependent on bankers, especially bankers whom he did not control'.[52] In fact, Philip didn't like anything he couldn't control.

Seen in the context of his other persecutory projects, Philip's attack on the Templars looks like part of an orchestrated campaign to increase his own might, turning the pope's enforcement of orthodoxy into an instrument of Capetian power. Philip and his ministers had begun spreading rumours of the Templars 'ill repute' when they first met Pope Clement at Lyon in the autumn of 1305, but they increased the pressure in 1308, around the time that they first broached the subject of Guichard of Troyes's diabolical dealings against the queen.[53] That was also when they began pressing Clement to open an investigation into the late and unlamented Boniface's heresies.[54] (The point of trying the dead pope was that, if convicted, his corpse would be exhumed and burned at the stake, a most satisfying demonstration that Philip and Nogaret had been right all along.) The Templars' annihilation was just the most spectacular miscarriage of justice produced by this policy intended to demonstrate Philip's authority over matters spiritual as well as temporal. Their downfall, judges a recent historian of the affair, had 'nothing to do with the order. It had everything to do, by contrast, with the Capetian monarchy.'[55]

In Philip's mind, the Capetian monarchy embodied God's will on earth and he embodied the Capetian monarchy. He saw himself as 'divinely deputized' to carry out the celestial plan.[56] He could imagine no meaningful distinction between his own objectives and Christ's. Both sought the world's salvation, its purification of sin, and the punishment of sinners. As the most Christian king of the most Christian kingdom, Philip knew that he bore a unique right and duty to defend the faith against its many and varied enemies, to ferret them out wherever they might be hiding, and to cleanse the world of their filth by fire. The Church's job was to help him carry out the work, ideally at his direction.

His grandfather Louis had not thought much differently. Louis had considered himself especially responsible for the spiritual health of all Christendom. He had persecuted heretics and Jews, and he had clashed with popes when need be. His confessor had written of how the saintly king had even exercised 'a priestly rule or a royal priesthood', a sort of 'pious usurpation' (*pia usurpatione*) of the Church's spiritual prerogatives.[57] Philip's policies 'did not spring suddenly out of the heads of a few shyster lawyers'.[58] They continued – though also expanded – those of his grandfather before him. Louis, however, had been an easier man in an earlier age. He had (mostly) tortured himself, not other people, and he ran a government that was still very much personally directed. He did not operate the kind of administrative machinery that would have, for example, allowed him to execute simultaneous dawn raids in every corner of the kingdom against well-respected men trained for warfare. But Philip, enabled by his advisors' ambition and ingenuity, directed all his rage and sorrow outward. His France became the site of 'secret denunciations, prompted or received under the pretext of maintaining the purity and unity of the faith; arrests, torture, efforts to rouse popular anger against the accused, *autos-da-fé*, expulsions, spoliation', and his Paris one where 'all stories and all fights were ultimately about royal power'.[59] At least, that's what it looked like to his victims. And there were more of those all the time.

18.

A Family Affair
Philip IV

Everyone was having so much fun, or so claimed a chronicler who wrote his account of Philip's reign in rhyming verse. This part of the poem goes on for pages, describing how Paris's avenues were hung with banners of every colour and lit up night and day with thousands of candles paid for by rich citizens, how a fountain of wine, decorated with mermaids, leopards, lions, civet-cats, and other 'fabulous beasts', gushed freely for the inebriation of all, and how nobles changed their outfits three times a day, while wealthy burghers' wives sang and span in their finery and rowdy boys danced in their shirts.[1] Even for those without an invitation to one of the royal banquets or guild-hall feasts, there was food for the taking on open-air tables. And there were wonderful things to see everywhere you looked. Actors staged a miniature Heaven, where ninety angels and saved souls sang sweetly, while smoke billowed from a stinking Hell and a hundred or more demons tormented the damned. The Magi visited the Virgin. Herod slaughtered the Innocents. The Resurrection was re-enacted, and the Apocalypse came at last. The fabled Renard the Fox played doctor, and Hersent the She-Wolf spun wool. The craftsmen processed in their finery and the city watchmen in theirs. Small children fought a play-tournament. Nightingales and parrots sang. Trumpets sounded. Drums beat. Bells chimed. Paris could remember nothing like it.[2]

The party had begun on Pentecost, a moveable feast that fell on 3 June in that year of 1313. King Edward II and Queen Isabelle of England had arrived in the city just the day before, escorted to their lodgings at Saint-Germain-des-Prés by a procession of proud Parisians. King Philip's only living daughter, Queen Isabelle had come to see her three brothers knighted. Louis, the eldest at twenty-four and already King of Navarre since their mother's passing in 1305, was joined by his brothers Count Philip of Poitiers and Count Charles of la Marche, as well as their cousin Philip of Valois, son of King Philip's favourite brother Charles. No one would have guessed it that day, but all four men would be King of France in their turn. Two hundred other young men of eligible age and background joined them in their overnight vigil in Notre-Dame cathedral, where they kept prayerful watch before the ceremony of dubbing and belting that signalled their entry into elite Christian manhood the next day. Three days later, having thoroughly enjoyed themselves in the interim, they took the cross along with King Philip, King Edward, and an innumerable mass of enthusiastic others, who made a solemn vow to depart in no more than six years' time. Their wives promised the same the next day in the Sainte-Chapelle, though Queen Isabelle overslept and missed the ceremony. She and Edward, said a chronicler, may have been having a little too much fun.[3]

The party had been planned for most of a year. Philip's half-brother Louis of Évreux seems to have thought it up while he was in England to help reconcile Edward and the Scots.[4] The eight days of festivities were meant to impress the English ruler, and they certainly did so. Watching the processions from windows above the streets, Edward and the other English barons had been bowled over. They could scarcely believe that a single city could put on such a show.[5] But there was also serious business to be done while Edward was in France. Once the public festivities ended, the three kings – Edward of England, Philip of France, and young Louis of Navarre – made their way to Pontoise, the old Capetian palace some 30 kilometres northwest of Paris. There they talked about England's problems with the Scots and France's problems with the Flemings. Philip and Louis were already planning to invade Flanders at the end of July, and Edward promised to harry the Flemish coastline on their behalf. Only a promise of better behaviour from the Flemings – not kept, sniffed a chronicler – put the attack on hold.[6]

Not that Pontoise was all work and no fun. On 19 June, Edward was entertained by fifty-four naked dancers led by a minstrel named Bernard the Fool, an exotic treat – Bernard and his dancers were French – that cost him only a few gold florins and silver pennies.[7] It's hard to imagine that puritanical Philip witnessed the show, and that we know about it only from an English account-book entry suggests that he was not meant to. No hypocrite, despite his many other failings, Philip applied his stern morality to his own life as strictly as he did to others. Celibate since the death of his wife eight years earlier, Philip continued the Capetian tradition of chastity unbroken since the reign of his great-grandfather Louis VIII a century before. It's surprising that he had let the Pentecost party happen at all. The only nod to his austerity was the replacement of a proper tournament – a pastime that Philip had repeatedly outlawed as violent and wasteful – with a play version fought between little children.[8] Probably the fact that other people paid for most of the festivities, and that the knighting ceremony allowed him to collect taxes from his people and the crusade vow to access a 10 per cent levy on clerical revenues, convinced him it was worth his while to impress Edward and celebrate Louis in such flamboyant fashion.[9]

Philip knew that Louis did not follow in his footsteps. He had often reprimanded his son for being 'wasteful and exceedingly childish'.[10] On his deathbed he would beg him not to behave 'like an entertainer or an actor, but like the son of a king'.[11] Maybe Philip also suspected that Louis's sexual morality deviated from chaste Capetian precedent. A daughter, born to Louis's married mistress in 1315 or 1316, would be the first known bastard sired by a Capetian king since Philip Augustus's affair with the mysterious lady of Arras at the beginning of the previous century.[12] What Philip the Fair knew or suspected about his son-in-law Edward II's sexual proclivities is less clear, surprisingly so given Philip's suspicious nature. But maybe he was just so pleased to have a pliable young man take the place of iron-willed Edward I that he turned a blind eye. Or maybe, as some historians think, what Philip knew depended entirely on what his ministers wanted him to know.[13] Nefarious Nogaret had died a few months before Edward's visit, but the king's chamberlain, Enguerran de Marigny, had replaced him at Philip's side. Called a 'second little king' in one chronicle, red-headed Enguerran had wits as foxy as his hair and financial interests in England besides.[14] Perhaps he and his helpers found Edward too useful for their own purposes to let stray whispers reach the king's ear. For if Philip was ignorant, wilfully or otherwise, of Edward's particular predilections, in many circles the English king's behaviour was already causing considerable consternation.

Edward had recently had a child with Isabelle and, like his brother-in-law Louis, he also later produced a bastard with an illicit liaison – there is no doubt that Edward II had sex, and enjoyed sex, with women – but he also had sex with men, too. Only a year before his French visit, Edward's devotion to his childhood companion, a Gascon named Piers Gaveston, had incited a baronial rebellion in England. In July 1312, on the very day that the salacious dancing would take place at Pontoise a year later, the Earl of Warwick had ordered Piers run through and decapitated. Piers's sins had included amassing treasure at the kingdom's expense, including the rubies, emeralds, pearls, and sapphires discovered on him at the time of his arrest, and behaving in a high-handed way toward his more nobly born betters.[15] But it was also how he monopolized Edward's attention that irked the English barons. Edward had eyes for no one else. It was said that he loved Piers with a love beyond the kind that men have for women, a love like that of Achilles for Patroclus, but more so. 'I do not remember having heard that one man so loved another,' worried a chronicler, who added that even Achilles and Patroclus had not done anything 'beyond what was usual'.[16] So immoderate was the obsession that Piers kindled in Edward, it made people think of sorcery.

Accusations of sorcery and sodomy against a political enemy went together like hand in glove in the fourteenth century, as Bishop Guichard of Troyes and Pope Boniface VIII could well have testified, so some historians have argued that the rumours of homosexuality were fabricated for political purposes.[17] That seems unlikely to me, given the extent of the evidence, but it is certainly true that Edward had enemies and that his subjects considered him a bad king and a strange man, aside from any thoughts they might have had about his sexuality.[18] He didn't hunt. He went swimming. He enjoyed peasant pursuits like hedging and ditching. He liked cart racing. He hung out with low lifes: 'Shunning the company of nobles,' recounted a later chronicler, 'he sought the society of jesters, singers, actors, carriage-drivers, diggers, oarsmen, sailors and the practitioners of other kinds of mechanical arts.'[19] The naked Pontoise dancers must have fitted right in.

But Edward's wife, Isabelle, seems at this juncture to have been no more perturbed by him than Philip was. To the contrary. Seventeen years old, a woman who inherited her famous beauty from her fair father, Isabelle had been delivered of her first child, a boy named Edward after her husband, the previous November. She had been married to seal the peace between England and France after the Gascon war of 1294–7, the wedding having taken place with great fanfare and no little expense in 1308. Despite the brouhaha over Piers among Edward's barons – and indeed some concern among Isabelle's relatives at the time of wedding – her marriage seems to have been so far untroubled and her queenship well established.[20] When a fire broke out in their chambers at Pontoise, Edward had had no thought but for her safety and heroically carried her out of the burning building. There was as yet no indication that the marriage would fail spectacularly or that Isabelle was the kind of woman who might flaunt an extramarital affair, depose her husband in partnership with her lover, and then arrange to have him murdered. During her father's lifetime anyway, Isabelle was the very model of Capetian chastity. So much so that when she uncovered adultery at the heart of the French kingdom, she went straight to her father with the evidence.

The sad and sordid story began when Isabelle came back to France by herself in March 1314, arriving just a few days after Philip ordered the last of his Templar victims burnt on an island in the Seine.[21] Her husband's Gascon subjects had cases pending in the Parlement that would benefit from a welcome word in Philip's ear. As always, Philip was delighted to see his only daughter. He gave her everything she asked for and entertained her *en famille* in the palace that his minister Enguerran de Marigny had recently renovated. Isabelle had a royal's taste for the rare and exotic – while she was there, she bought a wall hanging embroidered with baboons[22] – but she also had her father's eye for the suspicious and the strange. Isabelle, said the rhyming chronicler, 'revealed many things to the royals that turned out to be true'.[23] As even cautious historians have concluded, the infidelity of her two sisters-in-law must have numbered among these revelations.

Isabelle's suspicions were supposedly aroused by the fate of two preciously decorated purses that she had given to the wives of her oldest and youngest brothers the previous year.[24] For some reason, a pair of household knights now carried them. Why she assumed the re-gifted purses were lovers' favours and evidence of clandestine affairs that threatened her lineage's legitimacy is unknown. Or perhaps this detail – which has become so famous as to be assumed factual despite its appearance in only one, very unreliable source – is just a later chronicler's imaginative embellishment. Maybe it was instead palace gossip that came to Isabelle's ears. Later events make it seem that Enguerran de Marigny might have passed on a rumour. Or maybe it was some other, incongruent element that caught Isabelle's eye. The rhyming chronicler, writing much nearer to the time, simply said that 'there is no fire without smoke', meaning the ladies and their lovers had left clues, though of what kind, he failed to specify.[25]

Whatever it was that drew Isabelle's attention, she moved carefully and discreetly when bringing it to Philip's notice. Her household accounts for April 1314 record payments to 'various boys carrying torches' who accompanied her on several night-time visits from her lodgings to the palace where she spoke to her father in private.[26] Isabelle probably had no motivation other than morality for reporting the scandal. The advantages that eventually accrued to her and her son could not have been foreseen at the time and were minimal in any case. One wonders if she harboured regrets. Had she imagined what Philip would do? Would she still have mentioned it to him had she known? That she was near, but not too near, when he took action suggests that she feared how horrible the consequences would be.

It was not long after Isabelle left Paris for pilgrimage sites near Pontoise that Philip's agents burst into the nearby nunnery of Maubuisson, a place that served as something of a high-class hotel for noble ladies, and arrested Louis's wife, Marguerite, and Charles's wife, Blanche. These women were of great lineages. Marguerite's father was the Duke of Burgundy and her mother was Saint Louis's daughter. Blanche's father was the Count of Burgundy. (Today called Franche-Comté, the county of Burgundy was distinct from the duchy of the same name.) Her mother was Countess Mahaut of Artois, granddaughter of Saint Louis's reckless brother Robert. But their proud parentage did not protect them. Philip had their heads shaved for shame and their royal robes exchanged for 'vile rags'.[27] Then he shipped the two young women down the Seine to Château Gaillard, the giant castle in Normandy built by Richard Lionheart to taunt Philip Augustus an age before. Blanche protested her innocence and never ceased doing so, but Marguerite confessed her guilt over and over with screams and sobs. Probably she lost her mind, and soon she lost her life, dying – perhaps of misery, perhaps of murder – little more than a year later. There was no adulterous accusation against Isabelle's third sister-in-law, young Philip of Poitiers's wife Joan, who was Blanche's sister and heiress to the county of Burgundy. But she, too, found herself imprisoned at the king's orders. The charge against her was unspecified. Perhaps it was thought that she had helped Marguerite and Blanche cover up their crimes.

The royal ladies got off more lightly, much more lightly, than their alleged lovers. They, a pair of brothers named Philippe and Gautier d'Aulnay, were from a minor noble family of the Paris region favoured by King Philip's beloved brother Charles of Valois.[28] Most likely in their thirties, the Aulnay brothers were considerably older than either of the women they were supposed to have slept with, though some suspected Marguerite of initiating the depraved affair. King Philip had the two men seized at Pontoise on the same day that he ordered his daughters-in-law arrested. Then he probably had them tortured, as was done to their suspected helpers, some of whom were boiled alive.[29] The Aulnays held out for three days, and then they confessed. Philip's victims almost always did. According to the rhyming chronicle, Philip made their father announce the sentences against them.[30] His boys were to be skinned alive, castrated (penis and testes both), and decapitated. Their headless bodies were then to be dragged to the gallows, where they would be hung up by their shoulders with their heads displayed on pikes beside them. How they must have screamed, first in terror and then in agony, as the sentence was carried out immediately and publicly in the centre of Pontoise. Their genitals were thrown to the dogs; their corpses became carrion for the crows. Philip, it seems, stayed to watch.[31]

The scandal is now known as the Tour de Nesle affair, after the tower in Paris where the secret trysts supposedly took place. (Long ago demolished, it formed part of Philip Augustus's wall on the Left Bank, facing the Louvre across the Seine.) A play of that name by Alexandre Dumas, author of *The Three Musketeers* and other swashbuckling historical fictions, introduced Marguerite to nineteenth-century audiences as a murderous sex addict who had her lovers assassinated and their bodies thrown into the Seine on a nightly basis. The legend only grew in the twentieth century with Maurice Druon's seven-volume series *The Cursed Kings* (*Les Rois Maudits*). Translated into English and twice adapted for French television, the first book recounts the adultery scandal in lurid and much embroidered detail, though Druon had the Aulnay brothers executed a little more mercifully than Philip did. He, at least, had them knocked unconscious before the knives came out. Modestly, he spared their manhoods, too.

That the story lived on might not have displeased Philip. He seems to have wanted people to know. He could have hushed up the affair, but instead he gave it maximum publicity. He tasked Isabelle with spreading the news via letters to the good and the great among their relatives and other rulers. He also ensured that word got out quickly among the common people by staging the Aulnay brothers' arrests and spectacular executions at Pontoise, where he had been holding a session of Parlement attended by Parisian townsmen.[32] The good citizens had surely numbered among the crowd summoned to witness the Aulnays' gruesome end and could be relied upon to recount what they saw. The only explanation for Philip's willingness to publicize the scandal must be his moral fanaticism, the pig-headed pursuit of purity that drove him again and again to hound his real and imagined enemies to their literal deaths. He gained no advantage from airing his family's very dirty laundry in public like this. To the contrary, it made him and his sons look like men who couldn't govern a household, let alone a kingdom, and it cast doubt on the legitimacy of his lineage.

By the time the Aulnay brothers met their maker, Philip's daughters-in-law had given him a handful of grandchildren. His eldest son Louis's wife, Marguerite, had produced a girl, Joan of France and Navarre, in 1312. The wife of the middle son, Philip, also named Joan, had had several daughters before the scandal and gave birth to another baby around the time it broke.[33] Perhaps due to the stress that she was under, the child died soon after. Blanche, the wife of Philip's youngest son, Charles, was only seventeen at the time of the arrests but had already had at least one and perhaps as many as four children, none of whom survived childhood. She gave birth again about a year into her imprisonment, probably to a boy, but no one at the time or since has been sure who the father was or what happened to the child later in life.[34] Was it fathered by a servant?, wondered a chronicler; or maybe by her husband, who never really believed the charges against her?[35] Of these children, Louis and Marguerite's daughter Joan would have had the best claim to the throne should her father predecease her, as he eventually did. Or she would have had the best claim, were it not for the scandal's stain on her parentage. One chronicler accused the Aulnay brothers outright of impregnating their royal paramours.[36] Others merely implied as much by reporting the relationships had lasted two and half years or three years.[37] Long enough, that is, to make people wonder who fathered Marguerite's and Blanche's children.

Of course, Philip might well have felt secure enough about the succession in 1314 not to worry about the consequences for the next generation. After all, he had three adult sons. This was a wealth of heirs for a Capetian. The line had never needed more than one living male per generation. Each king had produced a son to take up his throne and produce a son in turn. The evidence of this unbroken line of succession marched around the Great Room (*Grand' Salle*) of the palace where gilded statues depicting each of the kings of France stood in majesty above pillars on the wall.[38] That Philip's sons were all to die without male heirs of their own over the next fourteen years was an unimaginable possibility. Except that it fulfilled a prophecy that Philip laboured under his whole life and a new curse that had just been laid against him.

Philip had done his best to suppress the old story spun in the dynasty's earliest days that the Crown of France would return to the Carolingian line after seven generations. The infusion of Carolingian blood that his great-great-grandmother Elizabeth of Hainaut had bequeathed to Louis VIII had helped to explain the dynasty's continuation to the eighth generation and beyond in the thirteenth century, and Philip's sainted grandfather Louis IX had viewed the Capetians' continued rule as a bracing incitement to moral rectitude lest God remove his favour from their family. Philip, however, wanted the whole thing forgotten. He preferred a version of the story that cast the Capetians not as the Carolingians' replacement but as their continuators. He had his chroniclers write that the dynasty's founder Hugh Capet had Carolingian blood through his mother. He had his artists inscribe Saint Louis's reliquary with the names of *all* the French and Frankish kings, not just the Capetian ones. And he had the tombs at Saint-Denis rearranged to mix the Capetians with the Carolingians, as if they were a single lineage.[39]

Yet the story had staying power. When Philip had the Bishop of

Pamiers arrested for fomenting rebellion a decade earlier, fanning the flames of his fatal conflict with Boniface VIII, one of the charges laid against the bishop was that he said Philip was not of the 'true lineage of French kings'.[40] Worse, the bishop had claimed – and many witnesses confirmed this – that Saint Louis himself had predicted the dynasty's end would come during Philip's time, when the king strayed from the path of righteousness. For the Capetians' enemies, a group that grew daily larger, the proof of this prediction was everywhere to be seen. The dynasty's original sin of usurpation was compounded by the more recent offences that Philip's agents committed against Boniface and those that his taxes and monetary manipulations visited upon his people. Chroniclers from Normandy to Italy would point to the Tour de Nesle scandal as proof of how deep the rot already went.[41] And then there was Philip's treatment of the Templars.

Just weeks before the Tour de Nesle scandal was revealed, Philip had two of the last Templars in his custody burned on a small island in the Seine. One of these men, aged and infirm after many years imprisonment, was the Grand Master of the Temple himself, Jacques de Molay. He had previously confessed to the charges laid against him but then recanted at the last minute and protested his innocence. As soon as the news reached Philip's ears, he had ordered the old man executed and his bones ground to dust. He allowed no time for an inquisitorial trial to be convened. Due process be damned; Philip wanted de Molay wiped from existence without delay. The old Templar had suffered so much already as to be sanguine in the face of death. As he was led to the stake, he commended himself to the Virgin and predicted that God would soon avenge the Templars against their wrongful persecutors.[42] Some years later, the story became more specific and more menacing: de Molay had cursed Pope Clement and Philip both on the pyre. He had promised he would see them answer for their sins before God's tribunal within the year.[43] This prophecy came true, as all *post hoc* predictions do. Clement died the next month, and Philip did not live to see Christmas.

What happened to cut Philip's life short at only forty-six is unclear.[44] It seems that some misadventure befell him while he was out hunting in the old forests north of Paris early in November 1314. Some accounts claim he was thrown – 'trebucheted' says the rhyming chronicle – from his horse.[45] Many chroniclers laid the fall at the feet of a wild boar, as did Dante, who blamed 'a blow of the boar's hide', perhaps recalling the misadventure of Philip's long-ago princely namesake with the diabolic pig careening through Paris.[46] But a Majorcan diplomat, who talked to members of the king's household immediately afterward, said Philip hadn't been thrown at all. Rather, during the hunt his 'heart was suddenly overwhelmed', robbing him of speech for a long time.[47] A chronicler at Saint-Denis said that he was seized with a stomach flux, loss of appetite, and an insatiable thirst.[48] Later there were rumours of poison. Today, we might diagnose a heart attack, but although his doctors took Philip's pulse and examined his urine (by smell and taste, as well as colour), they professed themselves confounded as to the ailment's cause.[49]

Philip, impatient with himself as well as others, refused to be invalided. He left his hunting lodge and travelled by boat to Poissy, the site of Saint Louis's birth where Philip had recently founded a nunnery. He stayed at Poissy for ten days, hoping to be healed by the saint's curative powers and the nuns' prayers. Having regained some strength there, he then rode south to Essonne on horseback, a journey of some 60 kilometres. It was too much for him. He had to be carried by litter from Essonne to his birthplace at Fontainebleau, where he succumbed on 29 November.[50] Released from earthly cares, Philip went at last to see what treasure, if any, he had stored up in Heaven.

Released from Philip, the kingdom's subjects, too, had treasure in mind, specifically that which the Crown had taken from them over the past year. In the final months of Philip's reign, assemblies had been meeting in Burgundy and Champagne to protest against the taxes that the Crown had levied for yet another Flemish invasion which failed to materialize.[51] In his previously planned but ultimately aborted effort to punish Flanders for its failure to implement the Treaty of Athis (1305) in 1313, Philip had returned the money collected after he called off the expedition. But this time the taxes had not been returned. The discontent spread with speed to other parts of the kingdom. From Vermandois to Languedoc, Philip's furious subjects were putting together petitions and forming leagues to voice their grievances. The rhyming chronicle claims some noblemen had even come to confront the king on his sickbed at Poissy.[52] In one of his last acts, Philip had promised them a hearing, but he'd also reasserted his right to levy those taxes.[53] And it was that kind of unapologetically arrogant attitude that inflamed the rebellion brewing across France as Philip took his final breaths.

The leagues decided that they wanted more than their money back. They also wanted a return not just to what they imagined as the lower taxation of Philip's predecessors, but also to their allegedly looser style of government. Nobles, among them the now nonagenarian Jean de Joinville, had spearheaded the movement, and they had particular grievances on this score. They fought, they claimed, not only for themselves but also for the 'freedom of the fatherland' (*patriae libertate*).[54] Philip's famous ancestors, they believed, had not run roughshod over the regional customs and local interests that Philip's agents so brutally disregarded. Philip Augustus and Blanche of Castile, let alone sainted Louis himself, would never have allowed them to be 'unduly oppressed and molested in violation of their ancient and approved freedoms, privileges, usages, and customs' by upstart officers the way Philip did.[55] Up until now, they had been left in peace to govern their lands as they saw fit. Or so they claimed. Apparently, these noble lords no longer sang their ancestors' caustic songs against Saint Louis's infringements of their liberties. Nor did they realize just how many of Philip's innovations were simply extensions of his predecessors' inventions. But they were right about one thing: Philip had overreached. Seeking to perfect his predecessors' legacy, he had carried his house to the edge of destruction.

PART SIX

Cursed Kings

(1314–1328)

Simplified Capetian family tree

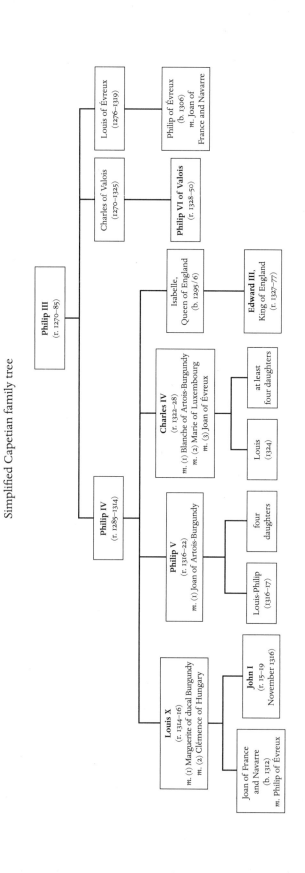

19.

Bad Omens

Louis X

On 1 December 1314, Philip the Fair's lifeless body was loaded on a boat and shipped down the Seine from Fontainebleau to Paris. Wrapped in cloth of gold and covered with an ermine-lined cloak, a five-foot-long gilded sceptre in its right hand and a gorgeous crown gracing its brow, the corpse was carried with great solemnity to Notre-Dame, where it lay in state overnight. After Mass the next morning, 400 Parisians bearing torches joined the cortege led by Philip's black-clad sons and brothers, winding its way north through the city along the road to Saint-Denis. There among his ancestors, Philip was laid to rest to the left of Saint Louis's grave, with few but his immediate family looking on. His heart and entrails, removed when the body was prepared for burial, were taken for separate burial at Poissy, where Saint Louis had been born and where Philip's little son Robert had been buried in 1308. A Majorcan diplomat, to whose correspondence we owe most of these details, reported that his heart was said to be as small as that of a bird or a newborn child.[1]

Walking beside the bier with his face hidden in the folds of a black cowl pulled up over his head, the new king, Louis X, cannot have helped but remember his father's last words to him. In his dying days at Fontainebleau, Philip had summoned his three sons, blessed them, and given special instructions to Louis, his heir. Under pain of 'every curse a father might lay on a son', he had commanded him to love God, to protect the Church, and to reign for God's glory and his subjects' benefit, 'just as blessed Louis, his grandfather, had done'.[2] Lamenting his own greed, he had advised Louis to renounce avarice, not to listen to bad counsellors, and to carry out the crusading vow they had taken together two years earlier. Growing more personal, he had begged his son to leave aside his dissolute companions, to dress properly, behave maturely, and to listen to his uncles' advice. He had evoked Louis's future coronation at Reims and then given him the secret instructions for healing the sick with his royal touch. This Louis must do with reverence and with hands free from sin. "'Think, Louis!'" Philip had implored his son, "think what it is to be king of the French!"'[3]

To judge by his actions in the wake of his father's death, Louis did think about it. In fact, he wondered whether he was up to the task. He procrastinated taking up the formal signs of kingship. He did not have a new royal seal made with his image to certify his acts until the following May, nor did he make any arrangements for his coronation. This delay, much remarked on by the chroniclers, also confused the Majorcan diplomat. He had thought the coronation might take place at Epiphany on 6 January but then wrote that he had heard it had been delayed 'for a reason' (*ex causa*), which he was unable or unwilling to specify.[4] In the end, Louis did not go to Reims until August 1315, nine months after his father's death. It was not only the diplomat who was puzzled by this behaviour. Without the ceremony of coronation, was Louis even king? The diplomat thought so; he spoke of Louis as reigning from the time of his father's funeral. But others – allegedly including a demon who discussed this with the royal minister Enguerran de Marigny – felt that in the interim, France had no king. 'Until he has the crown,' the demon said, 'no one will call him king of France.'[5]

Only twenty-five when he had kingship thrust upon him, Louis had surely expected his middle-aged father to live on for at least another decade. True, Louis had had a kingdom of his own, Navarre, to practise with for almost a decade.[6] (It was his Navarrese seal that he used until finally having the new French one made.) But that modest realm was nothing like the vast and varied expanse of France, nor was its Crown imbued with the moral and miraculous expectations incumbent on a French Capetian. Philip's deathbed advice had emphasized the importance of moral rectitude and personal purity. But Louis was tainted, tainted by the sins of his wife, the wretched Queen Marguerite.[7] Louis's sister-in-law Joan, wife of his brother Philip of Poitiers, was cleared of the lesser charges against her in December, but Marguerite, like the other sister-in-law Blanche, remained imprisoned in Château Gaillard for her alleged adultery. Marguerite's sin stained Louis by association, and it also stained their two-year-old daughter Joan, at present Louis's only heir.

Louis's marital situation was his first order of business. Little more than a week after his father's funeral, he dispatched an embassy to sue for the hand of the titular King of Hungary's daughter Clémence. Already twenty-two and the orphaned child of a man who never managed to rule, Clémence was probably not the most precious prize on the medieval marriage market, but she was from the lineage of Saint Louis on her father's side and a Hapsburg on her mother's.[8] And anyway, the still-married Louis was in no position to be picky. Quite how he hoped to resolve the matter of Marguerite is unclear. The fourteenth-century Church did not consider adultery sufficient grounds for an annulment. Other reasons might be found, but the pope's blessing would be required to dissolve the marriage. Unfortunately for Louis, the papal see had been vacant since Clement V's death that spring, and the cardinals showed no sign of agreeing on a successor. The only way out of his conjugal conundrum would be if Marguerite were to die, a prospect that seemed unlikely without outside intervention. And yet, Marguerite did die the next April, a scant six months after Louis's accession. Maybe she was murdered – strangled with a towel, claims a chronicler – or maybe the rigours of Château Gaillard were too much for her delicate constitution.[9] Certainly, it was a lucky break for Louis.

Just before her death, Marguerite had sent her confessor to Louis with a secret letter. No one but the king was allowed to look at it, and no one but he ever knew what was in it.[10] But much like the mysterious box that held secrets damning Philip III's minister Pierre de la Broce to death, Marguerite's letter told Louis something about his father's old official, Enguerran de Marigny, too terrible to tolerate. At the time that Louis received the letter, Marigny was already

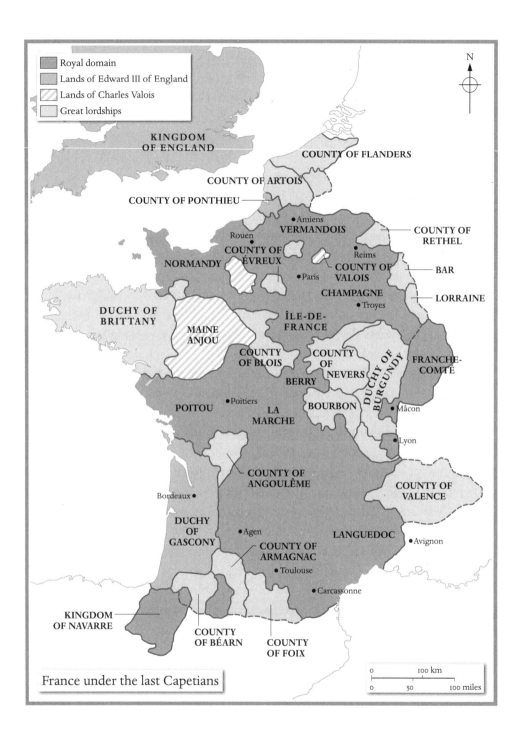

Legend:
- Royal domain
- Lands of Edward III of England
- Lands of Charles Valois
- Great lordships

N

KINGDOM
OF ENGLAND

COUNTY OF FLANDERS

COUNTY OF ARTOIS

COUNTY OF PONTHIEU

• Amiens
VERMANDOIS

Rouen •

COUNTY OF RETHEL

COUNTY OF
ÉVREUX

• Reims

NORMANDY

• Paris

COUNTY OF
VALOIS

BAR

LORRAINE

CHAMPAGNE

• Troyes

DUCHY OF
BRITTANY

MAINE
ANJOU

ÎLE-DE-
FRANCE

COUNTY
OF BLOIS

COUNTY
OF
NEVERS

DUCHY OF BURGUNDY

FRANCHE-
COMTÉ

BERRY

POITOU

• Poitiers

LA
MARCHE

BOURBON

• Mâcon

• Lyon

COUNTY OF
ANGOULÊME

Bordeaux •

COUNTY OF
VALENCE

DUCHY
OF
GASCONY

• Agen

COUNTY OF
ARMAGNAC

LANGUEDOC

• Avignon

• Toulouse

KINGDOM
OF NAVARRE

COUNTY
OF BÉARN

COUNTY
OF FOIX

• Carcassonne

France under the last Capetians

0   100 km

0   50   100 miles

in a heap of trouble. The king's influential uncle Charles of Valois had long hated Marigny, as did the people of Paris and the provincial leagues still angry over the taxes levied for Flanders. But while Philip IV lived, no one had been allowed to breathe a word against him. At Philip's side even on his deathbed, Marigny had begged the dying king to recommend him to Louis. Philip had done so but to little effect. Suspected of embezzlement and of treasonous dealings in Flanders, Marigny had been ordered not to leave court until he submitted his accounts to the Crown and not to touch the royal treasury.[11]

When Louis sat down with his ministers to look at the books after Philip's death, he'd learned that his coffers were empty and his cupboards bare. 'Where are the taxes collected in the time of my father?' Louis demanded to know. 'Where are the profits from changing the currency so often?'[12] Marigny was probably not (much) to blame, but Louis's uncle Charles of Valois thought he was.[13] At a meeting of the royal council in March 1315, Marigny had patiently explained that he had done what he had done at old King Philip's request. Charles had shouted, 'You lie!', Marigny had replied 'No, you lie!', and Charles had launched himself at Marigny.[14] Although prevented from murdering the man on the spot, as people feared he might do, Charles swore never to return to the council if Marigny was going to be there, too. The inexperienced young king may not have wholly believed that his father's trusted counsellor was the treacherous thief that Charles made him out to be, but he had promised his father to listen to Charles in all things. In the second week of March, he ordered Marigny arrested and imprisoned.

Marigny and his family did everything they could to save him. Prohibited from answering the charges or even receiving a copy of them, he offered to prove his innocence by judicial duel. That request was refused. His wife tried more nefarious means, dedicating waxen images to a demon in order to kill Louis and Charles of Valois. She was discovered and imprisoned, and the sorceress who helped her was burned. Marigny's brothers, both bishops, begged Louis simply to banish Enguerran to an island in the eastern Mediterranean. But in the end, Charles of Valois got his way. Marguerite's letter, which 'greatly aggravated the case against Enguerran', may have swayed Louis toward his uncle's opinion, though the demonic activities alleged against Marigny's wife helped, too. In a pattern all too familiar in fourteenth-century France, secrets and sorcery were marshalled against the accused to fatal effect.[15]

On 30 April, perhaps the very day of Queen Marguerite's death, a cart carried Marigny to the gallows. The poor of Paris hurled abuse at him as he passed. They blamed him for the high taxes and monetary manipulations that had driven them to the brink of starvation. They remembered, too, how an uprising against those measures had been brutally suppressed, the bodies of its executed leaders left exposed at the city gates as a warning to others.[16] Now what had happened to them was happening to him. The people cheered as the noose tightened around Marigny's neck and his feet kicked frantically in the air for a moment or two before he went limp and life left him. His corpse, clad in costly multi-coloured clothing prohibited to most people, was left to rot on the gibbet. When thieves came and stripped those clothes from his body, leaving it lying naked on the ground, a cheap poncho (*cloche*) was made and the body hung back up again.[17] It stayed exposed there for two years, far longer than was customary.[18] If the display was intended as an edifying example, many must have found Marigny's rotting body, eventually only recognizable by the wisps of bright red hair still clinging to its skull, a satisfying sight.

Perhaps Louis was among them, for with the double demise of Marigny and Marguerite he had stepped out of the shadow of two of the most offensive figures from his father's reign and seems finally to have gained confidence in his kingship. He wanted a fresh start, not just for himself, but for his dynasty, which he knew had veered from the right path ever since the death of Saint Louis. Louis now renewed his crusading vow, had more of his father's bad counsellors seized and tortured, and reconfirmed his namesake's *Grande Ordonnance*. Striking out on his own, he repealed the Jews' expulsion for a period of twelve years, and he freed all the remaining serfs in the royal domain. These measures brought Louis considerable profits – he charged the serfs for their freedom and the Jews paid him a lump sum of 25,000 *livres* plus 10,000 *livres* per year – but these were not just pecuniary ploys.[19] Louis, who said he modelled his Jewish policy after Saint Louis's, still required Jews to wear a badge – a piece of cloth shaped like a coin – and he forbade the Talmud, but he did allow them their other books and to repurchase the synagogues sold before departure.[20] The serfdom decree, too, expresses laudable sentiments, observing that 'according to natural law everyone ought to be born free *(franc)*', especially in France, which is called 'the kingdom of the *Francs*'.[21]

As a sign of this new beginning, Louis at last had a great royal seal designed that named him King of France, as well as Navarre, one that communicated the 'advent of our new government' *(la venüe de nostre nouvel gouvernment)*, and he used this seal for the first time on documents meant to resolve the dispute with the regional leagues that had been at a stand-off since his father's death the previous November (Plate 20).[22] The Majorcan diplomat had reported that few nobles and barons had attended Philip's burial. Perhaps they were dissuaded by news of the threats of violence that Louis had made against the leagues of Champagne who wanted their taxes refunded in Philip's dying days.[23] In the ensuing months, querulous complaints had continued to be made by the leagues and half-soothing, half-aggravating answers offered by the Crown. This acrimony could not continue. A medieval king could not rule without the cooperation of his subjects, particularly his nobles. It was they who staffed his army and his administration, and they who governed the patchwork of lordships that made up the political and legal geography of a medieval kingdom.[24] Louis had to have the barons back onside. He ordered his agents to investigate their claims and promised to discontinue 'any novelty made during the time of our lord father'.[25] On 17 May they accepted the Crown's promises to respect their rights and turned over their acts of confederation to Charles of Valois. In the remaining year of his short life, Louis would grant charter after charter recognizing the leagues' local customs and special privileges. They never did get their money back, though.

Another thorny problem that Louis settled in May 1315 was his search for a wife worthy of the name. The negotiations for Clémence of Hungary were brought to a successful conclusion, and she took ship for France on 1 June. If any grand plans were made for the royal wedding, they were probably scuttled when the unfortunate bride was delayed by shipwreck off Italy, escaping with her life but losing 'all her best and most beautiful jewels' at sea.[26] After she finally made landfall at Marseille, Louis met her on the road in Champagne and married her in an almost scandalously simple ceremony at a country house outside Troyes on 31 July. The rhyming chronicle reports that there wasn't even any dancing.[27] The dress that Clémence planned to wear on her wedding day, perhaps similar to the gowns of violet and vermilion velvet that she favoured later in life, had probably gone down with her ship, but she did at least have a little pearl-embroidered purse to carry.[28] She long cherished it as a reminder of the day, even if it had not been the grand occasion she might have expected. Perhaps it was a present from her otherwise inattentive groom.

Louis's mind was evidently elsewhere. Taking no time for a honeymoon or even a lie-in, Louis had his new wife up at dawn the next day to ride at speed toward Reims, where he had at last arranged for their double coronation for 3 August. In contrast with his no-frills second wedding, this ceremony must have been lavish since it cost over 21,000 *livres parisis*, though sadly the only source describing it (besides the Crown's account book) is a citizen's cranky complaint about the outrageous expense.[29] Maybe the chroniclers passed over it in silence out of embarrassment about the contrast between this lavish display and the rest of the reign's meagre accomplishments, for Louis's coronation was meant merely as an interim destination on the way to his ultimate goal: Flanders. And there his high hopes of finally finishing what his father had started were to be deeply disappointed.

Louis had planned his route toward the rebellious county carefully, so as to maximize its symbolic impact. On his departure from Paris, he had gone first to Saint-Denis to receive the Oriflamme from its abbot in the ancient tradition of his ancestors.[30] (The banner seems somehow to have been miraculously reconstituted after its destruction in Egypt during Louis IX's chaotic retreat up the Nile.) Collecting a queen and a crown along the way, his voyage under the banner's blood-red silk was meant to demonstrate his credentials as the world's most Christian king, such that God would grant him victory in battle, the ultimate sign of political legitimacy for a medieval ruler.[31] After his wedding and anointing with the heavenly oil that accompanied his coronation, he had only one thing left to prove before exposing himself to the judgement of battle: did he possess the healing power of the Capetian kings to cure those afflicted with scrofula? His father had passed on to him the sacred words that accompanied the ritual, but Louis had not yet dared to use them. The risks were enormous. If the scrofulaic recovered at his touch on their throat (or thought that they did, anyway), he could be sure that God considered him worthy. But what if God withheld the miraculous power from him? It would deal a blow to his kingship from which it could never recover.

The heavenly chrism that had anointed his brow was thought to unlock this mystical ability, but even then, Louis was still not entirely sure of himself.[32] Before putting his powers to the test, he rode some 20 kilometres north from Reims to the little town of Corbeny to venerate the remains of Saint Macroul, a relic much visited by his sainted great-grandfather Louis and one closely connected with the Capetian kings' thaumaturgical talents.[33] Only once fortified by the saint's favour did he lay his hands on the swollen necks of those suffering from the 'king's evil'. He must have been nearly as relieved as his patients when his first efforts were successful. After stopping in towns along his way to heal not only locals but foreigners brought in specially for the occasion, Louis at last pitched his tents little more than a stone's throw from Courtrai. He could now feel certain that God would grant him victory.

Louis had been keen to fight the Flemish the year before, when his father had squeezed the country hard for the invasion only for it to be cancelled by a truce negotiated by the late and unlamented Marigny.[34] As usual, the Flemings had not fulfilled their side of the bargain, a circumstance so predictable that Marigny's misplaced faith in the truce later seemed treacherous. Louis did not intend to repeat his father's mistakes, but it was neither the Flemings' military nor their diplomatic talents that bested him. It was the weather. That summer was so stormy that the grain and vines were beaten into the ground and the whole world, said the rhyming chronicle, was 'cast into torment'.[35] Processions of barefoot people wound their way through towns all over France, begging God for better weather, to no avail. In Flanders, the fields that Louis meant to fight on turned to mud. Men and horses waded through the stuff up to their knees, and the army could not find food for love nor money. There was nothing for it. The French burnt their tents and headed home under cover of darkness. 'To be honest,' said the rhyming chronicler, 'the way they left was extremely shameful.'[36]

The fresh start that Louis had envisaged for his reign had instead proved a false one. The little time left to him was spent parrying the consequences of bad politics and worse weather. That autumn he tried to avoid an open war between the nobles of Artois and their Countess Mahaut. The nobles had accused her of ignoring their customary liberties and riled up the common people against her. Her son had arrested two of them on spurious grounds, and they had reacted by stealing her horses and cattle, killing her game warden, and frightening her daughter's companion into a miscarriage. Louis brokered a compromise, which Countess Mahaut refused to accept, leaving Louis little choice but to sequester the county.[37] The daughter and granddaughter of the rash Roberts of Artois who had lost their lives at Courtrai and Mansoura, Mahaut shared her forefathers' predilection for rushing headlong into danger. Her proud refusal to accept the king's compromise might have been her undoing, except that she was also the mother of the wives of Louis's brothers.

The common people were even more discontented than the barons and with good reason. Louis's failed Flemish invasion had required taxes they were in no mood to support, especially that cold, wet year when everyone could see there would be no harvest. He had returned from Flanders to find complaints against his agents had piled up. Seeking scapegoats, he had many of his tax collectors hanged.[38] He also cracked down on the bakers who mixed pig shit into their dough to make more bread out of less flour and punished the merchants hoarding salt, a once commonplace but suddenly precious commodity in those damp days.[39] And he sent ships after the Flemish pirates who commandeered food shipments from Gascony, the only part of the kingdom to produce wheat and wine that year.[40] People died of starvation in the streets anyway or turned to crime and even cannibalism to keep themselves alive.[41]

The winter of 1315–16, one so cold that some saltwater harbours froze solid, must have been a miserable one for travellers, but Louis spent it on the move, trying to shore up his subjects' support following the Flemish fiasco. After celebrating Christmas at the abbey of Our Lady of the Lily in Melun south of Paris, he traversed the heartlands of his kingdom in a clockwise circle, heading first to Orléans, then north to Rouen in Normandy and east to Meaux, before turning south again to Sens and Bourges. Everywhere he went Louis granted local demands to reject his father's excesses and return to the more liberal policies of his earlier ancestors.[42] There are few sources aside from these grants that tell us what he was doing during these months. His Parlement did not sit, and his chancery register is blank following a final entry from Arras on 1 September 1315, as if no one thought it necessary to record royal business after that point.[43] Nor do the chronicles have much to say about that dark time. Aside from the weather and the growing famine, only a comet's coming caused much comment.[44]

This astronomical event turned out to be an omen portending the king's premature death on 5 June 1316. Like the cause of his father's death, the reason for Louis's early demise is a little unclear. Probably, he died of an infection, as even young people sometimes do. It is possible that he died of poison administered by an agent of Countess Mahaut of Artois, as a popular rumour had it, though she was later cleared of the charges. It is very unlikely that he died from drinking too much wine in an overly cold cellar following a sweaty game of *paume* (medieval tennis), though that is the explanation many chroniclers plumped for.[45] In any case, it was a surprisingly sudden death for a twenty-six-year-old man apparently otherwise in good health.

Although the funeral had to be thrown together with very little notice and although his eighteen-month reign was the second short-est, and arguably the least successful, of any Capetian king, Louis's funeral was every bit as much the ceremonial occasion as the obse-quies for his much more formidable father. On 7 June his corpse was carried to Saint-Denis clothed in a surcoat edged with fur and a gold-fringed ermine mantle. He carried a silver sceptre in his right hand, and on his head he wore a double crown, signifying his rule of both France and Navarre. No expense was spared. The precious fabrics needed to dress and display his body included twenty-one Turkish cloths, eighteen lengths of heavy blue silk, two of vermil-ion, one of black, and one woven or embroidered with golden fleurs-de-lys, worth nearly 300 *livres parisis* in total. The *son et lumière* of his obsequies cost over 2,500 *livres parisis*, which went on bell-ringers in Paris and Saint-Denis, torches and torch-bearers, as well as over 8,000 pounds of wax that had to be procured from various merchants since no single one could source it all.[46] And yet, his brother Philip of Poitiers judged that Louis was not yet mourned enough, for Philip, who had not been in Paris for the funeral, had missed his chance to demonstrate his pre-eminent place among the remaining royals at a moment when perception was everything.[47]

Everyone knew that the succession was in question, for Louis had not yet fathered a son. He had, however, left Queen Clémence pregnant. Medieval pregnancy being a chancy thing, Louis had in the meantime recognized the legitimacy of his four-year-old daugh-ter Joan from his disgraced first wife, Marguerite. He may even have designated Joan heir to the Crown of Navarre. Joan's uncle,

Duke Eudes of Burgundy, thought she also had a right to France, especially if Clémence had another girl or if the baby died. Nor was he alone in that opinion. Women had inherited other European Crowns, and many of France's lordships, great and small, were in female hands. Such was the practice, Eudes correctly claimed, 'in empires, kingdoms, peerages, and baronies for such a long time that there is no memory to the contrary'.[48] Only a year before, Louis X had affirmed that 'logic and natural law require that if there are no male heirs, the females must inherit', in a grant he had made to his brother Philip so that Philip's daughters could inherit the county of Poitiers, revoking a deathbed act of their father's to the contrary.[49] Whether a woman might inherit the Crown of France was simply not a question that had ever been posed because it had never needed to be answered. But for the moment, the point was moot until Clémence had her baby. The immediate issue was not who would be king or queen, but who would be regent.

Charles of Valois ought to have been the obvious choice. A senior statesman, he was by most reckonings the closest to the throne. He had the support of Charles of la Marche (Philip the Fair's youngest son) and of Clémence, who had a claim to the regency herself as mother to the likely heir to France.[50] And yet Philip of Poitiers somehow convinced the barons that he should be the regent. When Louis died, Philip had been at Lyon, where he was encouraging the cardinals at last to elect a pope. Having locked the recalcitrant clerics in a convent to finish their deliberations, he left Lyon on 2 July and rode hard to reach Paris ten days later. He went first to speak with Charles of Valois and Clémence at Vincennes, then to Saint-Denis, where he arranged for that unprecedented second funeral for Louis. After that, he headed straight to the palace and made himself comfortable. He may not have had to fight his way in or fight to keep others out, as later and foreign accounts claim, but his possession of the palace represented a *fait accompli* that would be hard to reverse. Almost all the remaining resistance to his regency collapsed at a conclave on 16 July when the realm's great barons appointed him to the office for the duration of Clémence's pregnancy. They also agreed that if the baby was male, Philip's regency would continue until the child reached his twenty-fourth year. They may also have agreed – though on this point accounts differ – that, should it be female, Philip would be proclaimed king.[51]

The child was male, but he never made it to his twenty-fourth year or even his twenty-fourth day. Born either too weakened from his mother's long and fevered labour or too inconvenient for his ambitious uncle's allies, the baby king John I died five days after his birth on 14 November 1316. There had not been time to crown him, of course, but his funeral was fit for a king, albeit a very little one. Enveloped in heavy black silk, his tiny coffin lay overnight under a blue canopy embroidered with lilies before being covered with costly filigreed gold cloth and transported to Saint-Denis.[52] There, he was laid at the feet of his father, his grave adorned with a statue that makes him look like the jolly three-year-old he never got to be (Plate 21). A tragedy in human terms, little John's death marked the beginning of an era's end for France. For over three centuries, ever since Robert the Pious succeeded Hugh Capet in 996, when *Francia* was not yet France and the Capetians were little more than ambitious upstarts, the kingdom had passed smoothly from father to son. Now, that long, lucky line had been broken. The omen was an ill one, and so it proved.

20.

Poisoned Waters

Philip V

All through that frigid December and into January 1317, the palace's drapers and furriers, its goldsmiths and leatherworkers, its tailors and seamstresses, and its carpenters, too, had worked flat out to outfit their new king and queen in the finest fashions for their coronation at Reims. Philip V's long and lanky form was resplendent in an outfit of azure velvet luxuriously lined in soft white vair. Under these robes, he wore a tunic of the taffeta-like silk called samite and over it a mantle of vermilion silk – it, too, lined in vair – with a furred hood to match. His wife, Joan, wore a gown of the gold-filigreed silk known as Turkish cloth, again lined in fur. Around her waist was a belt embellished with rubies and emeralds. Their eldest daughters were dressed in yellow velvet. The furnishings for the coronation and the feast that followed were likewise covered in silks and velvets of gold, scarlet, or sky-blue made especially for the occasion. That night the newly crown queen retired to a bedroom draped in vermilion velvet decorated with 1,321 parrots (the king's emblem), 661 butterflies (the queen's), and 7,000 trefoils, all of them made of silk and gold. Her husband went separately to his own bed of blue and yellow silk covered in a counterpane strewn with red, white, and blue silk lilies.[1] Who knows if they slept, but it had certainly been a busy day.

The coronation had been planned for 6 January, the Feast of Epiphany, an auspicious day for the anointing of a new king, but it had been pushed back three days, to the 9th, for reasons no source cared to explain. Maybe Philip got stage fright. Or maybe, in that winter of relentless snowstorms, the weather had just been too inclement to bear despite all the fur lining their garments. Or maybe

Philip was hoping more guests would arrive. If it was the last, he was disappointed. Few nobles had accompanied Philip on his journey from Paris to Reims, a normally celebratory progress that this time took place under armed guard for fear of opposition.[2] Attendance at the ceremony was sparse enough for even sympathetic chroniclers to comment on it. Many of the no-shows must have had doubts about Philip's right to the throne, doubts incited or magnified by the Burgundians still supporting his four-year-old niece Joan, who was, after all, the sister of the last king and the daughter of the one before that.

Joan's uncle, Duke Eudes of Burgundy, had rushed to Paris to safeguard her claims as soon as he had news of baby John I's death. By Christmas he was certain that Philip planned not only to keep the French Crown for himself but also that of Navarre and the counties of Champagne and Brie that ought to have been Joan's. He quit Paris in disgust at midday on 26 December to seek counsel among his people in Burgundy. Although he 'had been much pressured to attend the coronation', as he wrote to the Count of Flanders, he had not gone, feeling that to do so would violate his honour.[3] Eudes's mother, Agnes, Joan's grandmother, took an even stronger line. Declaring Joan 'the rightful heir to the realms of France and Navarre and the counties of Champagne and Brie', she wrote to the great barons of France to insist that there should be no coronation of any sort until her granddaughter's claims had been thoroughly investigated.[4] Agnes was one of the last living children of Saint Louis, and her words carried weight. All but two of the letters' recipients stayed away from Reims.

Philip's family was also unhappy. Both of his uncles, Charles of Valois and Louis of Évreux, had accompanied him to Reims, but Charles must have put on a long face, for chroniclers noted how little he wished to be there.[5] Whether he was upset because he thought his nephew a usurper or because he disliked how much Philip favoured Louis d'Évreux is hard to know. Likewise, although Philip's younger brother Charles of la Marche had accompanied him to Reims, he left the city in a very bad temper at sunrise the next day. Charles had used the journey from Paris to lobby his brother for better lands and was less than happy when Philip fobbed him off. Charles had a hard exit. Fearing armed opposition to Philip's coup d'état, Reims' citizens had closed the city's gates and set an armed watch. Charles and his people had to scale the walls and nearly broke their necks on the descent.[6]

Besides the royal couple themselves, perhaps the only person who really felt celebratory was Philip's mother-in-law, the mighty and mulish Countess Mahaut of Artois. She had such pull in the new king's court that people called Philip 'King Mahaut' behind his back.[7] During the ceremony she had carried the crown before Philip. It was a gesture that signalled the role she planned to play in the kingdom now that her daughter was queen, and one that 'made many indignant', according to the monks of Saint-Denis.[8] It was thought that she had procured her daughter's reconciliation with Philip through sorcery, and she had not yet been cleared of the allegations that she had poisoned Louis X.[9] Now, it was also being whispered that she had smothered baby John, too. Both stories probably stemmed less from any actual homicidal activity on the countess's part than from irritation at her difficult personality and the high-handed way she treated her county's nobles. It was especially annoying that, while her son-in-law had captured the Crown by disregarding the rights of female heirs, she had taken possession of Artois after her brother's death by excluding his grandson from the succession.

Philip's coronation, a 'furtive and shameful' affair in the judgement of one historian, had only inflamed his opponents' feelings.[10] On his return to Paris he made good on a promise to Eudes of Burgundy, calling together the realm's princes and prelates, representatives from the University of Paris, and the city's citizens to consider Joan's claims. Eudes hoped at least to safeguard her claims to Navarre and Champagne and to retain the right to challenge for France itself when she came of age. He maintained that this course of action had been agreed in words – but not, as even he acknowledged, in writing – back in July in the event that Clémence were to have a son who died.[11] Philip's position, however, was that the July agreement was irrelevant. It 'had regulated Louis X's succession, but not that of his son'.[12]

Much to Eudes's disgust, the meeting that Philip convened on or around 2 February was essentially for show. Called in the tradition of Philip the Fair's assemblies, it was intended to make a public demonstration of support for a decision already determined. Philip had packed the meeting with his allies, not least the burghers of Paris, who had welcomed him back to the city from his coronation with a celebratory enthusiasm that had been all too lacking at the ceremony itself. Even so, the assembly's decision was not unreasonable. Made to choose between a little girl of dubious parentage supported by the lord of a far-off territory, on the one hand, and an adult man of certain pedigree who was now anointed with the heavenly chrism, on the other, they understandably approved Philip accession. But they also recognized Philip's eight-month-old son Louis-Philip as heir to the realm. That act transformed what might have been a one-off decision into an enduring principle. 'And so,' concluded the chroniclers at Saint-Denis, 'it was declared that women do not succeed in the kingdom of France.'[13]

A verdict of monumental importance, the consequences of this flat denial of a woman's right to rule France have echoed down the centuries, even to the present day.[14] But opposition lingered, for Philip's claim, said a chronicler, 'could not be easily proven'.[15] Indeed, there was no proof. Philip did not invoke the so-called 'Salic Law', a long-defunct sixth-century legal compilation which had little relevance to the case at hand. The first such reference to the Salic Law did not come until forty years later, and it was rarely cited until the fifteenth century.[16] Unsubstantiated as well as unprecedented, Philip's power-play worried some people and angered others. Although the masters of the University of Paris had acquiesced in Philip's *fait accompli* at his assembly, they refused to endanger their souls by swearing to it. (They did, however, decide it wise to send a fawning letter acknowledging his succession's legitimacy on other grounds.)[17] In Champagne, which ought to have been Joan's, and in the duchy of Burgundy, where Eudes and Agnes remained unreconciled, nobles revived their leagues and prepared for another confrontation with the Crown, this time perhaps a violent one.

That Philip's only male child, the infant Louis-Philip, died a fortnight after the assembly's decision, seemed to some like God's judgement against the king. Philip was left with four daughters, whose right to succeed he had just abolished, and although he could not know it at the time he would never have another son. The royal chronicle, compiled well after the fact, recounts Louis-Philip's death immediately after its account of the assembly, giving a palpable sense that this tragedy not only followed the assembly excluding women from the succession but in some way followed *from* that decision, as if in answer to its hubris.[18] In the earlier chronicles it drew from, the baby's death is sandwiched between an earthquake in Philip's own county of Poitiers after the assembly and a description of that terrible winter when it began to storm non-stop from November onward, that is to say, from the moment that Philip seized the throne.[19] These were worrisome signs that even nature disapproved of the turn things were taking. As superstitious as the father whose name he bore (and whose ghost he sometimes talked to), Philip could hardly ignore these portents, let alone the storm brewing among the nobles in the kingdom's east.[20] But he had not come this far to back down now. He garrisoned the castles along the border with Champagne and summoned 3,000 soldiers to assemble at Mâcon in Burgundy.[21] If he had to go to war to keep his crown, so be it.

Philip moved first, but Joan's supporters were quick to answer. In April, the nobles of Champagne wrote a letter calling their lords and allies to arms against Philip in support of the little girl's rights to France and Navarre. These crowns were Joan's, declared the letter in ringing tones, 'by divine right' (*droit divin*), by law and custom, and by the terms agreed between Philip and Eudes the year before.[22] The lords of Champagne were eager to support the would-be countess of their once-independent land, which had only been absorbed by the French Crown as part of the dowry of Philip IV's wife thirty years before. They were joined by the son of the Count of Flanders, Louis, who held the county of Nevers in central France along with that of Rethel in its east. Even if Louis of Nevers did not join forces with his father, whom he did not much like, his lands joined with Burgundy and Champagne to create a vast crescent-shaped region ready to defy Philip.

With Countess Mahaut of Artois's lands still effectively embroiled in civil war, sharp-witted Philip decided to divide and conquer. He seized Nevers and Rethel from Louis and forcibly installed his officers in the counties' castles. But Eudes and Agnes he sought to sweeten. Principled people, they were already uneasy about their alliance with Louis of Nevers because of the way his soldiers rampaged across the countryside, kidnapping and torturing the locals, and they were scandalized by how he treated his wife, whom he had repudiated and impoverished for no good reason. Philip promised to put off his invasion, and Eudes agreed to negotiations in July. This initial rapprochement was aborted, for neither was willing to give ground. But then Philip had a stroke of luck. Countess Mahaut's only son suddenly died in September – we know not of what – leaving her county's fate in Philip's hands. The king had already promised his eldest daughter (who, like her mother, her cousin, and half the women of the period, was also called Joan) to Eudes as a sop to smooth their relationship the previous autumn and had endowed her with the county of Burgundy. He now offered to add Artois to the girl's dowry, more than doubling its worth. How could the good duke refuse?

Even so, Eudes drove a hard bargain on his niece's behalf, ensuring that, if she could not have Champagne, she could at least have great lands, and if she could not have France or Navarre, she could at least be married to a man of royal blood. In a treaty agreed in March 1318, Philip gave Joan the county of Angoulême, 50,000 *livres tournois* with which to buy another barony of her choice, and Louis of Évreux's twelve-year-old son Philip.[23] Although Joan was only six, she and her ten-year-old cousin of the same name were married off in a double ceremony in June to seal the peace. The pope had to grant dispensations for their youth, as well as the multiple consanguineous ties between them. People were shocked at these proceedings and 'rightly so' (*merito*), commented a chronicler, but the marriages did end the open opposition to Philip's succession.[24] He could at last turn his attention to ruling the kingdom he'd fought so hard to capture.

As he saw it, the first task was to undo his brother's mistakes. Philip brought back counsellors from his father's reign who had been not just sidelined but imprisoned and even tortured during the reign of his older brother, and he had Marigny's mouldering corpse cut down from the gibbet where it had been hanging since 1315 and buried with honour.[25] But he also demanded that those who had profited on the sly from his predecessors' largesse – here he named the heirs of his brother's and father's favourites, including Flote and Nogaret – were to return those 'gifts' by which the Crown had been 'defrauded and deceived most greatly'.[26]

For above all, Philip needed to get the Crown's finances back in order. He reformed the running of the royal households and the Exchequer, and he gave special attention to the royal forests, a rich source of potential income that had to be made to pay. There was a fundamental mismatch between the Crown's revenues, which were often irregular and hard to collect, and its expenditure, especially the huge sums spent on armies and on administrators handling everything from the king's fish weirs to his papal diplomacy. This problem was structural, and no medieval state really had an answer to it. Philip was also badly burdened by his father's and brother's wills. To save their souls, both had left enormous bequests to religious foundations, to the crusade, to those wronged by their taxes, and even to those harmed by the exotic beasts kept in their parks. In total, about half the Crown's already insufficient revenues had been earmarked for these projects.[27] Philip could not honour these in full, but neither could he ignore them without endangering his predecessors' salvation and his own. So financially embarrassed was Philip that he had to beg the pope for a tax on the clergy just to fund a few of these testamentary projects and to cover his wife and Clémence's household expenditures.

The pope granted Philip's petition, but only 'so that he could more freely and expeditiously attend to preparing for the crusade'.[28] Invoking the crusade was a tried-and-true strategy straight from his father's playbook. Although popes generally allowed kings to tax the clergy only for the purpose of crusading, it could always be argued that putting some of the sums toward other business was necessary to clear the way for the expedition. If that sounds a little cynical, Philip probably didn't think of it that way. Crusade was central to Capetian kingship, and he was not cynical about that at all.[29] One of his very first acts as regent in 1316 had been to confirm the crusading vow he had made as a new knight at the Pentecost celebrations in 1313.[30] Philip had continued thinking about the crusade even over that hard winter of 1317 when he was insecure on the throne and his heir died. In March that year he had outlawed tournaments and jousts in the hopes that people might use the money they saved for the voyage to the Levant.[31] By autumn 1318, Philip had named Louis of Bourbon, a grandson of Saint Louis, to head the expedition. Everything suggests that Philip really did intend to go East someday, maybe even someday soon. First, though, he had to deal with Flanders.

The Flemish Count Robert of Béthune was nearing eighty. Having succeeded his father just before the Peace of Athis in 1305, his relations with France had steadily worsened since the failed truces of the final years of Philip's father. As regent, Philip had negotiated yet another of these ineffectual agreements, but Robert, who shared Eudes of Burgundy's doubts about Philip's legitimacy as king, refused to attend the coronation, allowed Flemish attacks against French positions, and encouraged his officers to punish French sympathizers in Ghent, a city that favoured Philip. As Philip's fortunes improved, however, Robert became more pliable, as did his son, the erratic if powerful Louis of Nevers. Robert agreed to let the pope suggest a settlement, and Louis accepted a marriage proposal between his son and one of Philip's many daughters. Becoming increasingly hopeful about the crusade, Pope John XXII and Philip combined forces to pressure Robert into carrying out his end of the bargain. In the summer of 1319, John put Flanders under interdict and Philip began preparations to invade. Robert again agreed to terms, and this time he even did homage for Flanders.[32]

The peace wouldn't last – it never did – but Philip felt he could now turn his full attention to the crusade. He invited an array not just of prelates and barons, but also of lesser nobles and knights with crusading experience, to come to Paris in the winter of 1319–20 to make concrete plans for the expedition. There was even a former Templar among them. For the first time since the reign of Saint Louis, it began to seem like a French crusade might actually happen. Excitement mounted and not only among the elites at Paris. Word was spreading among the common people, too. The men who had attended these meetings and then gone home to the provinces no doubt 'brought the crusade close to the people and made it a topic for speculation, gossip, and debate'.[33]

Commoners, perhaps especially the poor among them, still carried in their hearts the embers of the fire that had lit the First Crusade. They sometimes had to be dissuaded from crusading, as did those too young, too old, too poor, too sick, or too simply female who wanted to join Louis VIII's expedition to Languedoc in the final phases of the Albigensian Crusade; and they sometimes came to grief, like those of the 1212 'Children's Crusade' who were sold into slavery. But often their enthusiasm was warmly welcomed, at least at first, just as Blanche of Castile welcomed the 'Shepherds' who had wanted to come to her son's rescue in 1251.[34]

Philip, however, did *not* welcome the popular crusaders who arose in the months following his assemblies. These young men and women also called themselves Shepherds, perhaps in imitation of their thirteenth-century predecessors but probably also because many of them *were* shepherds, or at any rate, pastoralists. Many had lost their sheep or cows in the terrible livestock pandemics that began in 1315, catastrophes that deepened the tragic effects of these years' repeated crop failures, when 10 per cent of northern Europeans died of starvation.[35] Made receptive to wondrous apparitions by these apocalyptic conditions, these second Shepherds had been inspired by an angelic vision ordering them to rescue the Holy Land. They were, nonetheless, not an ill-informed or uncritical rabble. Like most popular crusades, there were 'specific, immediate political agendas' behind their apparently irrational ideas.[36] Along with banners and pennants depicting the crucified Christ, they also carried many painted with the arms of Louis of Bourbon, the scion of Saint Louis whom Philip had appointed to head the crusade.[37] They expected to help Philip and that he would help them in turn.

But when they came to Paris in their hundreds or thousands in May of 1320, Philip did not come out to meet them. Instead, he stayed safely ensconced in his palace and ordered the Prévôt of Paris (essentially the head of the city's police force) to arrest them. This betrayal of expectations shattered the Shepherds' illusions about Philip. 'Cursing the king of France', the Shepherds broke into the prison where the Prévôt had incarcerated their leaders, and then they attacked the Prévôt himself in the street, 'defying and insulting the royal majesty' and killing some of his sergeants, too.[38] In some accounts, they also broke into his headquarters and threw him down the stairs. Abandoning their dreams of crusading with Philip, they marched out of Paris. Some of them may have joined Charles of Valois's son Philip in Italy, where he used them as cannon fodder in a 'political crusade' against the pope's enemies in Lombardy.[39] But most of them headed south into Gascony and Languedoc, where they began massacring Jews in some of the worst pogroms France ever witnessed.[40]

A reflection of the antisemitism that had metastasized in the hearts and minds of Christian France, these attacks also expressed the anger felt toward the Capetian Crown.[41] That there were even Jews in France to massacre was only because Louis had invited them back in 1315. Philip, too, had taken a relatively broad-minded approach, forbidding anyone but royal officers from laying hands on their persons, their goods or their books, and even allowing them to leave aside the Jewish badge on their clothing sometimes.[42] Louis had claimed that 'popular demand' (*commune clamour du pueple* [sic]) had moved him to allow Jews back in France, but there are many

signs that recent Capetian policies clashed with their people's prejudices.[43] The citizens of Montpellier had petitioned Philip to enforce
the wearing of the badge for fear, they claimed, that Catholic
women would be unwittingly seduced by Jewish men.[44] Adding to
such unease over social and sexual purity was the way the Crown
profited from Jews at its subjects' expense by collecting some of the
interest owed on Jewish loans to Christians. This did not sit well
with Philip's Christian subjects, most of whom were both econom-
ically insecure and fervently religious.

Aware of these royal policies in outline if not in detail, the Shepherds directed their violence against the infidels who lived among
them, unfathomably and infuriatingly at the will and under the protection of the most Christian kings of France. The Jews fled before
them, vainly seeking shelter in the king's castles where they were
besieged and murdered when they refused baptism. Few but Philip's agents came to their aid. In Carcassonne, the royal governor
sent warnings to all the towns to protect their Jews. Few of them
listened. The population was overwhelmingly sympathetic to the
Shepherds, both because they were avenging the crucifixion, as was
claimed in one town, and 'in defiance of the king', as was baldly
stated in another.[45] Royal authorities arrested hundreds of Shepherds, but when they brought them – all twenty-four wagon loads'
worth – to Toulouse, locals overwhelmed the guards and let them
loose on the city's Jews. Together they almost exterminated its
Jewish population, slaughtering them in the streets and outside the
cathedral, where the bodies lay piled up, sacking their houses and
burning both their religious books and their registers of debts.[46]

Faced with this popular crusade *cum* anti-royal rebellion, the provincial governor invoked his vice-regal powers and summoned an
army to crush the movement. Shepherds were hunted down and
hanged by the dozen, often from trees when no convenient gallows
could be found. Many escaped across the Pyrenees into Spain to
make new mischief there, but in France the military solution put an
end to the Shepherds' Crusade. By summer's end they had 'vanished like smoke' as the chroniclers liked to put it. What did not

vanish, however, was the paranoia and prejudices that had provoked the massacres. Less than a year passed before a new and even more murderous mass movement arose in its wake. Only this time those baying for blood had the full might of Philip's government behind them.

Somewhere and somehow – we never quite know the origins of these things – a bizarre rumour arose during the spring of 1321. It claimed the kingdom's lepers had conspired to poison the water supply.[47] Hoping either to kill everyone or infect them with leprosy, they had made a powder out of some combination of rotting bread, snakes, toads, urine, blood, faeces, women's hair, and consecrated communion hosts, and sprinkled this unholy concoction into the waters and wells all over France, especially in the south where the Shepherds had been the year before. Apprehended and tortured, one of these would-be poisoners confessed that the whole thing had been dreamt up by the Jews.[48] Further investigation turned up incriminating – though obviously forged – letters sent to the Jews by different Muslim princes, including the Sultan of Cairo and the King of Granada, promising to give them Jerusalem if they would kill the King of France and his Christian subjects. The Jews had protested that they would be too easily caught because the Christians had them under surveillance and instead proposed that the lepers would make more effective poisoners. In exchange, the lepers would rule France once all its non-leprous citizens were dead or infected.

If this conspiracy theory seems a bit baroque, even for fourteenth-century France, where people imagined demons, poisoners, sorcerers, and heretics around every corner, Philip at least believed the part about the lepers, if not the arguably even more far-fetched elements of a plot with Jews and Muslims.[49] He declared the supposed poisonings an act of *lèse-majesté* and ordered his officers to seize the lepers' property and to kill those guilty of the poisonings, extracting confessions by torture if necessary. Philip initially wanted these crimes only to be punished by royal officials, but public enthusiasm for the persecution overwhelmed his restrictions. By summer's end he was encouraging lords to hunt down guilty lepers in their

lands, 'so that the face of the earth may be cleansed of the iniquit-
ous putrefaction of the remaining stinking lepers'.[50] Hundreds of
lepers went to the stake, while those who escaped execution were
sentenced to permanent enclosure in their leprosaria. Jews, too,
were burned in great numbers all over France, including in Paris.
Philip may not have formally expelled those Jews who survived the
brutal summers of 1320–21, but the atmosphere was now so poisoned that those still able to escape probably did so.[51]

Philip, too, was poisoned, or maybe cursed, or so said a chronicler. He laid the blame not on the lepers, but on a conspiracy of
Philip's overtaxed subjects. They thought it 'better that one man
should die for the people than that so many people should be subject to such danger' as the taxes Philip wanted to raise for his
crusade.[52] Whether by these means or more natural causes, Philip
was taken with a 'bloody flux' that August from which he would
never recover. His doctors offered various medicines. The clergy of
Paris and the monks of Saint-Denis tried prayers and barefoot processions. Relics were brought to his bedside. Nothing helped. Still,
he struggled on for months, hoping that he might recover enough
to go on crusade and continuing to try to raise money for the project, despite his readily apparent illness and his subjects' obvious
opposition. At Orléans that autumn, the townsmen breezily promised to 'go with the king, fully armed for the host or for the
campaign, wherever he wanted to go, to the Levant or elsewhere',
but they would not put up any money in advance.[53] Their insolent
answer did not help Philip's increasingly anxious state of mind.
Having started his reign hoping to return the Crown to its former
glory, he had had time to accomplish very little and had in practice
presided over years of deepening paranoia, hatred, and misery, not
to mention outright starvation. And, of course, he had no son.

Taken to the nunnery of Longchamp founded by Saint Louis's
sister, Philip died around midnight on 2–3 January 1322, not quite
five years after his contested coronation. A funeral procession every
bit as grand as the coronation itself carried his body from Longchamp into Paris on a litter covered in gold cloths decorated with

fleur-de-lys. There it remained overnight at Notre-Dame, Philip's head resting on a silken pillow embroidered with the same parrots that had adorned his wife's ceremonial bed at Reims. In the morning, he was brought to his final resting place beside the main altar at Saint-Denis, his heart and entrails removed and divided between the Franciscan and Dominican churches of Paris.[54] Once the old king was interred, the new king's reign could begin. This time, there was no question about the succession. Philip's younger brother Charles of la Marche became the first Capetian king of France ever to bear Charlemagne's name. He would also be the last.

21.

End of the Line

Charles IV

Jourdain de l'Isle-Jourdain could not believe what was happening to him. Answering the king's summons in April 1323, he had come to Paris from the Languedoc in the full pomp and pride of his noble house, only to be seized and thrown into the Châtelet's dungeons and tried like a common criminal. Now, fifteen days later, his fine clothes confiscated, his little pouch holding relics of the Cross and Saint George taken from him, he was seated ignominiously on a cowhide with his hands bound and tied to the horses pulling him along the muddy road that led north toward Saint-Denis. Not much past Montmartre, his conveyance arrived before the king's gallows at La Villette, where a crowd of spectators awaited him. At this last stage, even the mercy of the cowhide was removed, and he was dragged through the dirt to the foot of the gibbet, where in his final moments he confessed to his sins. Yes, it was true that he had stolen from churches and extorted money from townsmen. Yes, he had been well pleased when his men killed women and little children and set fires. And yes, he had taken great satisfaction from the fate of a castellan hanged on his orders. 'But,' he said with a bewildered innocence that would be touching were it not so murderous, 'it was during war.'[1]

Jourdain's fate was nearly as shocking to others as it was to the condemned man himself. A Parisian chronicler commented that such a 'high and powerful nobleman' had not suffered such a downfall since Charlemagne tried Guenelon for treason.[2] (Indeed not even then, since that is an entirely fictional incident from the *Song of Roland*.) Neither the pope nor the Aragonese diplomat who reported it to his king could believe the news at first, and even centuries later, the case was considered unusual enough to be remembered as a *cause célèbre*.[3] Jourdain had certainly done bad things – the chroniclers accuse him of raping virgins and matrons alike, as well as those misdeeds he himself confessed – but he was right that they were no worse than other bad things that nobles and their soldiers did all the time in their innumerable wars with one another.[4] At most, they might have to pay compensation to the victims' families and a fine to the king. Explanations for Jourdain's harsh fate usually point to a chronicler's story about his grisly treatment of the king's officer, whom Jourdain supposedly killed with the 'mace enamelled with the fleur-de-lys' that the officer carried as a sign of his office, but there is no trace of such an act in the many royal records dealing with Jourdain's numerous wars and lawsuits.[5] Jourdain probably *was* guilty of killing two men after they appealed against his judgement to the king's court, and this was a serious matter, but it was not a hanging offence.

Jourdain's downfall was not for what he had done. It was that he found himself on the wrong side of powerful forces in the new regime of King Charles IV at just the wrong moment.[6] His family, the Isle-Jourdains, had been close to some of Philip V's counsellors, including that king's favourite uncle Louis of Évreux, who had intervened with the Crown on Jourdain's behalf in 1318, as had Philip himself in 1321.[7] But Louis of Évreux had died in 1319, and Charles IV, like his brothers before him, had begun his reign by clearing out the previous king's favourites. The old king's closest counsellors were excluded from court, many of them being imprisoned, tortured, and/or executed. Consequently, there was no one to plead on Jourdain's behalf when he was called to court in 1323. Jourdain's new lack of friends in Paris aggravated the effects of the enemies he'd made in Gascony, a place where King Charles and his uncle Charles of Valois were planning to move aggressively against the English king Edward II.[8]

Based west of Toulouse near the Gascon marches, the Isle-Jourdain family's interests created conflict with people that the king and his uncle needed as allies against England. Jourdain had long been at war with a nobleman under the protection of the most important noble family in English Gascony, the Albrets, who had been moving into the Capetians' orbit and were to be key French allies against Edward II. Then in 1322, just a year before Jourdain's execution, the Count of Isle-Jourdain (Jourdain's older brother) upped the ante by declaring war on the house of Albret itself, and a few months later Jourdain himself declared war on the Viscount of Lomagne, who was both a friend of the Albrets and an enemy of Pope John XXII, who was, in turn, a special patron of the Isle-Jourdain family.[9] Pope John had interceded with the Crown many times on Jourdain's behalf, writing in the weeks before his execution a flurry of letters to the king, the queen, Charles of Valois, and seemingly anyone he could think of to help his protégé.[10] John was so closely identified with the Isle-Jourdain family's interests that Jourdain went to the gibbet dressed in mocking papal livery.[11] Pope John, too, had made powerful enemies in the southwest by trying to clean up his Gascon predecessor's corruption, especially that bestowed upon the Viscount of Lomagne. The viscount now saw an opportunity to strike back not only at the Isle-Jourdains, but also at Pope John. He and the Count of Albret came to Paris for the trial, and Charles IV and Charles of Valois were convinced to sacrifice Jourdain's life to their allies' vendettas.[12] As for the pope, he was so alarmed by the situation that he immediately granted the crusading tax Charles had been demanding. The Aragonese diplomat commented that it was like an old proverb said: 'Hit the dog and scare the lion!'[13]

Not half a year after Jourdain's execution, a small but fateful incident occurred on the Gascon marches that allowed Charles to take a much more assertive stance in the duchy. In the early hours of 17 October, the lord of Montpezat, probably acting with the connivance of the English governor of Gascony, and forty of his men had ridden into a place called Saint-Sardos in the Agenais region of Gascony.[14] Shouting the Anglo-Gascon battle cry, 'Guyenne!', they had burned it to the ground and hanged a French royal officer next to a post painted with the fleurs-de-lys. This was an outrageous act.

Whether Saint-Sardos was under French or Anglo-Gascon rule had been a bone of contention for some time. The previous day this officer had driven the fleurs-de-lys-painted staff into the ground to mark the place where a new town (a *bastide*) was to be built under Capetian rule. Quite literally, he had staked France's claim to the land. Although perhaps not intended to be as incendiary as it turned out, this act was certainly meant to be provocative. King Edward still had not performed homage for Gascony to the new Capetian king, and Charles was becoming increasingly impatient with this failure. Just two weeks before the Saint-Sardos incident, Charles (or his proxies) had had his men overrun the island of Oléron off the Gascon coast, another pinprick provocation.[15]

Charles initially accepted Edward's protests that he had not consented to or even known about Montpezat's rash actions at Saint-Sardos, but he pointed out with some acerbity that the English king still had not done homage.[16] He ordered Edward to come

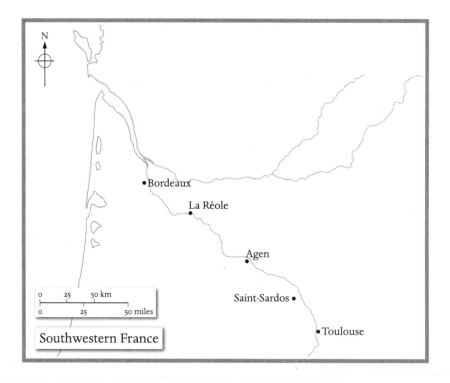

N

Bordeaux

La Réole

Agen

Saint-Sardos

Toulouse

0   25   50 km
0   25   50 miles

Southwestern France

to Amiens that summer to perform it, and he went south himself to monitor the situation from Toulouse. Not only did Charles wish to be close to the action, he also knew that success in Gascony would depend on the good will of his Occitan nobles, whose feathers had been seriously ruffled by Jourdain de l'Isle-Jourdain's execution. Toulouse had not seen its king since Philip the Fair had toured the south in 1303-4 on the eve of a Flemish invasion, so Charles's very presence in the city worked wonders on many, even if it did not reconcile the late Jourdain's retainers and relatives or one of the pope's nephews, who made 'images with magical characters' to kill the king.[17] Covert cross-border raiding continued throughout the winter, and Charles summoned before him the lord of Montpezat and others thought responsible for the Saint-Sardos outrage. When Montpezat did not appear, Charles banished him and ordered his castle seized. Montpezat's men refused to surrender it. Edward seemed unable or unwilling to make them do so. And a perfect pretext developed for the war that was to begin that summer.[18]

Charles must have felt pleased as he made his way home that March, but on the road northward tragedy struck, killing both his young wife and their newborn son. The couple had been married little more than a year, following Charles's successful campaign to convince Pope John to annul his first marriage to the allegedly adulterous Blanche of Artois, who had remained imprisoned in Château Gaillard. The efforts that Charles had made to be rid of Blanche during his brother's reign had foundered on the fact that John's predecessors had issued dispensations for the marriage's various illicit aspects, but soon after Charles's succession, someone suddenly remembered that Blanche's mother, Mahaut of Artois, had held Charles at the baptismal font. This made them 'spiritual kin', an impediment to legal marriage that previous dispensations had not mentioned.[19] If the claim seems suspiciously convenient, it certainly offered a more palatable solution to Charles's marital and reproductive predicament than strangulation, or whatever had happened to that other alleged adulteress, Louis X's wife Marguerite. Pope

John issued the annulment in May 1322, Blanche was released from her ordeal at Château Gaillard and sent to the nunnery of Maubuisson, and in September, Charles married sixteen-year-old Marie of Luxembourg. Marie was crowned in the Sainte-Chapelle nine months later and must have become pregnant soon thereafter.

Despite her condition, Charles took Marie south with him that winter, for a royal tour was nothing without a queen. But by the time they began their return, Marie was eight months pregnant, making travel uncomfortable, even dangerous on roads made treacherous with the thick mud of early spring. Perhaps some accident befell her carriage on the road, or perhaps, as a chronicle claims, the exertion of travel was just too much for her.[20] She went into premature labour at Issoudun, southwest of Bourges, and delivered a baby boy who died very soon thereafter. This short-lived child born too soon was the only son Charles would ever have, but of course he did not know that. Marie having almost immediately followed their infant son to the grave, Charles remarried as soon as he could, this time marrying one of the daughters of his half-uncle Louis of Évereux. Charles was only thirty years old and his new wife just fourteen, as young as a royal woman might begin childbearing. There was still hope.

By the time of that rushed wedding in July 1324, English diplomats at the French court were writing frantic letters to Edward II, informing him that Charles no longer believed his denial of involvement in the Saint-Sardos affair because he had not punished those responsible. A great French army had been summoned to meet at the border of the duchy at the beginning of August, and, they said, it appeared that Charles was readying his navy to invade by sea as well. Couching their words with expressions of affection and concern so as not to offend their sovereign, they told Edward that people were openly saying that 'you will lose your lands in France forever without hope of recovery'.[21] Tired of Edward's interminable excuses for neither having done homage nor surrendered those guilty of the Saint-Sardos outrage, Charles had dressed down Edward's high-born ambassadors, reminding them that the English king was nothing more to him than a 'vassal and subject of the king of France, who is emperor of his realm and has no sovereign under God'.[22]

Despite Charles's high-flown rhetoric and the ambassadors' anxieties, the War of Saint-Sardos was in the end a 'desultory affair' of limited results.[23] The French had neither the means nor, probably, the intention of conquering all of Gascony. What Charles wanted was the Agenais and for Edward to do homage as he ought. Edward, for his part, provided support both too little and too late to make much difference.[24] Agen and the area around Saintes surrendered to Charles of Valois, while the Atlantic coast from Bayonne to Bordeaux stayed loyal to Edward and in English hands. There were some naval engagements on the Garonne river and land-based skirmishes elsewhere, but the main event was a miserable siege of La Réole that began in late August. Led by Charles of Valois, the French forces sat outside the city walls for five weeks, eating rotten meat, drinking contaminated water, and fending off occasional sallies, a combination that killed many of them.[25] But the Anglo-Gascons, despairing of relief from England, surrendered on 22 September on the condition of a six-month truce, at the end of which Charles IV's sister, Queen Isabelle of England, came to Paris to negotiate a peace.

Isabelle had been glad to escape England, where her mercurial husband had fallen under the spell of Hugh Despenser the Younger, a man one chronicle refers to as 'the king's husband' and who was almost certainly his lover.[26] (Alternatively or additionally, Edward may have been sleeping with Despenser's wife.) Anger at the way that Despenser monopolized Edward's attentions and used his position to further his own interests incensed England's barons much as Edward's earlier favourite Piers Gaveston had done a decade before. Edward's losses to Robert Bruce in Scotland aggravated the growing anger at his chaotic misrule. England was a tinderbox, ready to explode into civil war. Isabelle hated Despenser and believed he wished her harm, but the atmosphere at Poissy, where she met her brother on 21 March 1325, was not initially very welcoming. Charles was deeply offended by her husband's behaviour and knew he held all the cards. The English were severely frightened, reporting rumours that Charles planned a two-pronged invasion of Gascony and England with the help of the Scots in the coming summer.[27] Under the circumstances, it is amazing that Isabelle managed to secure any terms at all. Those Charles offered 'on account of his love and regard for his sister' were harsh but not ruinous.[28] Edward was to cede his duchy to Charles, who would give it back to him when he came to France and performed homage by kneeling before the French king and placing his hands between Charles's hands. Charles would hold on to his conquests, at least until Edward paid him back for the costs of the French invasion. Montpezat was to be razed to the ground and the *bastide* at Saint-Sardos rebuilt.[29]

If these terms satisfied the kings' negotiators, they did nothing for the restive Gascon subjects, who continued to wage wars in which their own enemies and those of Capetian and Plantagenet regimes often became hopelessly intertwined. The war's many minor clashes had spawned a vast tangle of conflicting claims about injuries done and restitution owed both to and from Anglo-Gascons, whose loyalties toward the Capetians and the Plantagenets were fluid and often opportunistic. Only a year after peace was proclaimed, war broke out again in Gascony, which one chronicler pins on an alliance between the l'Isle-Jourdains and Anglo-Gascons avenging Jourdain's execution and others blame on a conspiracy of noble Gascon bastards, explanations which are not, of course, mutually exclusive.[30] The violent pursuit of individual grievances caused disorder in the duchy and created long-running lawsuits that could come before Parlement in ways awkward for their duke-king.[31] Closely tied to the intolerable burden of homage, France's supreme legal jurisdiction over England's continental fiefs was at the heart of the conflict between the two kingdoms. This was a problem that went right back to the reigns of Philip Augustus and John Lackland, when Philip confiscated Normandy because John refused to submit to his justice. It was a problem that would lead the two nations into the Hundred Years War little more than a decade later, a conflict the Saint-Sardos war foreshadowed and contributed to causing. Edward's ingenious solution to the issue of homage further complicated the situation by giving his Capetian wife the means to overthrow him.

Although he had agreed to meet Philip at Beauvais and perform the required ceremony, Edward very much did not want to go to France. It was not just that doing homage was humiliating. He also did not think it would be safe to leave England with his barons as unhappy as they were with him and his beloved Despenser, nor did he think it safe to be in France, where many of his enemies who had fled or been exiled from his kingdom were living. Chief among these exiles was Roger Mortimer, who had escaped imprisonment in the Tower of London two years earlier and found refuge across the Channel. Mortimer had not yet joined forces with Edward's increasingly estranged wife Isabelle – whose lover he was soon to become – but he was a danger to Edward's life in his own right. Rather than run these risks, Edward decided to bestow his continental fiefs on his twelve-year-old son, also named Edward, and send him to France to do homage. This was a neat get-out, but it was to prove a fatal mistake.

Young Prince Edward joined his mother at Vincennes and knelt before Charles at the end of September. But when King Edward then ordered his wife and son to return to England, Isabelle gave his messengers a shocking and very public reply that pointed an accusing finger at his extraordinary relationship with Despenser. 'I feel,' she said, 'that marriage is a union of a man and a woman, holding fast to the practice of a life together, and that someone has come between my husband and myself and is trying to break this bond; I declare that I will not return until this intruder is removed, but, discarding my marriage garment, shall put on the robes of widowhood and mourning until I am avenged.' Charles voiced his support for her position. 'The queen,' he said, 'has come of her own free will, she may freely return if she wishes. But if she prefers to remain in these parts, she is my sister, I will not expel her.'[32] Charles had a sincere affection for Isabelle, or at least he 'did what a good brother ought', supporting her expenses 'with good heart and will' when Edward cut her off.[33] A Capetian born and bred, she now fitted right in again with the busy social scene of her brother's court, dining regularly with their widowed sister-in-law, Clémence of Hungary, and Charles's young new wife, their cousin Joan of Évreux, as well as other refined women of noble blood.[34] But Isabelle was also a valuable weapon against Edward, and much more so now that her son, the heir to the English throne, was in their power.

According to some chronicles, Charles initially offered money and men to Isabelle to invade England. By the summer of 1326, however, something had turned him against his once-dear sister. Perhaps he was bribed by the precious presents sent by Edward's paramour Hugh Despenser, as a couple of chronicles say, or perhaps Isabelle's increasingly obvious attachment to Roger Mortimer outraged his morality, as historians sometimes suggest. Informed that Charles wanted to ship her back to England, Isabelle fled France with her son, Prince Edward, taking refuge in the imperial county of Hainaut where she and Mortimer had many supporters. There, or so the chronicler Jean Froissart charmingly imagined, the adolescent Edward fell in love with the count's daughter Philippa and she with him.[35] This story may actually be true since Philippa later became Froissart's patron, but even if it is, the teenagers' feelings for one another were irrelevant. The betrothal had been mooted months before they met. It was the price Isabelle had to pay for the count's support of her English invasion that autumn, and it proved good value. She and Mortimer stormed the country, executed Despenser in cruel and exemplary fashion, and imprisoned and deposed Edward II. In January 1327 they proclaimed her son King Edward III and began ruling on his behalf. Nine months later, Edward II himself was dead, probably on her orders.

If Charles was shocked by Isabelle's actions, no source comments on it. Their cousin, Philip of Valois, however, had offered her his secret support. He was the Count of Hainaut's brother-in-law, Isabelle's ally. But as the eldest grandson of Philip III, Philip may also have been acting with one eye already on the succession, seeking to sweeten Isabelle and Prince Edward in advance of a tricky situation. His father, the old warhorse Charles of Valois, had died of gout the previous December, making Philip the most senior prince of the blood. His mind turned naturally toward the future of France and his place in it.[36] Should King Charles die without a legitimate male heir of his body, Isabelle and her son would number high on the list of his rivals for the throne because they were the daughter and grandson respectively of Philip IV. It would be good to have them in his debt.

That once-unimaginable succession scenario was seeming increasingly likely. In August 1325, Queen Joan of Évreux had delivered a baby, 'whom the doctors and astronomers had predicted would be a boy', but who turned out to be a girl instead.[37] Pregnant again in 1326, she produced another girl early the next year. Charles, waiting anxiously outside the chamber, quit the palace in disgust as soon as he got the news. One cannot help but pity poor Joan, who, of course, was not at fault and whose firstborn, a two-year-old named Marie, was to die only a few months later. Joan was to become one of the most consequential political players of fourteenth-century France, but at this stage in life she had only one purpose. Not yet eighteen, she was pregnant again by midsummer 1327, for Charles was determined to ensure the succession. This reproductive snag was the last thing standing in the way of the royal legacy he imagined for himself.

Although a third son, Charles had shown the most confidence of Philip the Fair's children in his right to the throne. His reign had none of the hesitation of his brother Louis X, nor any of the underhanded harshness of that quasi-usurper Philip V. As the Saint-Denis chroniclers commented, Charles's succession had taken place 'without contradiction or opposition', a real contrast with the contested coronation of his older brother.[38] In his short time as king so far, Charles had put the pope in his place and made good the expansive ambitions of his ancestors in Gascony. He had appointed a leader for the crusade, should he ever manage to go on it. And now, as he waited for Joan to bear him the boy to which he knew he was entitled, he even had hopes of solving the long-running problem of Flanders.

France's relationship with Flanders had warmed under its new count, Louis of Nevers, the eighteen-year-old son of that vicious and unreliable Louis of Nevers whose opportunistic alliance with the Duke of Burgundy appeared in the previous chapter. Unlike the two most recent Flemish counts, always at war with the Capetians, Louis of Nevers was a Francophile. He had been raised at the Capetian court, was married to one of Charles's many nieces, and depended upon the French king's support against his uncle's claims to the county. In demonstration of his gratitude toward Charles, one of Louis's first acts as count was to reinstate instalments toward the still unpaid indemnities owed from the Peace of Athis. Unfortunately for Count Louis and King Charles both, the plan encountered violent resistance because Louis, on the advice of his counsellor, a nephew of Philip the Fair's old lawyer Pierre Flote, decided to raise the taxes by squeezing his rural subjects especially hard.[39] Medieval Flemish townspeople are justly famous for their uprisings, but the peasantry of coastal Flanders had a long tradition of resistance all their own.[40] They had been part of the great rebellion against Philip the Fair at the turn of the fourteenth century, and now they took the lead in a five-year uprising against Louis of Nevers and France, the first great peasant revolt of the late Middle Ages.

In the winter of 1324–5, although Charles's attention was focused on the Saint-Sardos affair, he was concerned enough to order Count Louis to get his people under control. Charles had feared that French peasants might rise up in sympathy, but it was the workers and middle classes of Bruges and Ypres who joined their rural counterparts and expanded the rebellion's reach in 1325. That July a rebel army had captured the count at Courtrai, scene of the Flemish commoners' great victory over Philip the Fair two decades earlier, and taken him back to Bruges as their prisoner. He was only freed in November after Charles prohibited trade between France and Flanders and had the county placed under interdict, an authority granted to him by compliant Pope John XXII.[41] Upon his release, Louis swore upon a relic of the Holy Blood not to take revenge against his subjects. This promise he did not keep. Instead, he departed immediately for Paris to seek Charles's armed intervention.[42]

Charles, again occupied by Gascon affairs, could not mount the invasion he and Louis desired, but in 1326 he imposed a peace treaty as punitive as anything his predecessors had inflicted. The count was to have 10,000 *livres* for his pain and suffering, plus another 100,000 *livres* for the burning of the port city of Sluys. Payments due to France for the Peace of Athis and all subsequent treaties were to resume, with arrears, plus an additional 200,000 *livres* due to the French Crown for its trouble.[43] Wealthy town merchants were willing to accept these hard terms in exchange for the restoration of trade, but they only exacerbated the peasants' grievances. It took a royal French army to crush their uprising. On 23 August 1328 heavy French cavalry outfoxed and outmanoeuvred the peasant forces assembled on a hill outside the city of Cassel. There, they killed somewhere between 3,000 and 12,000 rebels, while losing as few as seventeen men of their own. Crying '*Montjoie!*', the king himself had led the French forces, his holy Oriflamme banner flying above their slaughter of the enemy.[44] But this king was not Charles, for he had died almost eight months earlier.

Like his brothers before him, Charles had mysteriously sickened in the prime of life, but if anyone suspected poison, the story didn't catch on. The French chronicles say simply that a 'grave malady' came upon him in the middle of the night at Christmas.[45] Taken to Vincennes, he languished for a month before dying on 1 February 1328. His body was laid next to his brother Philip's at Saint-Denis. Charles's heart went to the Dominicans of Paris, his entrails to Maubuisson, where his disgraced first wife Blanche had died and was buried. Charles had left Joan of Évreux pregnant, and for two months the realm waited on tenterhooks to see what sex the child would be. On 1 April 1328 a messenger tore out of Vincennes and rode hard to Paris to cry the news: the queen had given birth to her child! It was a girl. Philip of Valois, who had been serving as regent, now became King Philip VI. In the space of fourteen years, all of Philip the Fair's fine sons had perished without heirs, a lamentable history that fulfilled the prophecies which had long dogged the dynasty and gave rise to new ones predicting awful calamities.[46]

'And so,' a chronicler concluded, 'the realm passed out of the direct line, so it seems to many people, out of which great wars arose and there occurred such great destructions of people and provinces in the realm of France as you will hear later on, for this is the foundation of that story.'[47]

Epilogue
The Last of the Lilies

The Capetian line didn't so much end as splinter. After Charles IV's death, there was in fact a surfeit of people who could claim to be Capetian, starting with Philip VI himself. Historians mark his reign as a dynastic break, a dividing line between the house of Capet and that of Valois. Philip himself didn't see it that way. He was a direct descendant of a Capetian king through that king's son, even if that son, his father, Charles of Valois, had not himself been king. Philip and his descendants considered themselves the Capetian dynasty's continuators, as did the Bourbons, descendants of Saint Louis's youngest son, who reigned after the Valois's extinction in 1589. There are still 'Capetian' claimants to the French throne today. All of these so-called Capetians were men tracing their descent from other men, for women could neither embody their family's dynastic claim nor transmit it. This principle had been proven first by the exclusion of Louis X's daughter Joan in 1316 and then by refusing claims from King Edward III of England, grandson of Philip IV by his daughter Isabelle, in 1328.[1] At least, it had been proved to the Valois's satisfaction. Others, many others, had doubts. The question of who, really, could claim to be Capetian plagued Philip and his successors well into the next century.

The best known of these would-be Capetians is, of course, Edward III of England. We could reasonably date the beginning of the Hundred Years War to January 1340, when he quartered the lions of England with the lilies of France on his coat of arms and made a speech before the townspeople of Ghent, claiming that he was the rightful heir to the French throne. For all the drama of this moment, Edward raised the claim with some reluctance, as a reliable chronicle says, and with little intention of making it good, as his later actions show.[2] He had bent the knee before Philip VI of Valois in 1329, and what had driven him to open war with France from 1337 was not a suddenly realization of his dynastic right but rather the usual conflicts over Gascony, further complicated by France's alliance with Scotland.[3] The move to claim the French Crown had been urged on Edward by the revolutionary leader of the latest Flemish uprising, a man who despite his origins in the weaving trades had become a key English ally. The Flemings hoped that Edward would finally overturn the Peace of Athis and provide them with a cheap and steady supply of English wool, while Edward used Flanders as an invaluable second front, diverting French forces from Gascony.

Edward claimed to be the rightful king of France to force Philip VI to give him what he really wanted: full sovereignty over an enlarged Gascony. When he got that, and much, much more besides, from Philip's successor in the Treaty of Brétigny of 1360, he agreed to renounce the claim to the French throne despite holding the French king captive in London at the time.[4] Edward's grandsons and successors, Richard II (d. 1399) and Henry IV (d. 1413), were never in any position to realize the claim, though they continued to make it. Only Henry V (d. 1422) made a treaty that gave him France, and even he never ruled it. By the terms of the Treaty of Troyes agreed in 1420, Henry was to rule France after the death of its then king Charles VI, but Henry died first. The only English king to wear the French crown, Edward's great-great-grandson Henry VI (d. 1471), inherited it as an infant and lost it before his majority. Although the dream of a cross-Channel double Crown had some enthusiastic proponents, it mostly served as a spectre to frighten the French into making concessions and a legal fiction giving the English greater latitude in the conduct of their wars.

The descendants of Philip III's third son, Louis of Évreux, posed at least as much of a potential threat to the Valois's new dynasty as did Edward III. Although Louis was the last-born of Philip's sons, his mother, Marie of Brabant (Philip's second wife), had been of better blood than the mother of Philip IV and Charles Valois,

Isabelle of Aragon. Marie could trace her descent from Charlemagne, while Isabelle's Aragonese ancestry was rumoured to be tainted with bastardry. Évreux's ties to the Capetian house were doubled when Louis's son Philip of Évreux married Joan, Louis X's daughter and only living heir. She gave him a son named Charles in 1332. This son was heir to the kingdom of Navarre, which was separated from the Crown of France and ceded to Joan and Philip of Évreux after Charles IV's death (1328) at the request of the Navarrese and in thanks for not pressing their claim to France.[5] That claim would have been an excellent one. Joan's claims as the firstborn child of Philip IV's firstborn heir and sister of his successor had been ignored when she was a girl of four in 1316, but in 1328 she was a woman grown and married to a man with a clear claim in his own right. Joan and Philip's son Charles, known unfairly and anachronistically by his sixteenth-century nickname 'the Bad', thus had a double claim to be the most Capetian heir to the French Crown.[6] As he himself put it in a stirring speech in Paris in 1358, he was 'descended from the lilies on both sides'.[7]

Like Edward III, however, Charles of Navarre mostly used his dynastic claim as leverage to win concessions from the Valois. The loss of his mother's lands in Champagne particularly angered him. These had been promised to her by the treaty of 1318 when she abandoned her claim to the Crown but were never restored or compensated for.[8] Unlike Edward, with whom he was often allied militarily, Charles came very close to seizing the throne. When the first two Valois kings proved hopelessly inept at politics and catastrophically incompetent at warfare, many good and thoughtful people began to wonder whether Charles of Navarre might make a better king than the one they had, especially after the English actually captured the Valois King John II at the Battle of Poitiers in 1356 and took him to London. Some of his support fell away after Charles made his ambitions clear in his speech invoking the lilies in Paris, but he came near to effecting a coup with the help of some of the city's great merchants in the summer of 1358, and then he waged open war on the Valois Crown in 1358–9.[9] The threat he posed was only definitively

Capetian, Valois, Plantagenet, and Évreux claimants

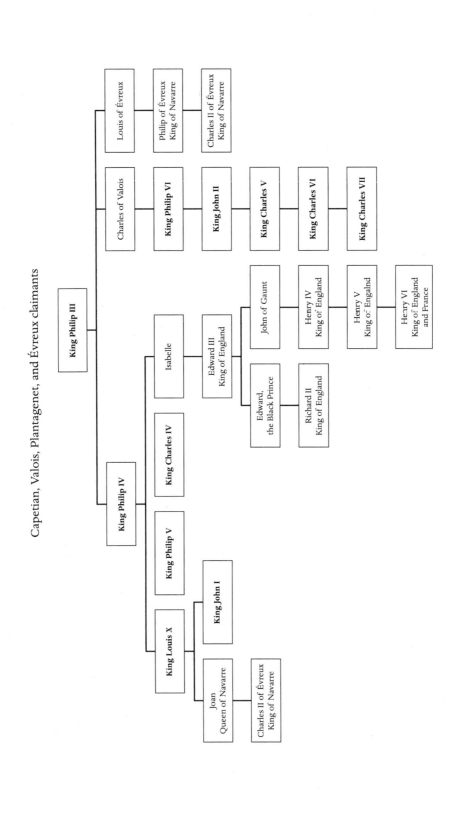

quelled in 1364, when his troops were routed at the Battle of Cocherel on the eve of the coronation of the third Valois king Charles V.[10]

The least-known, certainly the strangest, but just possibly the best claimant to the Capetian heritage appeared suddenly on the scene in 1360. Giannino di Guccio had grown up in Siena and had only recently learned that he was in fact King John I of France. Believed to have died in infancy, John had been switched with another infant, or so the story goes. According to one version, he had been smuggled out of the palace by his nursemaid to protect him from the murderous Countess Mahaut of Artois. The nursemaid put her own recently deceased baby in John's place, leaving the changeling to be buried in Saint-Denis. The real John was spirited away from Paris and then out of France to be raised by her lover and father of the dead baby, an Italian merchant who took him home to Siena.

Giannino knew nothing of this shocking history until he received a surprising letter in 1354 from a colourful character named Cola di Rienzo, himself something of an impostor, who was then ruling Rome. Initially dubious, Giannino was quickly convinced by Cola's story and threw his entire fortune, which was considerable, into the effort to reclaim his throne. Criss-crossing Europe in search of support, Giannino had secured a mercenary army and was preparing to take Lyon at the end of 1360 when a shift in circumstances led the mercenaries to join other freebooting bands attacking the pope near Avignon instead. Giannino was captured by the Provençals and shipped to Naples, where he died in prison soon thereafter. Nevertheless, his claim long lived on, not least through a copy of his own account of his incredible adventures.[11] His descendants are said to have borne a mark in the shape of cross on their shoulder, proving their descent from Saint Louis, and they carried the fleur-de-lys on their banners until their line ended in 1530.[12] Who knows if they were right, but they believed themselves the last true heirs to the house of lilies.

Notes

Abbreviations

AN: Paris, Archives nationales

BEC: *Bibliothèque de l'École des chartes*

BnF: Paris, Bibliothèque nationale de France

EHR: *English Historical Review*

HF: Dom Martin Bouquet et al. (eds), *Recueil des historiens des Gaules et de la France*, 24 vols (Paris 1737–1904)

JMH: *Journal of Medieval History*

LTC: Alexandre Teulet et al. (eds), *Layettes du Trésor des Chartes*, 5 vols (Paris 1863–1909)

Mansi: J. D. Mansi (ed.), *Sacrorum conciliorum nova et amplissima collectio*, 31 vols (Florence and Venice 1759–98)

MGH: Monumenta Germaniae Historica

  Capit.: Capitularia regum Francorum

  SS: Scriptores (in Folio)

  SS rer. Germ.: Scriptores rerum Germanicarum in usum scholarum separatim editi

Ord.: Eusèbe de Laurière, Denis-François Secousse et al. (eds), *Ordonnances des rois de France de la troisième race, recueillies par ordre chronologique*, 21 vols and supplement (Paris 1723–1849)

PL: Jacques Paul Migne (ed.), *Patrologia latina cursus completus* (Paris 1864–84)

RH: *Revue historique*

Prologue

1 *The Song of Roland*, ll. 115–19, trans. Robert Harrison (New York 1970), p. 35.

2 Patrick J. Geary, *Before France and Germany: The Creation and Transform-ation of the Merovingian World* (Oxford 1988), remains an excellent introduction.

3 François L. Ganshof, 'Les traits généraux du système d'institutions de la monarchie franque', *Settimane di studio del Centro italiano di studi sull'Alto Medioevo* 9 (1962), pp. 91–127; Jennifer R. Davis, *Charlemagne's Practice of Empire* (Cambridge 2015).

4 Dominique Barthélemy, *La France des Capétiens, 987–1214* (Paris 2012), p. 25; Ferdinand Lot, *Études sur le règne de Hugues Capet et la fin du Xe siècle* (Paris 1903), pp. 304–23.

5 Margret Lugge, *'Gallia' und 'Francia' im Mittelalter: Untersuchungen über den Zusammenhag zwischen geographischhistorischer Terminologie und politischem Denken vom 6.–15. Jahrhundert* (Bonn 1960).

6 Elizabeth M. Hallam, *Capetian France, 987–1328* (London 1980), pp. 330–31.

1. The Rise of the Robertians

1 Dante Alighieri, *Purgatorio*, canto 20, trans. Robert M. Durling (Oxford 2003), pp. 326–35.

2 Robert's origins are murky but probably pertain to a princely family close to the imperial retinue. Yves Sassier, *Hugues Capet* (Paris 1987), pp. 48–51, discusses the evidence.

3 Rosamond McKitterick, *The Frankish Kingdoms under the Carolingians, 751–987* (London 1983), pp. 258–77; Ferdinand Lot, *Les derniers Carolingiens: Lothaire, Louis V, Charles de Lorraine (954–991)* (Paris 1891), pp. 3–17.

4 Lot, *Les derniers Carolingiens*, pp. 18–93; Simon Maclean, *Ottonian Queen-ship* (Oxford 2017), pp. 67–94.

5 Simon Maclean, 'Shadow Kingdom: Lotharingia and the Frankish World, c.850–c.1050', *History Compass* 11 (2013), pp. 443–57.

6 Richer of Saint-Rémi, *Histories*, III.71, ed. and trans. Justin Lake, 2 vols (Cambridge, MA 2011), vol. 2, pp. 116–17; Theo Riches, 'The Carol-ingian Capture of Aachen in 978 and its Historiographical Footprint', in Paul Fouracre and David Ganz (eds), *Frankland: The Franks and the*

World of the Early Middle Ages: Essays in Honour of Dame Jinty Nelson (Manchester 2008), pp. 191–208.

7 Richer, *Histories*, III.88, ed. and trans. Lake, vol. 2, pp. 150–53. Emma was the daughter of Empress Adelheide, Otto I's wife, by her first husband, making her Otto II's stepsister.

8 Richer, *Histories*, III.96, ed. and trans. Lake, vol. 2, pp. 164–7.

9 Adelbert Davids (ed.), *The Empress Theophano: Byzantium and the West at the Turn of the First Millennium* (Cambridge 1995); Maclean, *Ottonian Queenship*, pp. 150–79.

10 Richer, *Histories*, III.86, ed. and trans. Lake, vol. 2, pp. 140–43; quote at Gerbert of Aurillac, *Lettres de Gerbert (983–997)*, ed. Julien Havet (Paris 1889), no. 48, p. 46; trans. Harriet Pratt Lattin, *The Letters of Gerbert, with his Papal Privileges as Sylvester II* (New York 1961), no. 55, p. 95.

11 Gerbert, *Lettres*, ed. Havet, no. 91, p. 83; trans. Lattin, *Letters*, no. 102, p. 137; Richer, *Histories*, III.95, ed. and trans. Lake, vol. 2, pp. 162–5.

12 Gerbert, *Lettres*, ed. Havet, no. 97, p. 89; trans. Lattin, *Letters*, no. 100, p. 135.

13 Robert-Henri Bautier, 'L'avènement d'Hugues Capet et le sacre de Robert le Pieux', in Michel Parisse and Xavier Barral i Altet (eds), *Le Roi de France et son royaume autour de l'an mil* (Paris 1992), pp. 27–37.

14 Richer, *Histories*, IV.2, ed. and trans. Lake, vol. 2, pp. 218–19. On Richer's and Adalbero's knowledge and use of classical rhetoric, see Justin Lake, *Richer of Saint-Rémi: The Methods and Mentality of a Tenth-Century Historian* (Washington, DC 2013), pp. 183–242.

15 Bautier, 'L'avènement d'Hugues Capet'.

16 Andrew W. Lewis, *Royal Succession in Capetian France: Studies on Familial Order and the State* (Cambridge, MA 1981), pp. 7–43.

17 Andrew W. Lewis, 'Anticipatory Association of the Heir in Early Capetian France', *American Historical Review* 83 (1978), pp. 906–27.

18 Gerbert, *Lettres*, ed. Havet, no. 120, p. 109; trans. Lattin, *Letters*, no. 129, p. 160.

19 Gerbert, *Lettres*, ed. Havet, no. 111, pp. 101–2; trans. Lattin, *Letters*, no. 119, pp. 151–2; A. A. A. Vasiliev, 'Hugh Capet and Byzantium', *Dumbarton Oaks Papers* 6 (1951), pp. 227–51.

20 Jan Dhondt, 'Sept femmes et un trio de rois', *Contributions à l'histoire économique et sociale* 3 (1964–65), pp. 37–70, at pp. 38–41.

21 Richer, *Histories*, IV.12, ed. and trans. Lake, vol. 2, pp. 222–3.

22 The ideals of early Capetian kingship are lucidly discussed in Geoffrey Koziol, 'The Conquest of Burgundy, the Peace of God, and the Diplomas of Robert the Pious', *French Historical Studies* 37 (2014), pp. 184–6.

23 Olivier Guillot, *Le comte d'Anjou et son entourage au XIe siècle*, 2 vols (Paris 1972), vol. 1, pp. 15–55; Bernard S. Bachrach, *Fulk Nerra, the Neo-Roman Consul, 987–1040: A Political Biography of the Angevin Count* (Berkeley, CA 1993).

24 Richer, *Histories*, IV.76–78, ed. and trans. Lake, vol. 2, pp. 364–9.

25 Richer, *Histories*, IV.96–97, ed. and trans. Lake, vol. 2, pp. 404–11.

26 Sassier, *Hugues Capet*, pp. 253–4.

27 Sassier, *Hugues Capet*, p. 250.

28 Christian Pfister, *Étude sur le règne de Robert le Pieux (996–1031)* (Paris 1885), pp. 314–15.

29 Helgaud of Fleury, *Vie de Robert le Pieux/Epitoma vitae regis Roberti pii*, ed. and trans. [into French] Robert-Henri Bautier and Gillette Labory (Paris 1965), pp. 96–9.

30 Alain Erlande-Brandenburg, *Le roi est mort: Étude sur les funérailles, les sépultures et les tombeaux des rois de France jusqu'à la fin du XIIIe siècle* (Geneva 1975), pp. 68–86.

31 Gerbert, *Lettres*, ed. Havet, no. 159, pp. 141; trans. Lattin, *Letters*, no. 168, pp. 197.

32 Karl Ferdinand Werner, 'Die Legitimität der Kapetinger und die Entstehung der "*Reditus regni Francorum ad stirpem Karoli*"', *Die Welt als Geschicte* 3 (1952), pp. 203–25; *Historia francorum senonensis*, trans. in Fraser McNair, 'A Post-Carolingian Voice of Dissent: The *Historia Francorum Senonensis*', *Journal of Medieval Latin* 28 (2018), p. 44; cf. Aimon of Fleury, *Les miracles de saint Benoît*, III.i, ed. E. de Certain (Paris 1858), p. 127.

2. Peace and Love at the Millennium

1 Helgaud of Fleury, *Vie de Robert le Pieux/Epitoma vitae regis Roberti pii*, ed. and trans. [into French] Robert-Henri Bautier and Gillette Labory (Paris 1965), pp. 92–3.

2 Frank Barlow, 'The King's Evil', *EHR* 95 (1980), pp. 3–27; Marc Bloch, *The Royal Touch: Sacred Monarchy and Scrofula in England and France*, trans. J. E. Anderson (London 1973), pp. 12–21, 36–48.

3 Geoffrey Koziol, 'The Conquest of Burgundy, the Peace of God, and the Diplomas of Robert the Pious', *French Historical Studies* 37 (2014), pp. 173–214.

4 Jan Dhondt, 'Sept femmes et un trio de rois', *Contributions à l'histoire économique et sociale* 3 (1964–5), pp. 42–6; David d'Avray, *Dissolving Royal Marriages: A Documentary History, 860–1600* (Cambridge 2014), pp. 44–6. Their common ancestor was Henry the Fowler, founder of the Ottonian dynasty.

5 Christian Pfister, *Étude sur le règne de Robert le Pieux (996–1031)* (Paris 1885), p. 49.

6 Helgaud of Fleury, *Vie de Robert le Pieux*, ed. and trans. Bautier and Labory, pp. 92–7.

7 Richer of Saint-Rémi, *Histories*, IV.87, ed. and trans. Justin Lake, 2 vols (Cambridge, MA 2011), vol. 2, pp. 385–7.

8 Pfister, *Étude sur le règne*, pp. 255–64; Rodulfus Glaber, *The Five Books of the Histories*, II.viii.15–16, ed. Neithard Bulst, trans. John France and Paul Reynolds (Oxford 1989), pp. 78–81.

9 Peter Damian, 'De variis miraculosis narrationibus', PL, vol. 145, col. 580.

10 Louis's wife was probably Constance's mother (Pfister, *Étude sur le règne*, pp. 62–3).

11 Penelope Ann Adair, 'Constance of Arles: A Study in Duty and Frustration', in *Capetian Women*, ed. Kathleen Nolan (Basingstoke 2003), pp. 9–26.

12 Glaber, *Five Books*, III.ix.32, 36, ed. Bulst, trans. France and Reynolds, pp. 152–3, 158–9; Helgaud of Fleury, *Vie de Robert*, ed. and trans. Bautier and Labory, pp. 74–75; Dhondt, 'Sept femmes', 51.

13 *Cartulaire de l'abbaye de Saint-Père de Chartres*, ed. Benjamin Guérard, 2 vols (Paris 1840), vol. 1, p. 115.

14 Helgaud, *Vie de Robert le Pieux*, ed. and trans. Bautier and Labory, pp. 64–5, 72–5.

15 Glaber, *Five Books*, II.ix.17, ed. Bulst, trans. France and Reynolds, pp. 80–83; Pierre Bonnassie, *From Slavery to Feudalism in South-Western Europe* (Cambridge 1991), pp. 288–313.

16 On earlier 'castles', see Simon Maclean, 'The Edict of Pîtres, Carolingian Defence against the Vikings, and the Origins of the Medieval Castle', *Transactions of the Royal Historical Association* 30 (2020), pp. 29–54; Luc Bourgeois, 'Les résidences des élites et les fortifications du haut Moyen Âge en France et en Belgique dans leur cadre européen: Aperçu historiographique (1955–2005)', *Cahiers de civilisation médiévale* 49 (2006), pp. 113–41.

17 There was much debate over this development and its relationship to castles and violence at the end of the twenty-first century. Representative views can be found in Thomas N. Bisson, 'The "Feudal Revolution"', *Past & Present* 142 (1994), pp. 6–42, and the ensuing debate, with contributions by Dominique Barthélemy, Stephen White, Timothy Reuter, and Chris Wickham, and a reply by Bisson in *Past & Present* 152 (1996), pp. 196–223, and 155 (1997), pp. 177–225. Charles West, 'Lordship in Ninth-Century Francia: The Case of Bishop Hincmar of Laon and his Followers', *Past & Present* 226 (2015), pp. 3–40, argues convincingly for the novelty of post-millennial lordship.

18 Geoffrey Koziol, *The Peace of God* (Leeds 2018); Thomas Head and Richard Landes (eds), *The Peace of God: Social Violence and Religious Response in France around the Year 1000* (Ithaca, NY 1992); Hartmut Hoffmann, *Gottesfriede und Treuga Dei* (Stuttgart 1964).

19 'Allocutio missi cuiusdam Divionensis', MGH, Capit., vol. 2, ed. Alfred Boretius and Victor Krause (Hanover 1897), p. 292; Jean Dunbabin, *France in the Making, 843–1180*, 2nd edn (Oxford 2000), pp. 150–54.

20 Helgaud of Fleury, *Vie de Robert le Pieux*, ed. and trans. Bautier and Labory, pp. 110–11.

21 Pfister, *Étude sur le règne*, no. XII, pp. lx–lxi; Theo Riches, 'The Peace of God, the "Weakness" of Robert the Pious and the Struggle for the German Throne, 1023–5', *Early Medieval Europe* 18 (2010), pp. 202–22; Élisabeth Magnou-Nortier, 'Les évêques et la paix dans l'espace franc (VIe–XIe siècles)', in *L'Évêque dans l'histoire de l'église* (Angers 1984), pp. 47–8, 50 n. 53, who notes that the Latin syntax clearly indicates that Warin swore the oath to Robert.

22 Dominique Barthélemy, 'The Peace of God and the Bishops at War in the Gallic Lands from the Late Tenth to the Early Twelfth Century', *Anglo-Norman Studies* 32 (2010), pp. 1–23.

23 Glaber, *Five Books*, III.iv.13, ed. Bulst, trans. France and Reynolds, pp. 116–17.

24 Richard Landes, 'The Fear of an Apocalyptic Year 1000: Augustinian Historiography, Medieval and Modern', *Speculum* 75 (2000), pp. 97–145, portents at p. 133; James T. Palmer, *The Apocalypse in the Early Middle Ages* (Cambridge 2014), pp. 189–226; Al-Hākim: Josef van Ess, *Chiliastische Erwartungen und die Versuchung der Göttlichkeit: der Kalif al-Hākim (386–411 H.)* (Heidelberg 1977).

25 E.g. Glaber, *Five Books*, II.xii.23, III.vii.24–25, ed. Bulst, trans. France and Reynolds, pp. 92–3, 133–7.

26 Dominique Barthélemy, *The Serf, the Knight, and the Historian*, trans. Graham Robert Edwards (Ithaca, NY 2009), esp. p. 283; Robert Chazan, '1007–1012: Initial Crisis for Northern European Jewry', *Proceedings of the American Academy for Jewish Research*, 38/39 (1970–71), pp. 101–17; R. I. Moore, *The Formation of a Persecuting Society: Authority and Deviance in Western Europe, 950-1250*, 2nd edn (Oxford 2006).

27 Adhemar of Chabannes, *Chronicon*, III.59, ed. Pascale Bourgain with Richard Landes and Georges Pon (Turnhout 1999), p. 180.

28 Michael D. Barbezat, 'The Fires of Hell and the Burning of Heretics in the Accounts of the Executions at Orléans in 1022', *JMH* 40 (2014), pp. 399–420.

29 Robert-Henri Bautier, 'L'hérésie d'Orléans et le mouvement intellectuel au début du XIᵉ siècle', *Actes du 95e Congrès national des sociétés savantes (Reims 1970), Section de philologie et d'histoire jusqu'à 1610* (Paris 1975), pp. 63–88.

30 W. Scott Jessee, 'A Missing Capetian Princess: Advisa Daughter of King Robert II of France', *Medieval Prosopography* 11 (1990), pp. 1–16.

31 Pfister, *Étude sur le règne*, p. 79; Marie Fauroux (ed.), *Recueil des actes des ducs de Normandie de 911 à 1066* (Caen 1961), no. 58, pp. 180–82; *The gesta normannorum ducum of William of Jumièges, Orderic Vitalis, and Robert of Torigni*, VI.6, ed. and trans. Elisabeth M. C. van Houts, 2 vols (Oxford 1992–5), vol. 2, pp. 52–3.

32 André of Fleury and Raoul Tortaire, *Les miracles de saint Benoît*, VII.i, VIII.i, ed. E. de Certain (Paris 1858), pp. 249–50, pp. 277–8. Odo is also known to have led French troops against Normandy under his brother's command, a more honourable but equally violent vocation that does not preclude sacrilegiously fatal banditry later on (William of Malmesbury, *Gesta regum anglorum: The History of the English Kings*, III.233, ed. and trans. R. A. B. Mynors, R. M. Thomson, and M. Winterbottom, 2 vols [Oxford 1998–99], vol. I, pp. 434–5).

33 Fulbert of Chartres, *The Letters and Poems of Fulbert of Chartres*, ed. and trans. Frederick Behrends (Oxford 1976), no. 101, pp. 182–5, no. 104, pp. 188–9.

34 Rudolph Glaber, 'The Life of St William', xi, in *Historiarum libri quinque/The Five Books of the Histories*, ed. Neithard Bulst and trans. John France and Paul Reynolds (Oxford 1989), pp. 284–5.

35 Fulbert of Chartres, *Letters and Poems*, ed. and trans. Behrends, no. 115, pp. 206–9.

36 Fulbert of Chartres, *Letters and Poems*, ed. and trans. Behrends, no. 124, pp. 222–5.

37 Glaber, *Five Books*, III.ix.35, ed. Bulst, trans. France and Reynolds, pp. 156–7.

38 Adalbero of Laon, *Poème au roi Robert*, ln. 389, ed. and trans. [into French] Claude Carozzi (Paris 1979), pp. 30–31.

3. A Stormy Season

1 André of Fleury, *Les miracles de saint Benoît*, VI.xi, ed. E. de Certain (Paris 1858), pp. 233–6, quote at p. 234.

2 Rudolph Glaber, *The Five Books of the Histories*, IV.iv.10–13, ed. Neithard Bulst and trans. John France and Paul Reynolds (Oxford 1989), pp. 187–93, quote at p. 189.

3 Richard Landes, 'The Fear of an Apocalyptic Year 1000: Augustinian Historiography, Medieval and Modern', *Speculum* 75 (2000), pp. 134–8; quote at Glaber, *Five Books*, IV.iv.16, ed. Bulst, trans. France and Reynolds, pp. 196–7.

4 For the Latin derivation of Molly, molly-houses, molly-boys, and the like, see Jonathon Green, *Cassell's Dictionary of Slang* (London 2000).

5 Robert-Henri Bautier, 'Anne de Kiev, reine de France, et la politique royale au XIᵉ siècle: Étude critique de la documentation', *Revue des études slaves* 57 (1985), p. 546.

6 Orderic Vitalis, *The Ecclesiastical History of Orderic Vitalis*, VII.14, ed. and trans. Marjorie Chibnall, 6 vols (Oxford 1969–80), vol. 4, pp. 74–9; Jan Dhondt, 'Une crise du pouvoir capétien, 1032–34', in *Miscellanea mediaevalia in memoriam Jan Frederik Niermeyer* (Groningen 1967), pp. 137–48, accepts the chronicler's account; cf. David Bates, *Normandy before 1066* (London 1982), pp. 71–3, who doubts it.

7 André of Fleury, *Miracles de saint Benoît*, VI.xv–xvi, ed. E. de Certain, pp. 241–3.

8 Michel Bur, *La formation du comté de Champagne, v. 905–v. 1150* (Nancy 1977), pp. 151–92.

9 Bernard S. Bachrach, *Fulk Nerra, the Neo-Roman Consul, 987–1040: A Political Biography of the Angevin Count* (Berkeley, CA 1993).

10 Glaber, *Five Books*, V.ii.19, ed. Bulst, trans. France and Reynolds, pp. 242–45; Olivier Guillot, *Le comte d'Anjou et son entourage au XIᵉ siècle*, 2 vols (Paris 1972), vol. 1, pp. 43–79.

11 William of Malmesbury, *Gesta regum anglorum: The History of the English Kings*, III.235, ed. and trans. R. A. B. Mynors, R. M. Thomson and M. Winterbottom, 2 vols (Oxford 1998–99), vol. 1, pp. 436–7.

12 Fulbert of Chartres, *The Letters and Poems of Fulbert of Chartres*, ed. and trans. Frederick Behrends (Oxford 1976), no. 51, pp. 90–93.

13 Bernard S. Bachrach, 'The Angevin Strategy of Castle Building in the Reign of Fulk Nerra, 987–1040', *American Historical Review* 88 (1983), pp. 533–60; Richard E. Barton, *Lordship in the County of Maine, c. 890–1160* (Woodbridge 2004).

14 Dhondt, 'crise du pouvoir', quote at p. 148.

15 Jane Martindale, 'Conventum inter Willelmum Comitem Aquitanorum et Hugonem Chiliarchum', *EHR* 84 (1969), pp. 528–48.

16 Dominique Barthélemy, *The Serf, the Knight, and the Historian*, trans. Graham Robert Edwards (Ithaca, NY 2009), quote at p. 65; Alice Rio, *Slavery after Rome, 500–1100* (Oxford 2017), pp. 107–14.

17 Alain Boureau, *The Lord's First Night: The Myth of the* droit de cuissage, trans. Lydia G. Cochrane (Chicago, IL 1998).

18 Paul Fouracre, 'Marmoutier and its Serfs in the Eleventh Century', *Transactions of the Royal Historical Society*, 6th ser., 15 (2005), pp. 29–49, at p. 38.

19 Adalbero of Laon, *Poème au roi Robert*, ln. 294, ed. and trans. [into French] Claude Carozzi (Paris 1979), pp. 22–3; André of Fleury, *Miracles de saint Benoît*, V.viii, VI.ii, ed. de Certain, pp. 205–7, 218–21; *The* gesta normannorum ducum *of William of Jumièges, Orderic Vitalis, and Robert of Torigni*, V.2, ed. and trans. Elisabeth M. C. van Houts, 2 vols (Oxford 1992–5), vol. 2, pp. 8–9; Georges Duby, *The Three Orders: Feudal Society Imagined*, trans. Arthur Goldhammer (Chicago, IL 1980).

20 David Bates, *William the Conqueror* (New Haven, CT 2017), pp. 16–48.

21 Bates, *William*, pp. 49–90.

22 Jan Dhondt, 'Henri Ier, l'Empire, et l'Anjou (1043–1056)', *Revue historique belge de philologie et d'histoire* 25 (1946), pp. 87–109.

23 Bates, *William*, pp. 129–46.

24 On Rus' and Rusian marital strategies, see Christian Raffensberger, *Reimagining Europe: Kievan Rus' in the Medieval World* (Cambridge, MA 2012).

25 Jean Dunbabin, 'What's in a Name? Philip, King of France', *Speculum* 68 (1993), pp. 949–68, quote at p. 953.

26 Talia Zajac, 'Remembrance and Erasure of Objects Belonging to Rus' Princesses in Medieval Western Sources: The Cases of Anastasia Iaroslavna's "Saber of Charlemagne" and Anna Iaroslavna's Red Gem', in *Moving Women, Moving Objects (400–1500)*, ed. Tracy Chapman Hamilton and Mariah Proctor-Tiffany (Leiden 2019), pp. 33–58.

27 Dunbabin, 'What's in a Name?'; Andrzej and Danuta Poppe, 'The Autograph of Anna of Rus', Queen of France', *Journal of Ukrainian Studies* 33/34 (2008/9), pp. 400–406.

28 Bautier, 'Anne de Kiev', pp. 554–60, 564.

29 *Chronique de Saint-Pierre-le-Vif de Sens, dite de Clarius/Chronicon Sancti Petri vivi Senonensis*, ed. and trans. [into French] Robert-Henri Bautier and Monique Gilles with Anne-Marie Bautier (Paris 1979), p. 126. The

marriage was consanguineous as well as bigamous since Anne and Raoul were related in the fifth degree.

30 Emily Joan Ward, 'Anne of Kiev (c. 1024–c. 1075) and a Reassessment of Maternal Power in the Minority Kingship of Philip I of France', *Historical Research* 89 (2016), pp. 435–53.

31 Gervase of Reims, 'Epistola ad Alexandrum II papam', *HF*, vol. ii, p. 499.

32 William of Malmesbury, *Gesta regum anglorum*, III.234, ed. and trans. Mynors, Thomson, and Winterbottom, vol. i, p. 437.

4. Philandering Philip

1 Richard A. Jackson (ed.), *Ordines coronationis franciae: Texts and Ordines for the Coronation of Frankish and French Kings and Queens in the Middle Ages*, 2 vols (Philadelphia, PA 1995), no. XVII, vol. i, pp. 226–32.

2 Orderic Vitalis, *The Ecclesiastical History of Orderic Vitalis*, XI.16, 34, ed. and trans. Marjorie Chibnall, 6 vols (Oxford 1969–80), vol. 6, pp. 76–7, 154–7; Guibert of Nogent, *Monodiae*, III.2, trans. Paul J. Archambault, *A Monk's Confession: The Memoires of Guibert of Nogent* (University Park, PA 1996), p. 123.

3 Michel Pastoureau, 'Le temps des rois obèses (XIe–XIIIe siècle)', *Micrologus* 19 (2011), pp. 259–76.

4 Augustin Fliche, *Le règne de Philippe Ier, roi de France (1060–1108)* (Paris 1912), p. 527.

5 François Neveux, *La Normandie des ducs aux rois, Xe–XIIe siècle* (Rennes 1998), pp. 285–6, 417–45; C. Warren Hollister, 'Normandy, France, and the Anglo-Norman *regnum*', *Speculum* 51 (1976), pp. 202–42.

6 William M. Aird, *Robert Curthose, Duke of Normandy, c. 1050–1134* (Woodbridge 2008); quote at David Bates, *William the Conqueror* (New Haven, CT 2017), p. 398.

7 Orderic Vitalis, *The Ecclesiastical History*, IV, ed. and trans. Chibnall, vol. 2, pp. 356–9.

8 Aird, *Robert Curthose*, pp. 99–147.

9 Robert Latouche, *Histoire du comté du Maine pendant le Xe et le XIe siècles* (Paris 1910), pp. 40–44; Fliche, *Le règne de Philippe Ier*, pp. 289–301.

10 Neveux, *Normandie des ducs*, pp. 417–68.

11 Orderic Vitalis, *Ecclesiastical History*, VIII.10, ed. and trans. Chibnall, vol. 4, pp. 186–7.

12 Olivier Guillot, *Le comte d'Anjou et son entourage au XIe siècle*, 2 vols (Paris 1972), vol. 1, pp. 102–24.

13 Matthew Gabriele, 'Not So Strange Bedfellows: New Thoughts on King Philip I of Francia's Marriage to Bertrada of Montfort', *JMH* 46 (2020), p. 505.

14 William of Malmesbury, *Gesta regum anglorum: The History of the English Kings*, III.257, ed. and trans. R. A. B. Mynors, R. M. Thomson, and M. Winterbottom, 2 vols (Oxford 1998–99), vol. 1, pp. 474–5.

15 Louis Halphen and René Poupardin (eds.), *Chroniques des comtes d'Anjou et des seigneurs d'Amboise* (Paris 1913), p. 65; Suger, *Gesta Ludovici grossi*, XVIII, ed. and trans. into French by Henri Waquet as *Vie de Louis VI le Gros* (Paris 1964), pp. 122–5.

16 Quoted in Fliche, *Le règne de Philippe Ier*, p. 45 n. 3.

17 Charles Verlinden, *Robert Ier le Frison, Comte de Flandre, Étude d'histoire politique* (Antwerp and Paris 1935), pp. 78–9.

18 Marie-Bernadette Bruguière, 'Canon Law and Royal Weddings, Theory and Practice: The French Example, 987–1215', *Proceedings of the Eighth International Congress on Medieval Canon Law*, ed. Stanley Chodrow (Vatican City 1992), pp. 473–96.

19 Olivier Guyotjeannin, 'L'épiscopat dans le domaine capétien (XIe–XIIe siècles): "Libertés" ecclésiastiques et service du roi', *Pouvoirs et libertés au temps des premiers Capétiens*, ed. Élisabeth Magnou-Nortier (Maulévrier 1992), pp. 215–30.

20 Ivo of Chartres, *Correspondance: Tome I (1090–1098)*, ed. and trans. [into French] Jean Leclercq (Paris 1949), no. 8, pp. 34–5.

21 Ivo of Chartres, *Correspondance*, no. 14, pp. 62–3.

22 Georges Duby, *Medieval Marriage: Two Models from Twelfth-Century France*, trans. Elborg Forster (Baltimore, MD 1978), pp. 29–45.

23 Brigitte Basdevant-Gaudemet, 'Le mariage d'après la correspondance d'Yves de Chartres', *Revue historique de droit français et étranger*, ser. 4, vol. 61

(1983), pp. 195–215; Christof Rolker, *Canon Law and the Letters of Ivo of Chartres* (Cambridge 2010), pp. 230–47; Fliche, *Le règne de Philippe Ier*, pp. 65–6.

24 Hans Eberhard Mayer, *The Crusades*, trans. John Gillingham, 2nd edn (Oxford 1988), pp. 1–7.

25 Robert Somerville, 'The Council of Clermont (1095) and Latin Christian Society', *Archivum historiae pontificae* 12 (1974), pp. 55–90.

26 Fulk le Réchin, 'Fragmentum historiae andegavensis', in Louis Halphen and René Poupardin (eds), *Chroniques des comtes d'Anjou et des seigneurs d'Amboise* (Paris 1913), p. 237.

27 Jay Rubenstein, *Armies of Heaven: The First Crusade and the Quest for Apocalypse* (New York 2011), p. 21.

28 The five main versions of the sermon are published in English translation in Edward Peters (ed.), *The First Crusade: The Chronicle of Fulcher of Chartres and Other Source Materials*, 2nd edn (Philadelphia, PA 1998).

29 Robert of Reims, 'The Historia Hierosolymitana', trans. in Peters (ed.), *The First Crusade*, p. 27.

30 Matthew Gabriele, *An Empire of Memory: The Legend of Charlemagne, the Franks, and Jerusalem before the First Crusade* (Oxford 2011), pp. 129–59.

31 Conor Kostick, *The Social Structure of the First Crusade* (Leiden 2008).

32 Quote from William of Malmesbury, *Gesta regum anglorum*, IV.348, ed. Mynors, Thomson and Winterbottom, vol. 1, p. 606.

33 Jean Flori, *Pierre l'ermite et la première croisade* (Paris 1999).

34 Robert Chazan, *European Jewry and the First Crusade* (Berkeley, CA 1987), pp. 85–114.

35 Anna Comnena, *The Alexiad of Anna Comnena*, X.5, ed. and trans. E. R. A. Sewter (New York 1989), pp. 308, 311. A recent re-assessment of Anna's often maligned history is Leonora Neville, *Anna Komnene: The Life and Work of a Medieval Historian* (Oxford 2016).

36 On tactics, see John France, *Victory in the East: A Military History of the First Crusade* (Cambridge 1994), and R. C. Smail, *Crusading Warfare, 1097–1193*, 2nd edn (Cambridge 1995).

37 Fulcher of Chartres, 'Gesta Francorum', trans. in Peters (ed.), *The First Crusade*, p. 91.

38 It is true that no kings from any kingdom went on the First Crusade, but Philip could not have done so even if he had wished to and the

only other likely royal candidate for the expedition was William Rufus, whose brother Robert Curthose went and who may well have been leery of leaving his kingdom unattended while the French king remained at home.

39 Suger, *Gesta Ludovici grossi*, XIII, ed. and trans. [into French] by Henri Waquet as *Vie de Louis VI le Gros* (Paris 1964), pp. 80–83, trans. [into English] by Richard Cusimano and John Moorhead as *The Deeds of Louis the Fat* (Washington, DC 1992), pp. 61–2; Orderic Vitalis, *The Ecclesiastical History*, XI.34, ed. and trans. Chibnall, vol. 6, pp. 154–5, corroborates Suger's account. For the tomb, excavated in the nineteenth century, see Fliche, *Le règne de Philippe Ier*, pp. 559–63.

5. The Knight-King

1 Suger, *Gesta Ludovici grossi*, XXIX, ed. and trans. into French by Henri Waquet as *Vie de Louis VI le gros* (Paris 1964), p. 236; trans. into English by Richard Cusimano and John Moorhead as *The Deeds of Louis the Fat* (Washington, DC 1992), p. 135.

2 Augustin Fliche, *Le règne de Philippe Ier, roi de France (1060–1108)* (Paris 1912), p. 85

3 Suger, *Gesta Ludovici*, I, ed. Wacquet, *Vie de Louis VI*, pp. 8–9, trans. Cusimano and Moorhead, *The Deeds of Louis*, p. 26.

4 Orderic Vitalis, *The Ecclesiastical History of Orderic Vitalis*, XI.9, ed. and trans. Marjorie Chibnall, 6 vols (Oxford 1969–80), vol. 6, pp. 50–55; scabies and rotten teeth, ibid., VIII.20, vol. 4, pp. 264–5.

5 Éric Bournazel, *Louis VI le gros* (Paris 2007), pp. 48–51.

6 Bournazel, *Louis VI*, pp. 41–3; 'Epistolae Lamberti Atrebatensis episcopi', 23, *HF*, vol. 15, p. 187.

7 Dominique Barthélemy, 'Rois et nobles au temps de la Paix de Dieu', in Rolf Große (ed.), *Suger en question: Regards croisés sur Saint-Denis* (Munich 2004), pp. 155–67.

8 Jean Flori, *L'essor de la chevalerie, XIe–XIIe siècles* (Geneva 1986).

9 Orderic Vitalis, *The Ecclesiastical History*, XI.34, ed. and trans. Chibnall, vol. 6, pp. 156–7.

10 Jean Dufour (ed.), *Recueil des actes de Louis VI roi de France (1108–37)*, 4 vols (Paris 1992–4), no. 58, vol. 1, p. 119.

11 Achille Luchaire, *Louis VI le gros: Annales de sa vie et de son règne (1081–1137)* (Paris 1890), no. 111, pp. 59–60.

12 Suger, *Gesta Ludovici*, XXIX, ed. Waquet, *Vie de Louis*, p. 238, trans. Cusimano and Moorhead, *The Deeds of Louis*, p. 136.

13 Fliche, *Le règne de Philippe*, pp. 90–91, 114. His third son, named Florus, married a minor heiress in Champagne (Andrew W. Lewis, *Royal Succession in Capetian France: Studies on Familial Order and the State* (Cambridge, MA 1981), p. 51).

14 James Naus, *Constructing Kingship: The Capetian Monarchs of France and the Early Crusades* (Manchester 2016).

15 Suger, *Gesta Ludovici*, IX, ed. Waquet, *Vie de Louis*, p. 48, trans. Cusimano and Moorhead, *The Deeds of Louis*, p. 45.

16 An episode nicely narrated in Peter Frankopan, *The First Crusade: The Call from the East* (Cambridge, MA 2012), pp. 161–3.

17 Anna Comnena, *The Alexiad of Anna Comnena*, XI.12, ed. and trans. E. R. A. Sewter (New York 1989), pp. 366–7.

18 Orderic Vitalis, *The Ecclesiastical History*, XI.12, ed. and trans. Chibnall, vol. 6, pp. 68–73.

19 Marion Facinger, 'A Study of Medieval Queenship: Capetian France, 987–1237', *Studies in Medieval and Renaissance History* 5 (1968), pp. 3–48; Fliche, *Le règne de Philippe*, p. 97.

20 Ivo of Chartres, *Epistolae*, PL, vol. 162, no. 89, col. 110C.

21 Jean Dufour, 'Étienne de Garlande', *Bulletin de la Société de l'histoire de Paris et de l'Île-de-France*, 122–4 (1999), pp. 39–53; Bournazel, *Louis VI*, pp. 56–68.

22 *Domesday Book*, vol. 17, *Herefordshire*, ed. Frank and Caroline Thorn with Veronica Sankaran (Chichester 1983), 29.16.

23 C. Warren Hollister, 'War and Diplomacy in the Anglo-Norman World: The Reign of Henry I', *Anglo-Norman Studies VI*, ed. R. Allen Brown (1984), pp. 72–88.

24 Orderic Vitalis, *The Eccclesiastical History*, XII.39, ed. and trans. Chibnall, vol. 6, pp. 352–3.

25 Suger, *Gesta Ludovici*, XVI, ed. Waquet, *Vie de Louis*, p. 104.

26 Daniel Power, *The Norman Frontier in the Twelfth and Early Thirteenth Centuries* (Cambridge 2004), pp. 374–5.

27 Suger, *Gesta Ludovici*, XXVI, ed. Waquet, *Vie de Louis*, p. 196, trans. Cusimano and Moorhead, *The Deeds of Louis*, p. 117.

28 François Neveux, *La Normandie des ducs aux rois, X^e–XIIe siècle* (Rennes 1998), pp. 481–3; quote at Orderic Vitalis, *Ecclesiastical History*, XII.18, ed. and trans. Chibnall, vol. 6, p. 241.

29 Orderic Vitalis, *Ecclesiastical History*, XII.26, ed. and trans. Chibnall, vol. 6, pp. 294–307, see p. 299 n. 3 for the lunar phase; William of Malmesbury, *Gesta regum anglorum: The History of the English Kings*, V.419, ed. and trans. R. A. B. Mynors, R. M. Thomson and M. Winterbottom, 2 vols (Oxford 1998–9), vol. 1, pp. 758–63.

30 Karl Leyser, 'The Anglo-Norman Succession, 1120–1125', *Anglo-Norman Studies 13*, ed. Marjorie Chibnall (Woodbridge 1991), pp. 225–41, quote at 232.

31 Orderic Vitalis, *The Ecclesiastical History*, XII.36, ed. and trans. Chibnall, vol. 6, pp. 340–43.

32 Ekkhard of Aura, 'Chronicon imperatorum ab origine Francorum ad anno 1114', ed. Cl. G. Waitz, MGH, SS, vol. 6 (Hanover 1844), pp. 262–3, quote at 262.

33 Dufour (ed.), *Recueil des actes de Louis VI*, no. 220, vol. 1, pp. 458–66.

34 Suger, *Deeds of Louis*, XXVIII, ed. Waquet, *La vie de Louis*, p. 222, trans. Cusimano and Moorhead, *The Deeds of Louis*, p. 129.

35 Laura Hibbard-Loomis, 'L'oriflamme de France et le cri "Munjoie" au XIIe siècle', *Le Moyen Âge*, 4th ser, vol. 65 (1959), pp. 469–99; 'The Oriflamme of France and the War-Cry "Monjoie" in the Twelfth Century', in Dorothy Miner (ed.), *Studies in Art and Literature for Belle Da Costa Green* (Princeton, NJ 1954), pp. 67–82.

36 *The Song of Roland*, ll. 3093–95, ed. and trans [into French] Ian Short, p. 208, trans. Robert Harrison (New York 1970), pp. 145–6.

6. Gothic Fabrications

1 'Annales de Saint-Denis', ed. Élie Berger, 'Annales de Saint-Denis, généralement connues sous le titre de Chronicon sancti Dionysii ad cyclos-paschales', *BEC* 40 (1879), p. 276.

2 Élisabeth Lalou, 'The Capetians and the River Seine (Thirteenth-Fourteenth Century)', in *Political Ritual and Practice in Capetian France: Studies in Honour of Elizabeth A. R. Brown*, ed. M. Cecilia Gaposchkin and Jay Rubenstein (Turnhout 2021), pp. 383–98.

3 Jean Guérout, *Le Palais de la Cité à Paris des origines à 1417: Essai topographique et archéologique* (Paris 1953), pp. 132–46.

4 Robert-Henri Bautier, 'Paris au temps d'Abélard', in *Abélard en son temps* (Paris 1981), pp. 21–77; Jacques Boussard, *Nouvelle histoire de Paris, de la fin du siège 885–886 à la mort de Philippe Auguste* (Paris 1976), pp. 89–155.

5 Constant J. Mews, 'The Voice of Heloise', *The Lost Love Letters of Heloise and Abelard*, 2nd edn (New York 2008), pp. 145–77.

6 Peter Abelard, *Historia calamitatum*, ed. David Luscombe and trans. Betty Radice, *The Letter Collection of Peter Abelard and Heloise* (Oxford 2013), pp. 36–9.

7 Derek Keen, 'Towns and the Growth of Trade', in *The New Cambridge Medieval History*, vol. 4 (Cambridge 2004), pp. 49, 53.

8 Boussard, *Nouvelle histoire de Paris*, pp. 268–71; Walter Map, *De nugis curialium*, V.5, ed. and trans. M. R. James as *Courtiers' Trifles*, rev. edn by C. N. L. Brooke and R. A. B. Mynors (Oxford 1983), pp. 457–8.

9 Suger, *Gesta Ludovici grossi*, XXXII, ed. and trans. into French by Henri Waquet as *Vie de Louis VI le gros* (Paris 1964), pp. 266, trans. into English by Richard Cusimano and John Moorhead as *The Deeds of Louis the Fat* (Washington, DC 1992), pp. 149–50.

10 *La Chronique de Morigny*, II.14, ed. Léon Mirot (Paris 1909), pp. 56–9.

11 Kathleen Nolan, 'The Tomb of Adelaide of Maurienne and the Visual Imagery of Capetian Queenship', in eadem (ed.), *Capetian Women* (Basingstoke 2003), pp. 45–76.

12 Philippe Plaigneux, 'Un chantier royal: Saint-Pierre de Montmartre (1131–1134): Louis VI le Gros et l'invention du gothique', *Bulletin monumental* 173 (2015), pp. 5–37, quote at p. 15. See also Marvin Trachtenberg, 'Suger's Miracles, Branner's Bourges: Reflections on "Gothic Architecture" as Medieval Modernism', *Gesta* 39 (2000), pp. 183–205.

13 Lindy Grant, *Abbot Suger of Saint Denis: Church and State in Early Twelfth-Century France* (London 1998); Andreas Speer, 'Les écrits de Suger comme source d'une esthétique médiévale: Une relecture critique', in

Rolf Große (ed.), *Suger en question: Regards croisés sur Saint-Denis* (Munich 2004), pp. 95–107.

14 Suger, 'De rebus in administratione sua gestis', XXIX, ed. and trans. Erwin Panofsky, *Abbot Suger on the Abbey Church of Saint-Denis and its Art Treasures*, 2nd edn by Gerda Panofsky-Soergel (Princeton, NJ 1979), pp. 52–3.

15 Blaise de Montesquiou-Fēzensac with Danielle Gaborit-Chopin, *Le Trésor de Saint-Denis: Inventaire de 1634*, 3 vols (Paris 1973–7).

16 Suger, 'De rebus administratione', XXIX, ed. and trans. in Panofsky, *Abbot Suger on the Abbey Church*, pp. 46–9.

17 Erwin Panofsky, Introduction to *Abbot Suger on the Abbey Church*, pp. 1–37; Michel Bur, *Suger: Abbé de Saint-Denis, régent de France* (Paris 1991).

18 Suger, *Gesta Ludovici*, XXIX, ed. Waquet, *Vie de Louis*, pp. 238–40, trans. Cusimano and Moorhead, *The Deeds of Louis*, p. 137.

19 Suger, *Gesta Ludovici*, I, ed. Wacquet, *Vie de Louis*, p. 10, trans. Cusimano and Moorhead, *The Deeds of Louis*, p. 27.

20 Gustav Braun von Stumm, 'L'origine de la fleur de lys des rois de France du point de vue numismatique', *Revue numismatique*, 5th ser., 13 (1951), pp. 43–58.

21 Anne Lombard-Jourdan, *Fleur de lis et oriflamme* (Paris 1991); Robert Bossaut, 'Poème latin sur l'origine des fleurs de lis', *BEC* 101 (1940), pp. 80–101.

22 Michel Pastoureau, *Le roi tué par un cochon* (Paris 2015), pp. 163–200; Colette Beaune, *The Birth of an Ideology: Myths and Symbols of Nation in Late-Medieval France*, trans. Susan Ross Huston, ed. Frederic L. Cheyette (Berkeley, CA 1991), pp. 204–10.

23 Lombard-Jourdan, *Fleur de lis*, p. 27.

24 Guillaume de Nangis, *Chronique latine de Guillaume de Nangis, de 1113 à 1300, avec les continuations de cette chronique, de 1300 à 1368*, ed. Hercule Géraud, 2 vols (Paris 1843), vol. I, pp. 14–15.

25 Suger, 'Libellus alter de consecratione ecclesiae Sancti Dionysii', III, ed. and trans. Panofsky, *Abbot Suger on the Abbey Church*, pp. 94–7.

26 Geoffrey Koziol, *The Peace of God* (Leeds 2018), ch. 3, summarizes the large literature on the subject.

27 Guibert of Nogent, *Monodiae*, III.7, trans. Paul J. Archambault as *A Monk's Confession: The Memoirs of Guibert of Nogent* (University Park, PA 1995), p. 146.

28 James Bruce Ross, 'Rise and Fall of a Twelfth-Century Clan: The Erembalds and the Murder of Count Charles of Flanders, 1127–1128', *Speculum* 34 (1959), pp. 367–90.

29 Galbert of Bruges, *De multro, traditione, et occisione gloriosi Karoli comitis Flandriarum*, [51], ed. Jeff Rider (Turnhout 1994), p. 100, trans. Jeff Rider as *The Murder, Betrayal, and Slaughter of the Glorious Charles, Count of Flanders* (New Haven, CT 2013), p. 87.

30 François-Louis Ganshof, 'Le roi de France en Flandre en 1127 et 1128', *Revue historique de droit français et étranger* 27 (1949), pp. 204–28; Galbert of Bruges, *De multro*, [57–8, 77, 80–81], ed. Rider, pp. 106–10, 129–31, 133, trans. Rider, *The Murder*, pp. 101–2, 133–5; Suger, *Gesta Ludovici*, XXX, ed. Wacquet, *Vie de Louis*, pp. 246–8, trans. Cusimano and John Moorhead, *Life of Louis*, p. 141. Suger's account of the dog is much more gruesome but much less reliable than that in Galbert of Bruges.

31 R. C. Van Caenegem, *Law, History, the Low Countries, and Europe*, ed. Ludo Milis and others (London 1994), p. 109

32 Galbert of Bruges, *De multro*, [106], ed. Rider, pp. 150–52, ed. and trans. James Bruce Ross, *The Murder of Charles the Good* (Toronto 1982), pp. 284–5.

33 Elizabeth A. R. Brown, *'Franks, Burgundians, and Aquitanians' and the Royal Coronation Ceremony in France* (Philadelphia, PA 1992), pp. 34–9, 50.

34 George T. Beech, 'The Eleanor of Aquitaine Vase: Its Origins and History to the Early Twelfth Century', *Ars Orientalis* 22 (1992), pp. 69–79. For the Madagascan origins of Sassanian crystal, see Stéphane Pradines, 'Islamic Archaeology in the Comoros: The Swahili and the Rock Crystal Trade with the Abbasid and Fatimid Caliphates', *Journal of Islamic Archaeology* 6 (2019), pp. 109–35.

35 Louis Grodecki, *Les vitraux de Saint-Denis: Étude sur le vitrail au XIIe siecle*, I (Paris 1976), pp. 115–21; Elizabeth A. R. Brown and Michael W. Cothren, 'The Twelfth-Century Crusading Window of the Abbey of Saint-Denis: *Praeteritorum enim recordatio futurum est exhibitio*', *Journal of the Warburg and Courtauld Institutes* 49 (1986), pp. 1–40, argues for a somewhat later dating.

36 Jens Peter Clausen, 'Suger, faussaire de chartes', in Große (ed.), *Suger en question*, pp. 109–16.

7. Bread, Wine, and Gaiety

1 Guy Devailly, *Le Berry du Xe siècle au milieu du XIIIe: Étude politique, religieuse, sociale et économique* (Paris 1973), pp. 381–400.

2 Jean-Hervé Foulon, 'La Nativité dans la prédication de Saint Bernard, abbé de Clairvaux', in Gilles Dorival and Jean-Paul Boyer (eds), *La Nativité et le temps de Noël, Antiquité et Moyen Âge* (Aix-en-Provence, 2003), pp. 213–29.

3 Kati Ihnat, 'The Middle Ages', Timothy Larsen (ed.), *The Oxford Handbook of Christmas* (Oxford 2020), pp. 15–26; Margot Fassler, 'The Feast of Fools and *Danielis ludus*: Popular Tradition in a Medieval Cathedral Play', in Thomas Forrest Kelly (ed.), *Plainsong in the Age of Polyphony* (Cambridge 1992), pp. 65–99.

4 Max Harris, *Sacred Folly: A New History of the Feast of Fools* (Ithaca, NY 2011), pp. 76–7; Henry Copley Greene, 'The Song of the Ass', *Speculum* 6 (1931), pp. 534–49, with evidence that the song may have been sung in Bourges.

5 Robert Branner, *The Cathedral of Bourges and its Place in Gothic Architecture*, ed. Shirley Prager Branner (New York and Cambridge, MA 1989), pp. 8–9, 15–17.

6 Guillaume de Nangis, *Chronique latine de Guillaume de Nangis, de 1113 à 1300, avec les continuations de cette chronique, de 1300 à 1368*, ed. Hercule Géraud, 2 vols (Paris 1843), vol. I, pp. 35, 38.

7 Otto of Freising, 'Gesta Friderici I imperatoris', I.35 ed. Georg Waitz and Bernhard von Simson, MGH, SS rer. Germ., vol. 46 (Hanover and Leipzig 1912), p. 54, trans. Charles C. Mierow with Richard Emery as *The Deeds of Frederick Barbarossa* (New York 1953), p. 70.

8 *La Chronique de Morigny*, III.7, ed. Léon Mirot (Paris 1909), p. 83; Eugenius III, 'Quantum praedecessores', *HF*, vol. 15, pp. 429–30.

9 Hans Eberhard Mayer, *The Crusades*, trans. John Gillingham, 2nd edn (Oxford 1988), pp. 58–92.

10 Odo of Deuil, *De profectione Ludovici VII in Orientem,* ed. and trans. as *The Journey of Louis VII to the East* by Virginia Gingerick Berry (New York 1948), pp. 6–7.

11 Odo of Deuil, *De profectione,* ed. and trans. Berry, pp. 6–7.

12 Otto of Freising, 'Gesta Friderici I imperatoris', I.35, ed. Waitz de Simson, p. 54, trans. Mierow with Emery, *The Deeds of Frederick Barbarossa,* p. 70.

13 Guillaume de Nangis, *Chronique latine,* ed. Géraud, vol. 1, p. 34

14 Ralph of Diceto, 'Abbreviationes chronicorum', in William Stubbs (ed.), *The Historical Works of Master Ralph de Diceto,* 2 vols (London 1876), vol. 1, p. 256.

15 Michel Bur, *La formation du comté de Champagne, v. 905–v. 1150* (Nancy 1977), pp. 283–307.

16 Marion Meade, *Eleanor of Aquitaine* (London 1977), did much to popularize the association, but see Jean Flori, *Eleanor of Aquitaine: Queen and Rebel,* trans. Olive Class (Edinburgh 2007), pp. 243–61, 266–72, on the problematic attributions of 'courtly love' to Eleanor's influence.

17 Yves Sassier, *Louis VII* (Paris 1991), pp. 112–24 for the dating.

18 Sassier, *Louis VII,* p. 91.

19 Geoffrey of Auxerre, *Vita et miraculis Sancti Bernardi,* 50, ed. and trans. [into French] by Raffaele Fassetta as *Notes sur la vie et les Miracles de Saint Bernard* (Paris 2011), pp. 162–5.

20 Bernard of Clairvaux, 'Epistola ad clerum et populum orientalis franciae', *HF,* vol. 15, p. 605.

21 Ralph of Diceto, 'Abbreviationes chronicorum', ed. Stubbs, *The Historical Works,* vol. 1, pp. 256–7.

22 Marcel Pacaut, *Louis VII et son royaume* (Paris 1964), pp. 55–56.

23 Odo of Deuil, *De profectione,* ed. and trans. Berry, pp. 14–17.

24 *Chronique de Morigny,* III.7, ed. Mirot, p. 85.

25 Quoted in Christopher Tyerman, *God's War: A New History of the Crusades* (London 2006), p. 336.

26 Achille Luchaire (ed.), *Études sur les actes de Louis VII* (Paris 1885), no. 224, pp. 171.

27 Aryeh Graboïs, 'The Crusade of King Louis VII: A Reconsideration', in Peter W. Edbury (ed.), *Crusade and Settlement* (Cardiff 1985), pp. 94–104.

28 Mayer, *The Crusades*, p. 103.

29 The movie's script embroidered on an already much embellished account ultimately drawn from a chronicle written more than a half century afterward, which simply states that there were armed female troops, riding astride their horses like Amazons, 'among them a second Penthesilia' (a famous Amazonian queen). See Flori, *Eleanor of Aquitaine*, pp. 43–5.

30 Flori, *Eleanor of Aquitaine*, pp. 209–38; John of Salisbury, *Historia pontificalis*, xxiii, ed. and trans. Marjorie Chibnall (Oxford 1986), p. 52.

31 John of Salisbury, *Historia pontificalis*, xxix, ed. and trans. Chibnall, pp. 61–2.

32 Elizabeth A. R. Brown, 'Eleanor of Aquitaine Reconsidered: The Woman and Her Seasons', in Bonnie Wheeler and John Carmi Parsons (eds), *Eleanor of Aquitaine, Lord and Lady* (Basingstoke 2002), p. 9.

33 Elizabeth Hallam and Charles West, *Capetian France, 987–1328*, 3rd edn (Abingdon 2020), p. 225.

34 Walter Map, *De nugis curialium*, V.5, ed. and trans. M. R. James as *Courtiers' Trifles*, rev. edn by C. N. L. Brooke and R. A. B. Mynors (Oxford 1983), pp. 450–51.

35 *Chronique de Morigny*, ed. Mirot, pp. 56–9, quote at p. 59.

36 'Comitia regni habita Suessone', *HF*, vol. 14, pp. 387–8; Aryeh Graboïs, 'De la trêve de Dieu à la paix du roi: Étude sur les transformations du mouvement de la paix au XIIe siècle', in *Mélanges offerts à René Crozet*, 2 vols (Poitiers 1966), vol. 1, pp. 585–96.

37 Pacaut, *Louis VII*, pp. 197–202. The phrase was bestowed by John of Salisbury, *Historia pontificalis*, v, ed. Chibanall, p. 11.

38 John W. Baldwin, *The Government of Philip Augustus: Foundations of French Power in the Middle Ages* (Berkeley, CA 1986), p. 368.

8. Augustus

1 E. M. Rose, 'Royal Power and Ritual Murder: Notes on the Expulsion of the Jews from the Royal Domain of France, 1182', in Katherine L. Jansen, Guy Geltner, and Anne E. Lester (eds), *Center and Periphery:*

Studies on Power in the Medieval World in Honor of William Chester Jordan (Leiden 2013), pp. 51–63, argues for Philip's fabrication of the story.

2 Rigord, *Gesta Philippi Augusti*, [5], ed. and trans. [into French] by Élisabeth Carpentier, Georges Pon, and Yves Chauvin as *Histoire de Philippe Auguste* (Paris 2006), pp. 130–33. There is now an English translation of Rigord's chronicle: *The Deeds of Philip Augustus: An English Translation of Rigord's* 'Gesta Philippi Augusti', trans. Larry Field, ed. M. Cecilia Gaposchkin and Sean Field (Ithaca, NY 2022).

3 Kenneth Stow, *Jewish Dogs: An Image and its Interpreters* (Stanford, CA 2006), p. 76 n. 4.

4 William Chester Jordan, *The French Monarchy and the Jews: From Philip Augustus to the Last Capetians* (Philadelphia, PA 1989), p. 30, for the dating to 1181 rather than 1180.

5 Robert Chazan, *Medieval Jewry in Northern France: A Political and Social History* (Baltimore, MD 1973), pp. 30–62.

6 'Epistola ad universos ecclesiae Dei fidelos', *HF*, vol. 16, p. 8; Walter Map, *De nugis curialium*, V.5, ed. and trans. M. R. James as *Courtiers' Trifles*, rev. edn by C. N. L. Brooke and R. A. B. Mynors (Oxford 1983), pp. 454–5.

7 Robert Chazan, 'The Bray Incident of 1192: Realpolitik and Folk Slander', *Proceedings of the American Academy for Jewish Research* 37 (1969), 1–18; Jordan, *The French Monarchy*, 35–7.

8 Quoted in Jordan, *The French Monarchy*, p. 37.

9 Rigord, *Gesta Philipi Augusti*, [11], ed. Carpentier, Pon, and Chauvin, *Histoire*, pp. 144–45; Jacques Krynen, *L'Empire du roi: Idées et croyances politiques en France, XIIIᵉ–XVᵉ siècle* (Paris 1993), pp. 54–5.

10 Rigord, *Gesta Philippi Augusti*, [9], ed. Carpentier, Pon, and Chauvin, *Histoire*, pp. 140–41.

11 Rigord, *Gesta Philipi Augusti*, [4], ed. Carpentier, Pon, and Chauvin, *Histoire*, pp. 128–31.

12 Jordan, *The French Monarchy*, p. 31; John W. Baldwin, *The Government of Philip Augustus: Foundations of French Power in the Middle Ages* (Berkeley, CA 1986), pp. 29, 51–2, 58.

13 Gislebert of Mons, *Chronicon Hannoniae*, 94, ed. Léon Vanderkindere as *La chronique de Gislebert de Mons* (Brussels 1904), p. 131, trans. Laura Napran as *Chronicle of Hainaut* (Woodbridge 2005), p. 75.

14 Chazan, *Medieval Jewry*, pp. 65–6; quote at Baldwin, *The Government of Philip Augustus*, p. 52.

15 Rigord, *Gesta Philipi Augusti*, [133], ed. Carpentier, Pon, and Chauvin, *Histoire*, pp. 352–3.

16 As estimated by Baldwin, *The Government of Philip Augustus*, pp. 160–61.

17 Colette Beaune, *The Birth of an Ideology: Myths and Symbols of Nation in Late-Medieval France*, trans. Susan Ross Huston, ed. Frederic Cheyette (Berkeley, CA 1991), pp. 226–44; Baldwin, *The Government of Philip Augustus*, pp. 372–3.

18 Michel Roblin, 'Cités ou citadelles? Les enceintes romaines du Bas-Empire d'après l'exemple de Paris', *Revue des études anciennes* 53 (1951), pp. 301–11.

19 Rigord, *Gesta Philipi Augusti*, [38], ed. Carpentier, Pon, and Chauvin, *Histoire*, pp. 192–3; Anne Lombard-Jourdan, *Paris – genèse de la 'ville': La Rive Droite de la Seine des origines à 1223* (Paris 1976), pp. 102–4.

20 Rigord, *Gesta Philipi Augusti*, [20], ed. Carpentier, Pon, and Chauvin, *Histoire*, pp. 160–63.

21 John Gillingham, *Richard I* (New Haven, CT 1999), p. 142 n. 5, argues for the truth of the charge.

22 Frank Barlow, *The Feudal Kingdom of England, 1042–1216*, 4th edn (Harlow 1988), p. 351.

23 Roger Howden, *Chronica*, ed. William Stubbs, 4 vols (London 1868–71), vol. 2, p. 345.

24 Baldwin, *The Government of Philip Augustus*, pp. 18–22.

25 Rigord, *Gesta Philipi Augusti*, [74], ed. Carpentier, Pon, and Chauvin, *Histoire*, pp. 270–71.

26 [Roger Howden], *Gesta regis Henrici secundi Benedicti abbatis / The Chronicle of the Reigns of Henry II & Richard I, AD 1169–1192*, ed. W. Stubbs, 2 vols (London 1867), vol. 2, p. 7.

27 Gillingham, *Richard I*, p. 84.

28 Rigord, *Gesta Philipi Augusti*, [63–66], ed. Carpentier, Pon, and Chauvin, *Histoire*, pp. 248–57, quote at p. 248; [Roger Howden], *Gesta regis*, ed. Stubbs, vol. 2, p. 33; Baldwin, *The Government of Philip Augustus*, pp. 52–4.

29 Rigord, *Gesta Philipi Augusti*, [76], ed. Carpentier, Pon, and Chauvin, *Histoire*, pp. 272–3.

30 Roger Howden, *Chronica*, ed. Stubbs, vol. 2, p. 335.

31 [Roger Howden], *Gesta regis*, ed. Stubbs, vol. 2, p. 160.

32 Henri-François Delaborde et al. (eds), *Recueil des actes de Philippe Auguste*, 6 vols (Paris 1916–2005), no. 376, vol. 1, pp. 464–6.

33 Ambroise, *L'Estoire de la Guerre Sainte*, ed. Gaston Paris (Paris 1897), ll. 4815–20, 4927–41.

34 Jean de Joinville, *Histoire de Saint Louis*, ed. Natalis de Wailly (Paris 1868), pp. 28, 198–200.

35 Baldwin, *The Government of Philip Augustus*, pp. 125–36. Rigord, *Gesta Philipi Augusti*, [77], ed. Carpentier, Pon and Chauvin, *Histoire*, pp. 276–85.

36 C. Warren Hollister and John W. Baldwin, 'The Rise of Administrative Kingship: Henry I and Philip Augustus', *American Historical Review* 83 (1978), pp. 867–905.

37 Baldwin, *The Government of Philip Augustus*, pp. 152–5, estimates the total.

38 Gillingham, *Richard I*, pp. 222–48; Gervase of Canterbury, *The Chronicle of the Reigns of Stephen, Henry II, and Richard I*, ed. William Stubbs, 2 vols (London 1879–80), vol. 1, pp. 515–16.

39 *LTC*, no. 412, vol. 1, pp. 175–6; [Roger Howden], *Gesta regis*, ed. Stubbs, vol. 2, p. 236.

40 Léon-Louis Borelli de Serres, *La Réunion des provinces septentrionales à la couronne par Philippe Auguste: Amiénois-Artois-Vermandois-Valois* (Paris 1899).

41 Rigord, *Gesta Philipi Augusti*, [02], ed. Carpentier, Pon and Chauvin, *Histoire*, pp. 118–19; Jim Bradbury, *Philip Augustus: King of France (1180–1223)* (London 1998), p. 220.

42 Élisabeth Carpentier, Georges Pon, and Yves Chauvin, 'Introduction' to *Histoire de Philippe Auguste* (Paris 2006), pp. 77–8; on Capetian 'imperial' usage from the reigns of Louis VI and VII cited in Elizabeth A. R. Brown and Michael W. Cothren, 'The Twelfth-Century Crusading Window of the Abbey of Saint-Denis: *Praetitorum enim recordatio futurum est exhibitio*', *Journal of the Warburg and Courtauld Institutes* 49 (1986), pp. 23–4.

43 Innocent III, *Regestri sive epistolae*, PL 214, col. 1130–34b, at col. 1132b.

44 Gillingham, *Richard I*, 244–8.

45 Thomas Riis, 'Autour du mariage de 1193: L'épouse, son pays et les relations franco-danoises', in Robert-Henri Bautier (ed.), *La France de Philippe Auguste: Le temps des mutations* (Paris 1982), pp. 341–62.

9. The Danish Witch

1 *Vita Innocenti*, XLIX, PL, 214, col. XCVa, trans. by James M. Powell as *The Deeds of Pope Innocent III* (Washington, DC 2004), p. 65.

2 Robert Davidsohn, *Philipp II: August von Frankreich und Ingeborg* (Stuttgart 1888), pp. 39–46, 297–306.

3 Rigord, *Gesta Philippi Augusti*, [99], ed. and trans. [into French] by Élisabeth Carpentier, Georges Pon, and Yves Chauvin as *Histoire de Philippe Auguste* (Paris 2006), pp. 320–21.

4 *Vita Innocenti*, XLVII, PL, 214, col. XCIVa.

5 William of Newburgh, *Historia rerum anglicarum*, IV.26, ed. Richard Howlett, 2 vols (London 1884–9), vol. 1, p. 368.

6 John W. Baldwin, *The Government of Philip Augustus: Foundations of French Royal Power in the Middle Ages* (Berkeley, CA 1986), p. 82.

7 Jean Gaudemet, 'Le dossier canonique du mariage de Philippe Auguste et d'Ingeburge de Danemark (1193–1213)', *Revue historique de droit français et étranger*, 4th ser., 62 (1984), pp. 15–29.

8 This explanation is advanced by Thomas Heebøll-Holm, 'A Franco-Danish Marriage and the Plot against England', *Haskins Society Journal* 26 (2014), pp. 249–70; William of Newburgh, *Historia rerum Anglicarum*, IV.26, ed. Howlett, vol. 1, pp. 368–9.

9 *Vita Innocenti*, XLVII, PL, 214, col. XCIVb.

10 Constance Rousseau, 'Neither Bewitched nor Beguiled: Philip Augustus's Alleged Impotence and Innocent III's Response', *Speculum* 89 (2014), pp. 410–36.

11 Baudouin d'Avesnes, 'chronique', manuscript variant edited in Alexander Cartellieri, *Philipp II: August, könig von Frankreich*, 4 vols (Leipzig 1899–1922), vol. 1, Appendix 13, pp. 87–8.

12 Aline G. Hornaday, 'A Capetian Queen as Street Demonstrator: Isabelle of Hainaut', in Katherine Nolan (ed.), *Capetian Women* (Basingstoke 2003), pp. 75–97; Darrel W. Amundsen and Carol Jean Diers, 'The Age of Menarche in Medieval Europe', *Human Biology* 45 (1973), pp. 363–9.

13 Gislebert of Mons, *Chronicon Hannoniae*, 108, ed. Léon Vanderkindere as *La chronique de Gislebert de Mons* (Brussels 1904), pp. 152–3, trans. Laura Napran as *Chronicle of Hainaut* (Woodbridge 2005), p. 86.

14 Rigord, *Gesta Philippi Augusti*, [60], ed. Carpentier, Chauvin, and Pon, pp. 242–3.

15 Pierre Battifol, 'Les fouilles du choeur de Notre-Dame de Paris en 1858 (d'après les notes de chanoine Ravinet)', *Mémoires de la Société des antiquaires de France* 75 (1918), pp. 247–66, at 256–7, 264–5.

16 Rigord, *Gesta Philippi Augusti*, [99], ed. Carpentier, Pons, and Chauvin, pp. 322–3.

17 David d'Avray, *Medieval Marriage: Symbolism and Society* (Oxford 2005).

18 *Constitutiones concilii quarti Lateranensis una cum commentariis glossatorum*, canon 50, ed. Antonio García y García (Vatican City 1981), pp. 359–61.

19 *Vita Innocenti*, XLVII, PL, 214, col. XCI–XCIIa.

20 Mansi, XXII, col. 707e-12.

21 Trans. David d'Avray, *Dissolving Royal Marriages: A Documentary History, 860–1600* (Cambridge 2014), pp. 62–8.

22 John W. Baldwin, 'La vie sexuelle de Philippe Auguste', in Michel Rouche (ed.), *Mariage et sexualité au Moyen Âge: Accord ou crise?* (Paris 2000), pp. 226–7.

23 Mansi, XXII, col. 709.

24 Gaudemet, 'Le dossier canonique', pp. 19–20.

25 William of Newburgh, *Historia rerum Anglicarum*, V.16, ed. Howlett, vol. 2, p. 459.

26 Innocent III, *Regestri sive epistolae*, PL, 214, col. 5. On the legitimation, see most recently Sara McDougall, *Royal Bastards: The Birth of Illegitimacy, 800–1200* (Oxford 2016), pp. 224–9.

27 Ingeborg of Denmark, *Regestri sive epistolae Innocenti*, PL, 215, col. 86c–88c.

28 George Conklin, 'Ingeborg of Denmark, Queen of France, 1193–1223', in Anne J. Duggan (ed.), *Queens and Queenship in Medieval Europe* (Woodbridge 1997), pp. 39–52.

29 Elizabeth Makowski, 'The Conjugal Debt and Medieval Canon Law', *JMH* 3 (1977), pp. 99–114.

30 Innocent III, *Regestri sive epistolae*, PL, 215, col. 1135c–36b.

31 Rousseau, 'Neither Bewitched nor Beguiled', p. 427.

32 Innocent III, *Regestri sive epistolae*, PL, 215, col. 680b–c.

33 Innocent III, *Regestri sive epistolae*, PL, 215, col. 1493c–d.

34 Innocent III, *Regestri sive epistolae*, PL, 216, col. 617b–18b.

35 Cartellieri, *Philipp II*, vol. 4, pp. 352–4; Jenny Benham, 'Philip Augustus and the Angevin Empire: The Scandinavian Connection', *Mediaeval Scandinavia* 14 (2004), 37–50.

36 Delaborde et al. (eds), *Recueil des actes de Philippe Auguste*, vol. 4, p. 471.

37 Kathleen S. Schowalter, 'The Ingeborg Psalter: Queenship, Legitimacy, and the Appropriation of Byzantine Art in the West', in Kathleen Nolan (ed.), *Capetian Women* (Basingstoke 2003), pp. 99–135.

10. *Trial by Battle*

1 Guillaume le Breton, 'Gesta Philipi Augusti', 183, ed. Henri-François Delaborde, *Oeuvres de Rigord et de Guillaume le Breton*, 2 vols (Paris 1882–5), vol. 1, pp. 269–70. Guillaume le Breton's prose narrative, along with a version in verse and nearly a dozen other chronicle accounts of the Battle of Bouvines, are excerpted and translated in Georges Duby, *The Legend of Bouvines: War, Religion and Culture in the Middle Ages*, trans. Catherine Tihanyi (New York 1990), pp. 37–54, 192–220.

2 J. F. Verbruggen, *The Art of Warfare in Western Europe during the Middle Ages, from the Eighth Century to 1340*, trans. Sumner Willard and Mrs R. W. Southern, 2nd edn (Woodbridge 1997), pp. 242–7.

3 Quoted in Colette Beaune, *The Birth of an Ideology: Myths and Symbols of Nation in Late-Medieval France*, trans. Susan Ross Huston, ed. Frederic Cheyette (Berkeley, CA 1991), p. 207.

4 Duby, *Legend of Bouvines*, p. 19; The Marchiennes chronicler, 'De pugna Bovinensi', MGH, SS, vol. 26 (Hanover 1882), p. 391.

5 Philippe Mousket, *Chronique rimée*, ln. 22036, ed. Frédéric de Reiffenberg, 2 vols (Brussels 1836–88), vol. 2, p. 369.

6 Guillaume le Breton, 'Philipidos', XI.36, ed. Delaborde, *Oeuvres*, vol. 2, p. 319; Mousket, *Chronique rimée*, ln. 21717, ed. de Reiffenberg, vol. 2, p. 357, also names it 'L'oriflambe de Saint Denise'.

7 Guillaume le Breton, 'Philipidos', XI.20–29, ed. Delaborde, *Oeuvres*, vol. 2, p. 318. That Charlemagne's Muslim opponent in *The Song of Roland* also carried a dragon banner cannot have been lost on the chronicler, though he did not highlight the parallel.

8 A point well made in Duby, *Legend of Bouvines*, pp. 110–13.

9 Kurt-Georg Cram, *Iudicium Belli: Zum Rechtscharakter des Krieges im Deutschen Mittelalter* (Münster and Cologne 1955).

10 John W. Baldwin, 'The Intellectual Preparation for the Canon of 1215 against Ordeals', *Speculum* 36 (1961), pp. 613–36; Dominique Barthélemy, 'Diversité des ordalies médiévales', *RH* 280 (1988), pp. 3–25.

11 Justine Firnhaber-Baker, 'The Judicial Duel in Later Medieval France: Procedure, Ceremony, and Status', in M. Cecilia Gaposchkin and Jay Rubenstein (eds), *Political Ritual and Practice in Capetian France: Essays in Honour of Elizabeth A. R. Brown* (Turnhout 2021), pp. 399–430.

12 The Marchiennes chronicler, 'De pugna Bovinensi', MGH, SS, vol. 26, p. 390.

13 Mousket, *Chronique rimée*, ll. 21782–7, ed. de Reiffenberg, pp. 359–60, trans. in Duby, *Legend of Bouvines*, p. 208.

14 Guillaume le Breton, 'Gesta', 188–9, ed. Delaborde, *Oeuvres*, vol. 1, p. 279–81.

15 Roger of Wendover, *The Flowers of History by Roger of Wendover from the Year of Our Lord 1154*, ed. Henry G. Hewlett, 3 vols (London 1886–9), vol. 2, p. 108; Guillaume le Breton, 'Gesta', 191, ed. Delaborde, *Oeuvres*, vol. 1, p. 282.

16 Guillaume le Breton, 'Gesta', 190, ed. Delaborde, *Oeuvres*, vol. 1, p. 281.

17 Guillaume le Breton, 'Gesta', 196, ed. Delaborde, *Oeuvres*, vol. 1, p. 288.

18 Guillaume le Breton, 'Philipidos', XII.34–36, ed. Delaborde, *Oeuvres*, vol. 2, p. 349.

19 Guillaume le Breton, 'Gesta', 198, ed. Delaborde, *Oeuvres*, vol. 1, p. 290. This is one of the earliest uses of this phrase in Capetian France.

20 The continuator of Guillaume le Breton, 'Gesta', 210, ed. Delaborde, *Oeuvres*, vol. 1, p. 302.

21 Guillaume le Breton, 'Philipidos', XII.47–50, ed. Delaborde, *Oeuvres*, vol. 2, p. 350.

22 Werner Goez, *Translatio Imperii: Ein Betrag zur Geschichte des Geschichts-denkens und der politischen Theorien im Mittelalter und in der frühen Neuzeit* (Tübingen 1958); Walter Ullmann, *The Growth of Papal Government in the Middle Ages: A Study in the Ideological Relation of Clerical to Lay Power*, 3rd edn (London 1970), esp. 99–102.

23 Guillaume le Breton, 'Philipidos', XII.225–56, ed. Delaborde, *Oeuvres*, vol. 2, pp. 356–7, trans. in Duby, *Legend of Bouvines*, pp. 204–5.

24 Roger of Wendover, *Flowers of History*, ed. Hewlett, vol. 2, pp. 105–9.

25 J. C. Holt, *The Northerners: A Study in the Reign of King John*, new edn (Oxford 1992), p. 100.

26 Charles Petit-Dutaillis, 'Les copies du traité de paix du Goulet (22 mai 1200): Variantes et falsifications', *BEC* 102 (1941), pp. 35–50, at p. 35; treaty at Henri-François Delaborde et al. (eds), *Recueil des actes de Philippe Auguste*, 6 vols (Paris 1916–2005), no. 633, vol. 2, pp. 178–85.

27 Maurice Powicke, *The Loss of Normandy, 1189–1204: Studies in the History of the Angevin Empire*, 2nd edn (Manchester 1961), pp. 134–8.

28 Delaborde et al. (eds), *Recueil des actes de Philippe Auguste*, no. 287, vol. 1, pp. 348–9.

29 Martin Aurell, *The Plantagenet Empire, 1154–1124*, trans. David Crouch (Harlow 2007), p. 126.

30 Elizabeth Hallam and Charles West, *Capetian France, 987–1328*, 3rd edn (Abingdon 2020), p. 192.

31 Powicke, *Loss of Normandy*, pp. 174–7.

32 Roger of Wendover, *Flowers of History*, ed. Hewlett, vol. 1, pp. 316–17.

33 William the Breton, 'Gesta', 121–9, ed. Delaborde, *Oeuvres*, vol. 1, pp. 212–20, who also claims that they ate a newborn baby.

34 Ralph of Coggeshall, *Chronicon anglicanum*, ed. Joseph Stevenson (London 1875), p. 146.

35 On the expansion between 1204 and 1214 and its political ramifications, see John W. Baldwin, *The Government of Philip Augustus: Foundations of Royal Power in the Middle Ages* (Berkeley, CA 1986), pp. 191–219.

36 Frank Barlow, *The Feudal Kingdom of England, 1042–1216*, 4th edn (Harlow 1988), p. 405.

37 'Extraits d'une chronique française des rois de France par un Anonyme de Béthune', *HF*, vol. 24, p. 770, trans. in Duby, *Legend of Bouvines*, p. 197.

38 Joseph R. Strayer, *The Administration of Normandy under Saint Louis* (Cambridge, MA 1932).

11. New Horizons

1 Cf. Andrew W. Lewis, 'Anticipatory Association of the Heir in Early Capetian France', *American Historical Review* 83 (1978), pp. 906–27, at pp. 923–4.

2 On Louis's tutelage in Artois, see Charles Petit-Dutaillis, *Étude sur la vie et le règne de Louis VIII (1187–1226)* (Paris 1894), pp. 205–8.

3 J. C. Holt, *The Northerners: A Study in the Reign of King John*, new edn (Oxford 1992), p. 138, for the date of this meeting.

4 Guillaume le Breton, 'Philipidos', XII.834–40, ed. Henri-François Delaborde, *Oeuvres de Rigord et de Guillaume le Breton*, 2 vols (Paris 1882–5), vol. 2, p. 380.

5 Lindy Grant, *Blanche of Castile, Queen of France* (New Haven, CT 2016), p. 55. On the claim, see also Catherine Hanley, *Louis: The French Prince who Invaded England* (New Haven, 2016), pp. 79–83.

6 Roger of Wendover, *The Flowers of History by Roger of Wendover from the Year of Our Lord 1154*, ed. Henry G. Hewlett, 3 vols (London 1886–9), vol. 2, pp. 183–90.

7 On the causes of John's death and later legends, see Frédérique Lachaud, *Jean sans Terre* (Paris 2018), pp. 341–9.

8 John W. Baldwin, *The Government of Philip Augustus: Foundations of French Royal Power in the Middle Ages* (Berkeley, CA 1986), pp. 335–6, weighs the evidence for Philip's involvement.

9 Guillaume le Breton, 'Gesta Philipi Augusti', 222, ed. H.-F. Delaborde, *Oeuvres de Rigord et de Guillaume le Breton*, 2 vols (Paris 1885), vol. 1, p. 313; Anonymous of Béthune, *History of the Dukes of Normandy and the Kings of England*, ed. Paul Webster, trans. Janet Shirley (London 2021), p. 176.

10 Anonymous of Béthune, *History of the Dukes*, ed. Webster, trans. Shirley, p. 177.

11 David A. Carpenter, *The Minority of Henry III* (Berkeley and Los Angeles, CA 1990), p. 396.

12 Guillaume le Breton, 'Gesta', 223, ed. Delaborde, *Oeuvres*, vol. 1, pp. 314–15.

13 Grant, *Blanche of Castile*, pp. 56–7.

14 Anonymous of Béthune, *History of the Dukes*, ed. Webster, trans. Shirley, p. 186.

15 Grant, *Blanche of Castile*, pp. 47–50; Robert Fawtier, 'Un fragment du compte de l'hôtel du prince Louis de France pour le terme de la Purification 1213', *Le Moyen Age* 43 (1933), pp. 225–50.

16 Guillaume de Nangis, *Chronique latine de Guillaume de Nangis, de 1113 à 1300, avec les continuations de cette chronique, de 1300 à 1368*, ed. Hercule Géraud, 2 vols (Paris 1843), vol. 1, p. 169.

17 Gerald of Wales, *De principis instructione/Instructions for a Ruler*, 1.XX, ed. and trans. Robert Bartlett (Oxford 2018), pp. 386–7.

18 Petit-Dutaillis, *Étude sur la vie et le règne de Louis VIII*, p. 222. Quote at *Récits d'un ménestrel de Reims au treizième siècle*, [309], ed. Natalis de Wailly (Paris 1876), pp. 161–2. This text has been recently translated by Samuel N. Rosenberg as *Tales of a Minstrel of Reims in the Thirteenth Century* (Washington, DC 2022).

19 Philippe Mousket, *Chronique rimée*, ll. 24193–7, ed. Frédéric de Reiffenberg, 2 vols (Brussels 1836–88), vol. 2, p. 442.

20 Nicolas de Bray 'Gesta Ludovici VIII, Francorum regis', ll. 67–99, *HF*, vol. 17, pp. 313–14.

21 Philippe Mousket, *Chronique rimée*, ll. 23727–30, ed. de Reiffenberg, vol. 2, p. 426.

22 Delaborde et al. (eds), *Recueil des actes de Philippe Auguste*, no. 1795, vol. 4, p. 471.

23 Carpenter, *Minority of Henry III*, pp. 309–11.

24 The best account of Louis's Poitou expedition remains Petit-Dutaillis, *Étude sur la vie et le règne de Louis VIII*, pp. 224–56, on which most of the next two paragraphs depend.

25 'Gesta Ludovici octavi Franciae regis', *HF*, vol. 17, pp. 305–6.

26 'Le serment de fidélité des habitants de La Rochelle au roi de France en 1224', *Archives historiques du Poitou* 20 (1889), pp. 234–61.

27 Robert Favreau, 'La Rochelle, port français sur l'Atlantique au XIIIe siècle', *L'Europe et l'Océan au Moyen Âge: Contribution à l'histoire de la navigation* (Paris 1988), pp. 49–76; Frédéric Boutoulle, 'La vigne et le négoce du vin en Bordelais et Bazadais (fin XIe-début XIIIe siècle)', *Annales du Midi* 112/231 (2000), pp. 275–98.

28 *Récits d'un ménestrel de Reims*, [330], ed. de Wailly, p. 171.

29 Laurent Macé, *Les Comtes de Toulouse et leur entourage (XIIe–XIIIe siècles): Rivalités, alliances et jeux de pouvoir* (Toulouse 2000), pp. 21–38.

30 Antonio Sennis (ed.), *Cathars in Question* (York 2016); Jean-Louis Biget, *Hérésie et inquisition dans le midi de la France* (Paris 2007).

31 Caesarius of Heisterbach, *Dialogus miraculorum/Dialog über die Wunder*, V.21, ed. and trans. [into German] Nikolaus Nösges and Horst Schneider, 5 vols (Turnhout 2009), vol. 3, p. 1026. As the editors note, this is a biblical quotation from 2 Timothy.

32 Jonathan Sumption, *The Albigensian Crusade* (London 1978).

33 *The Song of the Cathar Wars: A History of the Albigensian Crusade*, liasse 25, ed. and trans. Janet Shirley (Farnham 1996), p. 172.

34 Petit-Dutaillis, *Étude sur la vie et le règne de Louis VIII*, pp. 279–88.

35 The 'false Baldwin' of Flanders appears in many chronicles, including Philippe Mousket, *Chronique rimée*, ll. 24480–25324, ed. de Reiffenberg, vol. 2, pp. 452–85, and 'Gesta Ludovici VIII', *HF*, vol. 17, pp. 308–9, and documentary sources. Robert Lee Wolff, 'Baldwin of Flanders and Hainaut, First Latin Emperor of Constantinople: His Life, Death, and Resurrection, 1172–1225', *Speculum* 27 (1952), pp. 281–322, demonstrates conclusively that he was an imposter.

36 Guillaume le Breton, 'Philipidos', ll. 855–8, in Delaborde (ed.), *Oeuvres*, vol. 2, p. 381.

37 Guillaume le Breton, 'Gesta', in Delaborde (ed.), *Oeuvres*, vol. 1, p. 319.

38 Petit-Dutaillis, *Étude sur la vie et le règne de Louis VIII*, pp. 292–323, remains the fullest account of Louis's crusade.

39 *LTC*, vol. 2, no. 1742–3, pp. 68–70.

40 Sumption, *Albigensian Crusade*, p. 216.

41 Roger of Wendover, *Flowers of History*, ed. Hewlett, vol. 2, p. 309.

42 'Ex chronico Turonensi', HF, vol. 18, p. 314.

43 *Ord.*, vol. 12, pp. 319–20.

44 *LTC*, vol. 2, no. 1747–48, 1752–57, 1759, pp. 70–76, etc.

45 *LTC*, vol. 2, no. 1768, p. 79.

46 *LTC*, vol. 2, no. 1767, pp. 78–9.

47 Flies: 'Ex chronico Turonensi', *HF*, vol. 18, p. 317; *LTC*, vol. 2, no. 1794, p. 90.

48 Roger of Wendover, *Flowers of History*, ed. Hewlett, vol. 2, p. 313.

49 Petit-Dutaillis, *Étude sur la vie et le règne de Louis VIII*, pp. 325–7.

12. *Of Babies and Barons*

1 Sylvie Laurent, *Naître au Moyen Age: De la conception à la naissance: La Grossesse et l'accouchement (XIIᵉ–XVᵉ siècle)* (Paris 1989), pp. 184–236; Costanza Gislon Dopfel, Alessandra Foscati, and Charles Burnett (eds), *Pregnancy and Childbirth in the Premodern World: European and Middle Eastern Cultures, from Late Antiquity to the Renaissance* (Turnhout 2019).

2 Tracy Chapman Hamilton, 'Queenship and Kinship in the French *Bible Moralisée*: The Example of Blanche of Castile and Vienna ÖNB 2554', in Kathleen Nolan (ed.), *Capetian Women* (Basingstoke 2003), pp. 177–208, at 183–6.

3 Janna Bianchini, *The Queen's Hand: Power and Authority in the Reign of Berenguela of Castile* (Philadelphia, PA 2012); Lindy Grant, *Blanche of Castile, Queen of France* (New Haven, CT 2016), p. 165.

4 Jean Dunbabin, *Charles I of Anjou: Power, Kingship, and State-making in Thirteenth-Century Europe* (London 1998), p. 1; Grant, *Blanche of Castile*, p. 154, argues that the choice of Charles as the name for Louis VIII's posthumous son was Blanche's.

5 Élie Berger, *Histoire de Blanche de Castille, Reine de France* (Paris 1895), pp. 14–15.

6 Angelika Wulff, 'Wohin mit den Kindern? Die Kindergräber von Royaumont: Denkmäler des Widerstreits zwischen Familienzuhörigkeit und Königswurde', in Wolfgang Neumann (ed.), *Creating Identities: Die*

Funktion von Grabmalen und öffentlichen Denkmalen in Gruppenbildung-sprozessen (Kassel 2007), pp. 301–20; Grant, *Blanche of Castile*, pp. 224–5.

7 Philip Augustus had given his illegitimate son the name Pierre Char-lot, a reflection of his fascination with Charlemagne.

8 Initial 'c's in Frankish names often became silent, and an internal 'v' is interchangeable with a 'u', though some thirteenth-century people just thought that Clovis had changed his name to Louis after baptism. Andrew W. Lewis, *Royal Succession in Capetian France: Studies on Familial Order and the State* (Cambridge, MA 1981), p. 113. My thanks to Dr Nelson Goering for confirmation on the historical linguistics.

9 The one exception to this rule was Count Charles the Good of Flan-ders, whose assassination by the Erembalds in 1127 is recounted in Chapter 6 above. This Charles was born to the king of Denmark but his mother was a descendant of the Carolingian Charles the Bald's daughter Judith. On the name and its Carolingian associations, see Robert Bartlett, *Blood Royal: Dynastic Politics in Medieval Europe* (Cambridge 2020), pp. 292–6.

10 Gabrielle Spiegel, 'The *reditus regni ad stirpem Karoli Magni*: A New Look', *French Historical Studies* 7 (1971), pp. 145–75.

11 Guillaume de Nangis, 'Gesta Sancti Ludovici/Vie de Saint Louis', *HF*, vol. 20, pp. 314–15.

12 Sidney Painter, *The Scourge of the Clergy: Peter of Dreux, Duke of Brittany* (Baltimore, MD 1937), p. 55. Painter's book is the most lucid account of this confused period and much of the next several paragraphs draw upon it.

13 Judith Éverard, 'Le duché de Bretagne et la politique Plantagenêt aux XIIᵉ et XIIIᵉ siècles: Perspective maritime', in Martin Aurell and Noël-Yves Tonnerre, *Plantagenêts et Capétiens: Confrontations et héritages* (Turnhout 2006), pp. 193–210.

14 Guillaume de Nangis, 'Gesta/Vie', *HF*, vol. 20, pp. 312–13, places Philippe Hurepel on Louis and Blanche's side initially; Cash: *LTC*, no. 1920, vol. 2, pp. 118–19.

15 LeRoux de Lincy (ed.), *Recueil de chants historiques français* (Paris 1841), p. 170.

16 *Récits d'un ménestrel de Reims au treizième siècle*, [339], ed. Natalis de Wailly (Paris 1876), p. 176. This text has been recently translated by

Samuel N. Rosenberg as *Tales of a Minstrel of Reims in the Thirteenth Century* (Washington, DC 2022).

17 Jean de Joinville, *Histoire de Saint Louis*, ed. Natalis de Wailly (Paris 1868), pp. 26–7, trans. M. R. B. Shaw, *Joinville and Villehardouin, Chronicles of the Crusades* (London 1963), p. 182; cf. Guillaume de Nangis, 'Gesta / Vie', *HF*, vol. 20, pp. 314–15.

18 David A. Carpenter, *Henry III: The Rise to Power and Personal Rule, 1207–1258* (New Haven, CT 2020), pp. 77–97, quote at 93.

19 'Compotus Th. de Carnoto et Amarrici Pulli', *HF*, vol. 21, pp. 220–26.

20 Here I follow the chronology of Painter, *The Scourge of the Clergy*, ch. 3, and Jean Richard, *Saint Louis, roi d'une France féodale, soutien de la Terre sainte* (Paris 1983), p. 48, which fits with the chronology of Brittany's earlier marital efforts on his own and his daughter's behalf, rather than those historians who follow Joinville, *Histoire de Saint Louis*.

21 Thibaut IV of Champagne, *Les chansons de Thibaut de Champagne, roi de Navarre*, ed. Axel Wallensköld (Paris 1925), no. 50, pp. 172–6; Painter, *Scourge of the Clergy*, pp. 78–80.

22 Joinville, *Histoire de Saint Louis*, ed. de Wailly, p. 29, trans. Shaw, p. 184.

23 *Récits d'un ménestrel de Reims*, [336], ed. de Wailly, p. 174.

24 'Ex chronico Turonensi', *HF*, vol. 18, pp. 318–19.

25 LeRoux de Lincy (ed.), *Recueil de chants*, p. 171.

26 Roger of Wendover, *The Flowers of History by Roger of Wendover from the Year of Our Lord 1154*, ed. Henry G. Hewlett, 3 vols (London 1886–9), vol. 3, p. 4.

27 Joinville, *Histoire de Saint Louis*, ed. de Wailly, p. 26, trans. Shaw, p. 182; Geoffrey of Beaulieu, 'Vita Ludovici noni', *HF*, vol. 20, p. 4, trans. Larry F. Field, ed. M. Cecilia Gaposchkin and Sean L. Field, *The Sanctity of Louis IX: Early Lives of Saint Louis by Geoffrey of Beaulieu and William of Chartres* (Ithaca, NY 2014), p. 74.

28 Richard, *Saint Louis*, p. 40; Grant, *Blanche of Castile*, pp. 78–9.

29 *Récits d'un ménestrel de Reims*, [187], ed. de Wailly, p. 98.

30 Grant, *Blanche of Castile*, pp. 168–9.

31 Quote at Painter, *Scourge of the Clergy*, p. 43.

32 Robert Fawtier, *The Capetian Kings of France: Monarchy and Nation, 987–1328*, trans. Lionel Butler and R. J. Adam (London 1960), p. 28.

33 Guillaume le Breton, 'Gesta Philipi Augusti', 152, ed. Henri-François Delaborde, *Oeuvres de Rigord et de Guillaume le Breton*, 2 vols (Paris 1882–5), vol. 1, p. 230.

34 Hastings Rashdall, *The Universities of Europe in the Middle Ages*, 3 vols (Oxford 1895), vol. 1, pp. 296–304.

35 Sophie Cassagnes-Brouquet, *La violence des étudiants au Moyen Âge* (Rennes 2012).

36 Rashdall, *The Universities*, vol. 1, pp. 335–6.

37 Matthew Paris, *Chronica majora*, ed. Henry Richards Luard, 7 vols (London 1872–84), vol. 3, p. 167.

38 Matthew Paris, *Chronica majora*, ed. Luard, vol. 3, p. 169.

39 Guillaume de Nangis, *Chronique latine de Guillaume de Nangis, de 1113 à 1300, avec les continuations de cette chronique, de 1300 à 1368*, ed. Hercule Géraud, 2 vols (Paris 1843), vol. 1, pp. 182–3. This passage is not in every manuscript of the chronicle and may be a later addition.

40 Gavin Langmuir, '"Judei nostri" and the Beginning of Capetian Legislation', *Traditio* 16 (1960), pp. 203–39, at 214–15 n. 52

41 William Chester Jordan, *The French Monarchy and the Jews: From Philip Augustus to the Last Capetians* (Philadelphia, PA 1989), pp. 129–36.

42 *LTC*, no. 2083, vol. 2, pp. 192–3.

43 William Chester Jordan, 'Jew and Serf in Medieval France Revisited', in Arnold Franklin, Roxani Margariti, Marina Rustow, and Uriel Simonsohn (eds), *Jews, Christians, and Muslims in Medieval and Early Modern Times* (Leiden 2014), pp. 248–56.

44 *LTC*, no. 2319–20, vol. 2, pp. 276–7.

45 *LTC*, no. 2270, vol. 2, p. 260.

46 Joinville, *Histoire de Saint Louis*, ed. de Wailly, p. 217, trans. Shaw, p. 316.

13. Chosen Ones

1 Emily Guerry, '"A Path Prepared for Them by the Lord": King Louis IX, Dominican Devotion, and the Extraordinary Journey of Two Preaching Friars', in Eleanor J. Giraud and Christian T. Leitmeir (eds),

The Medieval Dominicans: Books, Buildings, Music, and Liturgy (Turnhout 2021), pp. 167–211.

2 Jannic Durand, Marie-Pierre Laffitte, and Dorota Giovannoni (eds), *Le Trésor de la Sainte-Chapelle* (Paris 2001), pp. 55–60.

3 Gautier Cornut, 'Translatio corone sancte domini', ed. and trans. M. Cecilia Gaposchkin, 'Between Historical Narration and Liturgical Celebrations: Gautier Cornut and the Reception of the Crown of Thorns in France', *Revue Mabillon*, new ser., 30 (2019), pp. 121–39, at 136.

4 Cornut, 'Translatio', ed. Gaposchkin, p. 137.

5 Claudine Billot, 'Des reliques de la Passion dans le royaume de France', in Jannic Durand and Bernard Flusin (eds), *Byzance et les reliques du Christ* (Paris 2004), pp. 239–48.

6 Gaposchkin, 'Between Historical Narration and Liturgical Celebrations', p. 91.

7 Meredith Cohn, 'An Indulgence for the Visitor: The Public at the Sainte-Chapelle of Paris', *Speculum* 83 (2008), pp. 882, 883.

8 Cohen, 'An Indulgence for the Visitor', p. 881.

9 Meredith Cohen, *The Sainte-Chapelle and the Construction of Sacral Monarchy: Royal Architecture in Thirteenth-Century Paris* (Cambridge 2015), p. 153.

10 Cohen, 'An Indulgence for the Visitor', p. 847.

11 Durand, Laffitte and Giovannoni (eds), *Le Trésor de la Sainte-Chapelle*, pp. 18–95.

12 Yves Christe, 'Un autoportrait moral et politique de Louis IX: Les vitraux de sa chapelle', in Christine Hediger (ed.), *La Sainte-Chapelle de Paris: Royaume de France ou Jérusalem céleste?* (Turnhout 2007), p. 256.

13 Alyce A. Jordan, *Visualizing Kingship in the Windows of the Sainte-Chapelle* (Turnhout 2002), pp. 52–5; M. Cecilia Gaposchkin, 'Louis IX, Crusade, and the Promise of Joshua in the Holy Land', *JMH* 34 (2008), pp. 245–74.

14 Marcel Aubert, Louis Grodecki, Jean Lafond and Jean Verrier, *Les Vitraux de Notre-Dame et de la Sainte-Chapelle de Paris* (Paris 1959), pp. 295–304; Jordan, *Visualizing Kingship*, pp. 58–69, argues that the restoration narrowed the window's subject from the history of the kings of France more generally to that of the acquisition of the crucifixion relics under Louis.

15 David Townsend, 'The "Versus de corona spinea" of Henry of Avranches', *Mittellateinisches Jahrbuch* 23 (1988), pp. 157–9.

16 Cornut, 'Translatio', ed. Gaposchkin, p. 125; Cohen, 'An Indulgence for the Visitor', p. 883.

17 Among many others, M. Cecilia Gaposchkin, 'Louis IX, Heraclius, and the True Cross at the Sainte-Chapelle', in M. Cecilia Gaposchkin and Jay Rubenstein (eds), *Political Ritual and Practice in Capetian France* (Turnhout 2021), pp. 264–99; Joseph R. Stayer, 'France: The Holy Land, the Chosen People, and the Most Christian King', in Thomas N. Bisson and John F. Benton (eds), *Medieval Statecraft and the Perspectives of History* (Princeton, NJ 1971), pp. 300–314.

18 *LTC*, no. 2835, vol. 2, pp. 416–18.

19 Michelle Perrot, 'Le people hébreu dans les vitraux de la Sainte-Chapelle', in Paul Salmona and Juliette Sibon (eds), *Saint Louis et les Juifs: Politique et idéologie sous le règne de Louis IX* (Paris 2015), p. 120. There were other markers of Jewishness in medieval Christian iconography, such as law scrolls or bags of money, but these, too, are absent from the Sainte-Chapelle's decoration. Sara Lipton, *Images of Intolerance: The Representation of Jews and Judaism in the* Bible moralisée (Berkeley, CA 1999), is a good introduction to those employed by the Capetians.

20 William Chester Jordan, *The French Monarchy and the Jews: From Philip Augustus to the Last Capetians* (Philadelphia, PA 1989), pp. 149–50.

21 Robert Chazan, 'Trial, Condemnation, and Censorship: The Talmud in Medieval Europe', in *The Trial of the Talmud: Paris, 1240* (Toronto 2012), pp. 1–92.

22 Yossef Schwartz, 'Authority, Control, and Conflict in Thirteenth-Century Paris: Contextualizing the Talmud Trial', in Elisheva Baumgarten and Judah D. Galinsky (eds), *Jews and Christians in Thirteenth-Century France* (Basingstoke 2015), pp. 93–110; cf. Jordan, *The French Monarchy and the Jews*, p. 138.

23 Peter Schäfer, *Jesus in the Talmud* (Princeton, NJ 2007), p. 90.

24 'The Disputation of Rabbi Yehiel of Paris', trans. Jean Connell Hoff in *The Trial of the Talmud*, p. 140. In fact, most men named Louis in France at this time were either Capetian or converts from Judaism who had

taken the name at baptism to honour the king (Jordan, *The French Monarchy and the Jews*, p. 139).

25 Paul Lawrence Rose, 'When was the Talmud Burnt at Paris? A Critical Examination of the Christian and Jewish Sources and a New Dating: June 1241', *Journal of Jewish Studies* 62 (2011), pp. 324–39; Colette Sirat, 'Les manuscrits du Talmud en France du Nord au XIIIᵉ siècle', in Gilbert Dahan (ed.), *Le Brûlement du Talmud à Paris, 1242–1244* (Paris 1999), pp. 121–39.

26 Simon Schwarzfuchs, 'La vie interne des communautés juives du nord de la France au temps de Rabbi Yéhiel et de ses collègues', in Dahan (ed.), *Le Brûlement du Talmud*, pp. 23–37.

27 'The Dirge of Rabbi Meir of Rothenberg on the Burning of the Talmuds of Thirteenth-Century France by King Louis IX', trans. John Friedman in *The Trial of the Talmud*, p. 170; Susan Einbinder, *Beautiful Death: Jewish Poetry and Martyrdom in Medieval France* (Princeton, NJ 2002), pp. 70–99.

28 Guillaume de Chartres, 'Vita et actibus inclitae recordationis regis francorum Ludovici', *HF*, vol. 20, p. 34, ed. M. Cecilia Gaposchkin and Sean L. Field, trans. Larry F. Field, *The Sanctity of Louis IX: Early Lives of Saint Louis by Geoffrey of Beaulieu and William of Chartres* (Ithaca, NY 2014), p. 142.

29 Jean de Joinville, *Histoire de Saint Louis*, ed. Natalis de Wailly (Paris 1868), pp. 19–20, trans. M. R. B. Shaw, *Joinville and Villehardouin: Chronicles of the Crusade* (London 1963), p. 175.

30 Lindy Grant, *Blanche of Castile, Queen of France* (New Haven, CT 2016), pp. 197–201.

31 Rose, 'When was the Talmud Burnt at Paris?'.

32 Danièle Sansy, 'Marquer la différence: L'imposition de la rouelle aux XIIIᵉ et XIVᵉ siècles', *Médiévales* 41 (2001), pp. 15–36; quote from Jeremy Cohen, 'Christian Theology and Papal Policy in the Middle Ages', in Steven Katz (ed.), *The Cambridge Companion to Anti-Semitism* (Cambridge 2022), pp. 176–7.

33 Guillaume de Chartres, 'Vita et actibus', *HF*, vol. 20, p. 34, ed. Gaposchkin and Field, trans. Field, *The Sanctity of Louis IX*, p. 142.

34 Sean L. Field, *Isabelle of France: Capetian Sanctity and Franciscan Identity in the Thirteenth Century* (Notre Dame, IN 2006).

35 Anne-Marie Allirot, 'Isabelle de France, soeur de Saint Louis: La vierge savante', *Médiévales* 48 (2005), pp. 66–7.

36 Agnès d'Harcourt, 'Vie d'Isabelle de France', ed. Allirot, 'Isabelle de France', p. 170.

37 William Chester Jordan, *Louis IX and the Challenge of the Crusade: A Study in Rulership* (Princeton, NJ 1979), p. 3.

38 Daniel H. Weiss, *Art and Crusade in the Age of Saint Louis* (Cambridge 1998), p. 1.

39 Joinville, *Histoire de Saint Louis*, ed. de Wailly, p. 39, trans. Shaw, p. 191; quote at *Récits d'un ménestrel de Reims au treizième siècle*, [371], ed. Natalis de Wailly (Paris 1876), p. 191.

40 Jordan, *Louis IX*, pp. 35–104.

14. Death on the Nile

1 Jean de Joinville, *Histoire de Saint Louis*, ed. Natalis de Wailly (Paris 1868), pp. 102–3, trans. M. R. B. Shaw, *Joinville and Villehardouin: Chronicles of the Crusade* (London 1963), p. 236.

2 Joinville, *Histoire de Saint Louis*, ed. de Wailly, pp. 107–8, trans. Shaw, pp. 239–40.

3 M. Cecilia Gaposchkin, 'The Captivity of Louis IX', *Questiones Medii Aevi Novae* 18 (2013), pp. 85–114, lucidly brings together the evidence for this episode of the crusade. For the Oriflamme (*oloflamma*), Matthew Paris, *Chronica majora*, ed. Henry Richards Luard, 7 vols (London 1872–4), vol. 6 (additional documents), p. 195, trans. in Peter Jackson, *The Seventh Crusade, 1244–1254: Sources and Documents* (Farnham 2007), p. 102, a compendium that contains most of the Latin, French, and Arabic sources for the crusade.

4 William Chester Jordan, *Louis IX and the Challenge of the Crusade: A Study in Rulership* (Princeton, NJ 1979), pp. 65–7; John Pryor, 'The Crusade of Emperor Frederick II, 1220–29: The Implications of the Maritime Evidence', *The American Neptune* 52 (1992), p. 116.

5 Janet Shirley (trans.), *Crusader Syria in the Thirteenth Century: The Rothelin Continuation of the History of William of Tyre* . . . (Aldershot 1999),

pp. 68–9; Peter Jackson, *The Mongols and the West: 1221–1410*, 2nd edn (London 2018), pp. 103–6.

6 Pryor, 'The Crusade of Emperor Frederick II', pp. 116–19.

7 Matthew Paris, *Chronica majora*, ed. Luard, vol. 6, p. 162.

8 Jackson (trans.), *Seventh Crusade*, p. 131.

9 Matthew Paris, *Chronica majora*, ed. Luard, vol. 6, pp. 165–7; Jackson (trans.), *Seventh Crusade*, pp. 92–3.

10 Jean Richard, 'La fondation d'une église latine en Orient par saint Louis: Damiette', *BEC* 120 (1962), pp. 39–54; Christopher Tyerman, *God's War: A New History of the Crusades* (London 2006), pp. 799–801.

11 Matthew Paris, *Chronica majora*, ed. Luard, vol. 5, p. 107; vol. 6, p. 163, trans. Jackson, *Seventh Crusade*, p. 92.

12 Joinville, *Histoire de Saint Louis*, ed. de Wailly, p. 129, trans. Shaw, p. 255.

13 Joseph R. Strayer, 'The Crusades of Louis IX', in Thomas N. Bisson and John F. Benton (eds), *Medieval Statecraft and the Perspectives of History* (Princeton, NJ 1971), pp. 159–92.

14 Jackson (trans.), *Seventh Crusade*, pp. 102–3, 147; Joinville, *Histoire de Saint Louis*, ed. de Wailly, p. 106, trans. Shaw, p. 239, maintained a judicious neutrality about the source of the proposal.

15 On the date of departure, see Jackson (trans.), *Seventh Crusade*, p. 99 n. 154.

16 Joinville, *Histoire de Saint Louis*, ed. de Wailly, p. 64, trans. Shaw, p. 210.

17 Jackson (trans.), *Seventh Crusade*, p. 85.

18 Pryor, 'Crusade of Frederick II', pp. 122–3.

19 Joinville, *Histoire de Saint Louis*, ed. de Wailly, p. 73, trans. Shaw, p. 216.

20 Jackson (trans.), *Seventh Crusade*, p. 100.

21 Joinville, *Histoire de Saint Louis*, ed. de Wailly, p. 83, trans. Shaw, p. 223.

22 Shirley (trans.), *The Rothelin Continuation* p. 97.

23 Joinville, *Histoire de Saint Louis*, ed. de Wailly, pp. 79–80, trans. Shaw, p. 221.

24 Jackson (trans.), *Seventh Crusade*, p. 144.

25 Jackson (trans.), *Seventh Crusade*, p. 110

26 This operation is best described by Ibn Wasil's chronicle in Jackson (trans.), *Seventh Crusade*, p. 146.

27 'Dépenses de Saint Louis de MCCL à MCCLIII', *HF*, vol. 21, pp. 512–15; Joinville, *Histoire de Saint Louis*, ed. de Wailly, p. 120, trans. Shaw, pp.

249–50; Jean Richard, *Saint Louis: Roi d'une France féodale, soutien de la Terre sainte* (Paris 1983), p. 201, for annual revenues. Only half of the ransom was ever paid because the Egyptians did not fulfil their promises to guard the sick people, the war machines, and the victuals that the French had left in Damietta.

28 Géraud Sivéry, *Marguerite de Provence: Une reine au temps des Cathédrales* (Paris 1987), pp. 87–8, 92–3; cf. Louise Gay, 'Des commandements militaires féminins en guerre sainte: Marguerite de Provence et Sagar al-Durr lors de la septième croisade', *Royal Studies Journal* 7 (2020), p. 41.

29 Joinville, *Histoire de Saint Louis*, ed. de Wailly, pp. 120–21, trans. Shaw, p. 249.

30 Gay, 'Des commandements militaires', p. 49.

31 Joinville, *Histoire de Saint Louis*, ed. de Wailly, p. 142, trans. Shaw, p. 263.

32 Joinville, *Histoire de Saint Louis*, ed. de Wailly, pp. 134–6, trans. Shaw, pp. 258–9.

33 Joinville, *Histoire de Saint Louis*, ed. de Wailly, p. 141, trans. Shaw, p. 263.

34 André Du Chesne (ed.), *Historiae Francorum scriptores*, 5 vols (Paris 1636–49), vol. 5, pp. 429, 432.

35 Matthew Paris, *Chronica majora*, ed. Luard, vol. 5, pp. 107–9.

36 Joinville, *Histoire de Saint Louis*, ed. de Wailly, p. 143, trans. Shaw, p. 265.

37 Joinville, *Histoire de Saint Louis*, ed. de Wailly, p. 178, trans. Shaw, pp. 290–91.

38 Shirley (trans.), *The Rothelin Continuation*, p. 105.

39 Jackson, *Seventh Crusade*, pp. 126–8.

40 Jackson (trans.), *Seventh Crusade*, p. 113.

41 Jackson (trans.), *Seventh Crusade*, p. 114.

42 Guillaume de Nangis, 'Gesta Sancti Ludovici/Vie de Saint Louis', *HF*, vol. 20, pp. 382–3.

43 Gary Dickson, 'The Advent of the *Pastores* (1251)', *Revue belge de philologie et d'histoire* 66 (1988), pp. 249–67; Jackson (trans.), *Seventh Crusade*, pp. 179–89; Matthew Paris, *Chronica majora*, ed. Luard, vol. 5, pp. 246–54; 'Chronique anonyme des rois de France, finissant en MCCLXXXVI', *HF*, vol. 21, p. 83.

44 Jackson (trans.), *Seventh Crusade*, pp. 174, 176–7; Matthew Paris, *Chronica majora*, ed. Luard, vol. 5, pp. 169–70, 246 (quote).

45 Jackson (trans.), *Seventh Crusade*, p. 167.

46 Richard, *Saint Louis*, pp. 242–59.

47 Joinville, *Histoire de Saint Louis*, ed. de Wailly, p. 163, trans. Shaw, p. 278.

48 Richard Cassidy and Michael Clasby, 'Matthew Paris and Henry III's Elephant', https://finerollshenry3.org.uk/redist/pdf/fm-06-2012.pdf.

49 Joinville, *Histoire de Saint Louis*, ed. de Wailly, p. 175, trans. Shaw, p. 288.

50 William Chester Jordan, *The Apple of His Eye: Converts from Islam in the Reign of Louis IX* (Princeton, NJ 2019).

51 Matthew Paris, *Chronica majora*, ed. Luard, vol. 5, p. 280.

52 *Récits d'un ménestrel de Reims au treizième siècle*, [371], ed. Natalis de Wailly (Paris 1876), p. 192.

53 Richard, *Saint Louis*, p. 249.

54 *HF*, vol. 21, pp. 404, 515.

55 Joinville, *Histoire de Saint Louis*, ed. de Wailly, p. 166, trans. Shaw, p. 282.

56 Hans Eberhard Mayer, *The Crusades*, trans. John Gillingham, 2nd edn (Oxford 1998), p. 266.

57 Joinville, *Histoire de Saint Louis*, ed. de Wailly, p. 50, trans. Shaw, p. 199.

58 Xavier Hélary, 'Les rois de France et la Terre Sainte de la croisade de Tunis à la chute d'Acre (1270–1291)', *Annuaire-bulletin de la Société de l'histoire de France* (2005), pp. 21–104; Christopher Tyerman, 'The Holy Land and the Crusades of the Thirteenth and Fourteenth Centuries', in Peter W. Edbury (ed.), *Crusade and Settlement* (Cardiff 1985), pp. 105–12; James Magee, 'Crusading at the Court of Charles VI', *French History* 12 (1998), pp. 367–83.

15. A Guilty Conscience

1 Jean de Joinville, *Histoire de Saint Louis*, ed. Natalis de Wailly (Paris 1868), pp. 239–40, trans. M. R. B. Shaw, *Chronicles of the Crusade: Joinville and Villehardouin* (London 1963), p. 331.

2 Guillaume de Chartres, 'Vita et actibus inclitae recordationis regis francorum Ludovici', *HF*, vol. 20, p. 30, ed. M. Cecilia Gaposchkin and Sean L. Field, trans. Larry F. Field, *The Sanctity of Louis IX: Early Lives*

of Saint Louis by Geoffrey of Beaulieu and William of Chartres (Ithaca, NY 2014), p. 134.

3 Geoffrey de Beaulieu, 'Vita Ludovici noni', 17, *HF*, vol. 20, p. 10, ed. Gaposchkin and S. Field, trans. L. Field, *The Sanctity of Louis IX*, p. 89.

4 Mark P. O'Tool, 'The *povres avugles* of the Hôpital des Quinze-Vingts: Disability and Community in Medieval Paris', in Meredith Cohen and Justine Firnhaber-Baker (eds), *Difference and Identity in Francia and Medieval France* (Farnham 2010), pp. 168–9.

5 Guillaume de Chartres, 'Vita et actibus', *HF*, vol. 20, p. 35, ed. Gaposchkin and S. Field, trans. L. Field, *The Sanctity of Louis IX*, p. 145; Joinville, *Histoire de Saint Louis*, ed. de Wailly, p. 9, trans. Shaw, p. 169.

6 Jean Richard, *Saint Louis: Roi d'une France féodale, soutien de la Terre sainte* (Paris 1983), p. 252.

7 'Chronique anonyme des rois de France, finissant en MCCLXXXVI', *HF*, vol. 21, p. 83.

8 Matthew Paris, *Chronica majora*, ed. Henry Richards Luard, 7 vols (London 1872–84), vol. 5, p. 466.

9 Guillaume de Chartres, 'Vita et actibus, *HF*, vol. 20, pp. 31–2, ed. Gaposchkin and S. Field, trans. L. Field, *The Sanctity of Louis IX*, p. 138; Joinville, *Histoire de Saint Louis*, ed. de Wailly, p. 208, trans. Shaw, p. 310.

10 William Chester Jordan, *Louis IX and the Challenge of the Crusade* (Princeton, NJ 1979), p. 142.

11 Hans Eberhard Mayer, *The Crusades*, trans. John Gillingham, 2nd edn (Oxford 1998), p. 262; Jean Favier, 'Les finances de Saint Louis', in *Septième centenaire de la mort de Saint Louis* (Paris 1976), pp. 133–40.

12 Jordan, *Louis IX*, pp. 79–80; Joinville, *Histoire de Saint Louis*, ed. de Wailly, p. 151, trans. Shaw, p. 270.

13 Jordan, *Louis IX*, pp. 135–41.

14 Marie Dejoux, *Les enquêtes de Saint Louis: Gouverner et sauver son âme* (Paris 2014), esp. pp. 348–70; Charles-Victor Langlois, 'Doléances recueillies par les enquêteurs de Saint Louis et des derniers Capétiens directs', *RH* 100 (1906), pp. 63–95.

15 'Querimoniae', *HF*, vol. 24, pp. 531–7.

16 Jordan, *Louis IX*, pp. 147–52.

17 Louis Carolus-Barré, 'La grande ordonnance de 1254 sur la réforme de l'administration et la police du royaume', in *Septième centenaire*, pp. 85–96; Raymond Cazelles, 'Une exigence de l'opinion depuis Saint Louis: La réformation du royaume', *Annuaire-bulletin de la Société de l'histoire de France* (1962–3), pp. 91–99, cf. Marie Dejoux, 'La fabrique d'une loi: Retour sur la "grande ordonnance de réforme de 1254"', *Médiévales* 79 (2020), pp. 189–208. The law is published in *Ord.*, vol. 1, pp. 65–75.

18 *Ord.*, vol. 1, p. 74.

19 Joinville, *Histoire de Saint Louis*, ed. de Wailly, p. 247, trans. Shaw, p. 336.

20 Geoffrey of Beaulieu, 'Vita Ludovici noni', *HF*, vol. 20, p. 19, ed. Gaposchkin and S. Field, trans. L. Field, *The Sanctity of Louis IX*, pp. 110–11.

21 Géraud d'Auvergne, 'Chronicon', *HF*, vol. 21, pp. 215, 217.

22 Joinville, *Histoire de Saint Louis*, ed. de Wailly, pp. 21–2, trans. Shaw 177.

23 Jacques Le Goff, *Saint Louis*, trans. Gareth Evan Gollrad (Notre Dame, IN 2009), p. 245.

24 Thomas N. Bisson, 'Consultative Functions in the King's *parlements* (1250–1314)', *Speculum* 44 (1969), pp. 353–73; Gustave Ducoudray, *Les origines du Parlement de Paris et la justice aux XIIIe et XIVe siècles* (Paris 1902).

25 *Ord.*, vol. 1, pp. 72, 86–93; Justine Firnhaber-Baker, 'The Judicial Duel in Later Medieval France: Procedure, Ceremony, and Status', in M. Cecilia Gaposchkin and Jay Rubenstein (eds), *Political Ritual and Practice in Capetian France: Studies in Honour of Elizabeth A. R. Brown* (Turnhout 2021), pp. 401–5.

26 *Ord.*, vol. 1, p. 67.

27 Paris, BnF Latin 4651, fol. 74v; *Ord.*, vol. 1, p. 84; Justine Firnhaber-Baker, *Violence and the State in Languedoc, 1250–1400* (Cambridge 2014), pp. 26–35.

28 Claude Devic and Joseph Vaissette, *Histoire générale de Languedoc avec des notes et les pièces justificatives*, new edn by Auguste Molinier et al., 16 vols (Toulouse 1872–1904), vol. 8, columns 1393–4, 1410–12; Auguste-Arthur, le comte Beugnot (ed.), *Les Olim ou registres des arrêts rendus par la cour du roi . . .*, 3 vols in 4 (Paris 1839–48), vol. 1, pp. 270–71; Alexandre Germain, *Histoire de la commune de Montpellier, depuis ses origines jusqu'à son incorporation définitive à la monarchie française*, 3 vols (Montpellier 1851).

29 *LTC*, nos. 4411–12, vol. 3, pp. 405–9.

30 Jean Dunbabin, *France in the Making, 843–1180*, 2nd edn (Oxford 2000), pp. 75–8.

31 Devic and Vaissette, *Histoire générale*, vol. 6, pp. 858–61; Juan Reglà Campistol, *Francia, la corona de Aragon y la frontera pirenaica*, 2 vols (Madrid 1951), vol. 1, pp. 47–9.

32 *LTC*, no. 4416, 4554, vol. 3, pp. 411–13, 487–9; Pierre Chaplais, 'The Making of the Treaty of Paris (1259) and the Royal Style', *EHR* 67 (1952), pp. 235–53; Michel Gavrilovitch, *Étude sur le traité de Paris de 1259* (Paris 1899), pp. 55–61, for the price, worked out over several years.

33 Eudes Rigaud, 'Visitationibus', *HF*, vol. 21, p. 582; David Carpenter, 'Meetings between Henry III and Louis IX', in Michael Prestwich, Richard Britnell and Robin Frame (eds), *Thirteenth Century England* 10 (Woodbridge 2005), pp. 1–30.

34 Quoted in Gavrilovitch, *Étude sur le traité*, p. 65.

35 Joinville, *Histoire de Saint Louis*, ed. de Wailly, p. 245, trans. Shaw, p. 334; Matthew Paris, *Chronica majora*, ed. Luard, vol. 5, pp. 713–14.

36 *Les grandes chroniques de France*, ed. Jules Viard, 10 vols (Paris 1920–53), vol. 7, p. 192.

37 Edmond Faral, 'Le procès d'Enguerran IV de Couci', *Revue historique de droit français et étranger*, 4th ser., 25 (1948), pp. 213–58.

38 LeRoux de Lincy (ed.), *Recueil de chants historiques français* (Paris 1841), pp. 218–20.

39 Hans-Joachim Schmidt, 'La dévotion de Louis IX: Exception ou normalité?', in Christine Hediger (ed.), *La Sainte-Chapelle de Paris: Royaume de France ou Jérusalem céleste?* (Turnhout 2007), pp. 35–59.

40 Lester K. Little, 'Saint Louis' Involvement with the Friars', *Church History* 33 (1964), p. 127.

41 Salimbene de Adam, *Cronica*, ed. Giuseppe Scalia, 2 vols (Turnhout, 1998–99), vol. 1, p. 335.

42 Jean Favier, 'Les finances de Saint Louis', in *Septième centenaire*, pp. 133–40.

43 *Analecta Franciscana sive chronica aliaque varia documenta ad historiam Fratrum Minorum spectantia*, 18 vols (1885–2011), vol. 1, p. 413.

44 Geoffrey of Beaulieu, 'Vita Ludovici noni', *HF*, vol. 20, p. 7, ed. Gaposchkin and S. Field, trans. L. Field, *The Sanctity of Louis IX*, p. 80.

45 Geoffrey of Beaulieu, 'Vita Ludovici noni', *HF*, vol. 20, p. 7, ed. Gaposchkin and S. Field, trans. L. Field, *The Sanctity of Louis IX*, p. 79.

46 Louis Carolus-Barré, *Le procès de canonisation de Saint Louis (1272–1297): Essai de reconstitution* (Rome 1994), pp. 81–2.

47 Geoffrey of Beaulieu, 'Vita et conversatio', *HF*, vol. 20, p. 10, ed. Gaposchkin and S. Field, trans. L. Field, *The Sanctity of Louis IX*, pp. 87–88.

48 Joinville, *Histoire de Saint Louis*, ed. de Wailly, p. 248, trans. Shaw, p. 336.

49 Le Goff, *Saint Louis*, pp. 602–3.

50 Eudes Rigaud, 'Visitationibus', *HF*, vol. 21, p. 582; Louis Carolus-Barré, 'Le prince héritier Louis (1244–1260) et l'intérim du pouvoir royal, de la mort de Blanche de Castille (novembre 1252) au retour de Saint Louis en France (juillet 1254)', *Comptes rendus des séances de l'Académie des Inscriptions et Belles-Lettres* 104 (1970): 588–96

51 Joinville, *Histoire de Saint Louis*, ed. de Wailly, p. 213, trans. Shaw, p. 313.

52 Joseph R. Strayer, 'The Crusades of Louis IX', in Thomas N. Bisson and John F. Benton (eds), *Medieval Statecraft and the Perspectives of History* (Princeton, NJ 1971), p. 187.

53 Richard, *Saint Louis*, p. 540; Yves Dossat, 'Alfonse de Poitiers et la préparation financière de la croisade de Tunis: Les ventes de forêts (1268–70)' in *Septième centenaire*, pp. 121–32.

54 *Ord.*, vol. 1, pp. 99–102, 294; Danièle Sansy, 'Marquer la différence: L'imposition de la rouelle aux XIIIe et XIVe siècles', *Médiévales* 41 (2001), pp. 15–36.

55 Guillaume de Nangis, 'Gesta Sancti Ludovici/Vie de Saint Louis', *HF*, vol. 20, pp. 440–41.

56 Xavier Hélary, 'Les rois de France et la Terre Sainte de la Croisade de Tunis à la chute d'Acre', *Annuaire-bulletin de la Société de l'histoire de France* (2005), p. 26.

57 Jean Lognon, 'Les Vues de Charles d'Anjou pour la deuxième croisade de Saint Louis: Tunis ou Constantinople' in *Septième centenaire*, pp. 183–95; Xavier Hélary, *La dernière croisade: Saint Louis à Tunis (1270)* (Paris 2016).

58 Le Goff, *Saint Louis*, p. 225.

59 Guillaume de Nangis, 'Gesta/Vie', *HF*, vol. 20, pp. 456–7.

60 Guillaume de Saint-Pathus, *Vie de Saint Louis*, ed. Henri-François Delaborde (Paris 1899), p. 155.

61 'Chronique de Primat traduite par Jean du Vignay', *HF*, vol. 23, p. 58.

62 *HF*, vol. 23, pp. 68–9.

63 M. Cecilia Gaposchkin, *The Making of Saint Louis: Kingship, Sanctity, and Crusade in the Later Middle Ages* (Ithaca, NY 2008), pp. 28–30, 85–6.

64 Guillaume de Nangis, 'Gesta Sancti Ludovici', *HF*, vol. 20, pp. 438–9.

65 Joinville, *Histoire de Saint Louis*, ed. de Wailly, p. 2, trans. Shaw, p. 163.

66 'Chronique anonyme', *HF*, vol. 21, p. 85.

16. An Unhappy Childhood

1 Recounted in Sharon Farmer, 'Down, Out, and Female in Medieval Paris', *The American Historical Review* 103 (1998), pp 345–72.

2 Louis Carolus-Barré, *Le procès de canonisation de Saint Louis (1272–1297): Essai de reconstitution* (Rome 1994); M. Cecilia Gaposchkin, *The Making of Saint Louis: Kingship, Sanctity, and Crusade in the Later Middle Ages* (Ithaca, NY 2008), pp. 36–66.

3 Gaposchkin, *The Making of Saint Louis*, pp. 72–7, 100–124.

4 Colette Beaune, *The Birth of an Ideology: Myths and Symbols of Nation in Late-Medieval France*, trans. Susan Ross Huston, ed. Frederic Cheyette (Berkeley, CA 1991), pp. 90–125; Anja Rathmann-Lutz, *'Images' Ludwigs des Heiligen im Kontext dynastischer Konflikete des 14. und 15 Jahrhunderts* (Berlin 2010).

5 *Ord.*, vol. 1, pp. 354–68, 390.

6 M. Cecilia Gaposchkin, 'Boniface VIII, Philip the Fair, and the Sanctity of Louis IX', *JMH* 29 (2003), pp. 1–26.

7 Jean de Joinville, *Histoire de Saint Louis*, ed. Natalis de Wailly (Paris 1868), p. 268, trans. M. R. B. Shaw, *Joinville and Villehardouin: Chronicles of the Crusade* (London 1963), p. 351.

8 Elizabeth A. R. Brown, 'Philippe le Bel and the Remains of Saint Louis', *Gazette des Beaux-Arts* 97 (1980), pp. 175–82; Elizabeth A. R. Brown, 'Philippe le Bel et les restes de Saint Louis: Nouvel examen des sources', *BEC* 175 (2020), pp. 73–110.

9 Andrew W. Lewis, *Royal Succession in Capetian France: Studies on Familial Order and the State* (Cambridge, MA 1981), p. 143.

10 Gérard Sivéry, *Philippe III le hardi* (Paris 2003), pp. 12, 19.

11 Xavier Hélary, *L'ascension et la chute de Pierre de la Broce, chambellan du roi († 1278): Étude sur le pouvoir royal au temps de Saint Louis et de Philippe III (v. 1250–v. 1280)* (Paris 2021), pp. 21–34.

12 'Chronique anonyme finissant en MCCLXXXVI', *HF*, vol. 21, p. 92; *Les grandes chroniques de France*, ed. Jules Viard, 10 vols (Paris 1920–53), vol. 8, p. 4.

13 William Chester Jordan, 'The Struggle for Influence at the Court of Philip III: Pierre de la Broce and the French Aristocracy', *French Historical Studies* 24 (2001), pp. 439–68.

14 *Grandes chroniques*, ed. Viard, vol. 8, p. 61.

15 'Chronique anonyme finissant en MCCLXXXVI', *HF*, vol. 21, p. 92.

16 Elizabeth A. R. Brown, 'Vincent de Beauvais and the *reditus regni francorum ad stirpem Caroli imperatoris*', in Serge Lusignan, Alain Nadeau and Monique Paulmier-Foucart (eds), *Vincent de Beauvais: Intentions et réceptions d'une oeuvre encyclopédique au Moyen-Âge* (Paris 1990), pp. 167–96.

17 Hélary, *L'ascension et la chute*, p. 281, for the phrase in the sources.

18 *Grandes chroniques*, ed. Viard, vol. 8, pp. 50, 61–4; Xavier Hélary, 'La reine, le légat et le chambellan: un "péché contre nature" à la cour de Philippe III', in Bernard Andematten et al. (eds), *Passions et pulsions à la cour (Moyen Âge–Temps modernes)* (Florence 2015), pp. 159–70; Jordan, 'Struggle for Influence', p. 457, for the box.

19 Julien Théry, '"Innommables abominations sodomitiques": Les débuts de la repression. Autour de l'une des premières sentences conservées (justice épiscopale d'Albi, 1280)', in Michèle Fournié, Daniel Le Blévec, and Julien Théry (eds), *L'Église et la chair (XIIᵉ–XVᵉ siècle)* (Toulouse 2019), pp. 297–349.

20 Elizabeth A. R. Brown, 'The Prince is Father of the King: The Character and Childhood of Philip the Fair of France', *Mediaeval Studies* 49 (1987), p. 315.

21 Élisabeth Lalou, 'Le gouvernement de la reine Jeanne, 1285–1305', *Cahiers haut-marnais* 167 (1986), pp. 16–18.

22 Xavier Hélary, 'Pierre de la Broce, seigneur féodal, et le service militaire sous Philippe III: L'ost de Sauveterre (1276)', *Journal des savants* (2006), pp. 275–305.

23 Joseph R. Strayer, 'The Crusade against Aragon', *Speculum* 28 (1953), pp. 102–13.

24 *Grandes chroniques*, ed. Viard, vol. 8, p. 109.

25 Charles-Victor Langlois, *Le règne de Philippe III le hardi* (Paris 1887), pp. 153–65.

26 Farmer, 'Down, Out, and Female', pp. 347–8.

27 Bruce M. S. Campbell, *The Great Transition: Climate, Disease and Society in the Late-Medieval World* (Cambridge 2016).

28 *Grandes chroniques*, ed. Viard, vol. 8, pp. 81–2, 170.

29 Thomas K. Heebøll-Holm, *Ports, Piracy, and Maritime War: Piracy in the English Channel and the Atlantic, 1280–1330* (Leiden 2013), pp. 88–118, 269–75, at p. 272.

30 *Grandes chroniques*, ed. Viard, vol. 8, pp. 148–9; Auguste-Arthur, le comte Beugnot (ed.), *Les Olim ou registres des arrêts rendus par la cour du roi . . .*, 3 vols in 4 (Paris 1839–48), vol. 2, pp. 3–21, Fromage's story at p. 12.

31 Joseph R. Strayer, *The Reign of Philip the Fair* (Princeton, NJ 1980), p. 319.

32 Strayer, *Philip the Fair*, p. 320; Michael Prestwich, *Edward I* (New Haven, CT 1997), p. 340.

33 Claude Devic and Joseph Vaissette, *Histoire générale de Languedoc*, rev. edn Auguste Molinier, 16 vols (Toulouse and Paris 1868–1905), vol. 10, col. 292, 335–8.

34 *Chronique parisienne anonyme du XIVᵉ siècle*, ed. A. Hellot (Nogent-le-Rotrou 1884), p. 82.

35 *Grandes chroniques*, ed. Viard, vol. 8, p. 201, Jean de Saint-Victor, 'Excerpta e memoriali historiarum', *HF*, vol. 21, p. 634.

36 Jean Favier, *Philippe le bel*, rev. edn (Paris 1998), pp. 272–5.

37 Jan Dumolyn and Jelle Haemers, 'Patterns of Urban Rebellion in Medieval Flanders', *JMH* 31 (2005), pp. 369–93.

38 Jelle Haemers, 'A Moody Community? Emotion and Ritual in Late Medieval Urban Revolts', in Élodie Lecuppre-Desjardin and Anne-Laure

Van Bruaene (eds), *Emotions in the Heart of the City (14th–16th Centuries)* (Turnhout 2005), pp. 63–81.

39 *Grandes chroniques*, ed. Viard, vol. 8, p. 174; Frantz Funck-Brentano, *Les Origines de la guerre de Cent ans: Philippe le bel en Flandres* (Paris 1896).

40 *Annales Gandenses*, new edn, ed. Frantz Funck-Brentano (Paris 1896), pp. 13–14.

41 Giovanni Villani, *Nuova Cronica,* IX.55, ed. Giuseppe Porta, 3 vols (Parma 1990–91), vol. 2, p. 89.

42 *Annales Gandenses*, ed. Funck-Brentano, p. 25.

43 J. F. Verbruggen, *The Battle of the Golden Spurs (Courtrai, 11 July 1302): A Contribution to the History of Flanders' War of Liberation, 1297–1305*, ed. Kelly Devries, trans. David Richard Fergusson (Woodbridge 2002), pp. 220–23.

44 Jean de Saint-Victor, 'Excerpta', *HF*, vol. 21, p. 638.

45 *Annales Gandenses*, ed. Funck-Brentano, p. 32.

46 Strayer, *Philip the Fair*, p. 335.

47 Jean de Saint-Victor, 'Excerpta', *HF*, vol. 21, p. 636.

48 Funck-Brentano, *Les Origines de la guerre de Cent ans*, pp. 499–500; H. Van Werveke, 'Les charges financières issues du traité d'Athis (1305)', *Revue du Nord* 32 (1950), pp. 81–93.

17. *Angels and Antichrist*

1 Jean Coste (ed.), *Boniface VIII en procès: Articles d'accusation et dépositions des témoins (1303–1311)* (Rome 1995), pp. 191–7; Jean de Saint-Victor, 'Excerpta e memoriali historiarum', *HF*, vol. 21, p. 641; Charles-Victor Langlois, 'Une réunion publique à Paris, sous Philippe le Bel, 24 juin 1303', *Bulletin de la Société de l'histoire de Paris et de l'Île-de-France* 15 (1888), pp. 130–35.

2 Pierre Dupuy (ed.), *Histoire du différend d'entre le pape Boniface VIII et Philippe le Bel, roy de France* (Paris 1655), pp. 643–4, 656 (owl reference).

3 Dupuy (ed.), *Histoire du différend*, pp. 48–52.

4 Dupuy (ed.), *Histoire du différend*, p. 44; Georges Digard, *Philippe le Bel et le Saint Siège, de 1285 à 1304*, 2 vols (Paris 1936), vol. 2, pp. 94–6.

5 Georges Picot (ed.), *Documents relatifs aux États Généraux et assemblées réunis sous Philippe le Bel* (Paris 1901), no. 5, p. 6.

6 Picot (ed.), *Documents*, no. 6, p. 15.

7 Dupuy (ed.), *Histoire du différend*, p. 56. This bull is translated into English along with many of the other related documents in Brian Tierney (ed. and trans.), *The Crisis of Church & State 1050–1300* (Englewood Cliffs, NJ, 1964), pp. 188–9.

8 Elizabeth A. R. Brown, 'Moral Imperatives and Conundrums of Conscience: Reflections on Philip the Fair of France', *Speculum* 87 (2012), pp. 17–18.

9 Julien Théry-Astruc, 'The Pioneer of Royal Theocracy: Guillaume de Nogaret and the Conflicts Between Philip the Fair and the Papacy', in William Chester Jordan and Jenna Rebecca Williams (eds), *The Capetian Century* (Turnhout 2017), p. 246.

10 Coste (ed.), *Boniface VIII*, pp. 115–16; quoted in Julien Théry, 'A Heresy of State: Philip the Fair, the Trial of the "Perfidious Templars", and the Pontificalization of the French Monarchy', *Journal of Medieval Religious Cultures* 39 (2013), p. 131.

11 Jean de Saint-Victor, 'Excerpta', *HF*, vol. 21, pp. 639–40; Coste, *Boniface VIII*, pp. 78–9, 103–6.

12 Thomas N. Bisson, 'The General Assemblies of Philip the Fair: Their Character Reconsidered', in *Medieval France and her Pyrenean Neighbours: Studies in Early Institutional History* (London 1989 [1972]), pp. 97–122; Élisabeth Lalou, 'Les assemblées générales sous Philippe Le Bel' in *Recherches sur les états généraux et les états provinciaux de la France médiévale (110e congrès national des sociétés savantes, Montpellier, 1985)* (Paris 1986), pp. 7–29.

13 Coste (ed.), *Boniface VIII*, pp. 143–63.

14 Coste (ed.), *Boniface VIII*, p. 196. The accusations made on 24 June are only known from an Italian merchant's account of what he heard. Although written from memory by someone with imperfect French, it largely accords with what Plaisians is known to have said at the earlier assembly.

15 Picot (ed.), *Documents*, no. 99, p. 136.

16 Picot (ed.), *Documents*, no. 40, p. 80.

17 Picot (ed.), *Documents*, no. 124, pp. 190–92.

18 Examples at Picot (ed.), *Documents*, no. 551, p. 441 (towns); no. 123, pp. 184–5 (clerics).

19 Jean Favier, *Philippe le bel*, rev. edn (Paris 1998), pp. 381–2.

20 Robert E. Lerner, 'Jacob of Santa Sabina Warns Philip the Fair that Boniface VIII is Antichrist by Means of Scripture and the *Oraculum Cyrilli*', in M. Cecilia Gaposchkin and Jay Rubenstein (eds), *Political Ritual and Practice in Capetian France: Essays in Honour of Elizabeth A. R. Brown* (Turnhout 2021), p. 343.

21 Coste (ed.), *Boniface VIII*, pp. 33–63.

22 Peter Herde, *Cölestin V. (1294) (Peter vom Morrone) der Engelpapast* (Stuttgart 1981).

23 Dupuy (ed.), *Histoire du différend*, pp. 246, etc.

24 Robert Fawtier, 'L'Attentat à Anagni', *Mélanges d'archéologie et d'histoire* 60 (1948), pp. 153–79.

25 Giovanni Villani, *Nuova Cronica*, IX.63, ed. Giuseppe Porta, 3 vols (Parma 1990–91), vol. 2, p. 117, trans. Rose E. Selfe, ed. Philip H. Wicksteed as *Villani's Chronicle*, 2nd edn (London 1906), p. 348.

26 Henry G. J. Beck, 'William Hundleby's Account of the Anagni Outrage', *The Catholic Historical Review* 32 (1946), p. 194.

27 Villani, *Nuova Cronica*, IX.63, ed. Porta, vol. 2, p. 117; trans. Selfe, ed. Wicksteed, p. 349.

28 *Les grandes chroniques de France*, ed. Jules Viard, 10 vols (Paris 1920–53), vol. 8, p. 225, a poorly informed account for this incident; Beck, 'William Hundleby's Account', p. 213 n. 23.

29 Dupuy (ed.), *Histoire du différend*, p. 248.

30 Villani, *Nuova Cronica*, VIII.63, ed. Porta, vol. 2, p. 118.

31 Beck, 'William Hundleby's Account', p. 199.

32 Beck, 'William Hundleby's Account', p. 220 n. 48; Villani, *Nuova Cronica*, VIII.63, ed. Porta, vol. 2, p. 119, trans. Selfe ed. Wicksteed, p. 350, and *Grandes chroniques*, ed. Viard, vol. 8, p. 226, have similar stories.

33 Patrick N. R. Zutshi, 'The Avignon Papacy', *The New Cambridge Medieval History*, vol. 6, ed. Michael Jones (Cambridge 2000), pp. 657–8.

34 In fact, since he was Gascon, Clement was also a subject of the English king Edward I, whom he manifestly favoured: Sophia Menache, *Clement V* (Cambridge 1998), pp. 247–78.

35 Élisabeth Lalou, 'Le gouvernement de la reine Jeanne, 1285–1305', *Cahiers haut-marnais* 167 (1986), pp. 27–28; Amanda Luyster, 'The Place of a Queen/A Queen and her Places: Jeanne of Navarre's *Kalila and Dimna* as a Political Manuscript in Early Fourteenth-Century France', in Tracy Chapman Hamilton and Mariah Proctor-Tiffany (eds), *Moving Women, Moving Objects (400–1500)* (Leiden 2019), pp. 160–80.

36 Elizabeth A. R. Brown, 'The Prince is Father of the King: The Character and Childhood of Philip the Fair of France', *Mediaeval Studies* 49 (1987), p. 304 n. 75.

37 BnF Latin 4270, fol. 103r–104r, 250v; Brown, 'The Prince is Father of the King', pp. 305–6.

38 Elizabeth A. R. Brown, 'La mort, les testaments et les fondations de Jeanne de Navarre, reine de France (1273–1305)', in Anne-Hélène Allirot et al. (eds), *Une histoire pour un royaume, XII\u1d49–XV\u1d49 siècle: Actes du colloque Corpus Regni, organisé en hommage à Colette Beaune* (Paris 2010), pp. 131, 135–6.

39 Brown, 'The Prince is Father of the King', pp. 296, 309; Robert-Henri Bautier, 'Diplomatique et histoire politique: Ce que la critique diplomatique nous apprend sur la personnalité de Philippe le Bel', *RH* 259 (1978), pp. 19–27.

40 *La Chronique métrique attribuée à Geffroy de Paris*, ll. 2965–6, ed. Armel Diverrès (Paris 1956), p. 148.

41 Abel Rigault, *Le Procès de Guichard, évêque de Troyes (1308–1313)* (Paris 1896), pp. 21–44.

42 Rigault, *Procès*, pp. 61–9, 270–71.

43 Alain Provost, *Domus diaboli: Un évêque en procès au temps de Philippe le Bel* (Paris 2010); Rigault, *Procès*, pp. 125–7, 283–7 (incubus), 297–305 (witnesses); Monique Langlois and Yvonne Lanhers (eds), *Confessions et jugements de criminels au Parlement de Paris (1319–1350)* (Paris 1971), pp. 29–32.

44 *Grandes chroniques*, ed. Viard, vol. 8, p. 293–4; Rigault, *Procès*, pp. 220–21.

45 Melina Rokai, 'Constructing a Traitor: The Case of Guichard of Troyes, the Nominal Bishop of Bosnia in the Early Fourteenth Century', *Anali Pravnog fakulteta u Beogradu* 68 (2020), pp. 68–87.

46 Jules Michelet (ed.), *Le Procès contre les Templiers*, 2 vols (Paris 1841–51), vol. 1, pp. 90–96; Malcolm Barber, *The Trial of the Templars*, 2nd edn (Cambridge 2006), pp. 72, 202–16.

47 Lalou, 'Les assemblées générales', pp. 12–17.

48 *Chronique latine de Guillaume de Nangis, de 1113 à 1300, avec les continuations de cette chronique, de 1300 à 1368*, ed. Hercule Géraud, 2 vols (Paris 1843), vol. 1, p. 390.

49 Joseph R. Strayer, *The Reign of Philip the Fair* (Princeton, NJ 1980), p. 291 (quote); Barber, *The Trial*, pp. 283–5; Théry, 'Heresy of State', p. 125.

50 Barber, *The Trial*, pp. 270–72.

51 Céline Balasse, *1306, l'expulsion des Juifs du royaume de France* (Brussels 2008), at p. 203 for the profit.

52 Strayer, *Philip the Fair*, p. 288.

53 Alain Provost, 'On the Margins of the Templars' Trial: The Case of Bishop Guichard of Troyes', in Jochen Burgtorf, Paul F. Crawford, and Helen J. Nicholson (eds), *The Debate on the Trial of the Templars (1307–1314)* (Farnham 2010), pp. 123–5.

54 Théry, 'Heresy of State', p. 120.

55 Théry, 'Heresy of State', pp. 118–19.

56 *Ord.*, vol. 1, p. 390.

57 Guillaume de Chartres, 'Vita et actibus inclitae recordationis regis francorum Ludovici', *HF*, vol. 20, p. 32, ed. M. Cecilia Gaposchkin and Sean L. Field, trans. Larry F. Field, *The Sanctity of Louis IX: Early Lives of Saint Louis by Geoffrey of Beaulieu and William of Chartres* (Ithaca, NY 2014), p. 140.

58 Robert E. Lerner 'The Uses of Heterodoxy: The French Monarchy and Unbelief in the Thirteenth Century', *French Historical Studies* 4 (1965), p. 202.

59 Charles-Victor Langlois, 'L'affaire des Templiers', *Journal des Savants*, new ser., 6 (1908), pp. 417–35, at p. 433, quoted in translation by Brown, 'Moral Imperatives', p. 2; Sean L. Field, *The Beguine, the Angel, and the Inquisitor: The Trials of Marguerite Porete and Guiard of Cressonessart* (Notre Dame, IN 2012), p. 26.

18. A Family Affair

1 *La Chronique métrique attribuée à Geffroy de Paris*, ll. 5040–42, ed. Armel Diverrès (Paris 1956), p. 186.

2 Elizabeth A. R. Brown and Nancy Freeman Regalado, 'La grant feste: Philip the Fair's Celebration of the Knighting of His Sons in Paris at Pentecost of 1313', in Barbara A. Hanawalt and Kathryn L. Reyerson (eds), *City and Spectacle in Medieval Europe* (Minneapolis, MN 1994), pp. 56–85.

3 Jean de Saint-Victor, 'Excerpta e memoriali historiarum', HF, vol. 21, pp. 656–57; *Chronique métrique*, ll. 5057–62, ed. Diverrès, p. 187; Brown and Regnaldo, 'La grant feste', p. 64.

4 *Chronique métrique*, ll. 4644–82, ed. Diverrès, pp. 179–80.

5 Jean de Saint-Victor, 'Excerpta', HF, vol. 21, p. 657.

6 Jean de Saint-Victor, 'Excerpta', HF, vol. 21, p. 657.

7 Constance Bullock-Davies, *Register of Royal and Baronial Domestic Minstrels, 1272–1327* (Woodbridge, 1986), p. 9; Brown and Regalado, 'La grant feste', pp. 61, 72.

8 *Ord.*, vol. 1, pp. 328–9, 420–22, 426, 343–5, 491.

9 Brown and Regalado, 'La grant feste', pp. 72–3.

10 Jean de Saint-Victor, 'Excerpta', HF, vol. 21, p. 661.

11 Yves de Saint-Denis, 'Chronicon', HF, vol. 21, p. 206.

12 Elizabeth A. R. Brown, 'Philip the Fair of France and His Family's Disgrace: The Adultery Scandal of 1314 Revealed, Recounted, Reimagined, and Redated', *Mediaevistik* 32 (2019), p. 102 n. 98.

13 On the problem of discerning Philip's agency, see Elizabeth A. R. Brown, 'Réflexions sur Philippe le bel', *Annuaire-bulletin de la Société de l'histoire de France* (2014), pp. 7–24.

14 'Ex anonymo regum franciae chronico', HF, vol. 22, p. 19; Jean Favier, *Un conseiller de Philippe le Bel: Enguerran de Marigny* (Paris 1963), pp. 120–28.

15 Pierre Chaplais, *Piers Gaveston: Edward II's Adoptive Brother* (Oxford 1994), pp. 91–3.

16 *Vita Edwardi Secundi*, ed. and trans. N. Denholm-Young, re-ed. Wendy Childs (Oxford 2005), pp. 28–9.

17 Chaplais, *Gaveston*; Ian Mortimer, 'Sermons of Sodomy: A Reconsideration of Edward II's Sodomitical Reputation', in Gwilym Dodd and Anthony Musson (eds), *The Reign of Edward II: New Perspectives* (Woodbridge 2006), pp. 48–57, is a good empirical treatment of the tropes employed and their likely source in earlier, French weaponization of sodomy against political enemies.

18 W. Mark Ormrod, 'The Sexualities of Edward II', in Dodd and Musson (eds), *The Reign of Edward II*, pp. 22–47, is a sensitive treatment of the problem.

19 *Polychronicon Ranulphi Higden*, VII.41, ed. Joseph Lumby, 9 vols (Cambridge 1865–85), vol. 8, p. 298, quoted in Ormrod, 'Sexualities', p. 32.

20 Kathryn Warner, *Isabella of France: The Rebel Queen* (Stroud 2016), pp. 61–82.

21 Elizabeth A. R. Brown, 'Diplomacy, Adultery, and Domestic Politics at the Court of Philip the Fair: Queen Isabelle's Mission to the Court of France in 1314', in J. S. Hamilton and Patricia J. Bradley (eds), *Documenting the Past: Essays in Medieval History Presented to George Peddy Cuttino* (Woodbridge 1989), p. 66.

22 Brown, 'Diplomacy, Adultery', p. 55.

23 *Chronique métrique*, ll. 6375–8, ed. Diverrès, p. 211; Brown, 'Diplomacy, Adultery', p. 76.

24 Jean des Preis dit d'Outremeuse, *Ly myreur des histors*, ed. A. Borgnet and Stanislas Bormans, 7 vols (Brussels 1864–8), vol. 6, p. 197; Brown, 'Diplomacy, Adultery', p. 75.

25 *Chronique métrique*, ln. 5899, ed. Diverrès, p. 192.

26 Quoted in Brown, 'Diplomacy, Adultery', p. 66 n. 61.

27 Jean de Saint-Victor, 'Excerpta', *HF*, vol. 21, p. 658 (rags); *Chronique métrique*, ln. 5961, ed. Diverrès, p. 203 (shaved heads).

28 Richard C. Famiglietti, *Tales of the Marriage Bed from Medieval France (1300–1500)* (Providence, RI 1992), pp. 112–13.

29 Elizabeth A. R. Brown, 'His Family's Disgrace', p. 79; boiling water: *Chronique latine de Guillaume de Nangis, de 1113 à 1300, avec les continuations de cette chronique, de 1300 à 1368*, ed. Hercule Géraud, 2 vols (Paris 1843), vol. 1, p. 405.

30 *Chronique métrique*, ll. 5937–45, ed. Diverrès, p. 203.

31 Élisabeth Lalou, *Itinéraire de Philippe IV le Bel (1285–1314)*, 2 vols (Paris 2007), vol. 1, p. 103.

32 Brown, 'His Family's Disgrace', pp. 77–80.

33 Brown, 'His Family's Disgrace', p. 77.

34 Elizabeth A. R. Brown, 'The Children of Charles of la Marche and Blanche of Artois and Burgundy', *Medieval Prosopography* 34 (2019), pp. 151–74.

35 'Continuatio chronici Girardi de Francheto', *HF*, vol. 21, p. 43.

36 Jean de Saint-Victor, 'Excerpta', *HF*, vol. 21, p. 658.

37 *Chronique métrique*, ll. 5919–20, ed. Diverrès, p. 203; *Chronique latine de Guillaume de Nangis*, ed. Géraud, vol. 1, p. 405.

38 Herveline Delhumeau, *Le Palais de la Cité: Du Palais des rois de France au Palais de Justice* (Arles 2011), pp. 59–61.

39 Elizabeth A. R. Brown, 'La généalogie capétienne dans l'historiographie du Moyen Âge: Philippe le Bel, le reniement du *reditus* et la création d'une ascendance carolingienne pour Hugues Capet', in Dominique Iogna-Prat and Jean-Charles Picard (eds), *Religion et culture autour de l'an mil: Royaume capétien et Lotharingie* (Paris 1990), pp. 199–214.

40 Pierre Dupuy (ed.), *Histoire du différend d'entre le pape Boniface VIII et Philippe le Bel, roy de France* (Paris 1655), pp. 634–5.

41 Giovanni Villani, *Nuova Cronica*, VIII.64, ed. Giuseppe Porta, 3 vols (Parma 1990–91), vol. 2, pp. 120–21, trans. Selfe ed. Philip H. Wicksteed as *Villani's Chronicle*, 2nd edn (London 1906), p. 429; 'E chronico anonymi Cadomensis', *HF*, vol. 22, p. 25.

42 *Chronique métrique*, ll. 5725–30, ed. Diverrès, p. 199.

43 Frantz Funck-Brentano, 'La mort de Philippe le Bel', *Annales de la Société historique et archéologique du Gâtinais* 2 (1884), pp. 126–8; Malcolm Barber, *The New Knighthood: A History of the Order of the Temple* (Cambridge 1994), pp. 314–15, traces the curse to a Templar burned in the kingdom of Naples, which was ruled by the Capetian branch descended from Charles of Anjou. Alain Demurger, *Jacques de Molay: Le crépuscule des Templiers* (Paris 2002), pp. 273–4.

44 Charles Baudon de Mony, 'La mort et les funérailles de Philippe le Bel d'après un compte rendu à la cour de Majorque', *BEC* 58 (1897), pp. 5–14; Funck-Brentano, 'La mort de Philippe le Bel', pp. 83–129.

45 *Chronique métrique*, ln. 6386, ed. Diverrès, p. 211.

46 Villani, *Nuova Cronica*, X.66, ed. Porta, vol. 2, pp. 268–9, trans. Selfe, ed. Wicksteed, *Villani's Chronicle*, p. 428; Dante Alleghieri, *Paradiso*, canto 19, ln. 120, trans. Robert M. Durling (Oxford 2011), pp. 386–7.

47 Baudon de Mony, 'La mort et les funérailles', p. 13.

48 Yves de Saint-Denis, 'Chronicon', *HF*, vol. 21, p. 206.

49 'Continuatio chronici Girardi de Fracheto', *HF*, vol. 21, p. 42.

50 Lalou, *Itinéraire de Philippe IV*, vol. 2, pp. 426–7.

51 André Artonne, *Le mouvement de 1314 et les chartes provinciales de 1315* (Paris 1912); Elizabeth A. R. Brown, 'Reform and Resistance to Royal Authority in Fourteenth-Century France: The Leagues of 1314–1315', *Parliaments, Estates, and Representation* 1 (1981), pp. 109–37.

52 *Chronique métrique*, ll. 6443–714, ed. Diverrès, pp. 212–17.

53 Jean Roucaute and Marc Saché, *Lettres de Philippe le Bel relatives au pays de Gévaudan* (Mende 1896), no. 93, pp. 169–71.

54 'Continuatio chronici Girardi de Fracheto', *HF*, vol. 21, p. 42.

55 Edited in Brown, 'Reform and Resistance', appendix 6, p. 134.

19. Bad Omens

1 Charles Baudon de Mony, 'La mort et les funérailles de Philippe le Bel d'après un compte rendu à la cour de Majorque', *BEC* 58 (1897), pp. 11–12; *Istore et croniques de Flandres*, ed. J.-M.-B.-C. Kervyn de Lettenhove, 2 vols (Brussels 1879–80), vol. 1, p. 302.

2 Yves of Saint-Denis, 'Chronicon', *HF*, vol. 21, p. 206; Baudon de Mony, 'La mort et les funérailles', p. 12.

3 Yves of Saint-Denis, 'Chronicon', *HF*, vol. 21, pp. 206–7.

4 Baudon de Mony, 'La mort et les funérailles', p. 14.

5 *La Chronique métrique attribuée à Geffroy de Paris*, ll. 7095–6, ed. Armel Diverrès (Paris 1956), p. 224; Jean de Saint-Victor, 'Excerpta e memoriali historiarum', *HF*, 21, p. 661.

6 Olivier Canteaut, 'Louis X en majesté: Du royaume de Navarre au trône de France (1309–1315)', *Cahiers de recherches médiévales et humanistes/Journal of Medieval and Humanistic Studies* 31 (2016), pp. 45–9.

7 Elizabeth A. R. Brown, 'Kings like Semi-Gods: The Case of Louis X of France', *Majestas* 1 (1993), pp. 5–37.

8 Annie M. Huffelmann, *Clemenza von Ungarn, Königin von Frankreich* (Berlin and Leipzig 1911).

9 Giovanni Villani, *Nuova Cronica*, X.66, ed. Giuseppe Porta, 3 vols (Parma 1990–91), vol. 2, p. 269; Jean de Hocsem, *La chronique de Jean de Hocsem*, new edn by Godefroid Kurth (Brussels 1927), p. 151, also blamed strangulation, though he made no mention of a towel.

10 Jean de Saint-Victor, 'Excerpta', *HF*, vol. 21, p. 660.

11 Baudon de Mony, 'La mort et les funérailles', pp. 12–14.

12 Jean de Saint-Victor, 'Excerpta, *HF*, vol. 21, pp. 659–60.

13 Jean Favier, *Un conseiller de Philippe le Bel: Enguerran de Marigny* (Paris 1963), pp. 207–16.

14 *Les grandes chroniques de France*, ed. Jules Viard, 10 vols (Paris 1920–53), vol. 8, p. 306.

15 Favier, *Enguerran de Marigny*, pp. 213–14, 216.

16 *Grandes chroniques*, ed. Viard, vol. 8, p. 251.

17 Jean de Saint-Victor, 'Excerpta', *HF*, vol. 21, p. 661.

18 Favier, *Enguerran de Marigny*, p. 217; Alain Boureau, *Satan hérétique: Naissance de la démonologie dans l'Occident médiéval (1280–1330)* (Paris 2004).

19 William Chester Jordan, *The French Monarchy and the Jews: From Philip Augustus to the Last Capetians* (Philadelphia, PA 1989), p. 240.

20 *Ord.*, vol. 1, pp. 595–7.

21 *Ord.*, vol. 1, p. 583; vol. 11, p. 434.

22 Canteaut, 'Louis X', p. 53.

23 Elizabeth A. R. Brown, 'Reform and Resistance to Royal Authority in Fourteenth-Century France: The Leagues of 1314–1315', *Parliaments, Estates, and Representation* 1 (1981), p. 120 n. 38.

24 Hillary Zmora, *Monarchy, Aristocracy, and the State in Europe, 1300–1800* (London 2001); Wim Blockmans, André Holenstein and Jon Mathieu with Daniel Schläppi (eds), *Empowering Interactions: Political Cultures and the Emergence of the State in Europe, 1300–1900* (Farnham 2009).

25 *Ord.*, vol. 1, p. 569.

26 *Chronique métrique*, ll. 7426–7, ed. Diverrès, p. 231.

27 *Chronique métrique*, ll. 7411–12, ed. Diverrès, p. 230.

28 Huffelman, *Clemenza*, p. 28; Mariah Proctor-Tiffany, *Medieval Art in Motion: The Inventory and Gift Giving of Queen Clémence de Hongrie* (Philadelphia, PA 2019), pp. 17, 66–9.

29 Canteaut, 'Louis X', pp. 53–4 n. 6.

30 *Chronique latine de Guillaume de Nangis, de 1113 à 1300, avec les continuations de cette chronique, de 1300 à 1368*, ed. Hercule Géraud, 2 vols (Paris 1843), vol. 1, p. 422.

31 Brown, 'Kings like Semi-Gods', pp. 27–9.

32 Philippe Buc, 'David's Adultery with Bathsheba and the Healing Power of the Capetian Kings', *Viator* 24 (1993), pp. 101–21.

33 Canteaut, 'Louis X', pp. 54–5; Jean-Pierre Poly, 'La Gloire des rois et la parole cachée ou l'avenir d'une illusion', in Dominique Iogna-Prat and Jean-Charles Picard (eds), *Religion et culture autour de l'an mil: Royaume capétien et Lotharingie* (Paris 1990), pp. 167–88.

34 Frantz Funck-Brentano, *Les Origines de la guerre de Cent ans: Philippe le Bel en Flandres* (Paris 1896), pp. 660–63.

35 *Chronique métrique*, ln. 7540, ed. Diverrès, p. 233.

36 *Chronique métrique*, ln. 7540, ed. Diverrès, p. 232.

37 André Artonne, *Le Mouvement de 1314 et les chartes provinciales de 1315* (Paris 1912), pp. 125–45.

38 Jean de Saint-Victor, 'Excerpta', *HF*, vol. 21, p. 662.

39 Jean de Saint-Victor, 'Excerpta', *HF*, vol. 21, p. 663; *Ord.*, vol. 1, pp. 606–08.

40 Thomas K. Heebøll-Holm, *Ports, Piracy, and Maritime War: Piracy in the English Channel and the Atlantic, 1280–1330* (Leiden 2013), pp. 217–18; Jean de Saint-Victor, 'Excerpta', *HF*, vol. 21, pp. 662, 665.

41 Henry S. Lucas, 'The Great European Famine of 1315, 1316, and 1317', *Speculum* 5 (1930), pp. 343–77; William Chester Jordan, *The Great Famine: Northern Europe in the Early Fourteenth Century* (Princeton, NJ 1996).

42 Artonne, *Le Mouvement*, pp. 90–100.

43 Edgard Boutaric (ed.), *Actes du Parlement de Paris*, 2 vols (Paris 1863–7), vol. 2, pp. 141–2; Robert Fawtier et al. (eds), *Registres du Trésor des chartes*, 3 vols in 5 (Paris 1958–99), vol. 2.1, pp. vii–viii, 62.

44 'Continuatio chronici Girardi de Fracheto', *HF*, vol. 21, p. 45; 'Ex anonymo regum franciae chronico', *HF*, vol. 22, p. 20; Bernard Gui, 'E

floribus chronicorum', *HF*, vol. 21, p. 725; *Chronique latine de Guillaume de Nangis*, ed. Géraud, vol. 1, pp. 425–6; *Grandes chroniques*, ed. Viard, vol. 8, p. 327.

45 So claims *Chronique métrique*, ll. 7675–86; Jean de Saint-Victor, 'Excerpta', *HF*, vol. 21, p. 663; Gille le Muisit, *Chronique et annales*, ed. Henri Lemaître (Paris 1905), pp. 90–91.

46 François Maillard, (ed.), *Comptes royaux (1314–1328)*, 2 vols (Paris 1961), vol. 2, pp. 189–90.

47 Elizabeth A. R. Brown, 'The Ceremonial of Royal Succession in Capetian France: The Double Funeral of Louis X', *Traditio* 34 (1978), pp. 227–71, description of Louis's first funeral at pp. 228–31.

48 G. Servois, 'Documents inédits sur l'avènement de Philippe le Long', *Annuaire-bulletin de la Société de l'histoire de France*, vol. 2.2 (1864), no. 5, p. 71.

49 Dainville, Archives départmentales du Pas-de-Calais A 60, nos. 27–8; Paul Lehugeur, *Histoire de Philippe le Long, roi de France (1316–1322)*, 2 vols (Paris 1897–1931), vol. 1, p. 23; Favier, *Enguerran de Marigny*, no. 2, p. 232.

50 Heinrich Finke (ed.), *Acta aragonensia: Quellen zur deutschen, italienischen, französischen, spanischen, zur Kirchen- und Kulturgeschichte aus der diplomatischen Korrespondenz Jaymes II. (1291–1327)*, 3 vols (Berlin and Leipzig 1908–22), no. 137, vol. 1, p. 210.

51 Lehugeur, *Philippe le Long*, vol. 1, pp. 28–43; Brown, 'Double Funeral', pp. 257–9.

52 Louis Douët-D'Arcq (ed.), *Comptes de l'Argenterie des rois de France au XIVᵉ siècle* (Paris 1851), pp. 17–18.

20. Poisoned Waters

1 Louis Douët-D'Arcq (ed.), *Comptes de l'Argenterie des rois de France au XIVᵉ siècle* (Paris 1851), pp. 45–69. On the parrots and butterflies, see Elizabeth A. R. Brown, 'The Ceremony of Royal Succession in Capetian France: The Funeral of Philip V', *Speculum* 55 (1980), p. 280.

2 Jean de Saint-Victor, 'Excerpta e memoriali historiarum', *HF*, vol. 21, p. 665.

3 G. Servois, 'Documents inédits sur l'avènement de Philippe le Long', *Annuaire-bulletin de la Société de l'histoire de France*, vol. 2.2 (1864), no. 3, p. 67.

4 Servois, 'Documents inédits', no. 4, p. 68.

5 'Continuatio chronici Girardi de Fracheto', *HF*, vol. 21, p. 47; Jean de Saint-Victor, 'Excerpta', *HF*, vol. 21, p. 665.

6 'Ex anonymo regum franciae chronico', *HF*, vol. 22, p. 20.

7 Jean de Hocsem, *La chronique de Jean de Hocsem*, new edn by Godefroid Kurth (Brussels 1927), p. 151.

8 'Continuatio chronici Girardi de Fracheto', *HF*, vol. 21, p. 47; *Chronique latine de Guillaume de Nangis, de 1113 à 1300, avec les continuations de cette chronique, de 1300 à 1368*, ed. Hercule Géraud, 2 vols (Paris 1843), vol. 1, p. 432.

9 Paul Lehugeur, *Histoire de Philippe le Long, roi de France (1316–1322)*, 2 vols (Paris 1897–1931), vol. 1, pp. 168–74.

10 Paul Viollet, 'Comment les femmes ont été exclues, en France, de la succession à la couronne', *Mémoires de l'Institut national de France* 34 (1895), p. 139.

11 Servois, 'Documents inédits', no. 3, pp. 65–6.

12 Lehugeur, *Philippe le Long*, vol. 1, p. 79.

13 'Continuatio chronici Girardi de Fracheto', *HF*, vol. 21, p. 47; *Chronique latine de Guillaume de Nangis*, ed. Géraud, vol. 1, p. 434; *Les grandes chroniques de France*, Jules Viard, 10 vols (Paris 1920–53), vol. 8, p. 332.

14 Éliane Viennot, *La France, les femmes et le pouvoir: L'invention de la loi salique (V^e–XVIe siècle)* (Paris 2006).

15 Jean de Saint-Victor, 'Excerpta', *HF*, vol. 21, p. 665.

16 Richard Lescot, 'Genealogica aliquorum regum francie, per quam apparet quantum attinere potest regi francie rex navarre', appended to *Chronique de Richard Lescot, religieux de Saint-Denis (1328–1344), suivie de la continuation de cette chronique (1344–1364)*, ed. Jean Lemoine (Paris 1896), pp. 173–8, from BnF Latin 14663, fols 39–47, a manuscript of miscellaneous historical texts; Viollet, 'Comment les femmes', pp. 125–48; Craig Taylor, 'The Salic Law and the Valois Succession to the French Crown', *French History* 15 (2001), pp. 358–77.

17 Heinrich Denifle et al. (eds), *Chartularium Universitatis parisiensis*, 4 vols (Paris 1889–97), no. 737, vol. 2, pt 1, pp. 197–8. I am grateful to

Elizabeth A. R. Brown for our spirited discussion of this document, even if I am not sure we ever came to an agreement about it.

18 *Grandes chroniques*, ed. Viard, vol. 8, p. 332.

19 'Continuatio chronici Girardi de Fracheto', *HF*, vol. 21, p. 47; *Chronique latine de Guillaume de Nangis*, ed. Géraud, vol. 1, pp. 434–5.

20 Lehugeur, *Philippe le Long*, vol. 1, pp. 462–3.

21 Lehugeur, *Philippe le Long*, vol. 1, p. 94.

22 Edited in Alexandre Pinchart, 'Lettres missives tirées des archives de Belgique concernant l'histoire de France, 1317–24', *BEC* 45 (1884), p. 76.

23 Denis-François Secousse (ed.), *Recueil de pièces servant de preuves aux Mémoires sur les troubles excités en France par Charles II, dit le Mauvais, roi de Navarre et comte d'Évreux* (Paris 1755), pp. 6–10.

24 Jean de Saint-Victor, 'Excerpta', *HF*, vol. 21, p. 666.

25 Jean Favier, *Un conseiller de Philippe le Bel: Enguerran de Marigny* (Paris 1963), pp. 221–3.

26 *Ord.*, vol. 1, pp. 665–8; Olivier Canteaut, 'Hôtel et gouvernement sous les derniers Capétiens directs', *BEC* 168 (2010), pp. 385–7, 394.

27 Elizabeth A. R. Brown, 'Royal Salvation and Needs of State in Late Capetian France', in William Chester Jordan, Bruce McNab, and Teofilo F. Ruiz (eds), *Order and Innovation in the Middle Ages: Essays in Honor of Joseph R. Strayer* (Princeton, NJ 1976), pp. 365–84, 375, for the totals from Philip IV's testament.

28 Auguste Coulon and Suzanne Clémencet (eds), *Lettres secrètes et curiales du Pape Jean XXII (1316–1334), relatives à la France*, 10 vols (Paris 1900–72), nos 513–14, vol. 5, cols 433–36.

29 Christopher Tyerman, 'Philip V of France, the Assemblies of 1319–1320 and the Crusade', *Bulletin of the Institute of Historical Research* 57 (1984), pp. 15–34.

30 Elizabeth A. R. Brown, 'The Ceremonial of Royal Succession in Capetian France: The Double Funeral of Louis X', *Traditio* 34 (1978), p. 261.

31 *Ord.*, vol. 1, pp. 643–4.

32 Herman Vander Linden, 'Les relations politiques de la Flandre avec la France au XIVe siècle', *Compte-rendu des séances de la commission royale d'histoire*, 2nd ser., 3 (1893), pp. 476–94.

33 Tyerman, 'Philip V', p. 29

34 Christopher Tyerman, 'Commoners on Crusade: The Creation of Political Space?', *EHR* 136/579 (2021), pp. 245–75.

35 Bruce Campbell, *The Great Transition: Climate, Disease and Society in the Late-Medieval World* (Cambridge 2016), pp. 209–20; William Chester Jordan, *The Great Famine: Northern Europe in the Early Fourteenth Century* (Princeton, NJ 1996), pp. 36–9.

36 Tyerman, 'Commoners on Crusade', p. 272.

37 *Chronique parisienne anonyme du XIVᵉ siècle*, ed. A. Hellot (Nogent-le-Rotrou 1884), p. 47.

38 *Chronique parisienne*, ed. Hellot, pp. 47–8.

39 Henri Moranvillé (ed.), *Chronographia regum francorum*, 3 vols (Paris 1891–97), vol. 1, pp. 251–2; Jules Viard, 'Philippe de Valois avant son avènement au trône', *BEC* 91 (1930), pp. 315–17.

40 Georges Passerat, *La Croisade des Pastoureaux* (Cahors 2006), pp. 77–86.

41 David Nirenberg, *Communities of Violence: Persecution of Minorities in the Middle Ages*, new edn (Princeton, NJ 2015), pp. 43–68.

42 *Ord.*, vol. 1, pp. 645–7.

43 *Ord.*, vol. 1, p. 595; William Chester Jordan, *The French Monarchy and the Jews: From Philip Augustus to the Last Capetians* (Philadelphia, PA 1989), pp. 240–43.

44 *Ord.*, vol. 11, p. 447.

45 Passerat, *Croisade des Pastoureaux*, pp. 97, 106 n. 88, 108.

46 Passerat, *Croisade des Pastoureaux*, p. 97; Yves Dossat, 'Les Juifs à Toulouse: Un demi-siècle d'histoire communautaire', in *Juifs et judaïsme de Languedoc* (Toulouse 1977), pp. 117–39, for the pre-expulsion population, certainly much diminished after the 1306 expulsion.

47 Françoise Bériac, 'La persécution des lépreux dans la France Méridionale en 1321', *Le Moyen Âge* 93 (1987), pp. 203–21; Malcolm Barber, 'Lepers, Jews, and Moslems: The Plot to Overthrow Christendom in 1321', *History* 66 (1981), pp. 1–17.

48 On the Jewish connection and the development of this novel charge, see now Tzafrir Barzilay, *Poisoned Wells: Accusations, Persecution, and Minorities in Medieval Europe, 1321–1422* (Philadelphia, PA 2022).

49 Lehugeur, *Philippe le Long*, vol. 1, pp. 425–9.

50 *Ord.*, vol. 11, p. 482.

51 Elizabeth A. R. Brown, 'Philip V, Charles IV, and the Jews of France: The Alleged Expulsion of 1322', *Speculum* 66 (1991), pp. 294–329; Isidore Loeb, 'Les Expulsions des juifs de France au XIVᵉ siècle', in *Jubelschrift zum siebzigsten Geburtstage des Professors Dr. H. Graetz* (Breslau 1887), pp. 39–56.

52 Jean de Saint-Victor, 'Excerpta', *HF*, vol. 21, pp. 674–5, and *Chronique latine de Guillaume de Nangis*, ed. Géraud, vol. 2, p. 37; Isabelle Guyot-Bachy, '*Expediebat ut unus homo moreretur pro populo*: Jean de Saint-Victor et la mort du roi Philippe V', in Françoise Autrand, Claude Gauvard, and Jean-Marie Moeglin (eds), *Saint-Denis et la royauté: Études offertes à Bernard Guenée* (Paris 1999), pp. 493–504.

53 Quoted in Tyerman, 'Philip V', p. 30.

54 Brown, 'Funeral of Philip V', pp. 266–93.

21. End of the Line

1 Monique Langlois and Yvonne Lanhers (eds), *Confessions et jugements de criminels au Parlement de Paris (1319–1350)* (Paris 1971), pp. 38–9.

2 *Chronique parisienne anonyme du XIVᵉ siècle*, ed. A. Hellot (Nogent-le-Rotrou 1884), p. 88.

3 Auguste Coulon and Suzanne Clémencet (eds), *Lettres secrètes et curiales du Pape Jean XXII (1316–1334), relatives à la France*, 10 vols (Paris 1900–72), no. 1668, vol. 5, col. 246; Heinrich Finke (ed.), *Acta aragonensia. Quellen zur deutschen, italienischen, französischen, spanischen, zur Kirchen- und Kulturgeschichte aus der diplomatischen Korrespondenz Jaymes II. (1291–1327)*, 3 vols (Berlin and Leipzig 1908–22), no. 326, vol. 1, p. 490; AN U 785.

4 Georg Jostkleigrewe, 'Staatsbildung im Prozess? Neue Perspektiven auf eine Meistererzählung zur französischen Geschichte: Der Fall des Jourdain de l'Isle (1323)', *Historische Zeitschrift* 312 (2021), pp. 335–7; Justine Firnhaber-Baker, 'Techniques of Seigneurial War in the Fourteenth Century', *JMH* 36 (2010), pp. 90–103.

5 *Les grandes chroniques de France*, Jules Viard, 10 vols (Paris 1920–53), vol. 9, p. 17.

6 Jostkleigrewe, 'Staatsbildung im Prozess?'

7 Malcolm Vale, *The Origins of the Hundred Years War: The Angevin Legacy, 1250–1340*, new edn (Oxford 1996), p. 136; AN X1a 8844, fol. 44v.

8 Vale, *Origins*, pp. 133–9.

9 Jostkleigrewe, 'Staatsbildung im Prozess?', pp. 337–40.

10 Louis Guérard (ed.), *Documents pontificaux sur la Gascogne, d'après les archives du Vatican: Pontificat de Jean XXII (1316–34)*, 2 vols (Paris and Auch 1896–1903), nos 228–35, 237, vol. 2, pp. 77–83, 85–6.

11 Finke (ed.), *Acta aragonensia*, no. 326, vol. 1, p. 490; *Grandes chroniques*, ed. Viard, vol. 9, p. 18.

12 *Chronique latine de Guillaume de Nangis, de 1113 à 1300, avec les continuations de cette chronique, de 1300 à 1368*, ed. Hercule Géraud, 2 vols (Paris 1843), vol. 2, p. 46; 'Continuation anonyme de la chronique de Jean de Saint-Victor', *HF*, vol. 21, p. 680.

13 Finke (ed.), *Acta aragonensia*, no. 327, p. 493.

14 Pierre Chaplais (ed.), *The War of Saint-Sardos, 1323–1325: Gascon Correspondence and Diplomatic Documents* (London 1954), pp. 8, 186.

15 Vale, *Origins*, pp. 232–5.

16 Chaplais (ed.), *War of Saint-Sardos*, pp. 179–80.

17 Claude Devic and Joseph Vaissette, *Histoire générale de Languedoc*, rev. edn Auguste Molinier, 16 vols (Toulouse and Paris 1868–1905), vol. 10, cols 661–2.

18 Chaplais, *War of Saint-Sardos*, pp. xii–xiii.

19 Olivier Canteaut, 'L'annulation du marriage de Charles IV et de Blanche de Bourgogne: Une Affaire d'état?', in Emmanuelle Santinelli (ed.), *Répudiation, séparation, divorce dans l'Occident médiéval* (Valenciennes 2007), pp. 309–27; David d'Avray, *Dissolving Royal Marriages: A Documentary History, 860–1600* (Cambridge 2014), pp. 116–82.

20 'Continuation . . . de Jean de Saint-Victor', *HF*, vol. 21, p. 682.

21 Chaplais (ed.), *War of Saint-Sardos*, p. 190.

22 Chaplais (ed.), *War of Saint-Sardos*, p. 186.

23 Vale, *Origins*, p. 236.

24 Seymour Phillips, *Edward II* (New Haven, CT 2010), pp. 465–8; Françoise Bériac-Lainé, 'Une armée anglo-gasconne vingt ans avant la guerre de Cent ans', in Jacques Paviot and Jacques Verger (eds), *Guerre,*

pouvoir et noblesse au Moyen Âge: Mélanges en l'honneur de Philippe Contamine (Paris 2000), pp. 83–92.

25 Vale, *Origins*, p. 238.

26 Quote in J. R. S. Phillips, 'Introduction' to Dodd and Musson (eds), *Reign of Edward II*, p. 3 n.7.

27 Phillips, *Edward II*, pp. 469–73.

28 Chaplais (ed.), *War of Saint-Sardos*, pp. 202–4.

29 *Grandes chroniques*, ed. Viard, vol. 9, pp. 36–7.

30 Devic and Vaissette, *Histoire générale de Languedoc*, rev. edn Molinier, vol. 9, pp. 439–46; *Chronique parisienne*, 151, ed. Hellot, pp. 103–4.

31 Vale, *Origins*, pp. 241–4.

32 *Vita Edwardi Secundi*, ed. and trans. N. Denholm-Young, re-ed. Wendy Childs (Oxford 2005), pp. 242–3.

33 *Grandes chroniques*, ed. Viard, vol. 9, p. 43.

34 Phillips, *Edward II*, p. 485.

35 Jean Froissart, *Chroniques de J. Froissart*, ed. Siméon Luce et al., 16 vols (Paris 1869–1975), vol. 1, pt 2, p. 233, a variant adopted by 'Anciennes chroniques de Flandre', *HF*, vol. 22, p. 422.

36 Jules Viard, 'Philippe de Valois avant son avènement au trône', *BEC* 91 (1930), pp. 324–5.

37 'Continuation de . . . Jean de Saint-Victor', *HF*, vol. 21, p. 685.

38 'Continuatio chronici Girardi de Fracheto', *HF*, vol. 21, p. 57; *Chronique latine de Guillaume de Nangis*, ed. Géraud, vol. 2, p. 38; *Grandes chroniques*, ed. Viard, vol. 8, p. 366.

39 'Continuation de . . . Jean de Saint-Victor', *HF*, vol. 21, p. 681 and n. 2.

40 Bas J. P. van Bavel, 'Rural Revolts and Structural Change in the Low Countries, Thirteenth–Early Fourteenth Centuries', in Richard Goddard, John Langdon and Miriam Müller (eds), *Survival and Discord in Medieval Society: Essays in Honour of Christopher Dyer* (Turnhout 2010), pp. 249–68; Henri Pirenne, *Le Soulèvement de Flandre maritime de 1323–1328: Documents inédits* (Brussels 1900), pp. iv–xii.

41 William H. TeBrake, *A Plague of Insurrection: Popular Politics and Peasant Revolt in Flanders, 1323–1328* (Philadelphia, PA 1993), p. 95.

42 TeBrake, *A Plague of Insurrection*, pp. 43–107; Pirenne, *Soulèvement de Flandre*, pp. xv–xxvii.

43 TeBrake, *A Plague of Insurrection*, pp. 98–9.

44 Jules Viard, 'La guerre de Flandres (1328)', *BEC* 83 (1922), pp. 362–82; *Chronique latine de Guillaume de Nangis*, ed. Géraud, vol. 2, pp. 92–4.

45 *Chronique latine de Guillaume de Nangis*, ed. Géraud, vol. 2, p. 82; 'Continuatio chronici Girardi de Fracheto', *HF*, vol. 21, p. 69; Continuation de . . . Jean de Saint-Victor', *HF*, vol. 21, p. 688.

46 Colette Beaune, 'Perceforêt et Merlin: Prophétie, littérature et rumeurs au début de la guerre de Cent-Ans', in *Fin du monde et signes des temps* (Toulouse 1992), pp. 237–56.

47 Jean le Bel, *Chronique de Jean le Bel*, 1, ed. Jules Viard and Eugène Déprez, 2 vols, (Paris 1904–5), vol. 1, p. 8, trans. Nigel Bryant, *The True Chronicles of Jean le Bel (1290–1360)* (Woodbridge 2011), p. 24.

Epilogue

1 Paul Viollet, 'Comment les femmes ont été exclues, en France, de la succession à la couronne', *Mémoires de l'Institut national de France* 34 (1895), pp. 125–78.

2 Jean le Bel, *Chronique de Jean le Bel*, 33, ed. Jules Viard and Eugène Déprez, 2 vols (Paris 1904–5), vol. 1, pp. 166–8, trans. Nigel Bryant, *The True Chronicles of Jean le Bel (1290–1360)* (Woodbridge 2011), pp. 82–3; Henri Pirenne, 'Documents relatifs à l'histoire de Flandre pendant la première moitié du XIVᵉ siècle', *Bulletin de la commission royale d'histoire*, 2nd ser, vol. 7 (1897), pp. 30–33.

3 Jonathan Sumption, *The Hundred Years War*, 4 vols (Philadelphia, PA, and London, 1990–2015), vol. 1, pp. 100–152.

4 He did not, however, actually ever follow through on this promise. Roland Delachenal, *Histoire de Charles V*, 5 vols (Paris 1909–31), vol. 2; cf. John Le Patourel, 'The Treaty of Brétigny, 1360', *Transactions of the Royal Historical Society*, vol. 10 (1960), pp. 19–39.

5 Béatrice Leroy, 'À propos de la succession de 1328 en Navarre', *Annales du Midi: Revue archéologique, historique et philologique de la France méridionale* 82 (1970), pp. 137–46.

6 Suzanne Honoré-Duvergé, 'L'origine du surnom de Charles le Mauvais', *Mélanges d'histoire du Moyen Âge dédiés à la mémoire de Louis Halphen* (Paris 1951), pp. 345–50.

7 Roland Delachenal (ed.), *Chronique des règnes de Jean II et Charles V: Les grandes chroniques de France*, 4 vols in 3 (Paris, 1910–20), vol. I, p. 185.

8 Philippe Charon, *Princes et principautés au Moyen Âge: L'exemple de la principauté d'Évreux, 1298–1412* (Paris 2014), pp. 117–32, 231–51.

9 Raymond Cazelles, 'Le parti navarrais jusqu'à la mort d'Étienne Marcel', *Bulletin philologique et historique du Comité des travaux historiques et scientifiques (jusqu'à 1610), année 1960* (Paris 1961), pp. 839–69.

10 Delachenal, *Histoire de Charles V*, vol. 3, pp. 27–64.

11 Latino Maccari (ed.), *Istoria del re Giannino di Francia* (Siena 1893). The story has been retold many times, most recently by Tommaso di Carpegna Falconieri, *The Man Who Believed He Was King of France: A True Medieval Tale*, trans. William McCuaig (Chicago, IL 2008).

12 Louis-Jean-Nicolas Monmerqué, *Dissertation historique sur Jean Ier, roi de France et de Navarre* (Paris 1844), pp. 85–6, for the cross; Eugène Tavernier, 'Le roi Giannino', *Mémoires de l'Académie des sciences, agriculture, arts et belles-lettres d'Aix*, 12 (1882), pp. 211–99, at p. 294 for the lilies.

Acknowledgements

First and foremost, my thanks go to my family: James, Adryan, Sophie, and Hayden, whose love and support make everything possible and who give me so much joy. This book is dedicated to them.

My agent Adam Gauntlett had the bright idea that I should write this book. I am profoundly grateful for that and for finding me the perfect publisher.

Thank you to everyone at Allen Lane, especially Simon Winder, my editor, and his assistant Eva Hodgkin, as well as to Richard Duguid, Amelia Evans, and Pen Vogler, and to Cecilia McKay for her invaluable help with the images. I am also very grateful to my editor at Basic Books, Brian Distelberg, to his assistant Alex Cullina, and to Chin-Yee Lai for the gorgeous cover design, as well as to everyone else at Basic who brought this book to life in the US.

For their insights, comments, and helpful criticisms over many years, I thank my medievalist friends and colleagues on both sides of the Channel and of the Atlantic, particularly Frances Andrews, Thomas N. Bisson, Agnès Bos, Elizabeth A. R. Brown, Michael Brown, Frederik Buylaert, Meredith Cohen, Godfried Croenen, Jan Dumolyn, Cecilia Gaposchkin, Matt Gabriele, Erika Graham-Goering, Emily Guerry, Jelle Haemers, Julian Luxford, Simon Maclean, Sara McDougall, James Palmer, Levi Roach, Jay Rubenstein, Graeme Small, Angus Stewart, and all of my colleagues at St Andrews. I have learned a great deal, too, from the many students who have taken my class 'France from Philip Augustus to Philip the Fair' and from my PhD students over the years. I also thank Nelson Goering for some advice on historical linguistics. For advice and encouragement on writing, I am especially grateful to Elizabeth Boyle, Alexis Coe, Jasmine Guillory, and Kate Rundell.

I would also like to thank the staff of the Bodleian Library, the

Acknowledgements

Archives nationales and Bibliothèque nationale de France, as well as those of the Louvre and the Musée nationale du Moyen Âge (Cluny). The library staff at my own home institution of St Andrews deserve a medal, especially for sourcing my more recondite ILL requests. Without skilled librarians and curators like these, no historian could ever write anything worth reading. They are the power behind the throne.

Index

Aachen 6, 78

Abelard, Peter 81–2

Acre 119, 201–2, 216, 249

Adalbero, archbishop of Reims 7–11, 13

Adalbero, bishop of Laon 8, 18, 41

Adela of Aquitaine, queen of France 10–11, 69

Adela, countess of Blois 69, 76

Adela, daughter of Robert II 30

Adelaide of Maurienne 69–70, 83–4

Adelheid, western empress xx, 15–16

adultery xviii, 8, 45, 47, 55, 63, 90, 132, 174, 217, 248, 257, 259–60, 271, 301

see also Tour de Nesle scandal

Africa 195, 201, 203, 219

see also Egypt; Tunis

Agen, Agenais 299, 303

Agnes of Méran, queen of France 131, 133–4, 136, 148

Aigues-Mortes 192, 219

Albigensian Crusade *see* crusade: Albigensian

Alice, sister of Philip II Augustus 116, 118, 122

Alleghieri, Dante 3, 9, 18, 264

Alphonse of Poitiers 170, 175, 192, 201, 204, 218

Amiens 127, 137, 301

Anagni, 'outrage' of 244–6

see also Boniface VIII, pope

anathema 21, 48

Angoulême 288

see also Isabelle of

Anjou xxi, 15, 22, 35, 37–8, 50–51, 60, 74, 117, 146–9, 168, 175

see also Charles of, king of Sicily and Jerusalem; Fulk Nerra, count of; Fulk le Réchin, count of; Geoffrey Martel, count of; Geoffrey Plantagenet, count of

Anne of Kyiv, queen of France 44–6

annulment *see* divorce

anointing 9, 12–13, 16, 32, 47, 83, 104, 112, 156, 170–71, 241, 277, 283, 286

Antichrist 58, 113, 240, 243

Antioch 68, 96, 102, 218

antisemitism 29, 110–12, 179, 188, 292

see also pogroms; Shepherds' Crusade: First; Shepherds' Crusade: Second; Talmud

Apocalypse, apocalypticism 20, 26–8, 33, 57–8, 156, 185, 253, 291

Aquitaine 26, 31, 35, 37–40, 43, 47, 85–6, 91–2, 94, 102–3, 116, 119, 147–9, 161

see also Adela of; Bordeaux; Eleanor of; Gascony; Saint-Sardos; William V, duke of; William X, duke of

Arabic 195, 247

Justine Firnhaber-Baker is professor of history at the University of St. Andrews. A former fellow of All Souls College, Oxford, and a graduate of Harvard University, she is the author of two previous books on the history of medieval France. She lives in Scotland.